The Letters of

SAMUEL JOHNSON

SAMUEL JOHNSON

by James Barry, 1778–1780 (National Portrait Gallery, London)

The Letters of

SAMUEL JOHNSON

VOLUME II · 1773–1776

Edited by

BRUCE REDFORD

PRINCETON, NEW JERSEY

PRINCETON UNIVERSITY PRESS

MCM · LXXXXII

PUBLISHED BY PRINCETON UNIVERSITY PRESS, 41 WILLIAM STREET
PRINCETON, NEW JERSEY 08540

LIBRARY OF CONGRESS CATALOGING-IN-PUBLICATION DATA
(REVISED FOR VOLUMES 2 AND 3)

JOHNSON, SAMUEL, 1709–1784.
THE LETTERS OF SAMUEL JOHNSON.
INCLUDES BIBLIOGRAPHICAL REFERENCES AND INDEX.
CONTENTS: V. 1. 30 OCTOBER 1731 TO 15 DECEMBER 1772
—V. 2. 15 JANUARY 1773 TO 24 DECEMBER 1776—V. 3.
11 JANUARY 1777 TO 26 DECEMBER 1781.
ISBN 0–691–06928–X (V. 2)
1. JOHNSON, SAMUEL—1709–1784—CORRESPONDENCE.
2. AUTHORS, ENGLISH—18TH CENTURY—CORRESPONDENCE.
3. LEXICOGRAPHERS—GREAT BRITAIN—CORRESPONDENCE.
I. REDFORD, BRUCE. II. TITLE.
PR3533.A4 1992 828'.609 90–8806

PRINCETON UNIVERSITY PRESS BOOKS
ARE PRINTED ON ACID-FREE PAPER, AND MEET THE
GUIDELINES FOR PERMANENCE AND DURABILITY OF
THE COMMITTEE ON PRODUCTION GUIDELINES
FOR BOOK LONGEVITY OF THE COUNCIL
ON LIBRARY RESOURCES

PRINTED IN THE UNITED STATES OF AMERICA
BY THE STINEHOUR PRESS, LUNENBURG, VERMONT

1 3 5 7 9 10 8 6 4 2

CONTENTS

ILLUSTRATIONS

EDITORIAL PROCEDURES

POLICIES of annotation and transcription have been modeled on the style sheet for the Yale Research Edition of the Private Papers of James Boswell. The most detailed version in print appears in the front matter to *The Correspondence of James Boswell with David Garrick, Edmund Burke, and Edmond Malone*, ed. P. S. Baker et al. (1986). The statement that follows adheres closely to this version.

THE TEXTS

Choice and Arrangement of Letters

The letters are presented in chronological order. Letters written for others, as well as public dissertations in the guise of letters, have been excluded. Undated letters that cannot be assigned with confidence to a specific year appear in Appendix I, where they are ordered alphabetically by correspondent. Appendix II gathers together the evidence for letters whose texts have not been recovered. Translations of Johnson's letters in Latin appear in Appendix III.

The copy-text has been the MSS of letters sent, whenever such MSS were available. In the absence of originals, we have used MS copies. When no MSS at all have been recovered, we have used printed texts as copy.

Transcription

In accordance with the policy of the Yale Research Series, "manuscript documents in this edition have been printed to correspond to the originals as closely as is feasible in the medium of type. A certain amount of compromise and apparent inconsistency seems unavoidable, but change has been kept within the limits of stated conventions."

The following editorial conventions are imposed silently: *Addresses.* Elements appearing on separate lines in the MS are run together and punctuated according to modern practice. On franked covers, handwriting is that of the franker unless otherwise specified.

Datelines. Places and dates are joined at the head of the letter regardless of their position in the MS. Punctuation has been normalized.

Salutations. Abbreviations are expanded. Commas and colons after salutations are retained; in the absence of punctuation, a colon is supplied.

Complimentary closes. Abbreviations are expanded. Punctuation has been normalized. Elements appearing on separate lines in the MS are run together. Complimentary closes paragraphed separately in the MS are printed as continuations of the last line of text.

Endorsements. Handwriting is that of the recipient unless otherwise specified.

Punctuation. At the ends of completed sentences periods may replace commas or dashes and are always supplied when omitted. A sentence following a period always begins with a capital letter.

Changes. Substantive additions and deletions in Johnson's hand are recorded in the notes.

Lacunae. Words and letters missing through a tear or obscured by a blot are supplied within angle brackets. Inadvertent omissions are supplied within square brackets. Nonauthorial deletions are not reported unless the reading is in doubt.

Abbreviations, contractions, and symbols. The following abbreviations, contractions, and symbols, and their variant forms, are expanded: abt (about), acct (account), agst (against), Bp (Bishop), cd (could), compts (compliments), Dr (Dear), Ld (Lord), Lop (Lordship), Ly (Lady), Lyship (Ladyship), recd (received), sd (should), Sr (Sir), wc (which), wd (would), yr (your), & (and), &c (etc.). All retained abbreviations and contractions are followed by a period. Periods following ordinals have been removed.

Superior letters. Superior letters are lowered.

Brackets. Parentheses replace square brackets in the text, brackets being reserved for editorial use.

Spelling. The original spelling has been retained, except for obvious inadvertencies, which are corrected in the text and recorded in the notes.

Capitalization and paragraphing. Original capitalization and paragraphing have been retained.

ANNOTATION

Headnotes. Postmarks, although partly illegible on some letters, are left unbracketed when not in doubt. Marks on the wrappers other than addresses, postmarks, endorsements, and stamped and written franks have been ignored.

Footnotes. When an abbreviated source is given, the full citation may be found in the list of cue titles and abbreviations on pp. xv–xvii. All other reference titles in the footnotes are sufficiently complete to enable ready identification; for each letter, these citations are presented in full the first time they occur and are shortened in all subsequent occurrences in the notes to that letter. Except where a work has been directly quoted, no source is given when the information is available in the *Dictionary of National Biography,* an encyclopedia, or other general reference work.

Reference to all letters is made by correspondent and date. *Post* and *Ante* references supplement but do not replace the index, which should be consulted whenever the identity of names or places is in doubt.

CHRONOLOGY

1709	Is born at Lichfield, 18 Sept.
1717–25	Attends Lichfield Grammar School.
1728	Enters Pembroke College, Oxford, in October.
1729	Leaves Oxford in December.
1731	Death of his father Michael.
1732	Usher at Market Bosworth School.
1733	Resides in Birmingham; translates Lobo's *Voyage to Abyssinia.*
1735	Marries Elizabeth Porter; opens school at Edial.
1737	Leaves for London in March; begins work for Edward Cave.
1738	*London.*
1744	*An Account of the Life of Richard Savage*; *Harleian Miscellany.*
1746	Signs contract for the *Dictionary.*
1749	*Irene* produced; *The Vanity of Human Wishes.*
1750	Begins *Rambler.*
1752	Death of Elizabeth Johnson; final *Rambler.*
1755	Oxford M.A.; publication of the *Dictionary.*
1758	Begins *Idler.*
1759	Death of his mother Sarah; publication of *Rasselas.*
1760	Final *Idler.*
1762	Is granted annual pension.
1763	Meets James Boswell.
1764	Founding of The Club.
1765	Meets Henry and Hester Thrale; Dublin LL.D.; *The Dramatic Works of William Shakespeare.*
1770	*The False Alarm.*
1771	*Thoughts on the late Transactions respecting Falkland's Islands.*
1773	Hebridean tour.
1774	*The Patriot*; tour of Wales.
1775	*A Journey to the Western Islands of Scotland*; *Taxation No Tyranny*; Oxford D.C.L.; trip to Paris.

1777	Trial of Dr. Dodd; begins work on *Lives of the Poets*.
1779	First installment of *Lives*.
1781	Death of Henry Thrale; second installment of *Lives*.
1783	Founding of Essex Head Club.
1784	Final break with Hester Thrale; dies 13 Dec.

CUE TITLES AND ABBREVIATIONS

Adam Cat.	R. B. ADAM, *The R. B. Adam Library Relating to Dr. Samuel Johnson and His Era*, 4 vols., 1929–30.
Alum. Cant. I	JOHN and J. A. VENN, *Alumni Cantabrigienses*, Part I (to 1751), 4 vols., 1922–27.
Alum. Cant. II	J. A. VENN, *Alumni Cantabrigienses*, Part II (1752–1900), 6 vols., 1940–54.
Alum. Oxon. I	JOSEPH FOSTER, *Alumni Oxonienses ... 1500–1714*, 4 vols., 1891–92.
Alum. Oxon. II	JOSEPH FOSTER, *Alumni Oxonienses ... 1715–1886*, 4 vols., 1887–88.
Baker	*The Correspondence of James Boswell with David Garrick, Edmund Burke, and Edmond Malone*, ed. P. S. Baker et al., 1986.
Bibliography	W. P. COURTNEY and DAVID NICHOL SMITH, *A Bibliography of Samuel Johnson*, 1915, 1925.
Bibliography Supplement	R. W. CHAPMAN and A. T. HAZEN, *Johnsonian Bibliography: A Supplement to Courtney*, 1939.
Bloom	E. A. BLOOM, *Samuel Johnson in Grub Street*, 1957.
Burke's Correspondence	*The Correspondence of Edmund Burke*, ed. T. W. Copeland et al., 1958–70.
Chapman	*The Letters of Samuel Johnson, with Mrs. Thrale's Genuine Letters to Him*, ed. R. W. Chapman, 3 vols., 1952.
Clifford, 1952	J. L. CLIFFORD, *Hester Lynch Piozzi*, 2d ed., 1952.
Clifford, 1955	J. L. CLIFFORD, *Young Samuel Johnson*, 1955.
Clifford, 1979	J. L. CLIFFORD, *Dictionary Johnson*, 1979.
Croker	JAMES BOSWELL, *The Life of Samuel Johnson, LL.D.*, ed. J. W. Croker, rev. John Wright, 10 vols., 1868.
SJ's *Dictionary*	SAMUEL JOHNSON, *Dictionary of the English Language*, 4th ed., 1773.
DNB	*Dictionary of National Biography.*

Earlier Years	F. A. POTTLE, *James Boswell: The Earlier Years, 1740–1769*, 1966.
Fifer	*The Correspondence of James Boswell with Certain Members of The Club*, ed. C. N. Fifer, 1976.
Fleeman	SAMUEL JOHNSON, *A Journey to the Western Islands of Scotland*, ed. J. D. Fleeman, 1985.
GM	*The Gentleman's Magazine*, 1731–1907.
Greene, 1975	DONALD GREENE, *Samuel Johnson's Library*, 1975.
Hawkins	SIR JOHN HAWKINS, *The Life of Samuel Johnson, LL.D.*, 2d ed., 1787.
Hazen	A. T. HAZEN, *Samuel Johnson's Prefaces and Dedications*, 1937.
Hebrides	*Boswell's Journal of a Tour to the Hebrides with Samuel Johnson, LL.D., 1773*, ed. from the original MS by F. A. Pottle and C. H. Bennett, 1961.
Hendy	J. G. HENDY, *The History of the Early Postmarks of the British Isles*, 1905.
Hill	*Letters of Samuel Johnson, LL.D.*, ed. G. B. Hill, 1892.
Hyde, 1972	MARY HYDE, *The Impossible Friendship: Boswell and Mrs. Thrale*, 1972.
Hyde, 1977	MARY HYDE, *The Thrales of Streatham Park*, 1977.
JB	James Boswell.
Johns. Glean.	A. L. READE, *Johnsonian Gleanings*, 11 vols., 1909–52.
Johns. Misc.	*Johnsonian Miscellanies*, ed. G. B. Hill, 2 vols., 1897.
JN	*Johnsonian Newsletter.*
Later Years	FRANK BRADY, *James Boswell: The Later Years, 1769–1795*, 1984.
Life	*Boswell's Life of Johnson, Together with Boswell's Journal of a Tour to the Hebrides and Johnson's Diary of a Journey into North Wales*, ed. G. B. Hill, rev. L. F. Powell, 6 vols., 1934–50; vols. V and VI, 2d ed., 1964.
Lit. Anec.	JOHN NICHOLS, *Literary Anecdotes of the Eighteenth Century*, 9 vols., 1812–15.
Lit. Car.	F. A. POTTLE, *The Literary Career of James Boswell, Esq.*, 1929.
Lives of the Poets	*Johnson's Lives of the English Poets*, ed. G. B. Hill, 1905.

Lond. Stage — *The London Stage*, Part III (1729–47), ed. A. H. Scouten, 1961; Part IV (1747–76), ed. G. W. Stone, Jr., 1962; Part V (1776–1800), ed. C. B. Hogan, 1968.

Namier and Brooke — SIR LEWIS NAMIER and JOHN BROOKE, *The House of Commons, 1754–1790*, 3 vols., 1964.

OED — *Oxford English Dictionary.*

Piozzi, *Letters* — HESTER LYNCH PIOZZI, *Letters to and from the Late Samuel Johnson, LL.D.*, 2 vols., 1788.

Piozzi — Annotated presentation copy, given to Sir James Fellowes, of H. L. Piozzi's *Letters to and from the Late Samuel Johnson, LL.D.*, 1788 (Birthplace Museum, Lichfield).

Plomer — H. R. PLOMER et al., *Dictionary of Printers and Booksellers, 1668–1725; 1726–1775*, 2 vols., 1922, 1932.

Poems — *The Poems of Samuel Johnson*, ed. David Nichol Smith and E. L. McAdam, rev. J. D. Fleeman, 1974.

Reades — A. L. READE, *The Reades of Blackwood Hill and Dr. Johnson's Ancestry*, 1906.

RES — *Review of English Studies.*

SJ — Samuel Johnson.

Sledd and Kolb — J. H. SLEDD and G. J. KOLB, *Dr. Johnson's Dictionary*, 1955.

Thraliana — *Thraliana: The Diary of Mrs. Hester Lynch Thrale*, ed. K. C. Balderston, 1942.

TLS — *Times Literary Supplement.*

Waingrow — *The Correspondence and Other Papers of James Boswell Relating to the Making of the "Life of Johnson,"* ed. Marshall Waingrow, 1969.

Walpole's Correspondence, Yale ed. — *The Yale Edition of Horace Walpole's Correspondence*, ed. W. S. Lewis et al., 1937–83.

Wheatley and Cunningham — H. B. WHEATLEY and PETER CUNNINGHAM, *London Past and Present*, 3 vols., 1891.

Works, Yale ed. — *The Yale Edition of the Works of Samuel Johnson*, J. H. Middendorf, gen. ed., 1958–.

The Letters of

SAMUEL JOHNSON

John Hawkins

FRIDAY 15 JANUARY 1773

MS: Houghton Library.

ENDORSEMENT in an unidentified hand: 15th Jan. 1773, Dr. Johnson to Sir John Hawkins.

Dear Sir: Jan. 15, 1773

A young Woman of whose family I have some little knowledge, is, I believe, very injuriously and oppressively excluded from her little patrimoney, for which she sues in formâ pauperis.[1] Mr. Chambers has undertaken her cause, but we are in want of an Attorney.[2] I know very few attorneys, and none so well as Mr. Clark,[3] yet I cannot venture to ask him to do business for nothing, but should think it a great favour if you would recommend the cause to him.[4]

My compliments to Lady Hawkins.[5] I am, Sir, Your most humble servant,

SAM. JOHNSON

1. SJ refers to "Poll" Carmichael, "a Scotch Wench who has her Case as a Pauper depending in some of the Law Courts" (*Thraliana* I.184–85, 532); she joined SJ's household *c.* 1777 (*John. Misc.* I.205 n. 2; *Life* III.462–63). *Post* To Richard Clark, 31 Jan. 1774.

2. Because Robert Chambers was a barrister, he and SJ needed to secure the services of a solicitor.

3. Richard Clark (1739–1831), a London solicitor to whom SJ had been introduced by Hawkins; Clark later became Alderman (1776), Sheriff (1777), and ultimately Lord Mayor (1784).

4. *Post* To Richard Clark, 8 Feb. 1773.

5. In 1753 Hawkins had married Sidney Storer (1726–93), youngest daughter of Peter Storer, attorney of Highgate (Bertram Davis, *A Proof of Eminence: The Life of Sir John Hawkins*, 1973, pp. 57–58).

John Hawkesworth

WEDNESDAY 20 JANUARY 1773

MS: Hyde Collection.

ADDRESS: To Dr. Hawkesworth at Bromley in Kent.

POSTMARK: 20 IA.

Dear Sir: Jan. 20

You may by chance remember that I once mentioned in your grove[1] the fitness of an epitome of Chambers Dictionary,[2] which you said you would some time undertake. This gives you a right of refusing it to another, but if you have now, as I suppose you have, laid aside, all such thoughts, I would transfer it to a gentleman now out of business. Pray send me word.[3]

But send me word with more care of the health of dear Mrs. Hawkesworth. She is negligent of her self, and by consequence of you and me. I shall never love her when she is sick because she gets sick by her own fault. I am, Dear Sir, your most affectionate,

SAM. JOHNSON

1. *Ante* To John Hawkesworth, Early March 1756, n. 8.

2. The *Cyclopædia, or an Universal Dictionary* (1728) of Ephraim Chambers (d. 1740). "Johnson once considered making a revision of the *Cyclopædia*, which was in his library at his death and for which . . . he expressed a liking; and the tradition has persisted that he 'formed his style' on that of Chambers" (Sledd and Kolb, p. 19).

3. SJ duly transferred the project to the Rev. John Calder (1733–1815), D.D., dissenting minister and literary scholar, Deputy Librarian to the Duke of Northumberland (1773–75) (*Life* II.502–3). "One of the most important events of Dr. Calder's Literary Life was a contract which he made, in 1773, to prepare for the press a new Edition of Chambers's 'Cyclopaedia.' This project unfortunately terminated to the dissatisfaction of all parties (John Nichols, *Illustrations of the Literary History of the Eighteenth Century*, 1822, IV.800). *Post* To Archibald Hamilton, 13 Feb. 1776 and n. 1.

Hester Thrale

TUESDAY 26 JANUARY 1773

MS: Princeton University Library.

Madam: Tuesday, Jan. 26, 1773

The inequalities of human life have always employed the meditation of deep thinkers, and I cannot forbear to reflect on the difference between your condition and my own. You live upon Mock turtle, and stewed Rumps of Beef, I dined yesterday upon crumpets. You sit with parish officers, caressing and caressed, the idol of the table, and the wonder of the day. I pine in the solitude of sickness, not bad enough to be pitied, and not well enough to be endured.[1] You sleep away the night, and laugh or scold away the day. I cough and grumble, and grumble and cough. Last night was very tedious, and this day makes no promises of much ease. However I have this day[2] put on my shoe, and hope that Gout is gone. I shall have only the cough to contend with, and I doubt whether I shall get rid of that without change of place. I caught cold in the coach as I went away, and am disordered by very little things. Is it accident, or age? I am, dearest Madam, your most obedient and most humble Servant,

SAM. JOHNSON

1. "It seems to have been Mrs. Thrale's practice this winter to come in town every Tuesday for a brief stay at the Borough house, and it was Johnson's custom to dine with her there" (Clifford, 1952, p. 96).

2. MS: "d" superimposed upon "g"

Richard Clark

MONDAY 8 FEBRUARY 1773

MS: Houghton Library.

ADDRESS: To Mr. Clark.

ENDORSEMENT: 8th Feb. 1773, Dr. Johnson.

Dear Sir: Febr. 8, 1773

Sir John Hawkins told me that you would be so kind as to undertake the business which I recommended to him and you.[1] Mr. Chambers is now in town, and will be glad to consider the manner of proceeding with you. I am, Sir, Your most humble Servant,

SAM. JOHNSON

1. *Ante* To John Hawkins, 15 Jan. 1773.

Hester Thrale

FRIDAY 19 FEBRUARY 1773

PRINTED SOURCE: Piozzi, *Letters* I.72–73.

Madam, Feb. 19, 1773

I think I am better, but cannot say much more than that I think so.[1] I was yesterday with Miss Lucy Southwell and Mrs. Williams, at Mr. Southwell's. Miss Frances Southwell is not well.[2]

I have an invitation to dine at Sir Joshua Reynolds's on Tuesday. May I accept it?[3]

Do not think I am going to borrow the Roller.[4] I have undertaken to beg from you the favour of lending to Miss Reynolds Newton on the Prophecies,[5] and to Miss Williams

1. *Ante* To Hester Thrale, 26 Jan. 1773.

2. SJ refers to the brother and sisters of his late friend, Thomas (1698–1766), second Baron Southwell of Castle Mattress, Co. Limerick: the Hon. Edmond (b. 1705), the Hon. Frances (b. 1708), and the Hon. Lucia (b. 1710) (Edmond Malone's annotated copy of Piozzi, *Letters*, Dublin ed. I. 54: Georgetown University Library).

3. *Ante* To Hester Thrale, 26 Jan. 1773, n. 1.

4. *roller*: "any thing turning on its own axis, as a heavy stone to level walks" (SJ's *Dictionary*). "Mr. Thrale flew into a Rage always when anyone beg'd leave to borrow the Roller, and I used to be frighted and stop them slyly if I could" (annotated copy of Piozzi, *Letters*, I.72, Trinity College, Cambridge).

5. *Ante* To Frances Reynolds, 21 Dec. 1762, n. 6.

Burney's Musical Journey.[6] They are, I believe, both at Streatham.

Be pleased to make my most respectful compliments to dear Mrs. Salusbury. I wish I could send her any thing better.

Diversas hominum sortes.[7] Here am I, sitting by myself, uncertain whether I shall dine on veal or mutton; and there are you with the top dish and the bottom dish, all upon a card, and on the other side of the card Tom Lisgow.[8] Of the rest that dwell in darker fame why should I make mention. Tom Lisgow is an assembly. But Tom Lisgow cannot people the world. Mr. K—— must have a place.[9] The lion has his jackall.[10] They will soon meet.

And when they talk, ye gods! how they will talk.[11]

Pray let your voice and my master's help to fill the pauses. I am, etc.

SAM. JOHNSON

6. Charles Burney, *The Present State of Music in France and Italy: Or, The Journal of a Tour through those Countries, undertaken to collect Materials for a General History of Music* (1771).

7. *diversas hominum sortes*: "various are the fates of men" (proverbial).

8. "Tom Lisgow was a voter at the Southwark election. Mr. K[eep] was another. When they were entertained at Mr. Thrale's table, . . . [I] used to write the bill of fare on one side of a large blank card in a small character, the names of the company on the other side, and refer to it from time to time as it lay by [my] plate, that no mistakes might be made, or offence given from ignorance or forgetfulness; to this practice Mr. Johnson laughingly alludes" (Piozzi, *Letters* 1.73).

9. "Mr. Keep when he heard I was a native of North Wales, told me that his Wife was a Welsh woman: & desired to be buried at Ruthyn. So - says the Man I went with the Corpse myself because I thought it would be a *pleasant Journey*, & indeed I found Ruthyn is a very beautiful Place" (Piozzi 1.73).

10. *jackal*: "a small animal supposed to start prey for the lion" (SJ's *Dictionary*).

11. "Then he will talk, good gods, how he will talk!" (Nathaniel Lee, *The Rival Queens*, 1677, ed. P. F. Vernon, 1970, 1.ii.48). *Post* To Hester Thrale, 6 Oct. 1777.

James Boswell

WEDNESDAY 24 FEBRUARY 1773

PRINTED SOURCE: JB's *Life*, 1791, 1.389–90.

Dear Sir, London, Feb. 24, 1773

I have read your kind letter much more than the elegant Pindar which it accompanied.[1] I am always glad to find myself not forgotten, and to be forgotten by you would give me great uneasiness. My northern friends have never been unkind to me: I have from you, dear Sir, testimonies of affection, which I have not often been able to excite; and Dr. Beattie rates the testimony which I was desirous of paying to his merit, much higher than I should have thought it reasonable to expect.[2]

I have heard of your masquerade.[3] What says your Synod to such innovations?[4] I am not studiously scrupulous, nor do I think a masquerade either evil in itself, or very likely to be the occasion of evil; yet as the world thinks it a very licentious relaxation of manners, I would not have been one of the *first* masquers in a country where no masquerade had ever been before.[5]

A new edition of my great Dictionary is printed, from a copy which I was persuaded to revise; but having made no preparation, I was able to do very little.[6] Some superfluities I have

1. JB had last written SJ on 25 Dec. 1772 (*Life* II.203). For the volume of Pindar's *Works*, *Ante* To JB, 31 Aug. 1772, n. 3.

2. *Ante* To JB, 31 Aug. 1772 and n. 1. In his letter of 25 Dec. JB had quoted Beattie's response to SJ's praise: "'it is impossible for me to say how much I am gratified . . . ; for there is not a man upon earth whose good opinion I would be more ambitious to cultivate'" (*Life* II.203).

3. "Friday, [Jan.] 15. At Duff House . . . was exhibited the first masquerade ever seen in Scotland. . . . A number of dresses, rich genteel and curious, were exhibited. . . . [Including] Mr. Boswell, [as] a Dumb Conjuror" (*GM* 1773, p. 43). The masquerade, actually the second in Scotland (*London Magazine* 43, 1774, pp. 82–83), was given by Sir Alexander and Lady Macdonald, whom SJ and JB were soon to visit on Skye. *Post* To Hester Thrale, 6 Sept. 1773.

4. "Denounced from the pulpit as 'the encourager of intrigue, of libertinism, of debauchery,' it [the masquerade] encouraged, in fact, no more than fashionable, decorous insipidity" (*Later Years*, p. 44).

5. In an anonymous article that can be attributed confidently to him, JB echoes SJ's opinion: "In this [masking] there is nothing inherently evil; but it has no doubt been often made subservient to licentiousness of manners" (*London Magazine* 43, 1774, pp. 80–83; *Lit. Car.*, p. 223).

6. The fourth folio edition, revised from the first, appeared in March. This revision, the only one in SJ's lifetime, was in fact substantial, particularly in the

expunged, and some faults I have corrected, and here and there have scattered a remark; but the main fabrick of the work remains as it was. I had looked very little into it since I wrote it, and, I think, I found it full as often better, as worse, than I expected.

Baretti and Davies have had a furious quarrel; a quarrel, I think, irreconcileable.[7] Dr. Goldsmith has a new comedy, which is expected in the spring. No name is yet given it.[8] The chief diversion arises from a stratagem by which a lover is made to mistake his future father-in-law's house for an inn. This, you see, borders upon farce. The dialogue is quick and gay, and the incidents are so prepared as not to seem improbable.

I am sorry that you lost your cause of Intromission, because I yet think the arguments on your side unanswerable.[9] But you seem, I think, to say that you gained reputation even by your defeat; and reputation you will daily gain, if you keep Lord Auchinleck's precept in your mind, and endeavour to consolidate in your mind a firm and regular system of law, instead of picking up occasional fragments.[10]

My health seems in general to improve; but I have been

---

number of new quotations added (information supplied by Prof. Allen Reddick).

7. It is likely that this quarrel concerned Baretti's lack of progress on his translation of *Don Quixote*, for which Davies had been advancing him £10 a month (Lacy Collison-Morley, *Giuseppe Baretti*, 1909, p. 274).

8. Goldsmith's play was advertised as *The Mistakes of a Night*, and the final title, *She Stoops to Conquer*, was not fixed until just before the premiere, 15 Mar. (*Collected Works of Oliver Goldsmith*, ed. Arthur Friedman, 1966, v.88–89).

9. In the case of *Wilson* v. *Smith and Armour*, which came to trial in Jan. 1772, JB had argued in support of an "established principle" of Scots law, "that whoever intermeddled with the effects of a person deceased, with out the interposition of legal authority to guard against embezzlement, should be subjected to pay all the debts of the deceased, as having been guilty of what was technically called *vicious intromission*" (*Life* II.196; *Later Years*, p. 26). The Court of Session ruled against the principle, but SJ supported JB's position, and drew up a lengthy opinion in order to assist him in an "application to the Court for a revision and alteration of the judgement" (*Life* II.196). "This masterly argument, after being prefaced and concluded with some sentences of my own . . . was actually printed and laid before the Lords of Session, but without success" (*Life* II.200–201).

10. At this time, "Lord Auchinleck was not yet satisfied that Boswell had acquired a solid grounding in the law" (*Later Years*, p. 40).

troubled for many weeks with a vexatious catarrh, which is sometimes sufficiently distressful. I have not found any great effects from bleeding and physick; and am afraid, that I must expect help from brighter days and softer air.

Write to me now and then; and whenever any good befalls you, make haste to let me know it, for no one will rejoice at it more than, dear Sir, Your most humble servant,

SAM. JOHNSON

You continue to stand very high in the favour of Mrs. Thrale.[11]

11. During his London jaunt of 1772, Boswell visited the Thrales on three occasions, and "Mrs. Thrale expressed the hope that Mrs. Boswell would accompany her husband to London the next year. . . . It was a warm parting between Boswell and the Thrales, and the prospects of a solid friendship seemed quite possible" (Hyde, 1972, p. 18).

John Taylor

SATURDAY 27 FEBRUARY 1773

MS: Pierpont Morgan Library.

ADDRESS: To the Reverend Dr. Taylor in Ashbourne, Derbyshire.

POSTMARK: 27 FE.

ENDORSEMENTS: 1773, 27 Feby. 73.

Dear Sir: London, Febr. 27, 1773

Is it not a strange thing that we should visit, and meet, and live kindly together, and then part without any enquiry after each other?[1] This is surely not quite right, and therefore I will this day put an end to it, by desiring you to inform me about your health and your quiet, of both which I shall willingly hear the improvement and encrease.

As to my own health it has been pretty much interrupted by a cough which has hung on me about ten weeks, and for six or seven has been very violent.[2] I have been sometimes near

1. SJ had stayed with Taylor at Ashbourne from 27 or 28 Oct. until 2 Dec. 1772 (*Ante* To John Taylor, 19 Oct. 1772; *Ante* To Hester Thrale, 27 Nov. 1772).

2. MS: no punctuation

fainting, but have never fainted. My quiet nobody tries to interrupt, or if they try, I seldom hear of it.

When I had left you, I passed some days at Lucy's, and *lent* Mr. Greene the axe and lance.[3] I then went to Birmingham, and was a while with Hector.[4]

About three months ago the Schoolmaster who has dedicated his Spelling book to you, came to me with a request that I would put my name to a printed recommendation, which was to stand before it. This, you see was not fit for me to do. He was not importunate, but, I suppose, was not pleased. You will sometime let him see the impropriety of his request, that a man, who considers you as his friend, may not think himself unkindly treated.

My Cold was once so bad that I began to think of Country air, but then what country. I doubt Derbyshire is not the place that cures coughs. While I deliberated, I grew better, but perceive myself now not the match that I once was for wind and weather. Dr. Laurence laughs at me when he sees me in a great coat.

Infirmity has come somewhat suddenly, at least, unexpectedly upon me, and I am afraid that I suffer myself to be corroded with vain and idle discontent.

Let me hear from you. I am, Dear Sir, Your affectionate, humble servant,

SAM. JOHNSON

3. *Ante* To Lucy Porter, 12 July 1768, n. 2. The weapons were presumably intended for Greene's museum of antiquities and curiosities.

4. *Ante* To Edmund Hector, 5 Dec. 1772.

Phineas Bond[1]

THURSDAY 4 MARCH 1773

1. Phineas Bond (1749–1815), a Philadelphia attorney, came to England *c.* 1770 to study law and remained until after the American War. "We know relatively little about him . . . except that during the Revolution he remained a loyalist and after the war served as British consul in Philadelphia. The circumstances of his acquaintance with Johnson are also obscure" (Waingrow, p. 463 and n. 6;

MS: Haverford College. A copy in the hand of James Abercrombie.[2]

ADDRESS: To Mr. Bond.

London, Johnsons Court, Fleet Street,
March 4, 1773

Sir:

That in the hurry of a sudden departure, you should yet find leisure to consult my convenience, is a degree of kindness and an instance of regard not only beyond my claims, but above my expectation. You are not mistaken in supposing that I set a high value on my American Friends, and that you should confer a very valuable favor upon me, by giving me an opportunity of keeping myself in their memory.

I have taken the liberty of troubling you with a packet, to which I wish a safe and speedy conveyance, because I wish a safe & speedy voyage to him that conveys it.[3] I am, Sir, Your most humble servant,

SAM. JOHNSON

M. J. Quinlan, "Johnson's American Acquaintances," in *Johnson, Boswell and Their Circle*, 1965, pp. 196–97).

2. James Abercrombie (1758–1841), a Philadelphia businessman, copied this letter in 1792 for JB's use in the *Life* (Waingrow, pp. 462 and n. 1, 463).

3. SJ enclosed two letters to be taken to America. *Post* To William White, 4 Mar. 1773; *Post* To William Samuel Johnson, 4 Mar. 1773.

William White[1]

THURSDAY 4 MARCH 1773

MS: Hyde Collection.

ADDRESS: To the Reverend Mr. White.[2]

ENDORSEMENT: Dr. Samuel Johnson, 1773.

1. William White (1748–1836), first Bishop of Pennsylvania, arrived in England during the winter of 1770–71 to be ordained into the Anglican ministry. White left for America in June 1772. During his stay in England he occasionally visited SJ, who was "very civil" to him and "expressed a wish to see the edition of his *Rasselas*, which Dr. White told him had been printed in America" (JB's note, *Life* II.207 n. 2; J. H. Ward, *The Life and Times of Bishop White*, 1892, pp. 21, 23, 25).

2. *Ante* To Phineas Bond, 4 Mar. 1773 and n. 3.

To WILLIAM WHITE, 4 *March* 1773

Johnson's Court, Fleetstreet, London,
Dear Sir: March 4, 1773

Your kindness for your friends[3] accompanies you cross the Atlantick. It was long since observed by Horace, that no ship could leave care behind,[4] you have [been] attended in you[r] voyage by better powers, by Benevolence and Constancy, and I hope Care did not often show her face in their company.

I received the copy of Rasselas.[5] The impression is not magnificent, but it flatters an Authour, because the Printer seems to have expected that it would be scattered among the People.[6] The little Book has been well received, and is translated into Italian, French, German, and Dutch.[7] It has now one honour more by an American Edition.

I know not that much has happened since your departure, that can engage your curiosity. Of all publick transactions the whole world is now informed by the Newspapers. Opposition seems to despond, and the Dissenters though they have taken advantage of unsettled times, and a government much enfeebled, seem not likely to gain any immunities.[8]

3. MS: "friends" altered from "fiends"

4. *neque / decedit aerata triremi et / post equitem sedet atra Cura*: "nor does black Care quit the brass-bound galley and even takes her seat behind the horseman" (Horace, *Odes* III.i.38–40, trans. C. E. Bennett, Loeb ed.).

5. White had mentioned to SJ the existence of "a Philadelphia edition of his *Prince of Abyssinia*. He expressed a wish to see it. I promised to send him a copy on my return to Philadelphia, and did so" (Ward, *Bishop White*, p. 23). This edition, published by Robert Bell in 1768, was the first to describe the book on its title page as *The History of Rasselas* (*Works*, Yale ed. XVI.257 and n. 8).

6. Bell "patriotically announced on the title page that his version originated in 'America' and was 'printed for every purchaser'" (*Works*, Yale ed. XVI.257). See R. F. Metzdorf, "The First American *Rasselas* and Its Imprint," *Proceedings of the Bibliographical Society of America* 47, 1953, pp. 374–76.

7. By 1773, *Rasselas* had been translated into four European languages: Dutch (1760), French (1760), German (1762), and Italian (1764). SJ does not mention the Russian version, which appeared in 1764 (*Works*, Yale ed. XVI.254–57).

8. On 22 Feb. a bill instigated by the Dissenting denominations was introduced into the House of Commons. This Dissenters Bill would have removed the requirement that all officeholders must subscribe to the Thirty-Nine Articles of the Church of England. It passed the House of Commons on 25 Mar. but was rejected by the Lords on 2 Apr. (*Journals of the House of Commons* XXXIV, 1772–74, p. 146; *GM* 1773, pp. 197, 478). SJ firmly opposed any relaxation of the requirements.

Dr. Goldsmith has a new comedy in rehearsal at Covent garden,[9] to which the Manager predicts ill success. I hope he will be mistaken. I think it deserves a very kind reception.[10]

I shall soon publish a new Edition of my large Dictionary; I have been persuaded to revise it, and have mended some faults, but added little to its usefulness.[11]

No book has been published since your departure of which much notice is taken. Faction only fills the town with Pamphlets, and greater subjects are forgotten in the noise of discord.

Thus have I written only to tell you how little I have to tell. Of myself I can only add that having been afflicted many weeks with a very troublesome cough, I am now recovered.

I take the liberty which you give me of troubling you with a letter, of which you will please to fill up the direction.[12] I am, Sir, Your most humble Servant,

SAM. JOHNSON

9. *Ante* To JB, 24 Feb. 1773 and n. 8.

10. George Colman, who preferred "sentimental" to "laughing" comedy, had accepted *She Stoops to Conquer* with considerable reluctance. Convinced that the play would fail, "he refused to buy new costumes or settings" (R. W. Wardle, *Oliver Goldsmith*, 1957, pp. 232–33, 237). However, the comedy proved a great success and ran for seventeen performances that season (*Lond. Stage*, Part IV, iii.1702–34). According to SJ, "I know of no comedy for many years that has so much exhilarated an audience, that has answered so much the great end of comedy—making an audience merry" (*Life* II.233).

11. *Ante* To JB, 24 Feb. 1773 and n. 6.

12. *Post* To William Samuel Johnson, 4 Mar. 1773.

William Samuel Johnson[1]

THURSDAY 4 MARCH 1773

1. William Samuel Johnson (1727–1819), LL.D., served as agent in London for the Colony of Connecticut, 1766–71. One of Connecticut's first senators, Johnson went on to become the first President of Columbia College (1787). The circumstances of his acquaintance with SJ have not been determined; it is possible that the two men met at Oxford in 1767, when Johnson received his honorary doctorate (Mary Hyde, "Two Distinguished Dr. Johnsons," *Columbia Library Columns* 10, 1961, pp. 4, 10, 6).

To WILLIAM SAMUEL JOHNSON, 4 *March* 1773

MS: Rare Book and Manuscript Library, Columbia University.

ADDRESS: To Dr. Johnson [*added in the hand of William White*] in Stratford, Connecticut.[2]

POSTMARKS: PHILADELPHIA, NEW YORK, 4 MA, [Undeciphered].

ENDORSEMENT: Dr. Saml. Johnson, Fleet Street, London, March 4th, 1773.

Johnson's Court, Fleetstreet, London,
March 4, 1773

Sir:

Of all those whom the various accidents of life have brought within my notice there is scarce any man whose acquaintance I have more desired to cultivate than yours. I cannot indeed charge you with neglecting me, yet our mutual inclination could never gratify itself with opportunities; the current of the day always bore us away from one another. And now the Atlantick is between us.

Whether you carried away an impression of me as pleasing as that which you left me of yourself, I know not; if you did you have not forgotten me, and will be glad that I do not forget you. Merely to be remembred is indeed a barren pleasure, but it is one of the pleasures which is more sensibly felt, as human Nature is more exalted.

To make you wish that I should have you in my mind, I would be glad to tell you something which you do not know, but all publick affairs are printed; and as you and I had no[3] common friends I can tell you no private history.

The Government I think grows stronger, but I am afraid the next general election will be a time of uncommon turbulence, violence, and outrage.[4]

Of Literature no great product has appeared or is expected; the attention of the people has for some years been otherwise employed.

I was told two days ago of a design which must excite some

2. This letter was enclosed in To William White, 4 Mar. 1773.

3. MS: "not" del. before "no"

4. SJ's forebodings proved accurate: the election of Oct. 1774 brought to a head the conflicts between the Ministry and the "patriotic" Opposition, and riots ensued in London. SJ joined the fray by producing the second of his anti-Wilkes political tracts, *The Patriot* (*Works*, Yale ed. x.387).

curiosity. Two ships[5] are [in] preparation, which are under the command of Captain Constantine Phipps to explore the Northern Ocean, not to seek the Northeast or the Northwest passage, but to sail directly North, as near the pole as they can go. They hope to find an open Ocean, but I suspect it is one mass of perpetual congelation.[6] I do not much wish well to discoveries, for I am always afraid they will end in conquest and robbery.[7]

I have been out of order this winter but am grown better. Can I ever hope to see you again, or must I be always content to tell you that in another hemisphere I am, Sir, Your most humble servant,

SAM. JOHNSON

5. MS: final "s" superimposed upon "w"

6. The Hon. Constantine John Phipps (1744–92), R.N., later (1775) second Baron Mulgrave (peerage of Ireland), M.P. for Lincoln (1768–74), Huntingdon (1776–84), and Newark (1784–90) (Namier and Brooke III.277). From their two ships, the *Racehorse* and the *Carcass*, Phipps and his men were commissioned "to make such observations of every kind as might be useful to navigation, or tend to the promotion of natural knowledge" (Constantine Phipps, *A Voyage towards the North Pole*, 1774, in *A General Collection of the Best and Most Interesting Voyages*, ed. John Pinkerton, 1808, I.543). Phipps did indeed find the ice north of Spitzbergen impenetrable, and the expedition returned in October.

7. "If there is one aspect of Johnson's political thinking that is clearly defined and that does not vary from his earliest to his latest writings, it is his distrust of the foreign invaders of a land and his sympathy with those who originally occupied it" (D. J. Greene, *The Politics of SJ*, 1960, p. 165).

Hester Thrale

TUESDAY 9 MARCH 1773

MS: Hyde Collection.

Johnson's Court, Fleetstreet,
March 9, 1773

Dearest Madam:

Dr. James called on me last night, deep, I think, in wine.[1] Our dialogue was this

1. In 1779 SJ spoke of Robert James as "a physician who for twenty years was not sober" (*Life* III.389 and n. 2).

—You find the case hopeless.—Quite hopeless.—But I hope you can procure her an easier dismission out of life.—That, I believe is in our power.[2]

The rest of his talk was about other things.

If it can give the dear Lady any comfort, be pleased to let her know, that my grief for her is very serious and very deep. If I could be useful as you can be, I would devote myself to her as You must do. But all human help is little, her trust must be in a better Friend.

You will not let me burst in ignorance[3] of[4] your transaction with Alexander.[5] Surely my heart is with you in your whole System of Life. I am, Dear Madam, Your most humble Servant,

SAM. JOHNSON

I had written this letter before yours came. God bless you all.

2. James was attending Mrs. Salusbury in the final stage of her struggle with breast cancer. He apparently visited Streatham the same night: on 9 Mar. Hester Thrale wrote SJ, "James did come though late . . . he says we must purge her still more briskly" (MS: Rylands Library).

3. "Let me not burst in ignorance, but tell / Why thy canoniz'd bones, hearsed in death, / Have burst their cerements" (*Hamlet* I.iv.46–48).

4. MS: "of" repeated as catchword

5. In her own copy of *Letters*, 1788, H. L. Piozzi identifies Alexander as "the chymist in Long Acre" (I.74, Trinity College, Cambridge). Thomas Alexander (*fl.* 1748–90) and a Mr. Eyles had threatened to sue Henry Thrale for fraudulent business dealings. Hester Thrale was acting as intermediary in the dispute (Hester Thrale to SJ, 10 Mar. 1773, MS: Rylands Library; Clifford, 1952, p. 97; *The Piozzi Letters*, ed. E. A. Bloom and L. D. Bloom, 1989, I.245 n. 3). *Post* To Hester Thrale, 11 Mar. 1773.

Hester Thrale

THURSDAY 11 MARCH 1773

MS: Hyde Collection.

Dear Madam: March 11, 1773

Your negotiation will probably end as you desire.[1] I wish your

1. *Ante* To Hester Thrale, 9 Mar. 1773 and n. 5. On 10 Mar. she had informed SJ, "Your Advice was precisely right; upon my talking in a higher and more fearless Tone my friend Alexander was much disconcerted" (MS: Rylands Library).

pious offices might have the same success, but death is necessary, and your tenderness will make it less painful.[2] I am sorry that I can do nothing. The dear Lady has my wishes, and sometimes my prayers. I hope our prayers will be heard for her, and her prayers for herself. I am, Dear Madam, Your most humble servant,

SAM. JOHNSON

2. *Ante* To Hester Thrale, 9 Mar. 1773 and n. 2.

Hester Thrale

FRIDAY 12 MARCH 1773

MS: Hyde Collection.

Dear Madam: March 12, 1773

The pills certainly help her Stomach. Poor, dear, dear Lady, but if she grows weaker, the pills do not help, so much as the Disease wastes.[1] I am sorry the cough cannot yet mend. That perpetual irritation destroys all tranquillity either of life or death. But I hope nothing has been left to these dreadful moments. Dear Lady, how I now love her.[2] Does she ever name me?

⟨ ⟩[3] if any such design they have. I believe you must leave them for a time to their own res⟨oluti⟩ons, and think only on dear Mamma, u⟨nless⟩ you can spare a moment for, Madam, Your most humble Servant,

SAM. JOHNSON

1. "He [Dr. James] says we must purge her still more briskly, and when I urged her Inability to bear such rough Evacuation he only said that the Disease would weaken her still more than the Pills" (Hester Thrale to SJ, 9 Mar. 1773, MS: Rylands Library).

2. "My mother and he disliked one another extremely. . . . The domestic distresses of the year 1772 reconciled them" (*Johns. Misc.* I.234–35).

3. MS: mutilated: bottom quarter of sheet missing; jagged tear along left-hand margin

Hester Thrale

MONDAY 15 MARCH 1773

PRINTED SOURCE: Chapman 1.311–12.

Dear Madam: March 15, 1773

I am likewise sincerely glad of the prolongation of a life so dear on any terms. Dear, dear Lady. Methinks I should gladly see her again.

When the accumulated matter is discharged that which comes away through open orifices as fast as it is formed, will, I believe, be less fetid.[1]

Mr. Hector says, that a poultice of rasped carrots is very powerful to abate any offensive smell.[2] I think the London Chirurgeons use it.

May the poor Lady's pain and your cares end in happiness. I am, Madam, Your most humble Servant,

SAM. JOHNSON

1. A liquid discharge from the cancerous sore was thought to be one of the effects of purgatives (Robert James, *Medicinal Dictionary*, 1745, [2F1r]; *Ante* To Hester Thrale, 12 Mar. 1773, n. 1).

2. "A poultice of the root of garden carrot has been successfully used to cancerous . . . ulcers, the fætor of which it has not failed very speedily to remove, and generally with a great amendment of the state of the sore" (William Lewis, *Materia Medica*, 3d ed., 1784, p. 272).

Hester Thrale

TUESDAY 16 MARCH 1773

PRINTED SOURCE: Chapman 1.312.

Dear Madam: March 16, 1773

You are very kind in sending me such punctual accounts, though my solicitude for the dear Lady may almost presume to deserve them. All the advice that I can give is that by all means she allure herself to take nourishment. If the cough ceases, I hope she will be able to sleep, and if she could eat and sleep, we may hope for her continuance among us. I hope to morrow will be a good day.

My Master did not wish my stay, so I soon went away. But we totally forgot Eyles and Alexander as if they were out of Being.[1] Mr. Perkins says that the Customers are much pleased with their beer.[2] That is good news, and Perkins is always a credible witness. I am, Dear Lady, Your most obedient,

SAM. JOHNSON

1. *Ante* To Hester Thrale, 9 Mar. 1773, n. 5.

2. John Perkins (*c.* 1730–1812), manager of the Thrale brewery, went on to become a partner after Henry Thrale's death in 1781 (Peter Mathias, *The Brewing Industry in England, 1700–1830,* 1959, pp. 31, 272–73). The success of the beer came as a particular relief, for the previous year's supply had been entirely spoiled by Thrale's misguided attempts to brew without hops (Clifford, 1952, p. 93).

Hester Thrale

WEDNESDAY 17 MARCH 1773

MS: Hyde Collection.

Dear Madam: March 17, 1773

To tell you that I am sorry both for the poor Lady and for you is useless. I cannot help either of you. The weakness of mind is perhaps only a casual interruption or[1] intermission of the attention, such as we all suffer when some weighty care or urgent calamity has possession of the mind. She will compose herself. She is unwilling to dye, and the first conviction of approaching death raised great perturbation. I think she has but very lately thought death close at hand. She will compose herself to do that as well as she[2] can, which must at last be done. May she not want the Divine Assistance.

You, Madam, will have a great loss, a greater than is common in the loss of a parent. Fill your mind with hope of her happiness, and turn your thoughts first to Him who gives and takes away in whose presence the Living and Dead are stand-

1. MS: "or" written above "of" del.

2. MS: "she" repeated as catchword

ing together.[3] Then remember that when this mournful duty is paid, others yet remain of equal obligation, and, we may hope, of less painful performance. Grief is a species of idleness, and the necessity of attention to the present preserves us by the merciful disposition of providence from being lacerated and devoured by sorrow for the past. You must think on your Husband and your children, and do what this dear Lady has done for you.

Not to come to town while the great struggle continues is undoubtedly well resolved. But do not harrass yourself into danger, you owe the care of your health to all that love you, at least to all whom it is your duty to love. You cannot give such a Mother too much, if you do not give her what belongs to another. I am, Madam, Your most humble Servant,

SAM. JOHNSON

3. SJ is echoing phrasing and sentiments from "The Order for the Burial of the Dead" in the *Book of Common Prayer.*

Hester Thrale

FRIDAY 19 MARCH 1773

MS: Johnson House, London.
ADDRESS: To Mrs. Thrale.

Dear Madam: March 19, 1773

It is now two days since I heard of the poor dear Lady. I hope, I do not give you pain by enquiring after her. Let me know, if you please, what is to be known, I wish my expectations could flatter me with any amendment. There is no need of exhorting you to take care of her. Do not forget to take care of yourself. I am, Madam, Your most humble servant,

SAM. JOHNSON

If it be fit, tell her how much I love her and pity her.

John Taylor

SATURDAY 20 MARCH 1773

PRINTED SOURCE: Chapman 1.315.

We that have lived to lose many that might have cared for us, should care a little for one another.

Hester Thrale

SATURDAY 20 MARCH 1773

PRINTED SOURCE: Piozzi, *Letters* 1.78–79.

Madam, March 20, 1773, The Equinox

I have now heard twice to-day how the dear lady mends; twice is not often enough for such news. May she long and long continue mending.[1] When I see her again, how I shall love her. If we could keep a while longer together, we should all, I hope, try to be thankful. Part we must at last; but the last parting is very afflictive. When I see her I shall torment her with caressing her. Has she yet been down stairs?

On Tuesday morning I hope to see you.[2] I have not much to tell you, but will gather what little I can.

I shall be glad to see you, for you are much in my head, notwithstanding your negotiations for my master, he has mended his share for one year,[3] you must think of cutting in pieces and boiling him.[4] We will at least keep him out of J-ck-n's cop-

1. Hester Thrale had reported on 19 Mar. that Mrs. Salusbury was "vastly better these two Days thank God; I hope quite out of immediate danger" (MS: Rylands Library).

2. In her letter of 19 Mar. Hester Thrale had invited SJ to join her for breakfast at Southwark on the following Tuesday (MS: Rylands Library).

3. SJ may be referring to the dispute with Alexander and Eyles (*Ante* To Hester Thrale, 9 Mar. 1773, n. 5).

4. SJ may be alluding to the myth in which Tantalus cuts up his son Pelops and boils the pieces, feeding them to the unwitting gods in a stew (Robert Graves, *The Greek Myths*, 1955, II.25).

per.[5] You will be at leisure now to think of brewing and negotiating, and a little of, Madam, Your, etc.

5. Humphrey Jackson (1717–1801), F.R.S., experimental chemist, a friend of Henry Thrale at least since 1763, had encouraged him in his disastrous brewing experiments (J. H. Appleby, "Humphrey Jackson," *Notes and Records of the Royal Society of London* 40, 1986, p. 147; *Thraliana* I.307; Clifford, 1952, p. 93). Jackson had also persuaded Thrale to subsidize unsuccessful experiments in wood preservation that were designed to win a government contract. These experiments were performed under Jackson's supervision in large copper vessels, including one enormous vat in East Smithfield built by Thrale (*Autobiography Letters and Literary Remains of Mrs. Piozzi* [*Thrale*], ed. Abraham Hayward, 2d ed., 1861, II.25–26).

Hester Thrale

TUESDAY 23 MARCH 1773

MS: Hyde Collection.
ADDRESS: To Mrs. Thrale.

Dear Madam: March 23, 1773

The return of the dear Lady's appetite must prolong her life, unless some sudden rupture of the breast, or some other unexpected violence supervenes, and therefore I hope she will continue to eat.[1]

Ray and his people will perhaps have but a weeks work, and that will be but five pounds.[2] Never vex. To gain is the great point. My Master must gratify himself a little, now he is at liberty, else how will Liberty be enjoyed.[3] If we could once settle our gains, we would set expences at defiance.

Mr. Garrick has just now sent his brother to me with a con-

1. *Ante* To Hester Thrale, 9 Mar. 1773, n. 2.

2. At Streatham Park Henry Thrale was adding several rooms, including a new library (Hyde, 1977, pp. 52, 69). It is likely that the "Ray" to whom SJ refers is Richard Ray (d. 1795), a "wood mason" in Streatham (*The Piozzi Letters*, ed. E. A. Bloom and L. D. Bloom, 1989, I.237 n. 2).

3. SJ urges Hester Thrale to indulge her husband in his building schemes, now that the financial troubles of 1772 have been surmounted.

futation of Mr. Murphy to which I do not see what can be replied.[4]

Do not let vexation come near your heart. You have made this year a great progress in reformation, and to reform too violently has always been dangerous. To tell the truth I am not sorry that the neighborhood should see the usual degree of visible expence, and the stated process of annual operation; the continuance of the same appearances will discuss[5] any remains of suspicion, and settle us as we were before in the publick opinion. I am, Dear Madam, Your most humble servant,

SAM. JOHNSON

4. On 30 Dec. 1772 Arthur Murphy, exasperated by delays and disagreements over casting, had withdrawn his play, *Know Your Own Mind*, from rehearsal at Drury Lane. He then published a thinly veiled attack on David Garrick in the advertisement to *Alzuma*, which opened at Covent Garden on 23 Feb. 1773 (*Lond. Stage*, Part IV, iii.1696). SJ was called in to mediate the dispute, and Garrick's brother George (1723–79), assistant manager of Drury Lane, functioned as go-between (H. H. Dunbar, *The Dramatic Career of Arthur Murphy*, 1946, pp. 227–30, 232). Neither Garrick's "confutation" nor Murphy's answering pamphlet (*Post* To Hester Thrale, 25 Mar. 1773) appears to have been published.

5. *discuss*: "to disperse" (SJ's *Dictionary*).

Hester Thrale

THURSDAY 25 MARCH 1773

MS: Hyde Collection.

Madam: March 25, 1773

If my letters can do you any good it is not fit that you should want them. You are always flattering me with the good that I do without knowing it.

The return of Mrs. Salusbury's Appetite will undoubtedly prolong her life; I therefore wish it to continue or to improve. You did not say whether she went down stairs.

Harry will be happier now he goes to School and reads Milton.[1] Miss will want him for all her vapouring.

1. In order to give Mrs. Salusbury her "undivided Attention," Hester Thrale had enrolled Henry the younger in a local boys' school (Hyde, 1977, pp. 60–61).

Did not I tell you that I thought, I had written to Boswel?[2] he has answered my Letter.[3]

I am going this evening to put young Otway to school with Mr. Elphinston.[4]

Colman is so distressed with abuse about this play, that he has solicited Goldsmith to *take him off the rack of the newspapers*.[5]

Murphy is preparing a whole pamphlet against Garrick, and Garrick is, I suppose, collecting materials to confute Murphy.[6]

Jennens has published Hamlet, but without a preface, and Steevens declares his intention of letting him pass the rest of his life in peace.[7] Here is news. I am, Madam, Your most humble Servant,

SAM. JOHNSON

2. MS: question mark superimposed upon comma

3. *Ante* To JB, 24 Feb. 1773. JB responded on 19 Mar. (Register of Letters, MS: Beinecke Library).

4. According to SJ, "I would not put a boy to him [James Elphinston], whom I intended for a man of learning. But for the sons of citizens, who are to learn a little, get good morals, and then go to trade, he may do very well" (*Life* II.171).

5. George Colman was convinced on pragmatic grounds that *She Stoops to Conquer* would not succeed (*Ante* To William White, 4 Mar. 1773 and n. 10). It was widely believed, moreover, that he hoped the play would fail. Virulent "abuse" in the press prompted him to beg Goldsmith, "Either take me off the rack of the Newspapers, or give me the *Coup de Grace*" (*The Collected Letters of Oliver Goldsmith*, ed. K. C. Balderston, 1928, p. xlix). Though he was himself partly responsible for the anti-Colman campaign, Goldsmith declined to accuse the manager in the preface to the play, published on 26 Mar. (Balderston, *Letters of Goldsmith*, p. 1).

6. *Ante* To Hester Thrale, 23 Mar. 1773 and n. 4.

7. Charles Jennens (1700–1773), of Gopsal, Leicestershire, began an acrimonious public exchange with George Steevens in 1770 when (in his edition of *King Lear*) he disparaged the work of previous Shakespearean editors, including SJ. Jennens claimed in the preface "that no fair and exact collation of *Shakespeare* hath yet been presented to the public" [VII]. Jennens's editions of *Hamlet, Macbeth*, and *Othello* were published in 1773, his *Julius Caesar* posthumously in 1774 (Gordon Crosse, "Charles Jennens as Editor of Shakespeare," *The Library* 16, 1936, p. 239). Steevens's and SJ's own revised edition of SJ's *Shakespeare* appeared in 1773.

Hester Thrale

FRIDAY 2 APRIL 1773

MS: Birthplace Museum, Lichfield.
ADDRESS: To Mrs. Thrale.

Dear Madam: April 2, 1773

I cannot but hope that we may yet have the poor dear Lady a little longer; but long alas it cannot be. God bless you all.

The Dinner of tuesday is yet at a great distance, I shall not begin to long till monday.[1] Yesterday we dined very gaily, to day I have been learning Spanish of Mr. Baretti.[2] To morrow I dine at Mr. Hoole's, and to night I go to the club.[3]

Beyond to morrow where is the wonder that all is uncertainty; yet[4] I look beyond to morrow, and form schemes for tuesday. I am, Madam, your most humble servant,

SAM. JOHNSON

1. Hester Thrale had invited SJ to dine at Southwark on 6 Apr., "and hear all the Grievances" (29 Mar. 1773, MS: Rylands Library).

2. SJ already read Spanish fluently (*Life* 1.49, 526). At the time of his death his library contained editions of Cervantes and Feijóo (Greene, 1975, pp. 47, 58).

3. *Post* To Hester Thrale, 3 Apr. 1773.

4. MS: "yet" superimposed upon undeciphered erasure

Hester Thrale

SATURDAY 3 APRIL 1773[1]

MS: Pierpont Morgan Library.[2]

Dearest Madam:

Last night we chose Mr. Vesey an Irish Member of parliament into the Club.[3]

1. See below, n. 3. 2. MS: fragment

3. Agmondesham Vesey (d. 1785), M.P. for Harristown, Co. Kildare, and Kinsdale, Co. Cork, Accountant-General of Ireland (1767–85). In proposing him for membership, Edmund Burke attested that Vesey was "good humoured, sensible, well bred, and had all the social virtues" (*Letters of Sir Joshua Reynolds*, ed. F. W.

Hilles, 1929, pp. 33–34). According to Edmond Malone, Vesey was so eager to be elected to The Club that he "had couriers stationed to bring him the quickest intelligence of his success" (Edmond Malone to Lord Charlemont, 5 Apr. 1779, *Manuscripts and Correspondence of James, First Earl of Charlemont*, Historical Manuscripts Commission, 1891, I.344). Vesey was elected 2 Apr. (*Annals of The Club*, 1914, pp. 9, 139).

Oliver Goldsmith

FRIDAY 23 APRIL 1773

MS: Johnson House, London.

ADDRESS: To Dr. Goldsmith.

Sir: Apr. 23, 1773

I beg that you will excuse my Absence to the Club. I am going this evening to Oxford.

I have another favour to beg. It is that I may be considered as proposing Mr. Boswel for a candidate of our Society, and that he may be considered as regularly nominated.[1] I am, Sir, Your most humble Servant,

SAM. JOHNSON

1. On 30 Apr. JB, zealously supported by SJ and Topham Beauclerk, was elected a member of The Club (*Life* II.235). SJ admitted later to JB: "Several of the members wished to keep you out. . . . But, now you are in, none of them are sorry" (*Life* V.76).

John Hoole

FRIDAY 23 APRIL 1773

MS: Hyde Collection.

ENDORSEMENT: Letter to me after my recovery from illness.

Dear Sir: April 23, 1773

Mrs. Williams and I are both glad that You and Mrs. Hoole are safe at Stortford.[1] It is our joint request that you will keep

1. In 1757 Hoole had married Susannah Smith (?1718–98), who came from a

in a state of quiet till your health is completely reestablished. By attempting business before you are fit for it, you will be long before you are able to do it well, and will endanger a return of your fever. Take therefore great care of your self. Make my compliments to every body. I am, Sir, Your affectionate, humble Servant,

SAM. JOHNSON

Mrs. Williams sends her compliments along with mine.

---

leading Quaker family of Bishops Stortford, Hertfordshire (*Johns. Glean.* XI.438; *Lit. Anec.* II.405).

Hester Thrale

TUESDAY 27 APRIL 1773

MS: Hyde Collection.

Dear Madam: Apr. 27, 1773

Hope is more pleasing than fear, but not less fallacious, you know, when you do not try to deceive yourself, that the disease which at last is to destroy, must be gradually growing worse, and that it is vain to wish for more than that the descent to death may be slow and easy. In this wish I join with you, and hope it will be granted. Dear, dear Lady, whenever she is lost, she will be missed, and whenever she is remembered she will be lamented. Is it a good or an evil to me that she now loves me?[1] It is surely a good for you will love me better, and we shall have a new principle of concord; and I shall be happier with honest sorrow, than with sullen indifference; and far happier still than with counterfeited sympathy.

I am reasoning upon a principle very far from certain, a confidence of survivance. You, or I, or both, may be called into the presence of the Supreme Judge before her. I have lived a life of which I do not like the review. Surely I shall in time live better.

1. *Ante* To Hester Thrale, 12 Mar. 1773, n. 2.

I sat down with an intention to write high compliments, but my thoughts have taken another course, and some other time must now serve to tell you with what other emotions, what benevolence and fidelity, I am, Dear Madam, Your most humble Servant,

SAM. JOHNSON

Hester Thrale

TUESDAY 4 MAY 1773[1]

MS: Hyde Collection.

My dearest Lady: May 4

I wrote a letter to you this morning to tell you, that I could not well avoid dining in this neighborhood to morrow; but that I will wait on you early in the evening.[2] Early enough, I design, for tea and business. What we shall tell each other I know not, but hope we shall say nothing that can make us have less respect or kindness for one another than we have. I am, Madam, Your most humble Servant,

SAM. JOHNSON

1. In preparing this letter for publication in *Letters* (1788), H. L. Piozzi numbered it "72," then decided to omit it altogether. The published letters from 1773 are numbered 58–93.

2. This letter has not been recovered.

Thomas Bagshaw[1]

SATURDAY 8 MAY 1773

MS: Sarah Markham.

ADDRESS: To the Reverend Mr. Bagshaw at Bromley.

1. Thomas Bagshaw (1711–87), chaplain of Bromley College, Kent, and perpetual curate of Bromley Parish. In 1752 he had conducted the burial service for Elizabeth Johnson (*Post* To Thomas Bagshaw, 12 July 1784). Bagshaw was notable for his "absolute composure" and his "enthusiasm for philology" (Sarah Markham, *John Loveday of Caversham*, 1984, p. 70).

Sir: May 8, 1773

I return you my sincere thanks for your additions to my dictionary, but the new Edition has been published some time, and therefore I cannot now make use of them. Whether I shall ever revise it more I know not.[2] If many readers had been as judicious, as diligent, and as communicative as yourself, my work had been better. The world must at present, take it as it is. I am, Sir, Your most obliged and most humble Servant,

SAM. JOHNSON

2. The revised fourth edition of the *Dictionary* had appeared in March (*Ante* To JB, 24 Feb. 1773 and n. 6). SJ prepared further revisions sometime afterwards, but they were not incorporated into the *Dictionary* until after his death (G. J. Kolb and J. K. Sledd, "The Reynolds Copy of Johnson's *Dictionary*," *Bulletin of the John Rylands Library* 37, 1955, pp. 446–75).

Hester Thrale

SATURDAY 8 MAY 1773[1]

MS: Hyde Collection.[2]

I dined in a large company at a Dissenting Booksellers yesterday, and disputed against toleration, with one Doctor Meyer.[3]

1. It is likely that SJ refers to the dinner of 7 May 1773 described by JB (*Life* II.247–55). This dinner took place at the house of Edward Dilly (1732–79) and his brother Charles (1739–1807), booksellers in the Poultry.

2. MS: fragment

3. Presumably SJ refers to Henry Mayo (1733–93), D.D., LL.D., pastor of the Independent Congregation in Nightingale Lane, Wapping, London. SJ argued with Mayo against complete toleration of dissenters (*Life* II.249). According to JB: "Dr. Mayo's calm temper and steady perseverance, rendered him an admirable subject for the exercise of Dr. Johnson's powerful abilities. He never flinched: but, after reiterated blows, remained seemingly unmoved as at the first" (*Life* II.252 n. 3).

Hester Thrale

MONDAY 17 MAY 1773

MS: Houghton Library.

Madam: May 17, 1773

Never imagine that your letters are long, they are always too short for my curiosity; I do not know that I was ever content with a single perusal.

Of dear Mrs. Salusbury I never expect much better news than you send me, *de pis en pis* is the natural and certain course of her dreadful malady. I am content when it leaves her ease enough for the exercise of her mind.

Why should Mr. Thrale suppose that what I took the liberty of suggesting was concerted with you? He does not know how much I revolve [1] his affairs, and how honestly I desire his prosperity. I hope he has let the hint take some hold of his mind.[2]

Your declaration to Miss Fanny is more general than my opinions allow.[3] I think an unlimited promise of acting by[4] the opinion of another so wrong that nothing, or hardly any thing can make it right. All unnecessary vows are folly, because the[y] suppose a prescience of the future which has not been given us. They are, I think, a crime because they resign that life to chance which God has given us to be regulated by reason; and superinduce a kind of fatality, from which it is the

1. *revolve*: "to consider; to meditate on" (SJ's *Dictionary*).

2. SJ's "hint" apparently concerned Thrale's "connexions with Quack Chemists Quacks of *all sorts*" (Piozzi 1.83; *Ante* To Hester Thrale, 20 Mar. 1773, n. 5).

3. Frances Plumbe (1758–90), Henry Thrale's niece, had fallen in love with John Rice (*c*. 1752–1801), son of the distiller Morgan Rice (d. 1795) of Hill House, Tooting, High Sheriff of Surrey (1772), later (1776) Deputy Lieutenant (*Miscellanea Genealogica et Heraldica*, 3d ser., 1894–95, I.101; E. W. Brayley, *A Topographical History of Surrey*, 1850, III.487–88). Frances's father, Alderman Samuel Plumbe, was violently opposed to their marrying, ostensibly because Frances was only 15. The couple appealed to Henry Thrale to intercede on their behalf or to give his own consent to an elopement. Though she sympathized with their plight, Hester Thrale counseled them to respect "parental Authority" (Hester Thrale to SJ, *c*. 20 May 1773, MS: Rylands Library; Clifford, 1952, pp. 99–100).

4. MS: "by" altered from "of"

great privilege of our Nature to be free. Unlimited obedience is due only to the Universal Father of heaven and earth. My Parents may be mad or foolish; may be wicked and malicious; may be erroneously religious, or absurdly scrupulous. I am not bound to compliance with mandates either positive or negative, which either religion condemns, or reason rejects. There wanders about the world a wild notion which extends over marriage more than over any other transaction. If Miss Plumbe followed a trade, would it be said that she was bound in conscience to give or refuse credit at her Fathers choice? And is not marriage a thing in which she is more interested, and has therefore more right of choice? When I may suffer for my own crimes, when I may be sued for my own debts, I may judge by parity of reason, for my own happiness. The Parent's moral right can arise only from his kindness, and his civil right only from[5] his money.

Conscience cannot dictate obedience to the wicked, or compliance with the foolish; and of interest mere prudence is the judge.

If the daughter is bound without a promise, she promises nothing; and if she is not bound, she promises too much.

What is meant by tying up money in trade I do not understand. No money is so little tied as that which is employed in trade. Mr. Rice perhaps only means that in consideration of money to be advanced, he will oblige his son to be a trader.[6] This is reasonable enough. Upon ten thousand pounds diligently occupied they may live in great plenty and splendour without the mischiefs of idleness.

I can write a long letter as well as my Mistress, and shall be glad that my long letters may be as welcome as hers.

My Nights are grown again very uneasy and troublesome. I know not that the country will mend them, but I hope your company will mend my days. Though I cannot now expect much attention, and would not wish for more, than can be

5. MS: "from" superimposed upon "for"

6. *Post* To Hester Thrale, 22 May 1773.

spared from the poor dear Lady, yet I shall see you and hear you every now and then, and to see and hear you, is always to hear wit, and to see virtue.[7]

I shall, I hope, see you to morrow, and a little on the two next days, and with that little I must for the present try to be contented. I am, Madam, Your most obedient and most humble Servant,

SAM. JOHNSON

7. Cf. *Post* To Hester Thrale, Early June 1773 and n. 2.

Hester Thrale

SATURDAY 22 MAY 1773

MS: Berg Collection, New York Public Library.

Dear Lady: May 22, 1773

Dr. Lawrence is of your mind about the intermission,[1] and thought the bark would be best, but I have had so good a night as makes me wonder. Dr. Lawrence is just gone—he says I have no fever and may let bark alone, if I will venture, but it is meo periculo.[2]

Make my compliments to the dear lady.

I think Mr. Thrale has done right in not prohibiting at least Fanny's flight with her Lover.[3] There is no danger of Mr. Rice's taking care of his Son and of his Son's wife,[4] and as he is willing to receive a daughter in law without a fortune, he has a right to provide for her his own way. The great motive to his consent is, that his Son will engage in trade, and there-

1. *intermission*: "the space between the paroxysms of a fever" (SJ's *Dictionary*).

2. *meo periculo*: "at my own risk." SJ's intuition was correct: his fever had broken (*Post* To Hester Thrale, 23 May 1773).

3. Henry Thrale finally acquiesced in his niece's elopement with John Rice (*Ante* To Hester Thrale, 17 May 1773, n. 3) when he learned that Rice's father was willing and able to support them. The couple left for Calais on 23 or 24 May, and were married in Holland (Clifford, 1952, p. 100).

4. SJ means that Mr. Rice will not *fail* to take care of his son and daughter-in-law.

fore no doubt can be made, but he will enable him to do it, and whether at Midsummer, or Michaelmas, we have no need to care, nor right to prescribe. I am, Madam, Your most humble Servant,

SAM. JOHNSON

Hester Thrale

SUNDAY 23 MAY 1773

MS: Berg Collection, New York Public Library.

Dearest Lady: May 23, 1773

Still Flatter flatter? Why should the poor be flattered? The Doctor was with me again to day, and we both think the fever quite gone. I believe it was not an intermittent, for I took of my own head physick yesterday, and Celsus says, it seems, that if a cathartick be taken the fit will return certo certius.[1] I would bear something rather than Celsus should be detected in an errour. But I say it was a *febris continua* and had a regular crisis.[2]

What poor Nesbitt said, is worthy of the greatest mind, since the greatest mind can get no further.[3] In the highest and the lowest things we all are equal.

As to Mr. Plumbe, let him see a couple of fellows within call, and if he makes a savage noise, order them to come gradually nearer, and you will see how quiet he will grow.[4]

1. *certo certius*: "most certainly."

2. The *De Medicina* of Aulus Cornelius Celsus (*fl.* A.D. 14–37) contains detailed instructions on the treatment of various kinds of fever, including *febris continua* (e.g. II.i.7, III.viii). However, the passage to which SJ refers has not been traced. SJ quotes (inaccurately) from the *De Medicina* in his commentary on *Henry VIII* (*Works*, Yale ed. VIII.633); he owned a copy of Celsus at the time of his death (Greene, 1975, p. 47).

3. Probably Susanna Thrale Nesbitt (d. 1789), youngest sister of Henry Thrale and wife of Arnold Nesbitt (?1721–1779) (Hyde, 1977, p. 360). H. L. Piozzi described her as "a pretty, but paltry Creature" (*Thraliana* II.804).

4. On discovering his daughter's elopement (*Ante* To Hester Thrale, 22 May 1773 and n. 3), Plumbe assumed that Henry Thrale had driven the couple to Scotland to be married (Clifford, 1952, p. 100). Plumbe turned "his Wrath upon

Let the poor dear Lady know that I am sorry for her sorrows, and sincerely and earnestly wish her all good.[5]

Write to me when you can, but do not flatter me. I am sorry you can think, it pleases me. It is enough for one to be, as Mr. Evans[6] phrases it, Madam, Your friend and Servant,

SAM. JOHNSON

our House, where we stood a regular Seige" (Hester Thrale to Frances Rice, 1 June 1773, MS: Hyde Collection).

5. *Ante* To Hester Thrale, 9 Mar. 1773, n. 2.

6. James Evans (d. *c.* 1786), Rector of St. Saviour's and later (1777) of St. Olave's, Southwark, a friend and frequent guest of the Thrales.

Hester Thrale

MONDAY 24 MAY 1773

MS: Berg Collection, New York Public Library.

Dear Madam: May 24, 1773

My fever has departed but has left me a very severe inflammation in the seeing eye. I take physick, and do not eat.[1]

Recommend[2] me to the poor dear Lady, whom I hope to see again, however melancholy must be the interview, she has now quickly to do, what I cannot reasonably hope to put[3] off long,

res siqua diu mortalibus ulla est[4]

1. *Post* To John Taylor, 22 June 1773. The danger to SJ's eye was severe: the physician John Mudge feared "that unless Mr. Johnson took the greatest care to have the inflammation removed, the danger of his losing his sight was very great" (Giuseppe Baretti to Hester Thrale, 5 June 1773, MS: Hyde Collection). According to JB, SJ had lost all sight in his other eye as a consequence of the scrofula that afflicted him as an infant (*Life* I.41).

2. MS: "R" altered from "B"

3. MS: "putt"

4. *res si qua diu mortalibus ulla est*: "if to mortal beings aught be long" (Virgil, *Aeneid* X.861, trans. H. R. Fairclough, Loeb ed.).

and which is at no great distance from the youngest. I have the same hope with poor Nesbitt.[5]

You do not tell me whither the young Lovers are gone. I am glad Dr. Thomas is gone with them.[6] What a life do they image in futurity, how unlike to what they are to find it. But to morrow is an old deceiver, and his cheat never grows stale. I suppose they go to Scotland. Was Fanny dressed a la Nesbittienne?[7]

I shall not, I think, go into the country till you are so kind as to fetch me, unless some stronger invitation should be offered, than I have yet found.

The difference between praise and flattery, is the same as[8] between that hospitality that sets wine enough before the guest, and that which forces him to be drunk. If you love me, and surely I hope you do, why should you vitiate my mind with a false opinion of its own merit?[9] why should you teach [it] to be unsatisfied with the civility of every other place? You know how much I honour you, and you are bound to use your influence well.

I am glad that you made no struggle to dine with the Clerks;[10] I hope my Master will have no unpleasant week at his Restes.[11]

Do not let your own dear Spirits forsake you. Your task at present is heavy, and yet you purpose to take me, but I hope I shall take from it one way what I add another. I purpose to

5. *Ante* To Hester Thrale, 23 May 1773 and n. 3. The precise nature of their "hope" is undetermined.

6. *Ante* To Hester Thrale, 22 May 1773, n. 3. On their trip to the Continent, Frances Plumbe and John Rice had been chaperoned by the Streatham schoolmaster, the Rev. Dr. Thomas (Clifford, 1952, p. 100).

7. SJ refers to Susanna Thrale Nesbitt.

8. MS: "a" superimposed upon "w"

9. MS: question mark superimposed upon comma

10. The clerks at the brewery.

11. "When the master brewer goes round to his victuallers once a year, in order to examine the state of the trade, and the stock left on the hands of the alehouse-keeper, the expression used in the profession is, *that he takes up his restes*; a word borrowed from the French, and means the remainder—*les restes*" (Piozzi, *Letters* I.336 n. *).

watch the mollia tempora fandi,[12] and to talk, as occasions offer, to my Master. I think he will, by degrees, calculate his expences, and by his calculations regulate his privations.[13] I am, Madam, Your most humble Servant,

SAM. JOHNSON

12. *mollissima fandi / tempora*: "the happiest season for speech" (Virgil, *Aeneid* IV.293–94, trans. H. R. Fairclough, Loeb ed.).

13. *Ante* To Hester Thrale, 17 May 1773.

Hester Thrale

SATURDAY 29 MAY 1773

MS: Johnson House, London.

Madam: May 29, 1773

My eye is yet so dark that I could not read your note.[1] I have had a poor darkling week. But the dear Lady is worse. My eye is easier and bears light better, but sees little. I wish you could fetch me on Wednesday.[2] I long to be in my own room. Have you got your key?[3] I hope I shall not add much to your trouble, and will wish at least to give you some little solace or amusement. I long to be under your care. I am, Madam, your most etc.

SAM. JOHNSON

Let me hear daily ⟨what m⟩ay be read by Francis.

1. *Ante* To Hester Thrale, 24 May 1773 and n. 1.

2. In the event, SJ went to Streatham on Tuesday, 1 June (Margaret Forbes, *Beattie and His Friends*, 1904, p. 79).

3. *Post* To Hester Thrale, Early June 1773.

Hester Thrale

EARLY JUNE 1773[1]

1. The dating of this letter is problematic. J. D. Wright, who offers the most thorough survey of the evidence, argues that the letter "can hardly refer to the

MS: Rylands Library.

Madame trés honorée:

Puisque, pendant que je me trouve chez vous, il faut passer, tous les jours, plusieures heures dans une solitude profonde, dites moi, Si vous voulez que je vogue a plein abandon, ou que je me contienne dans des bornes prescrites.[2] S'il vous plaît, ma tres chere maîtresse, que je sois lassè a hazard. La chose est faite. Vous vous souvenez[3] de la sagesse de nôtre ami, *Si je ferai etc.* Mais, si ce n'est trop d'esperer que je puisse être digne, comme auparavent, des soins et de la protection d'une[4] ame si aimable par sa douceur, et si venerable par son elevation, accordez moi, par un petit ecrit, la connoisance de ce que m'est permis, et que m'est interdit. Et s'il vous semble mieux que je demeure dans un certain lieu, je vous supplie de m'epargner la necessitè de me contraindre, en m'ôtant le

earliest stages of his [SJ's] friendship with Mrs. Thrale, for he refers to her former care and protection" ("Unpublished Letters of Dr. Johnson," *Bulletin of the John Rylands Library* 16, 1932, p. 62). In addition, Wright links SJ's letter to an undated letter from Hester Thrale (MS: Rylands Library 539.30), "written in the crisis of her mother's illness" ("Unpublished Letters," p. 64). He places the Thrale letter sometime between 11 Dec. 1772, when SJ had returned to London from Lichfield, and the death of Mrs. Salusbury on 18 June 1773. Since the Thrale letter appears to respond directly to SJ's, both must belong to the same period. J. L. Clifford follows Wright in viewing the two documents as companion pieces, "probably written . . . for delivery inside the house" (Clifford, 1952, p. 102). Though not definitive, the findings of Wright and Clifford point toward a date between SJ's arrival at Streatham on 1 June and the 18th.

2. As W. J. Bate observes, this letter "can be understood only in the special context in which it was written—the fatal illness of Mrs. Thrale's mother, with whom Johnson felt a strong rivalry, and a childlike sulkiness and feeling of hurt that Mrs. Thrale is neglecting him when he himself is ill and lonely" (*Samuel Johnson*, 1977, p. 387). Katherine Balderston was the first to link the letter to SJ's fear of insanity and the padlock he entrusted to Hester Thrale in 1768 ("Johnson's Vile Melancholy," in *The Age of Johnson*, ed. F. W. Hilles and W. S. Lewis, 1949, pp. 3–14). Balderston interprets the letter as a "pathological document," one that suggests "erotic maladjustment" and masochistic fantasies ("Melancholy," pp. 8, 11–12). For a skeptical view, see James Gray, "*Arras/Helas!*, A Fresh Look at Samuel Johnson's French," in *Johnson After Two Hundred Years*, ed. P. J. Korshin, 1986, pp. 85–86.

3. MS: "ou" written above "u" del.

4. MS: "d'" altered from "de"

pouvoir de sortir d'ou vou[s] voulez que je sois. Ce que vous ne coûtera que la peine de tourner le clef dans la porte, deux fois par jour. Il faut agir tout a fait en Maîtresse, afin que vôtre jugement et vôtre vigilance viennent a secours de ma faiblesse.

Pour ce que regarde la table, j'espere tout de vôtre sagesse et je crains tout de vôtre douceur. Tournez, Madame tres honorèe, vos pensèes de ce côte la. Il n'y a pour vous rien de difficile; vous pourrez inventer une regime pratiquable sans bruît, et efficace sans peril.

Est ce trop de demander d'une ame telle qu'est la vôtre, que, maîtresse des autres, elle devienne maîtresse de soy-même, et qu'elle triomphe de cette inconstance, qui a fait si souvent, qu'elle a negligèe l[']execution de ses propres loix, qu'elle a oubliée tant de promesses, et qu'elle m'a[5] condamnè a tant de solicitations reiterèes que la resouvenance me fait horreur. Il faut ou accorder, ou refuser; il faut se souvenir de ce qu'on accorde. Je souhaite, ma patronne, que vôtre autoritè me soit toûjours sensible, et que vous me tiennez dans l'esclavage que vou[s] sçavez si bien rendre heureuse.[6] Permettez moi l'honeur d'être, Madame, vôtre très obeissant Serviteur.

5. MS: "m'a" altered from "me"

6. In her probable response to this letter, Hester Thrale urges SJ to "shake off these uneasy Weights, heavier to the Mind by far than Fetters to the body. Let not your fancy dwell thus upon Confinement and severity.—I am sorry you are obliged to be so much alone; I foresaw some ill Consequences of your being here while my Mother was dying thus" (MS: Rylands Library 539.30).

John Taylor

TUESDAY 22 JUNE 1773

MS: Pierpont Morgan Library.

ADDRESS: To the Reverend Dr. Taylor in Ashbourne, Derbyshire.

POSTMARKS: 22 IV, R X [Undeciphered].

ENDORSEMENTS: 1773, 23 June 73.

Dear Sir: June 22,[1] 1773

Sometime before Whitsuntide, I had, without knowing the cause, as I lay in bed a cold and hot fit of a fever; the disorder continued two or three days, and went away by sweat, with a regular crisis. Two days after I read for a very short time, in a book of a minute print,[2] and at night felt a pain in my eye, which was next day inflamed to a very great degree. I was blooded very copiously twice, and took about thirteen purges in fifteen days, and in three weeks was able to read a little. But my eye is, I fear still weak and misty. But it is recovering.[3]

Having thus told you my history, I expect in return to hear yours. We shall not easily at our age, find any that will interest themselves in our health or sickness, as we may reasonably interest ourselves in those of each other. If we do make any new friends, we may justly consider such acquisitions as uncommon instances of happiness.

Your last account of yourself was melancholy, sure summer and a proper regimen have done you good. You said nothing of Dr. Butter or his advice. Have you quitted him? Let me know how you go on, and if you are not better, write your case to Lawrence or Heberden,[4] and do not lye down and suffer without struggle or resistance. I have by some uncommon necessity been blooded five times this year, and I think have always been the better. Of Physick I keep no reckoning. I fancy that neither of us uses exercise enough; I know not well how to get more, but you have more in your power. It is not a very happy state, when the mere preservation of life becomes its chief business, yet such [is] the lot of many. I am, Dear Sir, Yours most affectionately,

SAM. JOHNSON

1. MS: "22" superimposed upon "19"

2. The book may well have been connected with SJ's attempt during this period "to learn the low Dutch Language" (*Works*, Yale ed. I.158).

3. The recovery was slow: a month later SJ's eyesight was still impaired (*Works*, Yale ed. I.158).

4. William Heberden (1710–1801), M.D., F.R.S., eminent and successful London physician, the first to describe angina pectoris. SJ called Heberden "*ultimum Romanorum*, the last of the learned physicians" (*Johns. Misc.* II.311), and bequeathed him a book in acknowledgment of his care (*Life* IV.402 n. 2).

James Boswell

MONDAY 5 JULY 1773

PRINTED SOURCE: JB's *Life*, 1791, I.424–25.

Johnson's-court,
Fleet-street, July 5, 1773

Dear Sir,

When your letter came to me,[1] I was so darkened by an inflammation in my eye, that I could not for some time read it.[2] I can now write without trouble, and can read large prints. My eye is gradually growing stronger; and I hope will be able to take some delight in the survey of a Caledonian loch.[3]

Chambers is going a Judge, with six thousand a year, to Bengal.[4] He and I shall come down together as far as Newcastle, and thence I shall easily get to Edinburgh.[5] Let me know the exact time when your Courts intermit.[6] I must conform a little to Chambers's occasions, and he must conform a little to mine. The time which you shall fix, must be the common point to which we will come as near as we can.[7] Except this eye, I am very well.

Beattie is so caressed, and invited, and treated, and liked,

1. "In a letter from Edinburgh, dated the 29th of May, I pressed him to persevere in his resolution to make this year the projected visit to the Hebrides, of which he and I had talked for many years" (*Life* II.264).

2. *Ante* To Hester Thrale, 24 May 1773 and n. 1.

3. Tentative plans for a Hebridean tour had been laid at least as far back as 1764 (*Boswell on the Grand Tour: Germany and Switzerland, 1764*, ed. F. A. Pottle, 1953, p. 280). "He had disappointed my expectations so long that I began to despair; but in spring 1773, he talked of coming to Scotland that year with so much firmness that I hoped he was at last in earnest" (*Hebrides*, p. 4).

4. Robert Chambers did not actually set sail for India until the following spring (*Post* To Warren Hastings, 30 Mar. 1774).

5. "Luckily Mr. Justice (now Sir Robert) Chambers, who was about to sail for the East Indies, was going to take leave of his relations at Newcastle, and he conducted Dr. Johnson to that town. Mr. [William] Scott of University College, Oxford ... accompanied him from thence to Edinburgh" (*Hebrides*, p. 6). *Post* To Hester Thrale, 12 Aug. 1773.

6. The summer term of the Court of Session in Edinburgh ran from 12 June to 11 Aug. (Appendix B, "The Scottish Courts and Legal System," in *Boswell for the Defence*, ed. W. K. Wimsatt and F. A. Pottle, 1959, p. 351).

7. SJ arrived in Edinburgh on 14 Aug. (*Hebrides*, p. 11).

and flattered, by the great, that I can see nothing of him. I am in great hope that he will be well provided for, and then we will live upon him at the Marischal College, without pity or modesty.[8]

——left the town without taking leave of me, and is gone in deep dudgeon to ——.[9] Is not this very childish? Where is now my legacy?[10]

I hope your dear lady and her dear baby are both well.[11] I shall see them too when I come; and I have that opinion of your choice, as to suspect that when I have seen Mrs. Boswell, I shall be less willing to go away. I am, dear Sir, Your affectionate humble servant,

SAM. JOHNSON

Write to me as soon as you can. Chambers is now at Oxford.

8. James Beattie, who had arrived in London on 7 May, was socially very much in demand. "While Beattie's days were thus passed in a constant succession of engagements . . . his friends were untiring in their efforts to procure for him such recognition for his services to the cause of religion as they considered him entitled to" (Margaret Forbes, *Beattie and His Friends*, 1904, pp. 75, 82). On 1 July he was confidentially informed that the King had granted him a pension of £200 per annum (Forbes, *Beattie*, p. 84). His continuing absence from Scotland, however, prevented him from entertaining JB and SJ in Aberdeen (*Post* To James Beattie, 5 Aug. 1773).

9. Bennet Langton had retired to Langton, his family home in Lincolnshire, having taken offense at SJ's rough handling of him during a discussion of the Trinity on 7 May (*Life* II.254).

10. On 10 May SJ had burst into laughter when he learned that Langton had solemnly made a will in favor of his three sisters: "'ha, ha, ha! I hope he has left me a legacy. I'd have his will turned into verse, like a ballad'" (*Life* II.261–62).

11. JB's eldest daughter, Veronica, was born 15 Mar. (*Later Years*, p. 46).

James Boswell

TUESDAY 3 AUGUST 1773

PRINTED SOURCE: JB's *Life*, 1791, I.425–26.[1]

Dear Sir, August 3, 1773

I shall set out from London on Friday the sixth of this month,

1. MS: enclosed with the following letter, *Post* To JB, 3 Aug. 1773

and purpose not to loiter much by the way.[2] Which day I shall be at Edinburgh, I cannot exactly tell.[3] I suppose I must drive to an inn, and send a porter to find you.[4]

I am afraid Beattie will not be at his College soon enough for us, and I shall be sorry to miss him;[5] but there is no staying for the concurrence of all conveniences. We will do as well as we can. I am, Sir, Your most humble servant,

SAM. JOHNSON

2. *Post* To Hester Thrale, 12 Aug. 1773.
3. *Ante* To JB, 5 July 1773, n. 7.
4. *Post* To JB, 14 Aug. 1773 and n. 1.
5. *Ante* To JB, 5 July 1773 and n. 8.

James Boswell

TUESDAY 3 AUGUST 1773

PRINTED SOURCE: JB's *Life*, 1791, I.426.

Dear Sir, August 3, 1773

Not being at Mr. Thrale's when your letter came, I had written the inclosed paper and sealed it;[1] bringing it hither for a frank, I found yours. If any thing could repress my ardour, it would be such a letter as yours.[2] To disappoint a friend is unpleasing: and he that forms expectations like yours, must be disappointed. Think only when you see me, that you see a man who loves you, and is proud and glad that you love him. I am, Sir, Your most affectionate

SAM. JOHNSON

1. *Ante* To JB, 3 Aug. 1773 and n. 1.
2. "I again wrote to him . . . expressing, perhaps in too extravagant terms, my admiration of him, and my expectation of pleasure from our intended tour" (*Life* II.265).

James Beattie

THURSDAY 5 AUGUST 1773

MS: Aberdeen University Library.

ADDRESS: To Dr. Beattie [*added in an unidentified hand*] at Sir Wm. Maynes, Arnos Grove, near Southgate, Midlesex.[1]

POSTMARKS: PENNY POST PAID, [Undeciphered].

Dear Sir: August 5, 1773

I shall set out to morrow with less cheerfulness, because I shall not find you and Mrs. Beattie at the College, but as my journey is regulated, by the Vacation of the Courts,[2] I cannot delay it.

It is very little for the honour of the age that you should meet with any delay or obstruction in the improvement of your fortune.[3] If I had power or influence, you should soon be raised above your difficulties, but I can do nothing more than encourage you not to be wanting to yourself, and wish that your perseverance may obtain success however[4] below your merit, yet equal to your desires.

Whatever good I wish you, I wish likewise to your Lady, for I hope you both[5] consider me, as, Your most affectionate and most humble Servant,

SAM. JOHNSON

1. From 12 July to 10 Aug. Beattie stayed with his friend Sir William Mayne (1722–94), Bt., of Arnos Grove, Middlesex, later (1776) first Baron Newhaven (Margaret Forbes, *Beattie and His Friends*, 1904, p. 89; Namier and Brooke III.125).

2. *Ante* To JB, 5 July 1773 and n. 6.

3. *Ante* To JB, 5 July 1773, n. 8.

4. MS: "however" superimposed upon "though far" partially erased

5. MS: "bothe"

John Taylor

THURSDAY 5 AUGUST 1773

MS: Berg Collection, New York Public Library.

ADDRESS: To the Reverend Dr. Taylor in Ashbourne, Derbyshire.

POSTMARK: 5 AV.

ENDORSEMENTS: 1773, 5 Augt. 73.

To JOHN TAYLOR, 5 *August* 1773

Dear Sir: Aug. 5, 1773

Your solicitude for me is a very pleasing evidence of your friendship. My eye is almost recovered, but is yet a little dim, and does not much like a small print by candlelight. You will however believe that I think myself pretty well, when I tell you my design.

I have long promised to visit Scotland, and shall set out to morrow on the journey. I have Mr. Chambers's[1] company as far as Newcastle, and Mr. Boswel an active lively fellow is to conduct me round the country.[2] What I shall see, I know not, but hope to have entertainment for my curiosity, and I shall be sure at least of air and motion.[3] When I come back, perhaps a little invitation may call me into Derbyshire, to compare the mountains of the two countries.[4]

In the mean time I hope you are daily advancing in your health. Drink a great deal, and sleep heartily, and think now and then of, Dear Sir, Your most humble servant,

SAM. JOHNSON

1. MS: "Chamberss's" 2. *Ante* To JB, 5 July 1773.

3. Six weeks earlier, SJ had complained to Taylor of a lack of healthful exercise (*Ante* To John Taylor, 22 June 1773).

4. SJ next visited Ashbourne with the Thrales in July 1774 (*Life* v.430).

Thomas Percy

MONDAY 9 AUGUST 1773

MS: Hyde Collection.

ADDRESS: To the Reverend Dr. Percy at Alnwick.

POSTMARK: NORTHALLERTON.

Dear Sir: Northallerton,[1] August 9, 1773

I am now at Northallerton on my way to Scotland, and expect to have a sight of Alnwick on the thirteenth or fourteenth.[2]

1. SJ stayed the night of 9 Aug. at the staging inn in Northallerton, a village in North Yorkshire (Fleeman, p. 286; *Post* To Hester Thrale, 12 Aug. 1773).

2. Alnwick Castle, dating from the twelfth century, was the seat of the Duke of

I hope, I shall find you there, and then we will spend two or three hours in seeing what you can show us.[3] I am, Sir, Your most humble servant,

SAM. JOHNSON

Northumberland, with whom Percy frequently resided in his capacity as chaplain (Nikolaus Pevsner, *Northumberland*, 1957, p. 68; Fleeman, p. 287).

3. Despite receiving word that Percy was not in residence, SJ visited Alnwick, where he was received by the Duke (*Post* To Hester Thrale, 12 Aug. 1773; 17 Aug. 1773).

James Boswell

WEDNESDAY 11 AUGUST 1773

PRINTED SOURCE: JB's *Life*, 1791, I.426.

Dear Sir, Newcastle, Aug. 11, 1771[1]

I came hither last night, and hope, but do not absolutely promise, to be in Edinburgh on Saturday.[2] Beattie will not come so soon. I am, Sir, Your most humble servant,

SAM. JOHNSON

My compliments to your lady.

1. Corrected to "1773" in fourth edition
2. *Post* To JB, 14 Aug. 1773.

Hester Thrale

THURSDAY 12 AUGUST 1773

MSS: Hyde Collection. Postscript, National Library of Scotland.

[Newcastle; postscript, Edinburgh]

Dear Madam: Aug. 12, 1773

We left London on Friday, the Sixth, not very early and travelled without any memorable accident through a country[1]

1. MS: "county"

which I had seen before. In the Evening I was not well, and was forced to stop at Stilton, one stage short of Stamford where we intended to have lodged.[2]

On the seventh We passed through Stamford and Grantham, and dined at Newark, where I had only time to observe that the Market place was uncommonly spacious, and neat.[3] In London we should call it a square, though the sides are neither straight nor parallel. We came at Night to Doncaster, and went to Church in the Morning where Chambers found the monument of Robert of Doncaster who says on his stone something like this

> What I gave, that I have; what I spent that I had; what I left that I lost. So saith Robert Berk who reigned[4] in the world sixty seven years, and all that time lived not one.[5]

Here we were invited to Dinner, and therefore made no great haste away.

We reached York however that night. I was[6] much disordered with old complaints. Next Morning we saw the Minster, an Edifice of loftiness, and elegance, equal to the highest hopes of architecture.[7] I remember nothing but the dome of

2. Traveling the Great North Road, SJ and Robert Chambers spent their first night at Stilton, Huntingdonshire, the center of distribution for the famous cheese. It is likely that they put up at the Angel, the town's staging inn (Fleeman, p. 285).

3. Newark, a market town in Nottinghamshire, is 18 miles northeast of Nottingham.

4. MS: "I" del. before "reigned"

5. The epitaph of Robin of Doncaster (d. 1590), alderman and three times mayor, was carved on the border of a tomb in the medieval church of St. George, destroyed by fire in 1853: "Howe nowe who is heare / I Robyn of Doncaster and Margaret my feare / That I spent that I had / That I gave that I have That I left that I loste." Added in the center of the tomb were the words: "Quod Robertus Byrkes who in this worlde dyd reyne thre skore yeares and seaven and yet lyved not one." SJ translated part of the epitaph into Latin (*Poems*, p. 228).

6. MS: single letter del. before "was"

7. York Minster, begun *c.* 1230 and virtually completed *c.* 1475, is "a cathedral almost exclusively Gothic, and for the Gothic style, or rather styles in England it tells a more consistent and complete story than any other cathedral" (Nikolaus Pevsner, *Yorkshire: York and the East Riding*, 1972, p. 78).

St. Pauls, that can be compared with the middle walk.[8] The Chapter house is a circular building very stately, but I think excelled by the chapter house of Lincoln.[9]

I then went to see the ruins of the Abbey which are almost vanished, and I remember nothing of them distinct.[10]

The next visit was to the jail which they call the castle, a fabrick built lately, such is terrestrial mutability out [of] the materials of the ruined Abby.[11] The underjailor was very officious to[12] show his fetters, in which there was no contrivance. The head jailor came in, and seeing me look, I suppose, fatigued, offered me wine, and when I went away, would not suffer his servant to take money. The jail is accounted the best in the kingdom, and you find the jailor deserving of his dignity.

We dined at York, and went on to Northallerton,[13] a place of which I know nothing but that it afforded us a lodging on Monday night,[14] and about two hundred and seventy years ago, gave birth to Roger Ascham.[15]

Next Morning we changed our horses at Darlington, where Cornelius Harrison a Cousin German of mine was perpetual Curate.[16] He was the only one of my relations who ever rose

8. SJ's definitions of *walk* in his *Dictionary* include "region; space." By "middle walk" he appears to mean "crossing" and / or "crossing tower."

9. The octagonal chapter house at York was completed before 1300 (Pevsner, *Yorkshire*, p. 85). Lincoln Cathedral has England's first polygonal chapter house; it "must have been begun before 1220. . . . The completing date is stylistic guesswork" (Nikolaus Pevsner and John Harris, *Lincolnshire*, 1964, pp. 122–23). SJ presumably visited Lincoln Cathedral during his visit to Bennet Langton in 1764.

10. St. Mary's Abbey was founded by William Rufus in 1088–89 for Benedictine monks (Pevsner, *Yorkshire*, p. 112).

11. The Debtors' Prison, distinguished by its "overpowering monumentality," was built in 1705, probably by William Wakefield (Pevsner, *Yorkshire*, pp. 130–31).

12. MS: "the"

13. *Ante* To Thomas Percy, 9 Aug. 1773.

14. MS: "Monday night" written above "the Ninth" del.

15. Roger Ascham (1515–68), author of *The Scholemaster* (1570), was born at Kirby Wiske, near Northallerton. In 1761 SJ had contributed a biography of Ascham to an edition of his English works (Hazen, pp. 19–20).

16. The Rev. Cornelius Harrison (1700–1748), Fellow of Pembroke Hall, Cambridge, and Perpetual Curate of Darlington, Co. Durham (1727–48), was SJ's first cousin (*Johns. Glean.* XI.205).

in fortune above penury or in character above neglect. The Church is built crosswise, with a fine spire, and might invite a traveller to survey it, but I perhaps wanted vigour, and thought I wanted time.[17]

The next stage brought us to Durham, a place of which Mr. Thrale bad me take particular notice. The Bishop's palace has the appearance of an old Feudal Castle, built upon an eminence and looking down upon the river upon which was formerly thrown a drawbridge, as I suppose, to be raised at night lest the Scots should pass it.[18]

The Cathedral has a massiness and solidity such as I have seen in no other place; It rather awes than pleases, as it strikes with a kind of gigantick dignity, and aspires to no other praise than that of rocky solidity, and indeterminate duration.[19] I had none of my friends resident, and therefore saw but little. The Library is mean and scanty.[20]

At Durham, beside all expectation, I met an old friend. Miss Fordice is married there to a Physician.[21] We met, I think, with honest kindness on both sides. I thought her much decayed, and having since heard that the Banker had involved her husband in his extensive ruin, I cannot forbear to think, that I

17. SJ admired the medieval church of St. Cuthbert, whose spire had been shortened and rebuilt in 1752 (Nikolaus Pevsner and Elizabeth Williamson, *County Durham*, 2d ed., 1983, p. 140).

18. The fortified palace of the Prince-Bishops of Durham was built by William I on a rocky promontory above the River Wear (Pevsner and Williamson, *Durham*, p. 212).

19. Durham Cathedral, a combination of Romanesque and Gothic, was begun *c.* 1093 and completed in the mid-twelfth century (Pevsner and Williamson, *Durham*, pp. 168–86).

20. In 1684 the refectory was converted into the Dean and Chapter Library. The library includes a distinguished collection of manuscripts, to which SJ could not have had access without official permission (Pevsner and Williamson, *Durham*, p. 203).

21. Elizabeth Fordyce (1731–77) was the sister of SJ's friend, James Fordyce (1720–96), and the aunt of another friend, George Fordyce (1736–1802), M.D., a member of The Club. In 1766 she married Joseph Spence (b. 1735), M.D.; the Spences had moved to Durham by 1770 (J. D. Fleeman, "Dr. Johnson and 'Miss Fordice,'" *Notes and Queries* 33, 1986, pp. 59–60).

saw in her withered features more impressions of sorrow than of time.[22]

Qua terra patet, fera regnat[23] Erinnys.[24]

He that wanders about the world sees new forms of human misery, and if he chances to meet an old friend, meets a face darkened with troubles.

On Tuesday night We came hither. Yesterday I took some care of myself, and today I am *quite polite*.[25] I have been taking a view of all that could be shewn me,[26] and find that all very near to nothing. You have often heard me complain of finding myself disappointed by books of travels,[27] I am afraid travel itself will end likewise in disappointment.[28] One town, one country is very like another. Civilized nations have the same customs, and barbarous nations have the same nature. There are indeed minute discriminations both of places and of manners, which perhaps are not unworthy of curiosity, but[29] which a traveller seldom stays long enough to investigate and compare. The dull utterly neglect them, the acute see a little, and supply the rest by fancy and conjecture.

I shall set out again to morrow, but I shall not, I am afraid see Alnwick, for Dr. Percy is not there.[30] I hope to lodge to morrow night at Berwick, and the next at Edinburgh, where I

22. "The Banker" was Elizabeth's brother, Alexander Fordyce. *Ante* To John Taylor, 15 Aug. 1772, n. 3.

23. MS: "Erynnys" del. after "regnat"

24. *Qua terra patet, fera regnat Erinys*: "Wherever the plains of earth extend, wild fury reigns supreme" (Ovid, *Metamorphosis* 1.241, trans. F. J. Miller, rev. G. P. Goold, Loeb ed.). *Post* To Hester Thrale, 16 Oct. 1777.

25. H. L. Piozzi's gloss provides a partial explanation: "A mistake of a Servant who said in reply to my Enquiries That the Dr. was quite polite to Day—we never knew what he meant exactly" (Piozzi 1.107).

26. "Wednesday was perhaps spent recuperating and Thursday with Chambers and his mother" (Fleeman, p. 286). On 3 Aug. Chambers had written to Anne Chambers, requesting her to entertain SJ (MS: Hyde Collection).

27. Cf. *Ante* To Hester Thrale, 20 July 1770.

28. SJ did not remain so pessimistic. *Post* To Hester Thrale, 25 Aug. 1773, n. 12; 21 Sept. 1773; *Post* To Saunders Welch, 3 Feb. 1778.

29. MS: "and" del. before "but"

30. *Ante* To Thomas Percy, 9 Aug. 1773, nn. 2, 3.

shall direct Mr. Drummond Bookseller at Ossian's Head, to take care of my letters.

I hope the little Dears are all well, and then my dear Master and Mistress may go somewhither. But wherever you be do not forget, Madam, Your most humble Servant,

SAM. JOHNSON

August 15th

Thus far I had written at Newcastle. I forgot to send it. I am now at Edinburgh, and have been this day running about. I run pretty well.

James Boswell

SATURDAY 14 AUGUST 1773

PRINTED SOURCE: JB's *Life*, 1791, I.426.

Saturday night

Mr. Johnson sends his compliments to Mr. Boswell, being just arrived at Boyd's.[1]

1. Boyd's Inn was called "The White Horse"; it stood at the head of the Canongate on the south side (*Hebrides*, p. 452).

Hester Thrale

TUESDAY 17 AUGUST 1773

MS: Hyde Collection.

ADDRESS: To Henry Thrale, Esq., in Southwark [*added in an unidentified hand*] London.

POSTMARKS: AU 17, 21 AV, FREE.

Dear Madam: Edinburgh, August 17, 1773

On the 13th I left Newcastle, and in the Afternoon came to Alnwick, where we were treated with great civility by the Duke. I went through the apartments, walked on the wall, and climbed the towers.[1] That night we lay at Belford,[2] and on the next night came to Edinburgh. On Sunday (15th) I went to the English Chapel.[3] After dinner Dr. Robertson came in and promised to shew me the place. On Monday, I saw their publick buildings. The Cathedral which I told Robertson I wished to see because it had been once a Church.[4] The Courts of Justice, the parliament house,[5] the Advocates Library, the Repository of Records, the Colege, and its Library,[6] and the Palace, particularly the old tower, where the king of Scotland seized David Rizzio[7] in the Queens presence.[8] Most of their buildings are very mean, and the whole town bears some resemblance to the old part of Birmingham.

Boswel has very handsome and spacious rooms level with

1. *Ante* To Thomas Percy, 9 Aug. 1773 and nn. 2, 3. Hugh Percy (1715–86), first Duke of Northumberland, had employed the architects James Paine and Robert Adam to repair and renovate Alnwick Castle (Nikolaus Pevsner, *Northumberland*, 1957, p. 69).

2. Belford, in northern Northumberland, a market town 15 miles southeast of Berwick-upon-Tweed.

3. The English Chapel stood on the corner of the High Street and Blackfriars Wynd. It was founded by John Smith (1657–1726), Lord Chief Baron of the Exchequer in Scotland, "for the service of the Church of England" (*Hebrides*, pp. 15, 453).

4. The Church of St. Giles (begun *c.* 1120) was the cathedral of the See of Edinburgh only briefly, from 1633 to 1639 and again from 1660 to 1689. Since 1707 it had been divided into four parochial (Presbyterian) churches (*Scotland*, ed. L. R. Muirhead, 3d ed., 1949, p. 46; David Daiches, *Edinburgh*, 1978, pp. 55, 104). SJ jested, "A Church will make many kirks" (*Hebrides*, p. 24 n. 8).

5. The Parliament House (1632–40) was designed by James Murray (John Gifford, Colin McWilliam, and David Walker, *Edinburgh*, 1984, p. 121). In 1773 it consisted of the Parliament Hall and the Laigh House (containing the Advocates' Library and the record repository), the Courts of Session and of Chancery, the Commissary Court, and the Court of Exchequer (*Hebrides*, p. 453).

6. The Old College of the University of Edinburgh, founded by James VI in 1582 (Gifford, McWilliam, and Walker, *Edinburgh*, p. 188 and n. ‡).

7. MS: "Rizzo" del. before "Rizzio"

8. David I founded the abbey of Holyrood in 1128, and it became a royal residence as early as the first decades of the fourteenth century. The "old tower" was added by James V between 1528 and 1532 (Gifford, McWilliam, and Walker, *Edinburgh*, p. 125). SJ refers to the murder of David Riccio (*c.* 1533–66), the favorite of Mary Queen of Scots, by the henchmen of her husband Lord Darnley ("the king").

the ground on one side of the house, and on the other four stories high.[9]

At diner on Monday were the Dutchess of Douglass, an old Lady who talks broad Scotch with a paralytick voice, and is scarce understood by her own countrymen.[10] The Lord Chief Baron,[11] Sir Adolphus Oughton,[12] and many more.[13] At supper there was such a Conflux of company, that I could scarcely support the tumult.[14] I have never been well in the whole Journey, and am very easily disordered.

This morning I saw at breakfast Dr. Blacklock the blind poet,[15] who does not remember to have seen light, and is read to by a poor S[c]holar in Latin, Greek,[16] and French. He was originally a poor scholar himself. I looked on him with reverence.

To morrow our Journey begins. I know not when I shall write again. I am but poorly. I am, Madam, Your most humble Servant,

SAM. JOHNSON

9. JB and his family occupied a large apartment in James's Court, on the north side of the Lawnmarket (*Hebrides*, p. 452).

10. Margaret (d. 1774), Duchess of Douglas, the widow of Archibald (1694–1761), the first Duke.

11. Robert Ord (1700–1778), Chief Baron of the Scottish Exchequer (1755–75) (Namier and Brooke III.232). JB reports that Ord "was on good terms with us all, in a narrow country filled with jarring interests and keen parties" (*Hebrides*, p. 16).

12. Sir James Adolphus Dickenson Oughton (1720–80), Governor of Edinburgh Castle and later (1778) Commander-in-Chief, North Britain. In JB's judgment, Sir Adolphus was "not only an excellent officer but one of the most universal scholars I ever knew" (*Hebrides*, p. 27).

13. The other dinner guests were the historian William Robertson, the banker Sir William Forbes (1739–1806), Bt., and Robert Cullen (d. 1810), advocate (*Hebrides*, p. 26).

14. The guest list at supper included Robert Cullen; his father, the physician William Cullen (1710–90); the philosopher Adam Ferguson (1723–1816); and two advocates, Andrew Crosbie (1736–85) and Charles Hay (1740–1811) (*Hebrides*, p. 27 and n. 12).

15. Thomas Blacklock (1721–91), D.D., Scots poet and classical scholar, had been blinded by smallpox at the age of six months. Blacklock's descriptive powers, as displayed in his verse and analyzed by Joseph Spence in *An Account . . . of Mr. Blacklock* (1754), had long intrigued SJ (*Life* I.466).

16. MS: undeciphered letter del. before "Greek"

Hester Thrale

WEDNESDAY 25 AUGUST 1773

MS: Pierpont Morgan Library.

ADDRESS: To Henry Thrale, Esq., in Southwark [*added in an unidentified hand*] London.

POSTMARKS: BANFF, AU 30, 3 SE, FREE.

Dear Madam: Bamff, Aug. 25, 1773

It has so happened that though I am perpetually thinking on you, I could seldom find opportunity to write.[1] I have in fourteen days sent only one Letter. You must consider the fatigues of travel, and the difficulties encountered in a strange Country.

August 18. I passed with Boswel the Firth of Forth, and began our Journey. In the passage We observed an Island which I persuaded my companions to survey. We found it a Rock somewhat troublesome to climb, about a mile long and half a mile broad; in the middle were the ruins of an old fort, which had on one of the stones Maria Re. 1564.[2] It had been only a blockhouse one story high. I measured two apartment[s] of which the walls were entire and found them 27 feet long and 23 broad. The Rock had some grass and many thistles,

1. According to J. D. Fleeman: "The contents of Johnson's documentary letters to Mrs Thrale suggest that they were written up as records from notes, and the different order of many of the details and items mentioned in the letters from the order in the *Journey* argues that the letters themselves were collateral descendants from the notebooks rather than intermediate sources for the eventual narrative manuscript of the *Journey*. Nevertheless there is presumptive evidence that the letters were consulted when the manuscript of the *Journey* was being written up" (Fleeman, p. xxxviii). Most of the geographical and architectural details recorded in these diary-letters have been exhaustively annotated in four scholarly editions: Mary Lascelles's edition of SJ's *Journey* and that of J. D. Fleeman; L. F. Powell's edition of JB's *Tour* (*Life* v.) and the edition of JB's *Journal* by F. A. Pottle and C. H. Bennett (*Hebrides*). Appendix C ("Chronology and Topography") in Fleeman's edition is of special importance. Given such copious and reliable commentary, it has seemed advisable to scale back the annotation of the Hebridean letters.

2. The fort on Inchkeith was built by the French, who occupied the island from 1549 to 1567. Though the inscription may refer to Mary of Guise, the likelier candidate is Mary Queen ["Reine"] of Scots (Fleeman, p. 152).

both cows and sheep were grazing. There was a spring of water. The name is Inchkeith. Look on your Maps.

This visit took about an hour. We pleased ourselves with being in a country all our own, and then went back to the boat, and landed at Kinghorn, a mean town, and travelling through Kirkaldie, a very long town meanly built, and Cowpar, which I could not see because it was night, we came late to St. Andrews, the most ancient of the Scotch Universities, and once the See of the Primate of Scotland.[3] The Inn was full, but Lodgings were provided for us at the house of the professor of Rhetorick,[4] a Man of elegant manners who showed us in the morning the poor remains of a stately Cathedral demolished in Knox's reformation, and now only to be imaged by tracing its foundation and contemplating the little ruins that are left.[5] Here was once a religious house.[6] Two of the vaults or cellars of the Subprior are yet entire. In one of them lives an old Woman who claims an hereditary residence in it, boasting that her husband was the fourth[7] tenant of this gloomy mansion in a lineal descent, and claiming by her marriage with this Lord of the cavern, an alliance with the Bruces.[8] Mr. Boswel staid awhile to interrogate her, because he understood her language. She told him, that she and her Cat lived together; that she had two sons somewhere, who might perhaps be dead; that when there were quality in the town, notice was taken of her; and that now she was neglected, but did not trouble them.

3. St. Andrews University was founded in 1412 by Bishop Henry Wardlaw. St. Andrews was named an archbishopric *c.* 1472; the last archbishop died in 1704 (C. J. Lyon, *History of St. Andrews*, 1843, I.233; Fleeman, p. 153).

4. Robert Watson (*c.* 1730–81), Professor of Logic, Rhetoric, and Metaphysics (1756–78) and later (1778–81) Principal of St. Andrews (*Life* V.481).

5. The Cathedral of St. Andrews (1160–1318), the largest in Scotland, was attacked in June 1559 and virtually destroyed after John Knox preached for four consecutive days on "The Cleansing of the Temple" (Fleeman, pp. 152–53).

6. SJ refers to the Priory of the Canons Regular of St. Augustine, founded *c.* 1120 (David Macgibbon and Thomas Ross, *The Ecclesiastical Architecture of Scotland*, 1896, II.6).

7. MS: "firth"

8. In 1787 it was found that, although Mrs. Bruce had been dead some years, "her vault was still occupied by one who claimed the same royal extraction" (Fleeman, p. 155).

Her habitation contained all that she had, her turf for fire was laid in one place, and her balls of coaldust in another, but her bed seemed to be clean. Boswel asked her if She never heard any noises, but she could tell him of nothing supernatural, though she sometimes wandered in the night among the graves and ruins, only she had some notice by dreams of the death of her relations.

We then viewed the remains of a Castle on the margin of the sea, in which the Archbishops resided, and in which Cardinal Beatoun was killed.[9]

The Professors, who happened to be resident in the vacation, made a publick dinner, and treated us very kindly and respectfully. The[y] Showed us their Colleges in one of which there is a library, that for luminousness and elegance may vie at least with the new Edifice at Streatham.[10] But Learning seems not to prosper among them, one of their Colleges has been lately alienated, and one of their churches lately deserted.[11] An experiment was made of planting a shrubbery in the church, but it did not thrive.

Why the place should thus fall to decay I know not, for Education, such as is here to be had, is sufficiently cheap. Their term or as they call it their session lasts seven months in the year which the Students of the highest rank, and greatest expence may pass here for twenty pounds in which are included, Board, Lodging, Books, and the continual instruction of three Professors.

20 We left St. Andrews well satisfied with our reception, and crossing the Firth of Tay, came to Dundee, a dirty despica-

9. David Beaton or Bethune (1494–1546), Archbishop of St. Andrews, was murdered on 29 May 1546: he had angered Knox and his supporters by exulting in the public burning of Knox's tutor and friend, George Wishart (Fleeman, p. 153).

10. The two remaining colleges at St. Andrews were St. Salvator's and St. Mary's. SJ praises St. Mary's library, most of which was constructed in 1764 (Fleeman, p. 153). For the new library at Streatham Park, *Ante* To Hester Thrale, 23 Mar. 1773, n. 2.

11. St. Leonard's College was dissolved into St. Salvator's in 1747. Its chapel was abandoned and largely demolished in 1761 (Fleeman, p. 153).

ble town. We past afterwards through Aberbrothick, famous once for an Abby of which there are only a few fragments left, but those fragments testify that the fabrick was once of great extent, and stupendous magnificence; two of the towers are yet standing though shattered, into one of them Boswel climbed, but found the stairs broken. The way into the other we did not see, and had not time to search, I believed it might be ascended but the top, I think, is open.[12]

We lay at Montross, a neat place, with a spacious area for the market, and an elegant townhouse.[13]

21 We travelled towards Aberdeen, another University, and in the way dined at Lord Monbodo's, the Scotch Judge who has lately written a strange book about the origin of Language, in which he traces Monkeys up to Men, and says that in some countries the human Species have tails like other beasts.[14] He enquired for these longtailed Men of Banks,[15] and was not well pleased, that they had not been found in all his peregrination. He talked nothing of this to me, and I hope, we parted friends, for we agreed pretty well, only we differed in adjusting the claims of merit between a Shopkeeper of London, and a Savage of the American wildernesses. Our opinions were, I think, maintained on both sides without full conviction; Monbodo declared boldly for the Savage, and I perhaps for that reason sided with the Citizen.[16]

12. Aberbrothick (or Arbroath) Abbey was founded in the late twelfth century by King William the Lion and dedicated to Thomas à Becket (Macgibbon and Ross, *Ecclesiastical Architecture* II.30). SJ was singularly impressed with the ruins: "I should scarcely have regretted my journey, had it afforded nothing more than the sight of Aberbrothick" (Fleeman, p. 8).

13. "The townhouse is a handsome fabrick with a portico" (Fleeman, p. 8). In his entry for 21 Aug., JB reports: "Before breakfast we went and saw the town hall, where is a good dancing-room and other rooms for tea-drinking" (*Hebrides*, p. 50).

14. James Burnett (1714–99), Lord Monboddo, Lord of Session from 1767, eccentric antiquary and author of the six-volume *Of the Origin and Progress of Language* (1773–92), whose evolutionary theories called forth SJ's frequent ridicule (*Hebrides*, p. 28). JB described Monboddo's country estate as "a wretched place, wild and naked, with a poor old house" (*Hebrides*, p. 53).

15. SJ refers to Joseph Banks, the distinguished naturalist.

16. According to JB's report of this meeting, SJ "was much pleased with Lord

We came late to Aberdeen, where I found my dear Mistress's Letter, and learned that all our little people, were happily recovered of the Measles.[17] Every part of your letter was pleasing. I am glad that the presents are made, and that Mr. Perkins is sent to Ireland, and sent with full powers both by my Master and you.[18] I do not well understand the question of the tithes, if you can follow Mr. Robson's advice without open war upon your unkle, it will be best to do it; but it would be wrong to raise new quarrels for a small matter.[19]

There are two Cities of the name of Aberdeen. The old town built about a mile inland, once[20] the see of a Bishop, which contains the King's College,[21] and the remains of the Cathedral,[22] and the new town which stands for the sake of trade upon a firth or arm of the Sea, so that Ships rest against the Key.

The two cities have their separate Magistrates, and the two Colleges, are in effect two Universities which confer degrees independently on each other.[23]

Now Aberdeen is a large town, built almost wholly of that Granite which is used for the new pavement in London, which,

---

Monboddo today. He said he would have pardoned him for a few paradoxes when he found he had so much that was good" (*Hebrides*, p. 57).

17. In her letter of 27 July Hester Thrale had reported, "My Children have got the Measles" (MS: Rylands Library).

18. On his way to brewery business in Ireland, John Perkins was deputized to stop in Wales and examine the Salusbury properties that Hester Thrale expected to inherit (Clifford, 1952, p. 106; *Ante* To Hester Thrale, 24 Oct. 1772 and n. 1).

19. The matter in dispute appears to have involved the payment of tithes from the Salusbury estate of Bach-y-Graig (Clifford, 1952, p. 106). Bateman Robson (*c.* 1719–91), attorney of Lincoln's Inn, helped to draw up a settlement "under which Johnson and [John] Cator were made trustees of all the Welsh property" (*Life* v.500).

20. MS: "which" del. before "once"

21. King's College, Aberdeen, was granted its charter in 1498 by James IV (Fleeman, p. 158).

22. The Cathedral of St. Mary's and St. Machar's, most of which dated to the fifteenth century, had been badly damaged by Cromwell's men (Fleeman, p. 292).

23. In his MS remarks on SJ's *Journey*, JB corrected this statement: "Old and new Aberdeen are not governed by the same Magistrates. The new town is a royal Borough. The old is only a Borough of Barony" (MS: Hyde Collection). Marischal College, in the New Town, was founded in 1593 (Fleeman, p. 159).

hard as it is, they square with very little difficulty. Here I first saw the women in plaids.[24] The plaid makes at once a hood and cloak without cutting or sewing, merely by the manner of drawing the opposite sides over the Shoulders. The maids at the Inns run over the house barefoot, and children, not dressed in rags, go without shoes or stockings. Shoes are indeed not yet in universal use. They came late into this country.[25] One of [the] Professors[26] told us, as we were mentioning a fort built by Cromwel, that the Country owed much of its present industry to Cromwel's soldiers. They taught us said he, to raise cabbage, and make shoes. How they lived without shoes may yet be seen, but in the passage through villages, it seems to him that surveys their gardens, that when they had not cabbage they had nothing.

Education is here of the same price as at St. Andrews only the session is but from the first of November to the first of April. The academical buildings, seem rather to[27] advance than decline. They showed their libraries which were not very splendid, but some manuscripts were so exquisitely penned, that I wished my dear Mistress to have seen them.[28]

I had an unexpected pleasure by finding an old acquaintance, now professor of physick in the King's College.[29] We were on both sides glad of the interview, having not seen nor perhaps thought on one another for many years. But we had

24. Cf. *Post* To Hester Thrale, 30 Sept. 1773.

25. "The Shoes anciently wore, were a piece of the Hide of a Deer, Cow or Horse, with the Hair on, being tied behind and before with a Point of Leather. The generality now wear Shoes, having one thin Sole only, and shaped after the right and left Foot, so that what is for one Foot, will not serve the other" (Martin Martin, *A Description of the Western Islands of Scotland*, 1703, p. 207).

26. Thomas Gordon (1714–97), Professor of Philosophy, one of the two clergymen serving the English chapel at Aberdeen (*Life* v.492).

27. MS: "to" altered from "it"

28. SJ was particularly impressed by two items, "a Hebrew manuscript of exquisite penmanship, and a Latin translation of Aristotle's Politicks by *Leonardus Aretinus*, written in the Roman character with nicety and beauty" (Fleeman, p. 11).

29. Sir Alexander Gordon (*c.* 1720–82), of Lismore, seventh Bt., Professor of Medicine, King's College, Aberdeen (1766–82) (*Life* v.493). Sir Alexander had been SJ's "acquaintance twenty years ago in London" (*Hebrides*, p. 60).

no mutation, nor had either of us risen to the others envy, and our old kindness was easily renewed.[30] I hope We shall never try the effect of so long an absence, and that I shall always be, Madam, Your most humble servant,

SAM. JOHNSON

30. In his *Journey* SJ observes, "Such unexpected renewals of acquaintance may be numbered among the most pleasing incidents of life" (Fleeman, p. 9).

Hester Thrale

SATURDAY 28 AUGUST 1773

MS: Beinecke Library.

ADDRESS: To Henry Thrale, Esq., in Southwark [*added in an unidentified hand*] London.

POSTMARKS: INVERNESS, SE 1, 6 SE, FREE.

Dearest Madam: Inverness, Aug. 28, 1773

August. 23. I had the honour of attending the Lord Provost of Aberdeen,[1] and was presented with the freedom of the city, not in a gold box but in good Latin. Let me pay Scotland one just praise. There was no officer gaping for a fee; this could have been said of no city on the English side of the Tweed. I wore my patent of freedom *pro more*[2] in my hat from the New town to the Old about a mile. I then dined with my friend the Professor of Physick at his[3] house,[4] and saw the Kings College.

Boswel was very angry that the Aberdeen Professors would not talk.[5]

When I was at[6] the English Church in Aberdeen, I happened to be espied by Lady Di. Middleton whom I had some-

1. James Jopp (1721–94) had been elected Sept. 1772 (Fleeman, p. 161 n. 8).

2. *pro more*: "according to custom"

3. MS: "his" superimposed upon "the"

4. *Ante* To Hester Thrale, 25 August 1773, n. 29.

5. "We had little or no conversation in the morning. Now we were but barren. The professors seemed afraid to speak" (*Hebrides*, pp. 65–66).

6. MS: "a" superimposed upon "th"

time seen in London.[7] She told what she had seen to Mr. Boyd, Lord Errols Brother,[8] who wrote us an invitation to Lord Errols house called Slanes Castle.[9] We went thither on the next day (Aug. 24) and found a house not old, except one tower, built upon the margin of the Sea upon a rock, scarce accessible from the sea; at one corner a tower makes a perpendicular continuation of the lateral surface of the rock, so that it is impracticable to walk round. The house incloses[10] a square court, and on all sides within the court is a piazza or gallery two stories high.

We came in, as we were invited, to Dinner, and after dinner offered to go, but Lady Errol[11] sent us word by Mr. Boyd, that if we went before Lord Errol came home, we must never be forgiven, and ordered out the Coach to show us two curiosities. We were first conducted by Mr. Boyd to Dunbuys, or the yellow rock. Dunbuys is a rock consisting of two protuberances each perhaps one hundred yards round, joined together by a narrow neck, and separated from the land by a very narrow channel or gully. These rocks are the haunts of Seafowl whose clang though this is not their season, we heard at a distance. The eggs, and the young are gathered here in great numbers at the time of breeding. There is a bird here called a Coote which though not much bigger than a duck, lays a bigger egg than a goose.[12]

We went then to see the[13] Buller or boulloir of Buchan. Buchan is the name of the district, and the Buller is a small

7. Lady Diana Grey Middleton (d. 1780), daughter of the third Earl of Stamford and wife (m. 1736) of George Middleton of Seaton.

8. The Hon. Charles Boyd (1728–82), younger brother of James Boyd (1726–78), fifteenth Earl of Errol and Lord High Constable of Scotland.

9. Slains Castle, Cruden parish, Aberdeenshire, was built in 1664 a few miles north of the old castle, destroyed in 1594 by James VI (*Ordnance Gazetteer of Scotland*, ed. F. H. Groome, 1895, VI.361; *Life* v.498).

10. MS: "incloses" altered from "inclosed"

11. Isabella (1742–1808), Countess of Errol, daughter of William Carr of Etall, Northumberland, second wife (m. 1762) of the fifteenth Earl (*Life* v.498).

12. *coot*: "the guillemot" (W. B. Grant and D. D. Murison, *The Scottish National Dictionary*, 1931–76).

13. MS: "th" superimposed upon "a"

creek or gulf into which the sea flows through an arch of the rock. We walked round it and saw it black at a great depth. It has its name from the violent ebullition of the water when high winds or high tides drive it up the arch into the bason. Walking a little further, I spied some boats, and told my companions that we would go into the Buller and examine it. There was no danger, all was calm. We went through the arch, and found ourselves in a narrow gulf surrounded by craggy rocks, of height not stupendous, but to a mediterranean[14] visitor uncommon. On each side was a cave of which the fishermen knew not the extent, in which smugglers hide their goods, and so⟨metimes⟩ parties of pleasure take a dinner.

I think I grow better. I am, Madam, Your most humble servant,

SAM. JOHNSON

14. MS: "mediterrranean"

Hester Thrale

MONDAY 6 SEPTEMBER 1773

MS: Hyde Collection.

ADDRESS: To Henry Thrale, Esq., in Southwark.

POSTMARKS: SE 22, 27 SE, SCONSER, FREE.

Dearest Madam: Skie, Sept. 6, 1773

I am now looking on the Sea from a house of Sir Alexander Macdonald in the Isle of Skie.[1] Little did I once think of seeing this region of obscurity, and little did you once expect a salutation from this verge of European Life. I have now the pleasure of going where nobody goes, and of seeing what nobody sees.

1. Sir Alexander Macdonald (1744–95), of Sleat, ninth Bt., later (1776) first Baron Macdonald, had invited SJ and JB to visit him on Skye, but when the travelers arrived on 2 Sept. they were inhospitably received. "When Mr. Johnson and I retired for rest, he said it grieved him to see the chief of a great clan in such a state; that he was just as one in a lodging-house in London" (*Hebrides*, p. 115). *Post* To Hester Thrale, 21 Sept. 1773.

Our design is to visit several of the smaller Islands, and then pass over to the Southwest of Scotland.

I returned from the sight of Bullers Buchan to Lord Errols and having seen his Library, had for a time only to look upon the Sea which rolled between us and Norway. Next morning August 25 We continued our journey through a country not uncultivated but so denuded of its Woods, that in all this journey I had not travelled an hundred yards between hedges or seen five trees fit for the Carpenter. A few small plantations may be found but I believe scarcely any thirty years old, at least, as I do not forget to tell they are all posteriour to the Union.[2] This day we dined with a Country Gentleman who has in his grounds the remains of a Druid's Temple,[3] which when it is complete is nothing more than a[4] circle or double circle of stones placed at equal distances, with a flat stone, perhaps an altar, at a certain point, and a stone taller than the rest at the opposite point. The tall stone is erected, I think, at the south. Of these[5] circles there are many in all the unfrequented parts of the Island. The Inhabitants of these parts respect them as memorials of the sepulture of some illustrious person. Here I saw a few trees. We lay at Bamff.

August 26[6] We dined at Elgin where we saw the ruins of a noble Cathedral.[7] The Chapterhouse is yet standing. A great part of Elgin is built with small piazzas to the lower story.[8]

2. In his letters and *Journey*, SJ frequently returns to the subject of deforestation and the lack of new plantation in Scotland. In the *Journey* he observes, "I believe few regions have been denuded like this, where many centuries must have passed in waste without the least thought of future supply" (Fleeman, p. 7). The "Union" of England and Scotland took place in 1707.

3. SJ and JB were entertained by Alexander Fraser (d. 1794) of Strichen, Aberdeenshire (*Life* v.500).

4. MS: undeciphered letter before "a"

5. MS: "this"

6. MS: "5" del. before "6"

7. Elgin Cathedral was begun in 1224. The central tower collapsed in 1711, destroying much of the nave (David Macgibbon and Thomas Ross, *The Ecclesiastical Architecture of Scotland*, 1896, II.121–23).

8. "In the chief streets of Elgin, the houses jut over the lowest story, like the old buildings of timber in London, but with greater prominence; so that there is sometimes a walk for a considerable length under a cloister, or portico" (Fleeman, p. 18).

We went on to Foris over the heath where Macbeth met the witches, but had no adventure. Only in the way we saw for the first time some houses with fruit trees about them. The improvements of the Scotch are for immediate profit. They do not yet think it worth while to plant what will not produce something to be eaten or sold in a very little time. We rested at Foris.

A very great proportion of the people are barefoot, and if one may judge by the rest of the dress, to send out boys without shoes into the streets or ways.[9] There are however more beggars than I have ever seen in England; they beg, if not silently, yet very modestly.

Next day we came to Nairn, a miserable town, but a royal burgh, of which the chief annual Magistrate is stiled Lord Provost. In the neighborhood we saw the castle of the old Thane of Cawder. There is one ancient tower with its battlements and winding stairs yet remaining, the rest of the house is though[10] not modern, of later erection.[11]

On the 28. We went to Fort George, which is accounted the most regular Fortification in the Island.[12] The Major of Artillery walked with us round the walls, and shewed us the principles upon which every part was constructed and the way in which it could be defended.[13] We dined with the Governer Sir Eyre Coote, and his Officers.[14] It was a very pleasant and in-

9. *Ante* To Hester Thrale, 25 Aug. 1773.

10. MS: "of" del. before "though"

11. Cawdor Castle, begun in 1454, was considerably expanded and remodeled between 1660 and 1670 (David Macgibbon and Thomas Ross, *Castellated and Domestic Architecture of Scotland from the 12th to the 18th Centuries*, 1887–92, II.315, 320).

12. Fort George, founded in 1748, "the most outstanding example in Britain of Hanoverian military architecture" (Fleeman, p. 295; John Tomes, *Scotland*, 1980, p. 307).

13. John Brewse (*fl.* 1745–85), Major in the Royal Engineers (1772–77), rose to the rank of Colonel and Chief Engineer before disappearing from the Army Lists after 1785 (*Life* v.509).

14. Eyre Coote (1726–83), Kt., Colonel of the Inniskillings, later (1777) Commander-in-Chief in India. Sir Eyre was not the governor of Fort George, but had taken charge because his "Regiment was lying here" (*Hebrides*, p. 91; Fleeman, p. 165).

structive day. But nothing puts my honoured Mistress out of my mind.

At night we came to Inverness, the last considerable town in the North, where we staid all the next day, for it was Sunday, and saw the ruins of what is called Macbeth's Castle. It never was a large house, but was strongly situated.[15] From Inverness we were to travel on Horseback.

Aug. 30. We set out with four horses.[16] We had two Highlanders to run by us, who were active, officious, civil, and hardy.[17] Our Journey was for many miles along a military way made upon the bank of Lough Ness, a Water about eighteen miles long, but not, I think, half a mile broad.[18] Our horses were not bad, and the way was very pleasant. The rock out of which the road was cut was covered with Birch trees, fern and heath. The lake below was beating its bank by a gentle wind, and the rocks beyond the water on the right, stood sometimes horrid and wild and sometimes opened[19] into a kind of bay in which there[20] was a spot of cultivated ground, yellow with corn. In one part of the way we had trees on both sides, for perhaps half a mile. Such a length of Shade perhaps Scotland cannot show in any other place.

You are not to suppose that here are to be any more towns or Inns. We came to a cottage which they call the Generals hut; where we alighted to dine, and had Eggs and Bacon, and Mutton, with wine, rum, and whiskey.[21] I had water.

At a bridge over the river which runs into the Ness, the

15. This fortification stood on a hill at the eastern edge of Inverness; it was popularly but mistakenly associated with Macbeth (Fleeman, pp. 295–96).

16. "We had three horses for Mr. Johnson, myself, and Joseph [JB's servant], and one which carried our portmanteaus. . . . Mr. Johnson rode very well" (*Hebrides*, p. 99).

17. SJ refers to John Hay and Lauchlan Vass (*Hebrides*, p. 99). "One of them was a man of great liveliness and activity, of whom his companion said, that he would tire any horse in Inverness" (Fleeman, p. 22).

18. In his published account SJ corrected these statistics: "*Lough Ness* is about twenty-four miles long, and from one mile to two miles broad" (Fleeman, p. 22).

19. MS: "opened" altered from "opening"

20. MS: "the"

21. According to SJ, the General's hut was "a house of entertainment for passengers, and we found it not ill stocked with provisions" (Fleeman, p. 25).

rocks rise on three sides with a direction almost perpendicular to a great height, they are in part covered with trees, and exhibit a kind of dreadful magnificence. Standing like the barriers of nature placed to keep different orders of Being in perpetual separation. Near this Bridge is the fall of Fiers, a famous Cataract, of which by clambering over the rocks we obtained the view. The water was low, and therefore we had only the pleasure of knowing that rain would make it at once pleasing and formidable. There will then be a mighty flood foaming along[22] a rocky channel frequently obstructed by protuberances, and exasperated by reverberation, at last precipitated with a sudden descent, and lost in the depth of a gloomy chasm.

We came somewhat late to Fort Augustus where the Lieutenant Governor met us beyond the gates,[23] and apologised that at that hour he could not by the rules of a Garrison admit us[24] otherwise than at a narrow door which only one can enter at a time. We were well entertained and well lodged,[25] and next morning after having viewed the fort we persued our journey.

Our way now lay over the mountains, which are ⟨to⟩ be passed not by climbing them directly, but by traversing, so that as we went forward, we saw our baggage following us below in a direction exactly contrary. There is in these ways much labour but little danger, and perhaps other places of which very terrifick representations are made, are not in themselves more formidable. These roads have all been made by[26] hewing the rock away with pickaxes, or[27] bursting them with Gunpowder. The stones so separated are often piled loose as a wall by the way side. We saw an inscription imparting the year in which

22. MS: "a" altered from "o"

23. Alexander Trapaud (*c.* 1712–96), Deputy Governor of Fort Augustus (1754–96) (*Life* v.512).

24. MS: "us us"

25. "It was comfortable to find ourselves in a well-built little square, a neat well-furnished house with prints, etc., a good supper (fricassee of moor-fowl, etc.); in short, with all the conveniencies of civilized life in the midst of rude mountains" (*Hebrides*, p. 101).

26. MS: "by" written above "but" del.

27. MS: "or" repeated as catchword

one of the regiments made two thousand yards of the road Eastward.

After tedious travel of some hours we came to what, I believe, we must call a village, a place where there were three huts built of turf, at[28] one of which we were to have our dinner and our bed, for we could not reach any better place that night. This place is called Enock in Glenmorrison. The house in which we lodged was distinguished by a chimney, the rest had only a hole for the smoke. Here we had Eggs, and Mutton, and a chicken, and a sausage, and rum. In the afternoon tea was made by a very decent Girl in a printed Linen.[29] She engaged me so much that I made her a present of Cocker's Arithmetick.[30] I am, Madam, Your most etc.

SAM. JOHNSON

28. MS: "at" written above "on" del.

29. SJ refers to the daughter of their landlord, Lauchlan Macqueen. "Her conversation, like her appearance, was gentle and pleasing. . . . She had been at *Inverness* to gain the common female qualifications" (Fleeman, pp. 28, 170).

30. At Inverness SJ had purchased a copy of *Cocker's Arithmetick* (1678), by Edward Cocker (1631–75). He later defended his choice to JB: "Why, sir, if you are to have but one book with you upon a journey, let it be a book of science. . . . a book of science is inexhaustible" (*Life* v.138 n. 2). Cf. *Post* To Hester Maria Thrale, 22 May 1783.

Robert Chambers

TUESDAY 14 SEPTEMBER 1773

MS: Loren Rothschild.

ADDRESS: To Robert Chambers, Esq., in Newcastle, Northumberland [*Readdressed in an unidentified hand*] No. 6 Kings Bench Walks, Inner Temple, London.

POSTMARKS: DUNVEGAN, NEWCASTLE, SE 23, 28 SE.

ENDORSEMENT in an unidentified hand: Doctor S. Johnson, d. Macleod's in Skie, 14 Sept. 1773.

Dear Sir: Macleod's in Skie,[1] Sept. 14, 1773

The post will not let me do more than entreat you, if you leave

1. *Post* To Hester Thrale, 14 Sept. 1773 and n. 3.

Newcastle before I can come, to let me know, and put up my things with yours to go to London, for if you are not at home, I shall probably go the other way.[2] Make[3] my Compliments to Mrs. Chambers and your Brother.[4] I am, Sir, Your affectionate Servant,

SAM. JOHNSON

2. As the altered address makes clear, Chambers had already departed for London. Nevertheless, SJ returned to London through Newcastle instead of going "the other way," presumably via Carlisle (*Hebrides*, p. 391).

3. MS: "M" superimposed upon "I"

4. SJ refers to Robert Chambers's mother (d. 1782) and his brother Richard.

Lord Elibank

TUESDAY 14 SEPTEMBER 1773

MS: Current location unknown. Transcribed from a photostat supplied by L. F. Powell.

ADDRESS: To the Right honourable Lord Elibank in Edinburgh [*Re-addressed in an unidentified hand*] Haddington.

POSTMARK: [Undeciphered].

ENDORSEMENT: Samuel Johnson.

My Lord: Skie, Sept. 14, 1773

On the rugged shore of Skie, I had the honour of your Lordship's Letter,[1] and can with great truth declare that no place is so gloomy, but that it would be cheered by such a testimony of regard, from a Mind so well qualified to estimate characters, and to deal out approbation in its due proportions. If I have more than my share it is your Lordships fault, for I have always reverenced your Judgement too much, to exalt myself in your presence by any false pretensions.

1. As part of his campaign to lure SJ to Scotland, JB had written to Lord Elibank but received no answer (*Life* v.14). At Portree on 12 Sept. both JB and SJ found letters from Elibank, who explained that he had arrived in Edinburgh only after the travelers had departed. Elibank told JB, "I shall be glad to go five hundred miles to enjoy a day of his [SJ's] company" (*Life* v.181). To SJ he wrote, "I value you more than any King in Christendom" (*Life* v.182).

Mr. Boswel and I are at present at the disposal of the winds, and therefore cannot fix the time at which we shall have the honour of seeing your Lordship,[2] but we should either of us think ourselves injured by the supposition that we would miss your Lordships conversation when we could enjoy it, for I have often declared that I never met you without going away a wiser man. I am, My Lord, Your Lordship's most obedient, and most humble servant,

SAM. JOHNSON

2. SJ and JB met Elibank in Edinburgh on 10 Nov. (*Hebrides*, p. 377). They also stayed at his home in Ballencrieff, 13–15 Nov. (Fleeman, p. 316).

Hester Thrale

TUESDAY 14 SEPTEMBER 1773

MS: Hyde Collection.

ADDRESS: To Henry Thrale, Esq., in Southwark.

POSTMARKS: DUNVEGAN, SE 22, 27 SE, FREE.

Dearest Madam: Skie, Sept. 14, 1773

The Post, which comes but once a week into these parts, is so soon to go that I have not time to go on where I left off in my last Letter. I have been several days in the Island of[1] Raarsa,[2] and am now again in the Isle of Skie, but at the other end of it. Skie is almost equally divided between the two great Families of Macdonald and Macleod,[3] other proprietors having

1. MS: undeciphered letter del. before "of"

2. JB and SJ arrived on Raasay 8 Sept. and departed for Skye on 12 Sept., landing at Portree (Fleeman, pp. 300–301; *Hebrides*, pp. 127, 154–56; *Post* To Hester Thrale, 21 Sept. 1773).

3. The Macdonalds of Sleat and the Macleods of Dunvegan were the two main branches of their respective families on Skye. Sir Alexander Macdonald (*Ante* To Hester Thrale, 6 Sept. 1773, n. 1) was head of the former, Norman Macleod (1754–1801), twenty-third Chief, of the latter. Until the eighteenth century the two families had disputed, usually by force of arms, for territory and control of portions of the island (Fleeman, pp. 264, 274–75; D. J. Macdonald, *Clan Donald*,

only small districts. The two great lords do not know within twenty square miles the contents of their own territories. Macdonald kept up but ill the reputation of highland hospitality,[4] we are now with Macleod quite at the other end of the Island, where there is a fine young Gentleman, and fine Ladies.[5] The Ladies are studying Earse. I have a cold and am miserably deaf, and am troublesome to Lady Macleod;[6] I force her to speak loud, but she will seldom speak loud enough.

Raarsa is an Island about 15 miles long, and 2 broad under the Dominion of one Gentleman, who has 3 sons, and 10 Daughters.[7] The Eldest is the beauty of this part of the world, and has been polished at Edinburgh.[8] They sing, and dance, and without expence, have upon their table most of what sea, air, or earth can afford. I intended to have written about Raarsa, but the post will not wait longer than while I send my compliments to my Dear Master, and little Mistresses. I am, Madam, Your most humble servant,

SAM. JOHNSON

You may, if you please, write to me at Mr. Drummond's Bookseller in Edinburgh.[9]

1978, pp. 398–416; I. F. Grant, *The Macleods*, 1959, p. 13; Donald Mackinnon and Alick Morrison, *The Macleods—The Genealogy of a Clan*, section 1, 1978, p. 38).

4. *Ante* To Hester Thrale, 6 Sept. 1773, n. 1.

5. *Post* To Hester Thrale, 30 Sept. 1773 and n. 31.

6. Emilia Brodie Macleod (1730–1802), the mother of the twenty-third Chief (Fleeman, pp. 191, 275).

7. John Macleod (*c.* 1714–86), eleventh Laird of Raasay, was the father of thirteen children: James, John, Malcolm, Flora, Margaret, Janet, Catherine, Isabella-Rose, Julia, Jane, Anne, Mary, and Christina (Fleeman, p. 277).

8. Flora Macleod (d. 1780), called "Princess." *Post* To Hester Thrale, 24 Sept. 1773.

9. *Ante* To Hester Thrale, 12 Aug. 1773.

Hester Thrale

TUESDAY 21 SEPTEMBER 1773

MS: Hyde Collection.

ADDRESS: To Henry Thrale, Esq., in Southwark [*added in an unidentified hand*] London.

POSTMARKS: DUNVEGAN, SE 29, 4 OC, FREE.

Dearest Madam: Skie, Sep. 21, 1773[1]

I am so vexed at the necessity of sending yesterday so short a Letter,[2] that I purpose to get a long letter beforehand by writing something every day, which I may the more easily do, as a cold makes me now too deaf to take the usual pleasure in conversation. Lady Macleod is very kind to me, and the place at which we now are, is equal in strength of Situation, in the wildness of the adjacent country, and in the plenty and elegance of the domestick entertainment, to a Castle in Gothick romances. The sea with a little Island is before us, cascades play within view. Close to the house is the formidable Skeleton of an old Castle probably Danish; and the whole mass of building stands upon a protuberance of rock, inaccessible till of late but by a pair of stairs on the Sea side, and secure in ancient times against any Enemy that was likely to invade the kingdom of Skie.[3] Macleod has offered me an Island,[4] if it were not too far off I should hardly refuse it; my Island would be pleasanter than Brighthelmston, if You and Master could come to it, but I cannot think it pleasant to live quite alone. Oblitusque meorum, obliviscendus et illis.[5] That I should be elated by the do-

1. SJ began writing this letter on 15 Sept. and completed it on the 21st.

2. *Ante* To Hester Thrale, 14 Sept. 1773.

3. Dunvegan, the oldest continuously inhabited castle in Scotland, has been occupied by the Macleods for over seven hundred years. The house in which SJ stayed was begun in the fifteenth century, and expanded and renovated frequently thereafter (W. H. Murray, *The Companion Guide to the West Highlands of Scotland*, 2d ed., 1969, pp. 266–67).

4. The island of Isa or Isay, in Loch Dunvegan, which Macleod offered to SJ on condition that he live there at least one month a year (*Hebrides*, p. 211).

5. *tamen illic vivere vellem / oblitusque meorum obliviscendus et illis*: "yet there would

minion of an Island to forgetfulness of my friends at Streatham,[6] and I hope never to deserve that they should be willing to forget me.

It has happened that I have been often recognized in my journey where I did not expect it. At Aberdeen I found one of my acquaintance [a] Professor of Physick.[7] Turning aside to dine with a country Gentleman, I was owned at table by one who had seen[8] me at a Philosophical Lecture.[9] At Macdonald's I was claimed by a Naturalist, who wanders about the Islands to pick up curiosities,[10] and I had once in London attracted the notice of Lady Macleod. I will now go on with my Account.

The Highland Girl made tea, and looked and talked not inelegantly.[11] Her father was by no means an ignorant or a weak man. There were books in the cottage, among which were some volumes of Prideaux's Connexion.[12] This man's conversation we were glad of while we staid. He had been *out* as they call it, in forty[13] five,[14] and still retained his old opinions. He was going to America, because his rent was raised beyond what he thought himself able to pay.

At night our beds were made, but we had some difficulty in persuading ourselves to lye down in them, though we had put on our own sheets. At last we ventured, and I slept very soundly, in the vale called Glenmorison amidst the rocks and mountains. Next morning our Landlord liked us so well, that

---

I live, and forgetting my friends and by them forgotten" (Horace, *Epistles* I.xi.8–9, trans. H. R. Fairclough, Loeb ed.).

6. MS: "Streatham" repeated as catchword

7. Sir Alexander Gordon. *Ante* To Hester Thrale, 25 Aug. 1773, n. 29.

8. MS: "s" superimposed upon "m"

9. One of Alexander Fraser's guests at dinner on 25 Aug. had been a certain "Dr. Fraser, who . . . remembered to have seen Mr. Johnson at a lecture on experimental philosophy at Lichfield" (*Hebrides*, p. 78). *Ante* To Hester Thrale, 6 Sept. 1773 and n. 3.

10. John Jeans (*c.* 1725–*c.* 1804), Scots mineralogist, "said he had been at Dr. Johnson's in London" (*Life* v.149, 517–18).

11. *Ante* To Hester Thrale, 6 Sept. 1773 and n. 29.

12. *The Old and New Testaments Connected* (1716–18) by Humphrey Prideaux (1648–1724).

13. MS: "45" del. before "forty"

14. See below, n. 16.

he walked some miles with us for our company through a country so wild and barren that the proprietor does not with all his pressure upon his tenants raise more than four hundred a year from near an hundred square miles, or sixty thousand acres. He let us know that he had forty head of black cattle, an hundred Goats, and[15] an hundred sheep upon a farm which he remembred let at five pounds a year, but for which he now paid twenty. He told us some stories of their march into England.[16] At last he left us, and we went forward, winding among mountains sometimes green and sometimes naked, commonly so steep as not easily to be climbed by the greatest vigour and activity. Our way was often crossed by little rivulets, and we were entertained with small streams trickling from the rocks, which after heavy rains must be tremendous torrents.

About noon, we came to a small glen, so they call a valley, which compared with other places appeared rich and fertile. Here our Guides desired us to stop that the horses might graze, for the journey was very laborious, and no more grass would be found. We made no difficulty of compliance, and I sat down to make notes on a green bank, with a small stream running at my feet, in the midst of savage solitude, with Mountains before me, and on either hand covered with heath. I looked round me, and wondered that I was not more affected, but the mind is not at all times equally ready to be put in motion.[17] If my Mistress, and Master, and Queeny had been there we should have produced some reflections among us either poetical or philosophical, for though *Solitude* be *the nurse of woe*,[18] conversation is often the parent of remarks and discoveries.

In about an hour we remounted, and persued our journey. The lake by which we had travelled from some time ended in

15. MS: "and and"

16. The Jacobite forces crossed the Tweed into England 6 Nov. 1745. They captured Carlisle and entered Derby, before retreating to Scotland 6 Dec.

17. "Whether I spent the hour well I know not; for here I first conceived the thought of this narration" (Fleeman, p. 31).

18. "The silent heart . . . learns to know / That solitude's the nurse of woe" (Thomas Parnell, *Hymn to Contentment*, ll. 19, 23–24).

a river, which we passed by a bridge and came to another Glen with a collection of huts, called Auknashealds, the huts were generally built of clods of earth held together by the intertexture of vegetable fibres, of which earth there are great levels in Scotland which they call mosses. Moss in Scotland, is Bog in Ireland, and Mosstrooper is Bogtrotter. There was however one hut built of loose stones piled up with great thickness into a strong though not solid wall. From this house we obtained some great pails of milk, and having brought bread with us, were very liberally regaled. The Inhabitants, a very coarse tribe, ignorant of any language but Earse, gathered so fast about us, that if we had not had Highlanders with us, they might have caused more alarm than pleasure. They are called the clan of Macrae.[19]

We had been told that nothing gratified the Highlanders so much as snuff and tobacco, and had accordingly stowed ourselves with both at fort Augustus. Boswel opened his treasure and gave them each a piece of tobacco roll. We had more bread than we could eat for the present, and were more liberal than provident. Boswel cut it in slices and gave each of them an opportunity of tasting wheaten bread for the first time. I then got some halfpence for a shilling and made up the deficiencies of Boswels distribution, who had given some money[20] among the children. We then directed that the mistress of the stone house should be asked what we must pay her, she who perhaps had never sold any thing but cattle before, knew not, I believe, well what to ask, and referred herself to us. We obliged her to make some demand, and our Highlanders settled the account with her at a shilling. One of the men advised her, with the cunning that clowns never can be without, to ask more but she said that a shilling was enough. We gave her half a crown and she offered part of it again. The Macraes were so well pleased with our behaviour, that they declared it the best day they had

19. "The Macraes, as we heard afterwards in the Hebrides, were originally an indigent and subordinate clan, and having no farms nor stock, were in great numbers servants to the Maclellans" (Fleeman, p. 33).

20. MS: "mon" superimposed upon "?far"

seen since the time of the old Laird of MacLeod,[21] who I suppose, like us, stopped in their valley, as he was travelling to Skie.

We were mentioning this view of the Highlander's life at Macdonald's, and mentioning the Macraes with some degree of pity, when a Highland Lady[22] informed us, that we might spare our tenderness, for she doubted not, but the Woman who supplied us with milk, was mistress of thirteen or fourteen milch Cows.

I cannot forbear to interrupt my Narrative. Boswel, with some of his troublesome kindness, has informed this family, and reminded me that the eighteenth of September is my birthday. The return of my Birthday, if I remember it, fills me with thoughts which it seems to be the general care of humanity to escape. I can now look back upon threescore and four years, in which little has been done, and little has been enjoyed, a life diversified by misery, spent part in the sluggishness of penury, and part under the violence of pain, in gloomy discontent, or importunate distress. But perhaps I am better than I should have been, if I had been less afflicted. With this I will try to be content.

In proportion as there is less pleasure in retrospective considerations the mind is more disposed to wander forward into futurity, but at Sixty four what promises, however liberal of imaginary good, can Futurity venture to make. Yet something will be always promised, and some promises will always be credited. I am hoping, and I am praying that I may live better in the time to come, whether long or short, than I have yet lived, and in[23] the solace of that hope endeavour to repose. Dear Queeney's day is next,[24] I hope, she at sixty four will have less to regret.

I will now complain no more, but tell my Mistress of my travels.

21. Norman Macleod (1705–72), twenty-second chief (Fleeman, pp. 173, 274).

22. Possibly Florence Macdonald, wife of Roderick Macdonald of Sandaig and sister-in-law of John Macleod of Raasay (Fleeman, p. 173).

23. MS: "in" written above "to" del.

24. Hester Maria Thrale's birthday was 17 Sept. (Hyde, 1977, p. 17).

After we left the Macraes, we travelled on through a country like that which we passed in the morning, the[25] highlands are very uniform, for there is little variety in universal barrenness. The rocks however are not all naked, some have grass on their sides, and Birches and Alders on their tops, and in the vallies are often broad and clear streams which have little depth, and commonly run very quick. The channels are made by the violence of wintry floods, the quickness of the stream is in proportion to the declivity of the descent, and the breadth of the channel makes the water shallow in a dry season.

There are Red Deer and Roebucks in the mountains, but we found only Goats in the road, and had very little entertainment as we travelled either for the eye or ear. There are, I fancy, no singing birds in the Highlands.

Towards Night we came to a very formidable hill named Rattiken, which we climbed with more difficulty than we had yet experienced, and at last came to Glanelg a place on the Seaside opposite to Skie. We were by this time weary and disgusted, nor was our humour much mended, by an inn, which, though it was built with lime and slate, the highlander's description of a house which he thinks magnificent, had neither wine, bread, eggs, nor any thing that we could eat or drink. When we were taken up stairs, a dirty fellow bounced out of the bed in which one of us was to lie.[26] Boswel blusterd, but nothing could he get. At last a Gentleman in the Neighbourhood who heard of our arrival sent us rum and white sugar.[27] Boswel was now provided for in part, and the Landlord prepared[28] some mutton chops, which we could not eat, and killed two Hens, of which Boswel made his servant broil a limb, with what effect I know not. We had a lemon, and a piece of bread, which supplied me with my supper.

25. MS: "for" del. before "the"

26. In his *Journey* SJ described this man as being "black as a Cyclops from the forge" (Fleeman, p. 39).

27. Murdoch Murchison of Beolary, Glenelg, "factor to the Laird of Macleod" (*Hebrides*, pp. 107, 111; Fleeman, p. 175).

28. MS: "pre" repeated as catchword

When the repast was ended, we began to deliberate upon bed. Mrs. Boswel had warned us that we should *catch something*, and had given us Sheets for our security; for Sir Alexander and Lady Macdonald,[29] she said, came back from Skie, so scratching themselves——. I thought sheets a slender defence, against the confederacy with which we were threatned, and by this time our Highlanders had found a place where they could get some hay; I ordered hay to be laid thick upon the bed, and slept upon it in my great coat. Boswel laid sheets upon his hay, and reposed in Linen like a Gentleman. The horses were turned out to grass, with a man to watch them. The hill Ratiken, and the inn at Glanelg, are the only things of which we or travellers yet more delicate, could find any pretensions to complain.

Sept. 2. I rose rustling from the hay, and went to tea, which I forget whether we found or brought. We saw the Isle of Skie before us darkening the horizon with its rocky coast. A boat was procured, and we launched into one of the Straits of the Atlantick Ocean. We had a passage of about twelve miles to the point where Sir Alexander resided, having come from his Seat in the midland part, to a small house on the shore, as we believe, that he might with less reproach entertain us meanly. If he aspired to meanness his retrograde ambition was completely gratified, but he did not succeed equally in escaping reproach. He had no cook, nor, I suppose, much provision, nor had the Lady the common decencies of her teatable. We picked up our Sugar with our fingers. Boswel was very angry, and reproached him with his improper parsimony.[30] I did not much reflect upon the conduct of a man with whom I was not likely to converse as long at any other time.

29. In 1768 Sir Alexander Macdonald had married Elizabeth Diana Bosville (1748–89), daughter of Godfrey Bosville (1717–84) of Gunthwaite, JB's "Yorkshire Chief" (Fleeman, p. 264; *Life* III.439).

30. On 3 Sept. JB "fell upon" Sir Alexander and reproached him for "the meanness of his appearance. . . . He was thrown into a violent passion" (*Hebrides*, p. 116). Their quarrel was revived as a result of JB's criticisms in his *Journal of a Tour to the Hebrides* (1785), and a duel might have ensued had not both men partially retracted their accusations (*Later Years*, pp. 306–11).

You will now expect that I should give you some account of the Isle of Skie, of which though I have been twelve days upon it, I have little to say. It is an[31] Island perhaps fifty miles long, so much indented by inlets of the Sea, that there is no[32] part of it removed from the water more than six miles. No part that I have seen is plain, you are always climbing or descending, and every step is upon rock or mire. A walk upon plowed ground in England is a dance upon carpets, compared to the toilsome drudgery, of wandering in Skie. There is neither town nor village in the Island, nor have I seen any house but Macleod's, that is not much below your habitation at[33] Brighthelmston. In the mountains there are Stags and Roebucks, but no hares and few rabbits, nor have I seen any thing that interested me, as Zoologist, except an Otter, bigger than I thought an otter could have been.

You are perhaps imagining that I am withdrawn[34] from the gay and the busy world into regions of peace and pastoral felicity, and am enjoying the reliques of the golden age; that I am surveying Nature's magnificence from a mountain, or remarking her minuter beauties on the flowery bank of a winding rivulet, that I am invigorating myself in the sunshine, or delighting my imagination with being[35] hidden from[36] the invasion of human evils and human passions, in the darkness of a Thicket, that I am busy in gathering shells and pebbles on the Shore, or contemplative on a rock, from which I look upon the water and consider how[37] many waves are rolling between me and Streatham.

The use of travelling is to regulate imagination by reality, and instead of thinking how things may be, to see them as they are. Here are mountains which I should once have climbed, but to[38] climb steeps is now very laborious, and to descend them dangerous, and I am now content with knowing that by

31. MS: "It is an" superimposed upon "Skie is"
32. MS: undeciphered deletion before "no"
33. MS: "of" del. before "at"
34. MS: "w" superimposed upon "g"
35. MS: "the" del. before "being"
36. MS: "from from"
37. MS: "h" superimposed upon "t"
38. MS: "the"

a Scrambling up a rock, I shall only see other rocks, and a wider circuit of barren desolation. Of streams we have here a sufficient number, but they murmer not upon pebbles but upon rocks; of flowers, if Chloris herself were here,[39] I could present her only with the bloom of Heath. Of Lawns and Thickets, he must read, that would know them, for here is little sun and no shade. On the sea I look from my window, but am not much tempted to the shore for since I came to this Island, almost every Breath of air has been a storm, and what is worse, a storm with all its severity, but without its magnificence, for the sea is here so broken into channels, that there is not a sufficient volume of water either for lofty surges, or loud roar.

On Sept 6 We left[40] Macdonald, to visit Raarsa, the Island which I have already mentioned.[41] We were to cross part of Skie on horseback, a mode of travelling very uncomfortable, for the road is so narrow, where any road can be found that only one can go, and so craggy that the attention can never be remitted, it allows therefore neither the gayety of conversation nor the laxity of solitude, nor has it in itself the amusement of much variety, as it affords only all the possible transpositions[42] of Bog,[43] Rock, and Rivulet. Twelve Miles, by computation, make a reasonable journey for a day.

At night we came to a tenants house of the first rank of Tenants where we were entertained better than the Landlords.[44] There were books, both English and Latin.[45] Company gathered about us, and we heard some talk of the Second sight and some talk of the events of forty five, a year which will not

39. Chloris, wife of Zephyrus and goddess of flowers.

40. MS: "set" del. before "left"

41. *Ante* To Hester Thrale, 14 Sept. 1773.

42. MS: initial "t" superimposed upon "s"

43. MS: "a" del. before "Bog"

44. SJ and JB spent the night of 6 Sept. at Coirechatachen, the farmhouse of Lachlan Mackinnon (*c.* 1710–89), a Jacobite who had fought in the '45 (*Life* v.520). Mackinnon's hospitality compared favorably with the miserly reception accorded the travelers by Sir Alexander Macdonald.

45. "There were several good books here: Hector Boethius in Latin, Cave's *Lives of the Fathers*, Baker's *Chronicle*, Jeremy Collier's *Church History*, Mr. Johnson's small Dictionary, several more books" (*Hebrides*, p. 121).

soon be forgotten among the Islanders. The next day we were confined by a storm, the company, I think, encreased and our entertainment was not only hospitable but elegant. At night, a Minister's sister in very fine Brocade, sung Earse songs.[46] I wished to know the meaning, but the Highlanders are not much used to scholastick questions,[47] and no translation could be obtained.

Next day, Sept. 8 the weather allowed us to depart, a good boat was provided us, and we went to Raarsa, under the conduct of Mr. Malcolm Macleod, a Gentleman who conducted Prince Charles through the mountains in his distresses.[48] The prince, he says, was more active than himself, they were at least one night, without any shelter.

The wind blew enough to give the boat a kind of dancing agitation, and in about three or four hours we arrived at Raarsa, where we were met by the Laird and his friends upon the Shore.[49] Raarsa, for such is his title, is Master of two Islands, upon the smaller of which, called Rona, he has only flocks and herds. Rona gives title to his eldest Son.[50] The money which he raises by rent from all his dominions which contain at least fifty thousand acres, is not believed to exceed two hundred and fifty pounds, but as he keeps a large farm in

46. Isabel Macpherson, sister of the Rev. Martin Macpherson (1743–1812), minister of Sleat and Lachlan Mackinnon's son-in-law (*Hebrides*, p. 120; *Life* v.547). "Mr. Johnson had always been merry with Miss Macpherson; asked her to go to London, and said many little jocular complimentary things to her which afforded us amusement" (*Hebrides*, p. 240).

47. MS: "ions" repeated as catchword

48. Malcolm Macleod (b. 1711), cousin to John Macleod of Raasay, assisted in the escape of Prince Charles Edward (1720–88), the Young Pretender, after the failure of the Jacobite Rebellion of 1745. He conducted the Prince from Skye to Raasay on 1 July 1746 and back again the next day. Macleod then led the Prince, who was disguised as his servant, to the house of John Mackinnon, Macleod's brother-in-law (*Life* v.190–98, 523; Henry Paton, *The Lyon in Mourning*, 1895, I.73–74, 130–42). After the failure of the rebellion, Macleod was arrested, brought to London, but then released for lack of evidence (Paton, *The Lyon in Mourning* I.145–46; *Post* To Hester Thrale, 30 Sept. 1773).

49. *Ante* To Hester Thrale, 14 Sept. 1773 and n. 7.

50. James Macleod (d. 1824), who on his father's death in 1786 became twelfth Chief (Fleeman, p. 277).

his own hands, he sells every year great numbers of cattle which he adds to his revenue, and, his table is furnished from the Farm and from the sea with very little expence, except for those things this count[r]y does not produce, and of these he is very liberal. The wine circulates vigorously, and the tea and Chocolate and Coffee, however they are got[51] are always at hand. I am, Madam, Your most obedient Servant,

SAM. JOHNSON

We are this morning trying to get out of Skie.[52]

51. MS: "got" repeated as catchword

52. It is not clear what SJ means by this statement. He and JB did not actually leave Skye until 3 Oct. (Fleeman, p. 304; *Hebrides*, p. 245). Between 21 Sept. and 3 Oct. they visited Ullinish, Talisker, Coirechatachen, Ostaig, and Armadale on what to some extent were planned visits (Fleeman, pp. 302–4).

Hester Thrale

FRIDAY 24 SEPTEMBER 1773

MS: Hyde Collection.

ADDRESS: To Henry Thrale, Esq., in Southwark.

POSTMARKS: OC 7, OC 11, SCONSER, FREE.

Dear Madam: Skie, Sept. 24, 1773

I am Still in Skie. Do you[1] remember the Song?

> Ev'ry Island is a prison
> Strongly guarded by the sea.[2]

We have at one time no boat, and at another may have too much wind, but of our reception here we have no reason to complain. We are now with Colonel Macleod in a more pleas-

1. MS: "your"

2. "Every island is a prison / Strongly guarded by the sea; / Kings and princes, for that reason, / Pris'ners are, as well as we." This song, which has been attributed to Charles Coffey (d. 1745), appeared in *The Charmer* (1749) (*Life* v.256 and n. 1).

ant place than I thought Skie able to afford.[3] Now to the narrative.

We were received at Raarsa, on the Seaside, and after clambering with some difficulty over the rocks, a labour which the traveller wherever he reposes himself on land, must in these islands, be contented to endure, we were introduced into the house, which one of the company called the court of Raarsa, with politeness, which not the court of Versailles could have thought defective. The house is not large though we were told in our passage that it had eleven fire rooms, nor magnificently furnished, but our utensils were commonly silver. We went up[4] into a dining room about as large as your blue room, where we had something given us to eat, and tea and coffee.

Raarsa himself is a man [of] no inelegant appearance, and of manners uncommonly refined. Lady Raarsa makes no very sublime appearance for a Sovereign, but is a good Housewife, and a very prudent and diligent conductress of her family.[5] Miss Flora Macleod is a celebrated Beauty, has been admired at Edinburgh, tosses her head very high, and has manners so Ladylike, that I wish her headdress was lower.[6] The rest of the nine Girls[7] are all pretty, the youngest is between Queeny and Lucy.[8] The youngest Boy,[9] of four years old, runs barefoot, and wandered with us[10] over the rocks to see a Mill. I believe he would walk on that rough ground without shoes, ten miles in a day.

3. John Macleod (1714–98), of Talisker, Skye (Fleeman, p. 278). After fighting on the side of the Government during the Jacobite Rebellion, Macleod joined the Scots Brigade in Holland, rising to the rank of Colonel. In 1772 he returned to Scotland to assist his Chief, Norman Macleod of Dunvegan, in managing his estates (*Life* v.524). According to JB, John Macleod and his wife, "in consequence of having lived abroad, had introduced the ease and politeness of the continent into this rude region" (*Life* v.256).

4. MS: "up" altered from "upon"

5. John Macleod had married Jane Macqueen of Totaroam (Fleeman, p. 278).

6. *Ante* To Hester Thrale, 14 Sept. 1773 and n. 8.

7. MS: "Girls" altered from "Gills"

8. *Ante* To Hester Thrale, 14 Sept. 1773, n. 7. If SJ was correct, then Christina Macleod was between four and nine years old.

9. Malcolm Macleod (*c.* 1769–1821) (Fleeman, p. 277).

10. MS: "u" superimposed upon "ov"

The Laird of Raarsa has sometimes disputed the chieftainry of the Clan with Macleod of Skie, but being much inferiour in extent of possessions, has I suppose, been forced to desist.[11] Raarsa and its provinces have descended to its present possessor through a succession of four hundred years, without any encrease or diminution. It[12] was indeed lately in danger of forfeiture, but the old Laird[13] joined some prudence with this zeal, and when Prince Charles landed in Scotland, made over his estate to his Son, the present Laird, and led an hundred Men[14] of Raarsa into the field, with officers of his own family. Eighty six came back after the last battle. The prince was hidden in his distress two nights at Raarsa, and the king's troops burnt the whole country, and killed some of the Cattle.

You may guess at the opinions that[15] prevail in this country, they are however content with fighting for their king, they do not drink for him, we had no foolish healths.

At night unexpectedly to us who were strangers, the carpet was taken up, the fidler of the family came up, and a very vigorous and general dance was begun. As I told you we were two and thirty, at supper, there were full as many dancers, for though all who supped did not dance, some[16] danced of the young people who did not come to supper. Raarsa himself danced with his children, and old Malcolm in his Fillibeg, was as nimble as when[17] he led the prince over the mountains.[18]

When they had danced themselves weary, two tables were Spread, and I suppose at least twenty dishes were upon them. In this country, some preparations of milk are always served

11. A similar claim in SJ's *Journey to the Western Islands of Scotland* caused Macleod of Raasay to protest to JB on 10 Apr. 1775 (Fleeman, p. 48; *Life* v.410–11). Informed of his mistake, SJ apologized to Raasay and retracted the statement in the *Caledonian Mercury* and the *Edinburgh Advertiser* (*Post* To John Macleod, 6 May 1775; Fleeman, p. 184). The retraction also was printed in a longer notice prefixed to the 1785 edition of the *Journey* (Fleeman, pp. 184, 186).

12. MS: "The" del. before "It"

13. Malcolm Macleod (d. 1761), tenth Chief (Fleeman, p. 276).

14. MS: "of" del. before "Men"

15. MS: "of" del. before "that"

16. MS: "s" superimposed upon "m"

17. MS: "when" written above "well" del.

18. Malcolm Macleod (*Ante* To Hester Thrale, 21 Sept. 1773, n. 48).

up as part of supper, and sometimes in the place of tarts at dinner. The table was not coarsely heaped, but at once plentiful and elegant. They do not pretend to make a loaf; there are only cakes, commonly of oats or barley, but they made me very nice cakes of wheat flower. I always sat at the left hand of Lady Raarsa, and young Macleod of Skie, the chieftain of the clan sat on the right.[19]

After supper a young Lady who was visiting, sung Earse songs, in which Lady Raarsa joined prettily enough, but not gracefully, the young Ladies sustained the chorus better. They are very little used to be asked questions, and not well prepared with answers. When one of the Songs was over, I asked the princess[20] that sat next me, *what is it*[21] *about*? I question, if she conceived that I did not understand it. For the entertainment of the company, said she. But, Madam, what is the meaning of it? It is a love song. This was all the intelligence that I could obtain, nor have I[22] ever been able to procure a translation of a line of Erse.

At twelve it was bedtime. I had a chamber to myself, which in eleven rooms to forty people was more than my share. How the company and the family were distributed is not easy to tell. Macleod the chieftain, and Boswel, and I, had all si[n]gle chambers on the first floor. There remained eight rooms for at least seven and thirty lodgers. I suppose they put up temporary beds in the dining room where they probably stowed all the young Ladies. There was a room above stairs with six beds in which they put ten Men. The rest in my next. I am, Madam, Your most humble servant,

SAM. JOHNSON

19. Norman Macleod, of Dunvegan (*Ante* To Hester Thrale, 14 Sept. 1773, n. 3).

20. Flora Macleod (*Ante* To Hester Thrale, 14 Sept. 1773, n. 8).

21. MS: "the" del. before "it"

22. MS: "of"

Macleod of Macleod[1]

TUESDAY 28 SEPTEMBER 1773

MS: Macleod of Macleod, Dunvegan.

Dear Sir: Ostig, Sept. 28, 1773

We are now on the margin of the sea, waiting for a boat and a wind. Boswel grows impatient, but the kind treatment which I find wherever I go makes me leave with some heaviness of heart an Island which I am not very likely to see again. Having now gone as far as horses can carry us, we thankfully return them. My Steed will, I hope, be received with kindness; he has born me, heavy as I am, over ground both rough and steep with great fidelity, and for the use of him, as for your other favours, I hope you will believe me thankful, and willing, at whatever distance we may be placed, to show my sense of your kindness by any offices of friendship that may fall within my power.

Lady Macleod and the young Ladies have by their hospitality[2] and politeness made an impression on my mind which will not easily be effaced. Be pleased to tell them that I remember them with great tenderness and great respect. I am, Sir, Your most obliged and Most humble Servant, SAM. JOHNSON

We passed two days at Talisker very happily, both by the perfectness of the place, and elegance of our reception.[3]

1. *Ante* To Hester Thrale, 14 Sept. 1773, n. 3.

2. MS: "hospi-" repeated as catchword

3. *Ante* To Hester Thrale, 24 Sept. 1773 and n. 3. SJ and JB arrived at Talisker 23 Sept. and departed 25 Sept. (Fleeman, p. 303).

Robert Chambers

THURSDAY 30 SEPTEMBER 1773

MS: Hyde Collection.

ADDRESS: To Robert Chambers, Esq., in the Temple, London.

POSTMARKS: SCONSER, 25 OC.

Dear Sir: Ostick, in Skie, Sept. 30, 1773

We are imp⟨risoned⟩[1] in Skie. The weather is such as no boat will venture to ⟨cross ov⟩er. Two have been lately lost in these equinoctial tempests. This restraint, which has all the alleviations that courtesy and hospitality can afford, is made very painful to me by the fear of not being able to take leave of you, before your departure.[2] If I am detained from you by insuperable obstructions, let this be witness that I love you, and that I wish you all the good that can be enjoyed through [the] whole of our Existence. You are going where there will be many opportunities of profitable wickedness, but you go with good principles, a confirmed and solid Christian. I hope to see you come [back] both with fortune encreased, and Virtue grown more resolute by contest.[3]

Do not forget young Laurence.[4] His Father has for more than twenty years been doing me all the good that he could, and I believe you will not look with indifference on the Son of a Man to whom I am desirous to give assistance in the only case, which can probably put assistance in my ⟨power⟩. If I do not come, be pleased to call on him as you very k⟨indly⟩ proposed.

If you go before I come⟨, write⟩ me a letter. I shall value it. I can say no more but tha⟨t again⟩ and again I wish you well. I am, Dear Sir, Most affectionately yours,

SAM. JOHNSON

1. MS: mutilated

2. Chambers did not in fact sail for India until the following April; he and SJ had a final meeting on 30 Mar. (*Post* To Robert Chambers, 30 Mar. 1774 and n. 2).

3. Chambers did not return from Calcutta until fifteen years after SJ's death.

4. William Chauncy Lawrence (d. 1783), Thomas Lawrence's second son, "had . . . fixed his mind upon trying his fortune" in India (*GM* 1787, p. 192). Several years after arriving in Calcutta, "young Laurence," who had received a legal education, became an advocate in the Supreme Court of Bengal. SJ recommended this "adventurer" to the notice of Warren Hastings (*Post* To Warren Hastings, 20 Dec. 1774), and continued to press Chambers to assist him (*Post* To Robert Chambers, 19 Apr. 1783).

Hester Thrale

THURSDAY 30 SEPTEMBER 1773

MS: Hyde Collection.

Dearest Madam: Ostick in Skie, Sept. 30, 1773

I am still confined in Skie.[1] We were unskilful travellers, and imagined that the sea was an open road, which we could pass at pleasure, but we have now learned with some pain, that we may still wait for a long time the caprices of the equinoctial winds, and sit reading or writing as I now do, while the tempest is rolling the sea, and roaring in the mountains. I am now no longer pleased with the delay, you can hear from me but seldom, and I cannot at all hear from you. It comes into my mind, that some evil may happen, or that I might be of use while I am away. But these thoughts are vain. The Wind is violent and adverse, and our Boat cannot yet come. I must content myself with writing to you, and hoping that you will sometime receive my Letter. Now to my Narrative.

Sept. 9. Having passed the night as is usual, I rose and found the Dining room full of company, we feasted and talked and when the Evening [came] it brought musick and dancing. Young Macleod, the great proprietor of Skie, and head of his clan, was very distinguishable, a young man of nineteen, bred a while at St. Andrews,[2] and afterwards[3] at Oxford,[4] a pupil of G. Strahan. He is a young man of a mind as much advanced as I have ever known, very elegant of manners and very graceful in his person. He has the full spirit of a feudal Chief, and I was very ready to accept his invitation to Dunvegan. All Raarsa's Children are beautiful. The ladies all except the eldest are in the morning dressed in their hair. The true High-

1. Delayed by bad weather, SJ and JB stayed from 28 Sept. until 1 Oct. at the home of the Rev. Martin Macpherson (1743–1812). They then proceeded to Armadale (Fleeman, pp. 304, 363).

2. According to St. Andrews's rolls for this period, Norman Macleod never officially matriculated.

3. MS: "afterwards" repeated as catchword

4. Norman Macleod matriculated at University College in Nov. 1770 but never took a degree (*Alum. Oxon.* II.iii.898).

lander never wears more than a riband on her head till she is married.

On the third day Boswel went out with old Malcolm[5] to see a ruined castle, which he found less entire than was promised, but he saw the country.[6] I did not go for the Castle was perhaps ten miles off and there is no riding at Raarsa, the whole Island being rock and mountain, from which the cattle often fall and are destroyed. It is very barren, and maintains as near as I could collect about seven hundred inhabitants, perhaps ten to a square mile. In these countries you are not to suppose that you shall find villages, or inclosures. The traveller wanders th[r]ough a naked desart, gratified sometimes, but rarely with the sight of cows, and now and then finds a heap of loose stones and turfs in a cavity between rocks, where a Being, born with all those powers which education expands, and all those sensations which culture refines, is condemned to shelter itself from the wind and rain. Philosophers there are who try to make themselves believe that this life is happy, but they believe it only while they are saying it, and never yet produced conviction in a single mind, he whom want of words or images sunk into silence, still thought, as he thought before, that privation of pleasure can never please, and that content is not to be much envied[7] when it has no other principle than ignorance of good.

This gloomy tranquillity which some may call fortitude, and others wisdom, was, I believe, for a long time to be very frequently found in these dens of poverty, every Man was content to live like his neighbour, and never[8] wandering from home saw no mode of life preferable to his own, except at the house of the Laird or the Laird's near relations, whom he considered as a superiour order of Beings, to whose luxuries or honours he had no pretensions.

5. Malcolm Macleod (*Ante* To Hester Thrale, 21 Sept. 1773, n. 48).

6. Brochel Castle, in the northeastern portion of Raasay, was reduced to "ruinous fragments: pieces of wall, pieces of stairs, a part of the battlement to the sea" (*Hebrides*, pp. 139 n. 1, 147).

7. MS: "to be much envied" written above "to be desired which" del.

8. MS: "saw" del. before "never"

But the end of this reverence and submission seems now approaching. The Highlanders have learned that there are countries less bleak and barren than their own, where instead of working for the Laird, every Man may till his own ground, and eat all the produce of his own labour. Great numbers have been induced by this discovery to go every year, for some time past to America. Macdonald and Macleod of Skie have lost Many tenants, and many Labourers, but Raarsa has not yet been forsaken by[9] a single inhabitant.[10]

Rona is yet more rocky and barren than Rarsa, and though[11] it perhaps contains perhaps four thousand acres, is possessed only by a herd of Cattle and the keepers.

I find myself not very able to walk upon the mountains, but one day I went out to see the walls yet standing of an ancient Chappel. In almost every Island the Superstitious votaries of the Romish Church, erected places of worship, in which the Drones of Convents or Cathedrals performed the Holy Offices; but by the active zeal of Protestant devotion, almost all of them have sunk into ruin. The Chappel at Rarsa is now only considered as the burying place of the family, and I suppose, of the whole Island.[12]

We could now have gone away, and left room for others to enjoy the pleasures of this little court, but the wind detained us till the 12th, when, though it was Sunday we thought it proper to snatch the opportunity of a calm day. Raarsay accompanied us in his six oar'd boat, which he said was his coach and six. It is indeed the vehicle in which the Ladies take the air, and pay their visits, but they have taken very little care for accommodations. There is no way in or out of the boat for a woman, but by being carried, and in the boat, thus dignified with a pompous name, there is no seat, but an occasional[13]

9. MS: "been forsaken by" written above "lost" del.

10. MS: "subj" del. before "inhabitant"

11. MS: "has" del. before "though"

12. The Chapel of St. Moluag, roofless and paved with gravestones, stands northeast of Raasay House (*Hebrides*, pp. 142–43, 470).

13. MS: "nal" repeated as catchword

bundle of straw. Thus we left Raarsa, the seat of plenty, civility, and cheerfulness.

We dined at a publick house at Portre, so called because One of the Scottish Kings landed there, in a progress through the Western Isles.[14] Raarsa paid the reckoning privately. We then got on horseback, and by a short, but very tedious journey, came to Kingsburgh, at which the same King lodged after he landed. Here I had the honour of saluting the farfamed Miss Flora Macdonald, who conducted the Prince dressed as her maid through the English forces from the Island of Lewes, and when she came to Skie,[15] dined with the English officers, and left her Maid below. She must then have been a young Lady, she is now not old, of a pleasing person and elegant behaviour.[16] She told me that she thought herself honoured by my visit, and I am sure that whatever regard she bestowed on me, was liberally repaid. "If thou likest her opinions thou wilt praise her virtue." She was carried to London, but dismissed without a trial, and came down with Malcolm Macleod, against whom sufficient evidence could not be procured.[17] She and her Husband are poor, and are going to try their fortune in America.[18] Sic rerum volvitur orbis.[19]

At Kingsburgh we were very liberally feasted, and I slept in the bed, on which the Prince reposed in his distress. The sheets which he used were never put to any meaner offices, but were

14. Portre was named after James V, whose visit occurred in 1540 (Derek Cooper, *Skye*, 1970, p. 105).

15. MS: "the" del. before "Skie"

16. In June 1746 Flora Macdonald (1722–90) helped the Young Pretender escape after the Battle of Culloden by smuggling him from Lewis to Portree. Prince Charles Edward was then met by Malcolm Macleod, who escorted him to Raasay (*Ante* To Hester Thrale, 21 Sept. 1773 and n. 48).

17. *Ante* To Hester Thrale, 21 Sept. 1773, n. 48.

18. In 1750 Flora Macdonald married Allan Macdonald (1726–92), of Kingsburgh, Skye. The couple's financial plight (due in large measure to the participation of Allan Macdonald's father in the '45) prompted them to emigrate to North Carolina in Aug. 1774. Flora returned to Britain in 1779; her husband joined her in 1784 (J. P. Maclean, *Flora Macdonald in America*, 1909, pp. 22–23, 30, 80; *Life* v.529–30).

19. *Sic rerum volvitur orbis*: possibly a translation of *Hamlet* III.ii.268 ("Thus runs the world away"). Cf. *Ante* To Hester Thrale, 5 Aug. 1771.

wrapped up by the Lady of the house, and at last, according to her desire, were laid round her in her grave.[20] These are not Whigs.

On the 13th, travelling partly on horseback where we could not row, and partly on foot where we could not ride, we came to Dunvegan, which I have described already.[21] Here though poor Macleod has been left by his Grandfather overwhelmed with debts,[22] we had another exhibition of feudal hospitality. There were two Stags in the house, and venison came to the table every day in its various forms. Macleod, besides his Estate in Skie, larger, I suppose than some English Counties, is Proprietor of nine inhabited Islands, and of his Islands uninhabited I doubt if he very exactly knows the number. I[23] told[24] him that he was a mighty monarch. Such dominions fill an Englishman with envious wonder, but when he surveys the naked mountain and treads[25] the quaking moor, and[26] wanders over wide[27] regions of gloomy[28] barrenness his wonder may continue, but his envy ceases. The unprofitableness of these vast domains can be conceived only by the means of positive instances. The Heir of *Col*[29] an Island not far distant has lately told me how wealthy he should be if he could let *Rum* another of his Islands, for two pence half-penny an acre; and Macleod has an estate which the Surveyer reports to contain eighty thousand acres, rented at Six hundred pounds a year.

While we were at Dunvegan, the wind was high and the rain violent so that we were not able to put a boat, to fish in the sea, or to visit the adjacent Islands, which may be seen from the house. But we filled up the time as we could, sometimes by talk sometimes by reading; I have never wanted books in the Isle of Sky.

20. SJ refers to Mrs. Alexander Macdonald (*c.* 1696–1759), Flora Macdonald's mother-in-law (*Life* v.190).

21. *Ante* To Hester Thrale, 21 Sept. 1773 and n. 3; Fleeman, p. 55.

22. SJ refers to Norman Macleod (1705–72), twenty-second Chief (Fleeman, p. 275).

23. MS: "I" superimposed upon "S"

24. MS: "uch" del. before "told"

25. MS: "the" del. before "treads"

26. MS: "his" del. before "and"

27. MS: "wide" altered from "wilde"

28. MS: "glo" written above "utm" del.

29. See below, n. 37.

We were visited one day by the Laird and Lady of Muack[30] one of the western Islands two miles long, and three quarters of a mile broad. He has half his Island in his own culture, and upon the other half live one hundred and forty dependants, who not only live upon the product but export corn sufficient for the payment of their rent.

Lady Macleod has a son and four Daughters,[31] they have lived long in England, and have the language and manners of English Ladies. We lived with them very easily. The hospitality of this remote region is like that of the golden age. We have found ourselves treated at every house as if we came to confer a benefit.

We were eight days at Dunvegan, but we took the first opportunity which the weather afforded after the first days, of going away, and on the 21st went to Ulinish, where we were well entertained, and wandered a little after curiosities.[32] In the afternoon an interval of calm sunshine courted us out to see a cave on the shore famous for its echo.[33] When we went into the boat One of our companions was asked in Earse by the boatmen who they were that came with him, he gave us characters, I suppose to our advantage, and was asked in the spirit of the highlands, whether I could recite a long series of Ancestors. The Boatmen said, as I heard afterwards, that they perceived the cry of an English Ghost, th⟨is⟩ Boswel says disturbed him. We came to the Cave and clambering up the rocks, came to an arch open at one end, one hundred and eighty feet long, thirty broad in the broadest part, and about thirty high. There was no echo, such is the fidelity of report,

30. Hector Maclean (d. 1780), of Muck, fourth Chief, married Isabella Macleod (d. 1780), of Talisker (Fleeman, pp. 270, 278).

31. Emilia Macleod had six children: Norman, Alexandra (d. 1810), Maria (d. 1809), Isabella (d. 1788), Ann (d. 1826), and Elizabeth (Fleeman, p. 275).

32. SJ and JB stayed with Alexander Macleod (?1690–1791), of Ullinish, Sheriff-Substitute for Skye, "a plain honest gentleman, a good deal like an English justice of peace" (Fleeman, pp. 58, 193, 279; *Life* v.235). The "curiosities" shown to them included an ancient Danish fort and an underground "house" (Fleeman, pp. 58–59, 303; *Hebrides*, pp. 199–200).

33. F. A. Pottle locates this cave on the island of Oronsay (*Hebrides*, p. 473).

but I saw, what I had never seen before, muscles and whilks in their natural state. There was another arch in the rock open at both ends.

Sept. 23. We removed to Talisker a house occupied by Mr. Macleod, a Lieutenant colonel in the Dutch service.[34] Talisker has been long in the hands of Gentlemen, and therefore has a garden well cultivated, and what is here very rare, is shaded by trees. A place where the imagination is more amused cannot easily be found. The Mountains about it are of great height, with waterfals succeeding one another so fast, that as one ceases to be heard another begins; between the mountains there is a small valley extended to the sea, which is not afar off beating upon a coast very difficult of access. Two nights before our arrival two boats were driven upon this coast by the tempest, one of them had a pilot that knew the passage, the second followed, but a third missed the true course, and was driven forward with great danger of being forced into the great Ocean, but however gained at last some other Island. The crews crept to Talisker almost lifeless with wet, cold, fatigue, and terrour, but the Lady took care of them. She is a woman of more than common qualifications; having travelled with her husband, she speaks four languages.[35]

You find that all the Islanders even in these recesses of life are not barbarians. One of the Ministers who has adhered to us almost all the time is an excellent Scholar.[36]

We have now with us the young Laird of *Col*, who is heir perhaps to two hundred square miles of land.[37] He has first

34. *Ante* To Hester Thrale, 24 Sept. 1773 and n. 3.

35. In 1745 John Macleod of Talisker had married Mary Maclean (b. *c.* 1725), of Coll (Fleeman, pp. 268, 278).

36. The Rev. Donald Macqueen (1716–85), Minister of Kilmuir, Skye, "whose knowledge and politeness give him a title equally to kindness and respect, and who, from this time, [at Raasay] never forsook us till we were preparing to leave Sky, and the adjacent places" (Fleeman, pp. 47, 282). Macqueen contributed the "Dissertation on the Government of the People in the Western Isles" to Thomas Pennant's *Tour in Scotland and Voyage to the Hebrides, 1772, Part II* (1776), and helped to translate the Pentateuch into Gaelic (*Life* v.522).

37. Donald Maclean (1750–74), eldest son and heir of Hugh Maclean, thir-

studied at Aberdeen, and afterwards gone to Hertfordshire to learn agriculture, being much impressed with desire of improvement. He likewise [has] the notions of a Chief, and keeps a piper. At Macleods the bagpipe always plaid while we were dining.[38]

Col has undertaken,[39] by the permission of the waves and wind, to carry us about several of the Islands, with which he is acquainted enough to show us whatever curious is given by Nature or left[40] by antiquity, but we grow afraid of deviating from our way home lest we should be shut up for months upon some little protuberance of earth, that just appears above the sea, and perhaps is scarcely marked upon a Map.

You remember the Doge of Genoa who being asked what struck him most at the French Court, answered, "Myself."[41] I can not think many things here more likely to affect[42] the fancy, than to see Johnson ending his Sixty fourth year in the wilderness of the Hebrides.

But now I am here, it will gratify me very little to return without seeing or doing my best to see what these places afford. I have a desire to instruct myself in the whole system of pastoral life, but I know not whether I shall be able to perfect the idea. However I have many pictures in my mind, which I could not have had without this Journey, and should have passed it with great pleasure had you and Master, and Queeney been in the party. We should have excited the attention, and

---

teenth Laird of Coll (Fleeman, p. 268). "Young Coll" was greatly interested in improving his family estates "without hurting the people or losing the ancient Highland fashions" (*Hebrides*, p. 213). *Post* To Hester Thrale, 15 Oct. 1773 and n. 4.

38. "I have had my dinner exhilirated by the bagpipe at *Armidale*, at *Dunvegan*, and in *Col*" (Fleeman, p. 85).

39. MS: "undertaken" altered from "undertaking"

40. MS: "f" del. before "left"

41. "Imperiale Lescaro, doge de Gênes, avec les sénateurs . . . vinrent à Versailles faire tout ce que le roi exigeait d'eux. . . . Ce doge était un homme de beaucoup d'esprit. Tout le monde sait que le marquis de Seignelai lui ayant demandé ce qu'il trouvait de plus singulier à Versailles, il répondit: *C'est de m'y voir*" (Voltaire, *Siècle de Louis XIV*, in *Oeuvres Complètes*, 1878, XIV.291).

42. MS: undeciphered deletion before "affect"

enlarged the observations of each other, and obtained many pleasing topicks of future conversation. As it is I travel with my mind too much at home, and perhaps miss many things observable, or pass them[43] with transient notice, so that the image, for want of that reimpression which discussion and comparison produce, easily fades away. But I keep a book of remarks, and Boswel writes a regular journal of our travels, which, I think, contains as much of what I say and do, as of all other occurrences together. —"For such a faithful Chronicler as Griffith."[44]

I hope, dearest Madam, you are equally careful to reposite proper memorials of all that happens to you and your family and then when we meet, we shall tell our stories. I wish you had gone this summer in your usual splendor to Brigh[t]-helmston.

Mr. Thrale, probably, wonders how I live all this time without sending to him for money. Travelling in Scotland is dear enough, dearer in proportion to what the[45] country affords, than in England, but residence in the Isles is unexpensive. Company is, I think, considered as a supply of pleasure and a relief of that tediousness of life which is felt in every place elegant or rude. Of Wine and punch they are very liberal, for they get them cheap, but as there is no custom house on the Island, they can hardly be considered as Smugglers. Their punch is made without lemons or any substitute.

Their tables are very plentiful, but a very nice man would not be pampered. As they have no meat, but as they kill it, they are obliged to live while it lasts, upon the same flesh. They kill a sheep and set mutton boiled and roast on the table together. They have fish both of the sea and of the brooks, but they can hardly conceive that it requires any sauce. To sauce in general they are strangers; now and then butter is melted, but I dare not always take, lest I should offend by disliking it.

43. MS: "them them"

44. "After my death I wish no other herald, / No other speaker of my living actions / To keep mine honour from corruption, / But such an honest chronicler as Griffith" (*Henry VIII* IV.ii.69–72).

45. MS: "the" altered from "this"

Barley broath is a constant dish, and is made well in every house. A stranger if he is prudent, will secure his share for it is not certain that he will be able to eat any thing else.

Their [meat] being often newly killed is commonly tough, and as nothing is sufficiently subdued by the fire, is not easily to be eaten. Carving is here a very laborious employment, for the knives are never whetted. Table knives are not of long subsistance in the highlands; every man while arms were a regular part of dress, had his knife and fork appendant to his dirk. Knives they now lay on the table, but the handles are apt to show that they have been in other hands, and the blades have neither brightness nor edge.

Of Silver there is no want, and it will last long for it is never cleaned. They are a Nation just rising from barbarity, long contented with necessaries, now somewhat studious of convenience, but not arrived at delicate discriminations. Their linen however is clean and fine.

Bread, such as we mean by that name, I have never seen in the Isle of Skie. They have ovens, for they bake pies, but they never ferment their meal, nor mould a loaf. Cakes, of oats and barley are brought to the table, but I believe wheat is reserved for strangers. They are commonly too hard for me, and therefore I take potatoes to my meat, and am sure to find them on almost every table.

They retain so much of the pastoral life that some preparation of milk is commonly one of the dishes both at dinner and supper. Tea is always drank at the usual times, but in the morning the table is polluted with a plate of slices of strong cheese. This is peculiar to the highlands; at Edinburgh there are always honey and sweetmeats on the morning teatable.

Strong liquors they seem to love; every Man, perhaps woman[46] begins the day with a dram, and the punch is made both at dinner and supper.

They have neither wood nor coal for fuel, but burn peat or turf in their chimnies. It is dug out of the moors or mosses

46. MS: "most" del. before "woman"

and makes a strong and lasting fire, not always very sweet, and somewhat apt to smoke the pot.

The houses of the inferiour Gentlemen are very small, and every room serves many purposes. In the bedrooms are perhaps laid up stores of different kinds. The parlour of the day is a Bedroom at Night. In the room which I inhabited last about fourteen feet square, there were three Chests of drawers, a long chest for larger cloaths, two closet cupboards, and the bed. Their rooms are commonly dirty, of which they have little sensibility, and if they had more, clean floors would be difficultly kept where the first step from the door is into the dirt. They are very much inclined to carpets, and seldom fail to lay down something under their feet, better or worse, as they happen to be furnished.

The Highland dress being forbidden by law is very little used. Sometimes it may be seen, but the English traveller is struck with nothing so much as with the nuditè des piès, of the common people.

Skie is the greatest Island or the greatest but one among the Hebrides. Of the soil I have already given some account. It is generally barren, but there are spots not unfruitful. The Gardens have apples and pears and Cherries, strawberries, raspberries, Currants, and Gooseberries, but all the fruit that I have [seen] is small. The[y] attempt to sow nothing but oats and barley; Oats constitute the breadcorn of the place. Their Harvest is about the beginning of October, and being so late is very much subject to disappointments from the rains that follow the equinox. This year has been particularly disastrous. Their rainy season lasts from autumn to spring, they have seldom very hard frosts, nor was it ever known that a lake was covered with ice strong enough to bear a Skater. The sea round them is always open. The snow falls but soon melts, only in 1771 they had a cold spring in which the Island was so long covered with it, that many beasts both wild and domestick perished, and the whole country was reduced to distress, from which I know not if it has yet recovered.

The animals here are not remarkably small, perhaps they

recruit their breed from the main Land. The cows are sometimes without horns. The horned and unhorned cattle, are not accidental variations, but different Species, they[47] will however bre[e]d together.

Oct. 3. The Wind is now changed, and if we snatch the[48] moment of opportunity, an Escape from this Island is become practicable. I have no reason to complain of my reception, yet I long to be again at home. You and my Master may perhaps expect after this description of Skie, some account of myself. My eye is, I am afraid, not fully recovered,[49] my ears are not mended, my nerves seem to grow weaker, and I have been otherwise not as well as I sometimes am, but think myself lately better. This Climate perhaps is not within my degrees of healthy Latitude.

Thus have I[50] given my most honoured Mistress the story of me and my little ramble. We are now going to some other Island to what we know not, the Wind will tell us. I am, Madam, Your most humble Servant,

SAM. JOHNSON

Compliments to Queeney and Jack[51] and Lucy and all.

47. MS: "but" del. before "they"

48. MS: "the the"

49. *Ante* To Hester Thrale, 24 May 1773 and n. 1.

50. MS: "I have I"

51. SJ may be referring to Sir John Lade. Chapman's identification ("Grinning Jack," the Thrales' "half-witted Cowman," 1.374 n. 12) seems highly unlikely.

Robert Chambers

FRIDAY 15 OCTOBER 1773

MS: Hyde Collection.

ADDRESS: To Robert Chambers, Esq., in King's Bench Walks, Temple, London.

POSTMARKS: INVERARY, NO 5, 9 NO.

ENDORSEMENT: Doctor Sam. Johnson, Isle of Mull, 15 Oct. 73.

Dear Sir: Isle of *Mull*, Oct. 15, 1773

We have been driven by the Wind out to *Coll*, an Island which has no communication with the world. We have now reached

Mull in a sloop which we hired on purpose.[1] We are hastening home as fast as we can.

Boswel will expect that I should pass a few days at his Father's, and by one step and another, we shall hardly see Edinburgh, before a letter from you may arrive. I beg that you will immediately write, if you are yet in London, and tell me the time fixed for your departure.[2] I am very desirous to take my leave of you, since You are going far off and I feel very sensibly the weight of time.

Be pleased before you write to call on Mrs. Williams, who may have something to say which she cannot well entrust to her ordinary secretaries. If they are in want of money, and you are not going, before I can see you, advance them what they cannot do without. Do not omit a post. I am, Dear Sir, Your humble servant,

SAM. JOHNSON

1. *Post* To Henry Thrale, 15 Oct. 1773; *Post* To Hester Thrale, 15 Oct. 1773.

2. *Ante* To Robert Chambers, 30 Sept. 1773 and n. 2.

Henry Thrale

FRIDAY 15 OCTOBER 1773

PRINTED SOURCE: Piozzi, *Letters* 1.166–7.

Dear Sir, Isle of Mull, Oct. 15, 1773

Since I had the honour of writing to my mistress,[1] we have been hindered from returning, by a tempest almost continual. We tried eight days ago to come hither, but were driven by the wind into the isle of *Col*, in which we were confined eight days.[2] We hired a sloop to bring us hither, and hope soon to get to Edinburgh.

1. *Ante* To Hester Thrale, 30 Sept. 1773.

2. *Post* To Hester Thrale, 15 Oct. 1773. On 3 Oct. SJ and JB attempted to reach Mull, but bad weather forced them to land on Coll, where they stayed with Donald Maclean (*Ante* To Hester Thrale, 30 Sept. 1773 and n. 37). After several more attempts, they finally arrived on Mull 14 Oct. (Fleeman, pp. 304–7).

Having for many weeks had no letter, my longings are very great to be informed how all things are at home, as you and mistress allow me to call it. A letter will now perhaps meet me at Edinburgh, for I shall be expected to pass a few days at Lord Auchenleck's, and I beg to have my thoughts set at rest by a letter from you or my mistress.

Be so kind as to send either to Mrs. Williams or Mr. Levett, and if they want money, advance them ten pounds.

I hope my mistress keeps all my very long letters, longer than I ever wrote before.[3] I shall perhaps spin out one more before I have the happiness to tell you at home that I am Your obliged humble servant.

3. *Ante* To Hester Thrale, 25 Aug. 1773, n. 1.

Hester Thrale

FRIDAY 15 OCTOBER 1773

MS: Beinecke Library.

Dear Madam: Mull, Oct. 15, 1773

Though I have written to Mr. Thrale,[1] yet having a little more time than was promised me, I would not suffer the Messenger to go without some token of my duty to my Mistress, who I suppose expects the usual tribute of intelligence, a tribute which I am not now very able to pay.

Oct. 3. After having been detained by Storms many days at Sky, we left it, as we thought, with a fair wind. But a violent gust which Bos. has a great mind to call a tempest, forced us into *Coll*, an obscure Island, on which *nulla campis*

Arbor æstivâ recreatur aurâ.[2]

1. *Ante* To Henry Thrale, 15 Oct. 1773.

2. *pone me pigris ubi nulla campis / arbor aestiva recreatur aura*: "place me on the lifeless plains where no tree revives under the summer breeze" (Horace, *Odes* I.xxii.17–18, trans. C. E. Bennett, Loeb ed.).

There is literally no tree upon the Island. Part of it is a sandy waste, over which it be really dangerous to travel in dry weather and a high wind. It seems to be little more than one continued rock, covered from space to space with a thin layer of earth. It is however, according to the highland notions,[3] very populous, and life is improved beyond the manners of Sky, for the huts are collected into little villages, and every one has a small garden of roots and cabbages. The Laird has a new house built by his Unkle, and an old Castle inhabited by his Ancestors.[4] The young Laird entertained us very liberally. He is heir perhaps to 300 square miles of Land, which at 10 shillings an acre, would bring him 96,000£ a year. He is desirous of improving the agriculture of his Country, and in imitation of the Czar travelled for improvement,[5] and worked with his own hands upon a farm in Hertfordshire in the neighbourhood of Sir Thomas Salusbury. He talks of doing useful things, and has introduced turnips for winter fodder. He has made a small essay towards a road.[6]

Coll is but a barren place, description has few opportunities here of spreading her colours. The difference of day and night is [the] only vicissitude. Of the Succession of Sunshine to Rain, or of calms to tempests, we have hardly known, wind and rain have been our weather.

At last after about nine days we hired a Sloop, and [having] lain in it all night, with such accommodations as those miserable vessels afford, were landed yesterday on the Isle of *Mull* from which we expect an easy passage to Scotland. I am sick in a Ship but recover by lying down.

3. MS: "notions" altered from "notion"

4. SJ and JB stayed at the "neat new house" constructed by Lauchlan Maclean (d. 1754), twelfth Laird of Coll and brother of Hugh (d. 1786), thirteenth Laird and father of their host—whom SJ mistakenly calls "the Laird" (Fleeman, pp. 222, 268). This modern seat stood near the fifteenth-century castle of Breachachadh, the previous "feudal residence" of the family (*Hebrides*, p. 266; Fleeman, p. 222).

5. To prepare himself for a campaign of modernization, Peter the Great (1672–1725), Tsar of Russia, worked at the Royal Navy yard at Deptford and as ship's carpenter in a Dutch East India Company shipyard.

6. "Young Coll" died before most of his schemes could be put into practice (*Post* To JB, 27 Oct. 1774 and n. 1).

I have not good health, I do not find that travelling much helps me. My nights are flatulent, though not in the utmost degree, and I have a weakness in my knees, which makes me very unable to walk.

Pray, dear Madam, let me have a long letter. I remember that you are now near a dangerous time, I hope the danger is quite over.[7] I am, Madam, Your most humble servant,

SAM. JOHNSON

7. Hester Thrale was pregnant with her ninth child (Ralph, b. 8 Nov.) (Hyde, 1977, p. xii).

Henry Thrale

SATURDAY 23 OCTOBER 1773

MS: Hyde Collection.

Dear Sir: Inverary, Oct. 23, 1773

We have gotten at last out of the Hebrides; some account of our travels I have sent to my Mistress. And I have inclosed an ode which I wrote in the Isle of Skie, because I suspect that she will ⟨*two or three words*⟩[1] in reading it.[2]

Yesterday we landed, and to day came hither. We purpose to visit Auchenlech, the seat of Mr. Boswel's Father, then to pass a day at Glasgow, and return to Edinburgh.[3]

About ten miles of this days journey were uncommonly amusing. We travelled with very little light, in a storm of wind and rain, we passed about fifty five streams that crossed our way, and fell into a river that for a very great part of our road, foamed and roared beside us, all the rougher powers of Nature, except thunder were in motion, but there was no danger. I should have been sorry to have missed any of the inconveni-

1. MS: heavy deletion

2. According to JB, it is likely that SJ composed this Latin ode, "Skia," on 5 Sept. (*Life* v.155; *Poems*, pp. 192–93).

3. In fact SJ and JB traveled first to Glasgow and then to Auchinleck (*Post* To Henry Thrale, 26 Oct. 1773; *Post* To Hester Thrale, 28 Oct. 1773).

ences, to have had more light, or less rain, for their cooperation crowded the scene, and filled the mind.

I long however to hear from you and from my Mistress; I have seen nothing that drives You from my thoughts, but continue in rain and sunshine, by night and day, Dear Sir, Your most obliged and most humble servant,

SAM. JOHNSON

Hester Thrale

SATURDAY 23 OCTOBER 1773

MS: Hyde Collection.

ADDRESS: To Henry Thrale, Esq., in Southwark [*added in an unidentified hand*] MP.

POSTMARKS: OC 27, 1 NO, FREE.

Honoured Mistress: Inverary, Oct. 23, 1773

My last letters to you and my dear Master were written from Mull,[1] the third Island of the Hebrides in extent; there is no post, and I took the opportunity of a Gentlemans passage to the main Land.

Oct. 16.[2] In Mull we were confined two days by the weather; on the third We got on horseback, and after a journey difficult and tedious over rocks naked and valleys untracked, through a country of barrenness and solitude, we came almost in the dark to seaside, weary and dejected having met with nothing but water falling from the mountains that could raise any image of delight. Our company was the young Laird of Coll and his servant. Coll[3] made every Maclean open his house and supply us with horses when we departed. But the horses of this country are small, and I was not mounted to my wish.

At the seaside we found the ferry boat departed, if it had been where it was expected, the[4] wind was against us, and the

1. *Ante* To Henry Thrale, 15 Oct. 1773; *Ante* To Hester Thrale, 15 Oct. 1773.
2. MS: "17" del. before "16"
3. MS: ", who" del. before ". Coll"
4. MS: "we" del. before "the"

hour was late, nor was it very desirable to cross the sea in darkness with a small boat. The Captain of a sloop that had been driven thither by the storms,[5] saw our distress and as we were hesitating and deliberating sent his boat, which by Coll's order, transported us to the Isle of *Ulva*; We were[6] introduced to Mr. Macquarry, the head of a small Clan, whose ancesters have reigned in Ulva beyond Memory, but who has reduced himself by his negligence and folly to the necessity of selling this venerable patrimony.[7]

On the next morning Oct. 17 We passed the strait to *Inch Kenneth* an Island about a mile in length, and less than half a mile broad, in[8] which Kenneth a Scottish Saint established a small clerical college of which the Chapell walls are still standing.[9] At this place I beheld a scene which I wish You and my Master and Queeney had partaken. The only family on the Island is that of Sir Allan the[10] chief of the ancient and numerous clan of Maclean,[11] the clan which claims the second place, yielding only to Macdonald, in the line of Battle. Sir Allan, a Chieftain, a Baronet, and a soldier, inhabits[12] in this insulated desart, a thatched hut with no chambers. Young Coll, who owns him as his chief and whose Cousin was his Lady,[13] had, I believe, given him some notice of our visit. He received us with the Soldier's frankness, and the Gentleman's elegance, and

5. "We should have been in a very bad situation had there not fortunately been lying in the little sound of Ulva an Irish vessel, the *Bonetta*, of Londonderry, Captain McClure, master" (*Hebrides*, p. 310).

6. MS: "We were" written above "and" del.

7. Lauchlan Macquarrie (*c.* 1715–1818), sixteenth Laird, of Ulva, told SJ and JB that "his family had possessed Ulva for nine hundred years" (*Hebrides*, p. 310). Macquarrie finally sold the island in 1777 (*Life* v.319, 556).

8. MS: "in in"

9. St. Kenneth or Canice, originally from Ireland, worked in the Western Isles and Scotland during the second half of the sixth century.

10. MS: "the" superimposed upon "Ma" del.

11. Sir Allan Maclean (*c.* 1710–83), sixth Bt., of Brolas, Mull, twenty-second Chief (Fleeman, p. 266). He began his military career in the Scots Brigade, then served in the British Army during the Seven Years' War (*Life* v.556).

12. MS: "lives" del. before "inhabits"

13. Una Maclean (d. 1760), daughter of Hector Maclean, eleventh Laird of Coll and Donald Maclean's great-uncle (Fleeman, p. 268).

introduced us to his daughters, two young Ladies who have not wanted Education suitable to their birth, and who in their cottage neither forgot their dignity,[14] nor affected to remember it.[15]

—Do not You wish to have been with us?—

Sir Allan's affairs are in disorder, by the fault of his ancestors, and while he forms[16] some scheme for retrieving them, he has retreated hither.[17] When our Salutations were over he showed us the Island. We walked uncovered into the chapel, and saw in the reverend ruin, the efforts of precipitate reformation. The floor is covered with ancient gravestones of which the inscriptions are not now legible, and without some of the chief families still continue the right of Sepulture. The altar is not yet quite demolished, beside it on the right side is a Bas relief of the Virgin with her Child, and an Angel hovering over her. On the other side still stands a hand bell, which though it has no clapper neither presbyterian bigotry, nor barbarian wantonness has yet taken away. The Chappel is about thirty eight feet long, and eighteen broad. Boswel, who is very pious, went into it at night to perform his devotions, but came back in haste for fear of Spectres.[18]

Near the chappel is a fountain to which the water, remarkably pure, is conveyed from a distant hill through pipes laid by the Romish Clergy, which still perform the office of con-

14. MS: "dignity" written above undeciphered deletion

15. SJ refers to Sir Allan's eldest daughter, Maria Maclean, and her sister Sibella (Fleeman, pp. 235, 266).

16. MS: "takes" del. before "forms"

17. In 1648 Sir Lachlan Maclean gave the Marquess of Argyll a bond for £30,000 in satisfaction of various claims. By 1674 the debt had grown to £120,000. Sir Allan's support for the Jacobite cause further exacerbated the family's financial problems and led to the forfeiture of his property to the Argylls. In 1777 he sued the fourth Duke of Argyll for the old Maclean estates; JB acted as one of his counsel. The suit was partially successful, recovering Brolas in 1783 (*Hebrides*, p. 428; *Boswell in Extremes*, ed. C. M. Weiss and F. A. Pottle, 1970, pp. 70 n. 1, 77, 85–89, 132 n. 7).

18. "I walked out in the dark to the cross, knelt before it, and holding it with both my hands, I prayed with strong devotion. . . . I was for going into the chapel; but a tremor seized me for ghosts, and I hastened back to the house" (*Hebrides*, p. 317).

veyance, though they have never been repaired since Popery was suppressed.

We soon after went in to dinner, and wanted neither the comforts nor the elegancies of life, there were several dishes, and variety of liquours. The Servants live in another cottage, in which I suppose the meat is drest.

Towards evening Sir Allan told us, that Sunday never passed over him like another day. One of the Ladies read, and read very well, the Evening service—And Paradise was open'd in the wild.[19]

Next day 18. We went and[20] wandered among the rocks on the Shore, while the boat was busy in catching oysters, of which there is a great bed. Oysters lye upon the sand one, I think, sticking to another, and Cockles are found a few inches under the sand. We then went in the boat to *Sondiland* a little Island, very near.[21] We found it a wild rock of about ten acres, part naked, part covered with sand, out of which we picked shells, and part cloathed with a thin layer of mould on the grass of which a few sheep are sometimes fed. We then came back and dined. I passed part of the Afternoon in reading, and in the evening One of the Ladies played on her harpsichord, and I believe Boswel danced with the other.[22]

On the 19th We persuaded Sir Allan to launch his boat again, and go with us to Icolmkil, where the first great Preacher of Christianity to the Scots built a Church, and settled a monastry.[23] In our way we stopped to examine a very uncommon

19. Pope, *Eloisa to Abelard*, l.134. The occasion prompted SJ to compose his "Latin verses," *Insula Sancti Kennethi* (*Poems*, pp. 195–96).

20. MS: "in a boat" del. before "and"

21. This "small spot" is called variously "Sannaland," "Sandyland," and "Samalan" (*Hebrides*, pp. 321, 480).

22. "I proposed a reel; so Miss Sibby and Coll and I danced, while Miss [Maria] Maclean played" (*Hebrides*, p. 323).

23. In 563 St. Columba founded a monastery on the island of Icolmkill (Iona), which then served as a base for converting the Northern Picts and eventually the rest of Scotland. Pillaged by Scandinavian pirates in the ninth century, the monastery was destroyed. In 1203 a new monastery and nunnery were founded by the Benedictines. These twin establishments were dissolved in 1560; the buildings

Cave on the coast of *Mull*.[24] We had some difficulty to make our way over the vast masses of broken rocks that lye before the entrance, and at the mouth were embarrassed with Stones which the sea had accumulated as at Brighthelmston, but as we advanced we reached a floor of soft sand, and as we left the light behind us, walked along a very spacious cavity vaulted over head with an arch almost regular, by which a mountain was sustained, at least a very lofty rock. From this magnificent cavern, went a narrow passage to the right hand, which we entered with a candle, and though it was obstructed with great stones, clambered over them to a second expansion of the Cave, in which there lies a great square stone which might serve as a table. The air here was very warm but not oppressive, the flame of the candle continued pyramidal. The cave goes onward to an unknown extent, but we were now 160 yards underground; we had but one Candle, and had never heard of any that went further and came back. We therefore thought it prudent to return.

Going forward we came to a cluster of rocks black and horrid which Sir Allan chose for the place where he would eat his dinner. We climbed till we got seats. The Stores were opened and the repast taken.

We then entered the boat again, the night came upon us, the wind rose, the sea swelled, and Boswel desired to be set on dry ground. We however persued our navigation, and passed by several little Islands in the silent solemnity of faint moonshine, seeing little, and hearing only the wind and the water. At last we reached the Island, the[25] venerable seat of ancient sanctity, where secret piety reposed, and where fallen greatness was reposited. The Island has no house of entertainment, and we[26] manfully made our bed in a Farmers Barn.

---

were then demolished (*Scotland*, ed. L. R. Muirhead, 1949, p. 345; F. M. MacNeill, *Iona*, 1920, 1973, pp. 25, 29, 49–57).

24. "We coasted along Mull till we reached Gribon, where is what is called Mackinnon's Cave, an *antrum immane* indeed, to which the one at Ullinish is nothing" (*Hebrides*, p. 324).

25. MS: "the the"

26. MS: "we we"

The Description I hope to give you another time.[27] I am, Madam, Your most obedient and most humble Servant,

SAM. JOHNSON

27. No epistolary account of Iona has been recovered. It is likely that SJ drew upon notebook materials for his published description.

Henry Thrale

TUESDAY 26 OCTOBER 1773

MS: Hyde Collection.

Dear Sir: Inverary, October 26, 1773

The Duke kept us yesterday,[1] or we should have gone forward. Inverary is a stately place.[2] We are now going to Edinburgh by Lochlomond, Glasgow, and Auchenlech.

I wrote to you from Mull, to send for Mr. Levet or Mrs. Williams, and let them have ten pounds if it was wanted.[3] I find that the passage of those insular letters is not very certain, and therefore think it necessary now to write again.

I do not limit them to ten pounds, be pleased to let them have what is necessary.

I have now not heard from London for more than two months, surely I shall have many letters at Edinburgh.[4] I hope my dear Mistress is well, with all her tribe. I am, Sir, Your most humble servant,

SAM. JOHNSON

1. On 25 Oct. SJ and JB dined with John Campbell (1723–1806), fifth Duke of Argyll.

2. Inveraray Castle, the seat of the Dukes of Argyll, had been replaced by a new castellated house, built by Robert Adam, 1746–50 (Fleeman, p. 311).

3. *Ante* To Henry Thrale, 15 Oct. 1773.

4. *Post* To Hester Thrale, 3 Nov. 1773.

The Duke of Argyll

WEDNESDAY 27 OCTOBER 1773

MS: Beinecke Library. A copy in JB's hand.

ADDRESS: To his Grace the Duke of Argyle.

My Lord, Rossdhu,[1] Oct. 27, 1773

That kindness which disposed your grace to supply me with the horse, which I have now returned, will make you pleased to hear that he has carried me well.[2]

By my diligence in the little commission with which I was honoured by the Duchess,[3] I will endeavour to shew how highly I value the favours which I have received, and how much I desire to be thought, my lord, your grace's most obedient, and most humble servant,

SAM. JOHNSON

1. Rossdhu, Dumbarton, the home of Sir James Colquhoun (*Post* To Hester Thrale, 28 Oct. 1773, n. 2).

2. "The Duke of Argyle was obliging enough to mount Dr. Johnson on a stately steed from his grace's stable. My friend was highly pleased" (*Life* v.362–63). *Post* To Hester Thrale, 28 Oct. 1773.

3. Elizabeth Gunning (1733–90), of Castle Coote, Roscommon, had first married the sixth Duke of Hamilton, and then (1759) the fifth Duke of Argyll. At dinner on 25 Oct., SJ had volunteered to procure her a copy of Archibald Campbell's *Doctrines of a Middle State* (1721) (*Life* v.356 and n. 2).

Hester Thrale

THURSDAY 28 OCTOBER 1773

MS: Hyde Collection.

ADDRESS: To Henry Thrale, Esq., in Southwark.

POSTMARKS: GLASGOW, 28 29, OC 29, 2 NO, FREE.

Dear Madam: Glasgow, Oct. 28,[1] 1773

I have been in this place about two hours.

1. MS: "28" written above "29" del.

On Monday 25. We dined with the Duke and Dutchess of Argyle, and the Duke lent me a horse for my next day's journey.

26. We travelled along a deep valley between lofty Mountains covered only with brown heath; entertained with a succession of cataracts on the left hand, and a roaring torrent on the other side. The Duke's horse went well, the road was good, and the journey pleasant except that we were incommoded by perpetual rain. In all September we had according to Boswels register, only one day and a half of fair weather, and in October perhaps not more. At night we came to the house of Sir James Cohune, who lives upon the banks of Loch Lomond,[2] of which the Scotch boast, and boast with reason.

27 We took a boat to rove upon the Lake which is in length twenty four miles, in breadth from perhaps two miles to half a mile. It has twenty four Islands of which twenty belong to Sir James. You[ng] Cohune[3] went into the boat with us but a little agitation of the water frighted him to shore. We passed up and down, and landed upon one small Island on which are the ruins of a Castle, and upon another much larger, which serves Sir James for a park, and is remarkable for a large wood of Eugh trees.[4] We then returned very wet to Dinner, and Sir James lent us his coach to Mr. Smollet's, a relation of Dr. Smollet for whom he has erected a monumental column on the banks of the Leven, a river which issues from the loch, this[5] was his native place.[6] I was desired to revise the inscription.[7]

2. Sir James Colquhoun (1714–86), Bt., of Rossdhu, Dumbarton, twenty-fifth Chief of the Colquhouns (*Life* v.563–64).

3. Ludovick Colquhoun, the youngest of Sir James's three sons (Fleeman, p. 243).

4. The castle ruins were probably those of Castle Galbraith on Inch Galbraith. Inchlonaig has been identified as the site of Sir James's deer park (Fleeman, p. 312).

5. MS: "whe" del. before "this"

6. The previous summer James Smollett (d. 1775), Commissary of Edinburgh, had set up a pillar to the memory of his cousin, the novelist Tobias (1721–71), on the outskirts of the town of Renton (*Life* v.564).

7. SJ did indeed correct the text of the Latin inscription; the final version as it appears on the monument shows further revisions by an unidentified hand (*Life* v.366–67 and n. 3, 564).

When I was upon the Deer Island,[8] I gave the keeper who attended me a shilling, and he said it was too much. Boswel afterwards offered him another, and he excused himself from taking it, because he had been rewarded already.

This day I came hither, and go to[9] Auchenlech on Monday. I am, Madam, your most humble servant,

SAM. JOHNSON

8. See above, n. 4. 9. MS: "M" del. before "to"

Hester Thrale

WEDNESDAY 3 NOVEMBER 1773

MS: Boston Public Library.

Honoured Mistress: Auchenlech, Nov.[1] 3, 1773

At Glasgow I received six letters of which the first was written August 23.[2] I am now at leisure to answer them in order.

Aug. 23. Mrs. Boswel has the mien and manners of a Gentlewoman, and such a person and mind, as would not be in any place either admired or contemned. She is in[3] a proper degree inferiour to her husband; she cannot rival him, nor can he ever be ashamed of her.

Little Miss, when I left her, was like any other Miss of seven months.[4] I believe she is thought pretty, and her father and mother have a mind to think her wise.

Your letter brought us the first certain intelligence of Dr. Beattie's pension.[5] He will now be a great man at Aberdeen, where every one speaks well of him.

1. MS: "Nov." superimposed upon "Sept."

2. These letters have not been recovered. H. L. Piozzi's *Letters* (1788) includes two from the period of the Hebridean tour (nos. 88 and 89); these are printed from holographs dated 23 Aug. and 7 Oct. respectively (MSS: Rylands Library). R. W. Chapman surmises that the original six formed "the basis" of these two (Chapman 1.384).

3. MS: "in" superimposed upon "to"

4. SJ refers to Veronica Boswell (*Ante* To JB, 5 July 1773, n. 11).

5. *Ante* To JB, 5 July 1773, n. 8; *Ante* To James Beattie, 5 August 1773.

Aug. 29. I am obliged to dear Queeney for her letter, and am sorry that I have not been able to collect more for her Cabinet, but I shall bring her something.[6]

What should Rice and his Wife do at the wrong end of the town, whither they can carry nothing that will not raise contempt and [from] which they can bring nothing that will not excite aversion. He is not to be either wit or statesman; his Genius, if he follow his direction, will bid him live in Lothbury, and measure brandy.[7]

Sept. 8. I first saw the account of Lord Littleton's death[8] in the Isle of Raarsa, and suspected that it had been hastened by the vexation which his son has[9] given him.[10] We shall now see what the young man will do, when he is left to himself.[11]

I am at a loss what to judge of Sir Thomas.[12] To doubt whether six thousand pounds have or have not been paid, as was directed, is absurd and childish;[13] he to whom they were

6. *Ante* To Hester Thrale, 31 Oct. 1772, n. 1.

7. "Fanny [Plumbe Rice] and her Husband set out very prettily, and will I hope stick to the City. Lothbury as you say" (Hester Thrale to SJ, MS: Rylands Library 538.8). *Ante* To Hester Thrale, 17 May 1773, n. 3. SJ used Lothbury Street, which ran along the north side of the Bank of England, as a synonym for the central business district ("the City") (Wheatley and Cunningham II.442).

8. MS: "done"

9. MS: "gave" del. before "has"

10. George Lyttelton (1709–73), fifth Bt., of Hagley Hall, cr. (1756) Baron Lyttelton, politician and man of letters, had died 22 Aug. (*GM* 1773, p. 414). His son and heir Thomas (1744–79), briefly (1768–69) M.P. for Bewdley, had acquired "the reputation of a rake and bounder" (Namier and Brooke III.76). On 2 Sept. Horace Walpole reported: "Lord Lyttelton is dead—His worthy son has added so much to his mass of character by histories too opprobrious to be entertaining, that even this age has the grace to shun him" (*Walpole's Correspondence*, Yale ed. XXIII.511).

11. "After succeeding to the peerage he [Thomas Lyttelton] led a more regular life, and took a prominent part in the debates of the House of Lords" (Namier and Brooke III.76).

12. *Ante* To Hester Thrale, 24 Oct. 1772, n. 1.

13. In early Sept. Sir Thomas's agent pressed Hester Thrale for "Papers relating to the [Welsh] Estate" (Clifford, 1952, p. 107 n. 1). At issue appears to have been the mortgage on the property that Sir Thomas paid off in 1755. At that time Hester Thrale's father "signed various papers admitting indebtedness to his brother for the whole amount" (Clifford, 1952, p. 19). After Sir Thomas's death his widow sued Hester Thrale for payment of the debt.

due can answer the question, and he by whom they were remitted can confirm or confute the answer. You should surely write to Mr. Bridge.[14]

Of Sir Thomas you had not left me any high notions, but I supposed him to be at least commercially honest, and incapable of eluding his own bond by fraudulent practices, yet I think Mr. Thrale's suspicion not to be slighted. Principles can only be strong, by the strength of understanding, or the cogency of religion.

I do not see how you can much offend by putting Harry's life into the lease, it puts no life out, and therefore dos not lessen Sir Thomas's interest.[15] I believe however you may depend better for peace upon the indifference of his indolence, than[16] the approbation of his judgement. I think it should not be neglected.

Sept. 14. I take great delight in your fifteen thousand trees;[17] the greater for having been so long in a Country, where trees and diamonds are equal rarities.

Poor Vansittart![18] There are not so many reasons as he thinks why he should envy me, but there are some; he wants what I have a kind and careful Mistress, and wants likewise what I shall want at my return. He is a good man, and when his mind is composed a man of parts.

Sept. 28. When I wrote an account of my intention to return, I little thought that I should be so long the plaything of the wind. Of the various accidents of our voyage I have been careful to give you an account and hope you have received it. My Deafness went away by degrees. Miss Macleod made

14. *Ante* To Hester Thrale, 24 Oct. 1772, n. 2.

15. To include Henry Thrale the younger in the lease would not threaten the established line of inheritance, since the Welsh estate "was entailed on Thomas and his sons" (Clifford, 1952, p. 19).

16. MS: "that"

17. This figure came from John Perkins, who had been examining the Welsh estate; the trees counted as an important financial asset (*Ante* To Hester Thrale, 25 Aug. 1773, n. 18; Clifford, 1952, pp. 165, 215).

18. Hester Thrale had described Robert Vansittart to SJ as "very ill, and very wild; I fancy *he* wants a governess" (23 Aug. 1773, MS: Rylands Library).

me a great flannel nightcap, which perhaps helped to set[19] me right.[20]

If Sir Thomas goes to Bath, it may deserve consideration whether you should not follow him. If you go, take two footmen, and dress in such a manner as he may be proud to see. The money that you stake is no great venture, nor will the want of it be felt, whether you gain or lose the purpose of your journey.

My poor little Lucy is, I hope, now quite recovered,[21] for I have brought no little maiden from the Highlands, though I might perhaps have had one of the princesses of Raarsa, who are very pretty people, and in that wild recess of life, put me in mind of your little tribe, by[22] the propriety of their behaviour.

Oct. 7. This is the last letter. I have done thinking of Sir Alexander, whom we now call Sir Sawney,[23] he has disgusted all mankind by injudicious parsimony, and given occasion to so many stories, that Boswel has some thoughts of collecting them, and making a novel of his life.[24]

Scrambling I have not willingly left off, the power of scrambling has left me. I have however been forced to exert it on many occasions. I am, I thank God, better than I was. I am grown very much superiour to wind and rain, and am too well acquainted both with mire and with rocks, to be afraid of a Welsh journey. I had rather have Bardsay than Macleod's Island,[25] though I am told much of the beauty of my new prop-

19. MS: "s" superimposed upon "r"

20. At Dunvegan "much care was taken of Mr. Johnson. He had hitherto most strangely slept without a night-cap. Miss MacLeod made him a large flannel one, and he was prevailed with to drink a little brandy when he was going to bed—all to do his cold good" (*Hebrides*, p. 173).

21. Lucy Thrale suffered from an infection of the middle ear. The infection grew into a mastoid abscess; this led to an abscess on the brain, which caused her death on 22 Nov. 1773 (Hyde, 1977, pp. 46, 84 and n. 9).

22. MS: "but"

23. *sawney*: "a derisive nickname for a Scotchman"—originally a variant of "Sandy," short for "Alexander" (*OED*).

24. *Ante* To Hester Thrale, 6 Sept. 1773, n. 1; 21 Sept. 1773, n. 30.

25. "When I am grown rich, we will buy Bardsey for you; perhaps a Sight of

erty, which the storms did not suffer me to visit. Boswel will praise my resolution and perseverance, and I shall in return celebrate his goodhumour and perpetual cheerfulness. He[26] has better faculties, than I had imagined, more justness of discernment, and more fecundity of images. It is very convenient to travel with him, for there is no house where he is not received with kindness and respect.

I wish Bridge success in his new Mine, and hope that the vein will be as rich as his wants prompt him to wish it.[27] I congratulate you likewise on the rising reputation of the Brewery, and hope that the sweets of doing right will so much engage us, that we shall never more allow ourselves to do wrong. Forty shillings is a frightful price for malt, but we must brew on, and brew well, and hold out to better times.

Thus, dear Madam, I have answered your six letters, in part too late to be of any use. The regard which you are pleased to express, and the kindness which you always show, I do not pretend to return otherwise than by warm wishes for your happiness.

I will now continue my Narrative.

Oct. 29 was spent in surveying the city and college of Glasgow. I was not much pleased with any of the Professors.[28] The town is opulent, and handsome.

30 We dined with the Earl of Loudon,[29] and saw his Mother

Wales in the mean Time may not be amiss" (Hester Thrale to SJ, 7 Oct. 1773, MS: Rylands Library). Bardsey Island lies off the coast of Gwynedd, Wales, which SJ and the Thrales visited the following summer. For "Macleod's Island," *ante* To Hester Thrale, 21 Sept. 1773 and n. 4.

26. MS: "w" del. before "He"

27. "Our old Friend B——, by the way, has found a Vein of Lead ore on his Estate" (Hester Thrale to SJ, 7 Oct. 1773, MS: Rylands Library). *Ante* To Hester Thrale, 24 Oct. 1772, n. 2.

28. "The general impression upon my memory is that we had not much conversation at Glasgow, where the professors, like their brethren at Aberdeen, did not venture to expose themselves much to the battery of cannon which they knew might play upon them" (*Hebrides*, p. 365).

29. John Campbell (1705–82), fourth Earl of Loudoun, former Commander-in-Chief in America and Governor of Virginia; from 1763 until his death Governor of Sterling and Edinburgh, and from 1770 Colonel of the Third Regiment of

the Countess, who at ninety three has all her faculties, helps at table, and exerts all the powers of conversation that she ever had.[30] Though not tall, she stoops very much. She had lately a daughter, Lady Betty,[31] whom at seventy, she used to send after supper early to bed, for girls must not use late hours, while she sat up to entertain the company.

31[32] Sunday. We passed at Mr. Cambel's who married Mrs. Boswels Sister.[33]

Oct. 1.[34] We paid a visit to the Countess of Eglington, a Lady who for many years, gave the laws of Elegance to Scotland.[35] She is in full vigour of mind, and not much impaired in form. She is only eighty three. She was remarking that her marriage was in the year eight, and I told her my birth was in nine. The[n], says she, I am just old enough to be your mother, and I will take you for my son. She called Boswel the boy, yes Madam, said I, we will send him to school. He is already, said she, in a good school, and expressed her hope of his improvement. At last night came, and I was sorry to leave her.

2 We came to Auchenlech. The house is like other houses in this country built of Stone, scarcely yet finished, but very magnificent and very convenient.[36]

We purpose to stay here some days, more or fewer as we are

Foot-Guards. Lord Loudoun, an Ayrshire neighbor of the Boswells, had long been an influential political patron of the family.

30. Lady Margaret Dalrymple (1684–1779), Dowager Countess of Loudoun and daughter of the first Earl of Stair.

31. Lady Elizabeth Campbell (d. 1771), daughter of the third Earl of Loudoun and sister of the fourth Earl (*Scots Magazine* 33, 1771, p. 221).

32. MS: "o" del. before "1"

33. Margaret Montgomerie Boswell's sister Mary (d. 1777) was the second wife of James Campbell of Treesbank (d. 1776) (*Life* v.566).

34. MS: "31" del. after "1"; month left unchanged

35. Susanna Kennedy (1689–1780), widow of the ninth Earl of Eglinton. "Her figure was majestic, her manners high-bred, her reading extensive, and her conversation elegant. She had been the admiration of the gay circles of life, and the patroness of poets" (*Hebrides*, p. 368).

36. JB's father had abandoned the family castle and constructed a house in the Adam style; it was finished in 1762 (*Earlier Years*, pp. 10, 454).

used.[37] I shall find no kindness such as will suppress my desire of returning home. I am, Dear Madam, Your most obedient and most humble Servant,

SAM. JOHNSON

37. SJ and JB left Auchinleck for Edinburgh on 8 Nov. During their visit with JB's father, SJ and Lord Auchinleck "came in collision" (*Hebrides*, pp. 375–77).

Hester Thrale

FRIDAY 12 NOVEMBER 1773

PRINTED SOURCE: Piozzi, *Letters* 1.201–3.

Dearest Madam, Edinburgh, Nov. 12, 1773

Among the possibilities of evil which my imagination suggested at this distance, I missed that which has really happened. I never had much hope of a will in your favour, but was willing to believe that no will would have been made.[1] The event is now irrevocable, it remains only to bear it. Not to wish it had been different is impossible; but as the wish is painful without use, it is not prudent, perhaps not lawful, to indulge it. As life, and vigour of mind, and sprightliness of imagination, and flexibility of attention, are given us for valuable and useful purposes, we must not think ourselves at liberty to squander life, to enervate intellectual strength, to cloud our thoughts, or fix our attention, when by all this expence we know that no good can be produced. Be alone as little as you can; when you are alone, do not suffer your thoughts to dwell on what you might have done, to prevent this disappointment. You perhaps could not have done what you imagine, or might have done it without effect. But even to think in the most reasonable manner, is for the present not so useful as not to think. Remit yourself solemnly into the hands of God, and then turn your mind

1. Sir Thomas Salusbury had died in October, leaving "all his personal Estate to his Wife, and his real Estate to her likewise *for her Life*, after which it goes to a distant relation in Wales" (Hester Thrale to SJ, 31 Oct. 1773, MS: Rylands Library).

upon the business and amusements which lie before you. "All is best," says Chene, "as it has been, excepting the errours of our own free will."[2] Burton concludes his long book upon melancholy with this important precept, "Be not solitary; be not idle."[3] Remember Chene's position and observe Burton's precept.

We came hither on the ninth of this month. I long to come under your care, but for some days cannot decently get away. They congratulate our return as if we had been with Phipps or Banks;[4] I am ashamed of their salutations.

I have been able to collect very little for Queeney's cabinet; but she will not want toys now, she is so well employed.[5] I wish her success; and am not without some thought of becoming her school-fellow. I have got an Italian Rasselas.[6]

Surely my dear Lucy will recover; I wish I could do her good.[7] I love her very much; and should love another godchild, if I might have the honour of standing to the next baby.[8] I am, etc.

2. "But every Thing is best as it has been, except the Errors and Failings of our own free Wills" (George Cheyne, *Essay of Health and Long Life*, 5th ed., 1725, p. xv).

3. "Only take this for a corollary and conclusion, as thou tenderest thine own welfare in this and all other melancholy, thy good health of body and mind, observe this short precept, give not way to solitariness and idleness. 'Be not solitary, be not idle.'" (Robert Burton, *The Anatomy of Melancholy*, ed. Holbrook Jackson, 1964, III.432).

4. *Ante* To William Samuel Johnson, 4 Mar. 1773, n. 6; *Ante* To Joseph Banks, 27 Feb. 1772, n. 1.

5. On 17 Oct. Queeney Thrale, at the urging of SJ, began to study Italian under Giuseppe Baretti's tutelage (Hyde, 1977, p. 76).

6. *Ante* To William White, 4 Mar. 1773 and n. 7.

7. *Ante* To Hester Thrale, 3 Nov. 1773, n. 21.

8. The Thrales did not act on this hint: Ralph's godfathers were Lord Sandys of Ombersley Court and William Henry Lyttelton of Little Hagley (Hyde, 1977, pp. 84–85).

Hester Thrale

THURSDAY 18 NOVEMBER 1773

MS: Beinecke Library.

My dearest Mistress: Edinburgh, Nov. 18, 1773

This is the last Letter that I shall write, while You are reading it, I shall be coming home.

I congratulate you upon your boy,[1] but you must not think that I will love him all at once as well as I love Harry, for Harry, you know, is so rational. I shall love him by degrees.

Poor, pretty, dear Lucy. Can nothing do her good? I am sorry to lose her.[2] But if she must be taken from us, let us resign her with confidence into the hands of Him who knows, and who only knows, what is best both for us and her.

Do not suffer yourself to be dejected. Resolution and Diligence will supply all that is wanting⟨, and all⟩ that is lost. But if your health should be impaired⟨, I know no⟩t where to find a substitute. I shall have no Mistress⟨, Mr. Thra⟩le will have no Wife, and the little fl⟨ock will have no m⟩other.

I long to be at home, and have taken place in the Coach for Monday. I hope therefore to be in London on Fryday the 26. in the Evening.[3] Please to let Mrs. Williams know. I am, dear Madam, your most humble servant,

SAM. JOHNSON

1. *Ante* To Hester Thrale, 15 Oct. 1773, n. 7.
2. *Ante* To Hester Thrale, 3 Nov. 1773, n. 21.
3. *Post* To JB, 27 Nov. 1773; *Post* To Robert Chambers, 27 Nov. 1773.

James Boswell

SATURDAY 27 NOVEMBER 1773

PRINTED SOURCE: JB's *Life*, 1791, I.428.

Dear Sir, Nov. 27, 1773

I came home last night, without any incommodity, danger, or weariness, and am ready to begin a new journey. I shall go to

Oxford on Monday.[1] I know Mrs. Boswell wished me well to go; her wishes have not been disappointed.[2] Mrs. Williams has received Sir A's letter.[3]

Make my compliments to all those to whom my compliments may be welcome.

Let the box be sent as soon as it can, and let me know when to expect it.[4]

Enquire, if you can, the order of the Clans: Macdonald is first, Maclean second; further I cannot go.[5] Quicken Dr. Webster.[6] I am, Sir, Yours affectionately,

SAM. JOHNSON

1. SJ intended to visit Robert Chambers, whose departure for India seemed imminent. However, Chambers was in London at the time (*Post* To Robert Chambers, 27 Nov. 1773). Although Chambers could not have received SJ's (readdressed) letter in time to stop him from leaving for Oxford, there is no reliable evidence to indicate that SJ did in fact go there.

2. "I wonder how he discovered her wishing for his departure [from Edinburgh]. The truth is, that his irregular hours and uncouth habits . . . could not but be disagreeable to a lady. Besides . . . she thought he had too much influence over her husband" (*Life* II.269 n. 1).

3. Mrs. Williams's correspondent was Sir Alexander Gordon of Aberdeen (*Life* II.269 n. 2).

4. "This was a box containing a number of curious things which he had picked up in Scotland, particularly some horn spoons" (*Life* II.269 n. 3).

5. JB responded, "A gentleman of the name of Grant tells me, that there is no settled order" (*Life* ii.269–70). SJ was collecting information with his *Journey* in mind.

6. On 17 Aug. JB had introduced SJ to the Rev. Alexander Webster (1707–84), D.D., Minister of the Tolbooth Church, Edinburgh (1737–84), and an expert on Scots demography (*Hebrides*, p. 32; *Life* v.472, 474). Webster "had promised him [SJ] information concerning the Highlands of Scotland" (*Life* II.269 n. 4).

Robert Chambers

SATURDAY 27 NOVEMBER 1773

MS: Hyde Collection.

ADDRESS: To Robert Chambers, Esq., at New Inn Hall, Oxford [*Readdressed in an unidentified hand*] No. 6 Kings Bench Walks, Inner Temple, London.

To ROBERT CHAMBERS, 27 *November* 1773

POSTMARKS: OXFORD, 27 NO, 29 NO.

ENDORSEMENT: Doctor Sam. Johnson, London, 27 Nov. 1773.

Dear Sir: Nov. 27, 1773

I came home last night no more weary than if I had not moved from the same place. I have desired Mr. Levett to take a place for me in Monday's coach. You will take care that we have our time to ourselves.[1] I am, Dear Sir, Your humble Servant,

SAM. JOHNSON

1. *Ante* To JB, 27 Nov. 1773, n. 1.

Elizabeth Montagu

TUESDAY 11 JANUARY 1774

MS: Huntington Library.

Madam: Jan. 11, 1774

Having committed one fault by inadvertence, I will not commit another by sullenness. When I had the honour of your card, I could not comply with your invitation, and must now suffer the shame of confessing that the necessity of an answer did not come into my mind.

This omission, Madam, you may easily excuse, as the consciousness of your own character must secure you from suspecting that the favour of your notice can ever miss a suitable return, but from ignorance or thoughtlessness, and to be ignorant of your eminence is not easy but to him who lives out of the reach of the publick[1] voice. I am, Madam, Your most obedient and most humble Servant,

SAM. JOHNSON

1. MS: "lick" repeated as catchword

John Taylor

SATURDAY 15 JANUARY 1774

MS: Hyde Collection.

ADDRESS: To the Reverend Dr. Taylor in Ashbourn, Derbyshire.

POSTMARK: 15 IA.

ENDORSEMENTS: 1774, 15 Jany. 74.

Dear Sir: Jan. 15, 1774

When I was at Edinburgh I had a letter from you, telling me that in answer to some enquiry you were informed that I was in the Sky. I was then I suppose in the western Islands of Scotland; I set out on the northern expedition August 6, and came back to Fleetstreet, November 26. I have seen a new region.

I have been upon seven of the Islands, and probably should have visited many more, had we not begun our Journey so late in the year, that the stormy weather came upon us, and the storms have I believe for about five months hardly any intermission.

Your Letter told me that you were better. When you write do not forget to confirm that account. I had very little ill health while I was on the journey, and bore rain and wind tolerably well. I had a cold and deafness only for a few days, and those days I passed at a good house.[1] I have traversed the east coast of Scotland from south to north from Edinburgh to Inverness, and the west coast from north to south, from the Highland to Glasgow, and am come back, as I went, Sir, Your affectionate, humble servant,

SAM. JOHNSON

1. *Ante* To Hester Thrale, 3 Nov. 1773 and n. 20.

James Boswell

SATURDAY 29 JANUARY 1774

PRINTED SOURCE: JB's *Life*, 1791, I.430.

Dear Sir, Jan. 29, 1774

My operations have been hindered by a cough; at least I flatter myself, that if the cough had not come, I should have been further advanced. But I have had no intelligence from Dr. W——, [Webster,] nor from the excise-office, nor from you.[1] No account of the little borough.[2] Nothing of the Erse language. I have yet heard nothing of my box.[3]

You must make haste and gather me all you can, and do it quickly, or I will and shall do without it.

Make my compliments to Mrs. Boswell, and tell her that I do not love her the less for wishing me away.[4] I gave her trouble enough, and shall be glad, in recompence, to give her any pleasure.

I would send some porter into the Hebrides, if I knew which way it could be got to my kind friends there.[5] Enquire, and let me know.

Make my compliments to all the Doctors of Edinburgh, and to all my friends from one end of Scotland to the other.

Write to me, and send me what intelligence you can: and if any thing is too bulky for the post, let me have it by the carrier. I do not like trusting winds and waves. I am, dear Sir, Your most, etc.

SAM. JOHNSON

1. SJ was continuing to collect information for use in his *Journey* (*Ante* To JB, 27 Nov. 1773).

2. JB identifies the "borough" as "the ancient Burgh of Prestick, in Ayrshire" (*Life* II.271 n. 4). However, SJ does not mention Prestwick in the *Journey*.

3. *Ante* To JB, 27 Nov. 1773, n. 4.

4. *Ante* To JB, 27 Nov. 1773 and n. 2.

5. Cf. *Post* To JB, 5 Mar. 1774.

Richard Clark

MONDAY 31 JANUARY 1774

MS: Houghton Library.

ADDRESS: To Mr. Clark.

Dear Sir: Jan. 31, 1774

I suppose you know that Mr. Chambers going to the Indies, has transferred Miss Carmichael's cause to Mr. Murphy.[1] On Wednesday evening at seven Mr. Murphy will be with me to consider the case. We shall have great need of your assistance and therefore I hope it will be convenient to you to call at the same hour, on, Sir, your humble servant,

SAM. JOHNSON

1. *Ante* To John Hawkins, 15 Jan. 1773 and n. 1. Arthur Murphy had been called to the bar in June 1762 (J. P. Emery, *Arthur Murphy*, 1946, p. 85).

James Boswell

MONDAY 7 FEBRUARY 1774

PRINTED SOURCE: JB's *Life*, 1791, I.431.

Dear Sir, London, Feb. 7, 1774

In a day or two after I had written the last discontented letter, I received my box, which was very welcome. But still I must entreat you to hasten Dr. Webster, and continue to pick up what you can that may be useful.[1]

Mr. Oglethorpe was with me this morning.[2] You know his errand. He was not unwelcome.

1. *Ante* To JB, 27 Nov. 1773; 29 Jan. 1774.

2. James Edward Oglethorpe (1696–1785), general, colonist of Georgia (1732–43), founder and first Governor of Savannah. In 1754, having lost his seat as M.P. for Haslemere, Oglethorpe retired from public life. Though never elected to The Club, he was well acquainted with several of its most distinguished members, including Goldsmith, who introduced him to SJ *c.* 1770 (*Boswell for the Defence*, ed. W. K. Wimsatt and F. A. Pottle, 1959, p. 86). SJ declared of Oglethorpe:

Tell Mrs. Boswell that my good intentions towards her still continue. I should be glad to do any thing that would either benefit or please her.

Chambers is not yet gone, but so hurried, or so negligent, or so proud, that I rarely see him. I have, indeed, for some weeks past, been very ill of a cold and cough, and have been at Mrs. Thrale's, that I might be taken care of. I am much better, *novae redeunt in praelia vires*;[3] but I am yet tender, and easily disordered. How happy it was that neither of us were ill in the Hebrides.

The question of Literary Property is this day before the Lords. Murphy drew up the appellants' case, that is, the plea against the perpetual right. I have not seen it, nor heard the decision.[4] I would not have the right perpetual.[5]

I will write to you as any thing occurs, and do you send me something about my Scottish friends. I have very great kindness for them. Let me know likewise how fees come in, and when we are to see you. I am, Sir, Yours affectionately,

SAM. JOHNSON

"I know no man whose Life would be more interesting. If I were furnished with materials, I should be very glad to write it" (*Life* II.351).

3. SJ alters Virgil's *novae rediere in pristina vires*: "newborn strength returned, as of yore" (*Aeneid* XII.424, trans. H. R. Fairclough, Loeb ed.); *in praelia*: "for battle."

4. According to the Copyright Act of 1709, "Copyright held for fourteen years and, if the author was still alive at the end of that period, could be extended for another fourteen" (*Later Years*, p. 87). However, London booksellers had long maintained that their common-law right to "literary property" in perpetuity was *not* affected by the act. In July 1773 the Court of Session ruled in favor of Alexander Donaldson of Edinburgh, who had challenged the validity of the claim to perpetual copyright. JB helped to argue Donaldson's case, and then published a pamphlet on the issue, *The Decision of the Court of Session upon the Question of Literary Property* (*Later Years*, pp. 87–88). At the beginning of 1774 Donaldson also had a copyright case pending before the House of Lords (on appeal from the Court of Chancery). The hearing began on 4 Feb.; Donaldson was represented by Arthur Murphy (J. P. Emery, *Arthur Murphy*, 1946, p. 140). On 22 Feb. the House of Lords ruled in favor of Donaldson (*Life* II.272 n. 2). "Thus it restored the letter of the Act of Anne and completely disposed of any possible legal claims to perpetuity. Literary monopolies were then ended in England, except for those granted to schools like Oxford, Cambridge, and Eton" (Bloom, p. 225).

5. *Post* To William Strahan, 7 Mar. 1774.

George Steevens

MONDAY 7 FEBRUARY 1774

MS: Hyde Collection.

ADDRESS: To George Steevens, Esq., at Hampstead.

POSTMARKS: PENY POST PAYD T MO, 9 O'CLOCK.

Sir: Febr. 7, 1774

If I am asked when I have seen Mr. Steevens, you know what answer I must give; if I am asked when I shall see him, I wish you would tell me what to say.

If you have Lesley's[1] history of Scotland[2] or any other book about Scotland, except Boetius[3] and Buchanan,[4] it will be a kindness, if you send them to, Sir, your humble servant,

SAM. JOHNSON

1. MS: "Lesley"

2. *De Origine Moribus et Rebus Gestis Scotorum* (1578) by John Lesley (1527–96). SJ refers to Lesley's treatise in his *Journey* (Fleeman, p. 131).

3. Hector Boece, or Boethius (*c.* 1465–1536), author of the *Scotorum Historiae* (1527). Although SJ cites Boethius's history in his *Journey*, he considered that its "fabulousness and credulity are justly blamed" (Fleeman, p. 10).

4. George Buchanan (1506–82), Latin poet and historian, author of *Rerum Scoticarum Historia* (1582). SJ, who believed that the name of Buchanan "has as fair a claim to immortality as can be conferred by modern latinity" (Fleeman, p. 3), owned a copy of Thomas Ruddiman's two-volume edition of Buchanan's works (Greene, 1975, p. 42).

George Steevens

MONDAY 21 FEBRUARY 1774

MS: Hyde Collection.

ADDRESS: To George Steevens, Esq., in Hampstead, Febr. 21, afternoon.

POSTMARKS: PENY POST PAYD T MO, 12 O'CLOCK.

Sir: Febr. 21, 1774

We are thinking to augment our Club,[1] and I am desirous of

1. According to Topham Beauclerk, writing on 12 Feb.: "Our club has dwin-

nominating you, if You care to stand the ballot, and can attend on Fryday night at least twice in five weeks, less than that is too little, and rather more will be expected. Be pleased to let me know before Friday. I am, Sir, your most etc.

SAM. JOHNSON

dled away to nothing. Nobody attends but Mr. Chambers, and he is going to the East Indies. Sir Joshua and Goldsmith have got into such a round of pleasures, that they have no time" (Francis Hardy, *Memoirs of the Earl of Charlemont*, 1812, I.350).

James Boswell

SATURDAY 5 MARCH 1774

PRINTED SOURCE: JB's *Life*, 1791, I.432–33.

Dear Sir, March 5, 1774

Dr. Webster's informations were much less exact and much less determinate than I expected: they are, indeed, much less positive than, if he can trust his own book which he laid before me, he is able to give.[1] But I believe it will always be found, that he who calls much for information will advance his work but slowly.

I am, however, obliged to you, dear Sir, for your endeavours to help me, and hope, that between us something will some time be done, if not on this, on some occasion.

Chambers is either married, or almost married, to Miss Wilton, a girl of sixteen, exquisitely beautiful, whom he has, with his lawyer's tongue, persuaded to take her chance with him in the East.[2]

1. JB identifies this book as "A manuscript account drawn up by Dr. Webster of all the parishes in Scotland, ascertaining their length, breadth, number of inhabitants, and distinguishing Protestants and Roman Catholicks. This book had been transmitted to government, and Dr. Johnson saw a copy of it in Dr. Webster's possession" (*Life* II.274 n. 2).

2. On 8 Mar. Robert Chambers married Frances Wilton (*c.* 1751–1839), only daughter of the sculptor Joseph Wilton (1722–1803).

We have added to the club, Charles Fox,[3] Sir Charles Bunbury,[4] Dr. Fordyce,[5] and Mr. Steevens.

Return my thanks to Dr. Webster. Tell Dr. Robertson that I have not much to reply to his censure of my negligence; and tell Dr. Blair that since he has written hither what I said to him, we must now consider ourselves as even, forgive one another, and begin again.[6] I care not how soon, for he is a very pleasing man. Pay my compliments to all my friends, and remind Lord Elibank of his promise to give me all his works.

I hope Mrs. Boswell and little Miss are well.—When shall I see them again? She is a sweet lady, only she was so glad to see me go, that I have almost a mind to come again, that she may again have the same pleasure.

Enquire if it be practicable to send a small present of a cask of porter to Dunvegan, Rasay, and Col. I would not wish to be thought forgetful of civilities. I am, Sir, Your humble servant,

SAM. JOHNSON

3. Charles James Fox (1749–1806), son of Lord Holland of Foxley, entered Parliament in 1768 and rapidly acquired a reputation as one of the foremost speakers of the day. In 1770 he joined Lord North's administration as one of the Lords of Admiralty; in 1772 he was appointed to the Treasury board, but was dismissed in Feb. 1774. Fox remained in opposition until 1782, when he took office as Foreign Secretary under Lord Rockingham. Burke, who had known him for at least eight years, proposed Fox for membership in The Club (Fifer, pp. xlviii–xlix; Namier and Brooke II.455–61).

4. Sir Thomas Charles Bunbury (1740–1821), sixth Bt., M.P. for Suffolk (1761–84, 1790–1812) and a friend of C. J. Fox (Namier and Brooke II.136–40).

5. George Fordyce (1736–1802), M.D., F.R.S., physician and chemist, a friend of Beauclerk and Goldsmith.

6. Hugh Blair (1718–1800), D.D., Regius Professor of Rhetoric and Belles Lettres at the University of Edinburgh (1762–83), one of the most prominent of the Scots literati. SJ, who had known Blair since 1763, spent a good deal of time with him in Edinburgh at the conclusion of the Hebridean tour (*Life* I.395; V.387, 394, 397–98). In his letter of 12 May JB responded, "Dr. Blair requests you may be assured that he did not write to London what you said to him, and that neither by word nor letter has he made the least complaint of you; but, on the contrary, has a high respect for you, and loves you much more since he saw you in Scotland" (*Life* II.278).

George Steevens

SATURDAY 5 MARCH 1774

MS: Hyde Collection.

ADDRESS: To George Steevens, Esq., in Hampstead, March 5 at 11 before noon.

POSTMARK: PENY POST PAYD T SA.

Sir: March 5, 1774

Last night you became a Member of the club; if you call on me on Fryday, I will introduce You. A Gentleman proposed after you was rejected.[1]

I thank you for Neander, but wish he were not so fine.[2] I will take care of him. I am, Sir, Your humble Servant,

SAM. JOHNSON

1. Goldsmith had proposed the historian Edward Gibbon (1737–94), but Gibbon was blackballed. (*Letters of David Garrick*, ed. D. M. Little and G. R. Kahrl, 1963, III.923). However, later that year Gibbon was elected to The Club (*Life* I.481 n. 3).

2. Edmond Malone (*Life* II.274 n. 1) identifies this book—a loan, not a gift—as the *Opus Aureum* (1577) of Michael Neander (1525–95). A copy, bound in morocco with gilt edges, was in Steevens's library at the time of his death (*Bibliotheca Steevensiana*, 1800, No. 265).

William Strahan[1]

MONDAY 7 MARCH 1774

MS: Hyde Collection.

Sir: March 7, 1774

I will tell you in a few words, what is, in my opinion, the most desirable state of Copyright or literary Property.

1. Following Bloom (pp. 226–29), I accept G. B. Hill's case for identifying the recipient of this letter as Strahan (*Johns. Misc.* II.442 n. 1). The letter was almost certainly written in response to a request for testimonials from authors, among them David Hume and William Robertson, against the ruling that literary property was not copyrighted to the original owner in perpetuity. These testimonials

The Authour has a natural and peculiar right to the profits of his own work.

But as every Man who claims the protection of Society, must purchase it by resigning some part of his natural right, the authour must recede from so much of his claim, as shall be deemed injurious or[2] inconvenient to Society.

It is inconvenient to Society that an useful book should become perpetual and exclusive property.

The Judgement of the Lords was therefore legally and politically right.[3]

But the Authours enjoyment of his natural right might without any inconvenience be protracted beyond the term settled by the Statute. And it is, I think, to be desired

1. That an Authour should retain during his life the sole right of printing and selling his work.

This is agreeable to moral right, and not inconvenient to the publick, for who will be so diligent as the authour to improve the book, or who can know so well how to improve it?

2. That the authour be allowed, as by the present act, to alienate his right only for fourteen years.

A shorter time would not procure a sufficient price, and a longer would cut off all hope of future profit, and consequently all solicitude for correction or addition.

---

were intended for use as evidence in the booksellers' attempt to overturn the House of Lords' decision. Though a bill in their favor passed the House of Commons that spring, it was rejected by the Lords. "So, late in the eighteenth century, the Battle of the Booksellers ended. Copyright had ceased to be a publisher's right and had become an author's right" (L. R. Patterson, *Copyright in Historical Perspective*, 1968, p. 179). *Ante* To JB, 7 Feb. 1774 and n. 4.

2. MS: "or" altered from "to"

3. "Johnson differed only on a philosophical plane from the opinion of Sir William Blackstone. . . . Blackstone assumed that an author retained exclusive possession of his manuscript, but that once it was published he could no longer claim proprietary rights except for those privileges accorded him under the statute of Queen Anne. After expiration of the legal privileges provided by the copyright act, Blackstone thought, the author's published work becomes a piece of public property. Under his interpretation of the law, therefore—the interpretation finally validated by the English court in 1774—ownership was a matter of temporary occupancy or proprietary right" (Bloom, p. 226).

3. That when after fourteen years the copy shall revert to the authour, he be allowed to alienate it again only for Seven years at a time.

After fourteen years the value of the work will be known, and it will be no longer bought at hazard. Seven years of possession will therefore have an assignable price. It is proper that the authour be always incited to polish and improve his work, by that prospect of accruing interest which those shorter periods of alienation will afford him.

4. That after the Authours death his work should continue an exclusive property capable of bequest and inheritance, and of conveyance by gift or sale for thirty years.

By these regulations a book may continue the property of the authour or of those who claim from him about fifty years, a term sufficient to reward the writer without any loss to the publick. In fifty years far the greater number of books are forgotten and annihilated, and it is for the advantage of learning that those which fifty years have not destroyed should become bona communia, to be used by every scholar as he shall think best.

In fifty years almost every book begins to require notes either to explain forgotten allusions and obsolete words; or to subjoin those discoveries which have been made by the gradual advancement of knowledge; or to correct those mistakes which time may have discovered.

Such Notes cannot be written to any useful purpose without the text, and the text will frequently be refused while it is any man's property. I am, Sir, Your humble servant,

SAM. JOHNSON

Hester Thrale

FRIDAY 11 MARCH 1774

MS: Hyde Collection.

Madam: March 11, 1774

Our Master is a very good Man, and contrives well for me. I have now a reason for doing on Monday, what I might have been persuaded against my will, to have delayed till tuesday. I hope on Monday to be your slave in the morning, and Mrs. Smith's[1] in the Evening, and then fall again to my true Mistress, and be the rest of the week, Madam, Your most obedient,

SAM. JOHNSON

1. It is likely that SJ refers either to Jane Smith (1727–81), widow of Henry Thrale's first cousin, Henry Smith (1724–68), or to Mary Smith (d. 1805), wife of another first cousin, Ralph (1727–1800) (Hyde, 1977, pp. 90, 367).

James Boswell

c. SATURDAY 19 MARCH 1774[1]

PRINTED SOURCE: JB's *Life*, 1791, I.433–35.

Dear Sir,

I am ashamed to think that since I received your letter I have passed so many days without answering it.[2]

1. In his *Life* JB describes this letter as "Not dated, but written about the 15th of March" (II.276). However, JB's Register records the arrival of the letter on 23 Mar. (MS: Beinecke Library), and the post from London to Edinburgh usually took between three and four days (Howard Robinson, *The British Post Office*, 1948, p. 139).

2. "On the 5th of March I wrote to him, requesting his counsel whether I should this spring come to London. I stated to him on the one hand some pecuniary embarrassments, which, together with my wife's situation at that time, made me hesitate; and, on the other, the pleasure and improvement which my annual visit to the metropolis always afforded me; and particularly mentioned a peculiar satisfaction which I experienced in celebrating the festival of Easter in St. Paul's cathedral; that to my fancy it appeared like going up to Jerusalem at the feast of the Passover" (*Life* II.275).

I think there is no great difficulty in resolving your doubts. The reasons for which you are inclined to visit London, are, I think, not of sufficient strength to answer the objections. That you should delight to come once a year to the fountain of intelligence and pleasure, is very natural; but both information and pleasure must be regulated by propriety. Pleasure, which cannot be obtained but by unseasonable or unsuitable expence, must always end in pain; and pleasure, which must be enjoyed at the expence of another's pain, can never be such as a worthy mind can fully delight in.

What improvement you might gain by coming to London, you may easily supply, or easily compensate, by enjoining yourself some particular study at home, or opening some new avenue to information. Edinburgh is not yet exhausted; and I am sure you will find no pleasure here which can deserve either that you should anticipate any part of your future fortune, or that you should condemn yourself and your lady to penurious frugality for the rest of the year.

I need not tell you what regard you owe to Mrs. Boswell's entreaties; or how much you ought to study the happiness of her who studies yours with so much diligence, and of whose kindness you enjoy such good effects. Life cannot subsist in society but by reciprocal concessions. She permitted you to ramble last year, you must permit her now to keep you at home.

Your last reason is so serious, that I am unwilling to oppose it. Yet you must remember, that your image of worshipping once a year in a certain place, in imitation of the Jews, is but a comparison, and *simile non est idem*;[3] if the annual resort to Jerusalem was a duty to the Jews, it was a duty because it was commanded; and you have no such command, therefore no such duty. It may be dangerous to receive too readily, and indulge too fondly, opinions, from which, perhaps, no pious mind is wholly disengaged, of local sanctity and local devotion. You know what strange effects they have produced over a great

3. *simile non est idem*: "a parallel case is not an identical case" (proverbial).

part of the Christian world. I am now writing, and you, when you read this, are reading under the Eye of Omnipresence.

To what degree fancy is to be admitted into religious offices, it would require much deliberation to determine. I am far from intending totally to exclude it. Fancy is a faculty bestowed by our Creator, and it is reasonable that all his gifts should be used to his glory, that all our faculties should co-operate in his worship; but they are to co-operate according to the will of him that gave them, according to the order which his wisdom has established. As ceremonies prudential or convenient are less obligatory than positive ordinances, as bodily worship is only the token to others or ourselves of mental adoration, so Fancy is always to act in subordination to Reason. We may take Fancy for a companion, but must follow Reason as our guide. We may allow Fancy to suggest certain ideas in certain places, but Reason must always be heard, when she tells us, that those ideas and those places have no natural or necessary relation. When we enter a church we habitually recal to mind the duty of adoration, but we must not omit adoration for want of a temple; because we know, and ought to remember, that the Universal Lord is every where present; and that, therefore, to come to Jona, or to Jerusalem, though it may be useful, cannot be necessary.[4]

Thus I have answered your letter, and have not answered it negligently. I love you too well to be careless when you are serious.

I think I shall be very diligent next week about our travels, which I have too long neglected.[5] I am, dear Sir, Your most, etc.

SAM. JOHNSON

Compliments to Madam and Miss.

4. SJ voices a less severe opinion in his *Journey*: "That man is little to be envied . . . whose piety would not grow warmer among the ruins of *Iona*!" (Fleeman, p. 124).

5. SJ delivered the manuscript of his *Journey* to the printer on 20 June (Fleeman, p. xviii; *Post* To JB, 21 June 1774).

John Taylor

SATURDAY 26 MARCH 1774

MS: Massachusetts Historical Society.

ADDRESS: To the Revd. Dr. Taylor.

ENDORSEMENTS: 1774, 26 March 74.

Dear Sir: March 26, 1774

I cannot wait on You to day for a reason that I will tell you when I see you. Let me [know] which day I shall come to you next week. Next Saturday will not be so fit. I am, Sir, Your most etc.

SAM. JOHNSON

Warren Hastings[1]

WEDNESDAY 30 MARCH 1774

MS: British Library.

ADDRESS: To the Honourable Warren Hastings, Esq.[2]

ENDORSEMENT: Mr. Saml. Johnson, March 30th 1774.

Sir: March 30, 1774

Though I have had but little personal knowledge of you, I have had enough to make me wish for more and though it be now a long time since I was honoured by your visit, I had too much pleasure from it to forget it.[3] By those whom we delight to remember we are unwilling to be forgotten, and therefore I cannot omit this[4] opportunity of reviving myself in your memory, by a letter which you will receive from the hands of my friend Mr. Chambers, a man whose purity of manners and

1. Warren Hastings (1732–1818) had risen through the ranks of the East India Company to become Governor-General of India (1773–85). It is likely that SJ met Hastings during his protracted stay in England, 1765–69 (see below, n. 9). The two remained cordial correspondents until SJ's death.

2. Address supplied from JB's *Life*, 1791, II.367.

3. See above, n. 1.

4. MS: "this" superimposed upon undeciphered erasure

vigour of mind are sufficient to make every thing welcome that he brings.

That this is my only reason for writing will be too apparent by the uselessness of my letter to any other purpose. I have no questions to ask, not that I want curiosity after either the ancient or present state of regions in which have been[5] seen all the power[6] and splendour of wide-extended empire; and which as by some grant[7] of natural superiority supply the rest of the world with almost all that pride desires and luxury enjoys; but my knowledge of them is too scanty to furnish me with proper topicks of enquiry. I can only wish for information, and hope that a Mind comprehensive like yours will find leisure amidst the cares of your important station to enquire into many[8] subjects of which the European world either thinks not at all, or thinks with deficient intelligence and uncertain conjecture. I shall hope that he who once intended to encrease the learning of his country by the introduction of the Persian language,[9] will examine nicely[10] the Traditions and Histories of the East, that he will survey the remains of its ancient Edifices, and trace the[11] vestiges of its ruined cities; and that at his return we shall know the arts and opinions of a Race of Men from whom very little has been hitherto derived.

You, Sir, have no need of being told by me how much may be added by your attention and patronage to experimental knowledge and natural history. There are arts of manufacture

5. MS: "in which have been" superimposed upon undeciphered erasure

6. MS: "power" superimposed upon undeciphered erasure

7. MS: "some grant" superimposed upon undeciphered erasure

8. MS: "many" altered from "may"

9. In a letter "On the Institution of a College in Bengal," Hastings reports: "About thirty-five years ago [*c.* 1766], I drew up a proposal for the establishment of a professorship of the Persian language in the University of Oxford. . . . It had the approbation of the Noble Lord who was the Chancellor of the University, and the late Dr. Johnson promised, if it took place, to frame a code of regulations for the conduct of it. It met with no other encouragement and therefore dropped" (W. H. Hutton, "A Letter of Warren Hastings on the Civil Service of the East India Company," *English Historical Review* 44, 1929, p. 640).

10. MS: "examine nicely" superimposed upon undeciphered erasure

11. MS: "the" superimposed upon undeciphered erasure

practised in the countries in which you preside which are yet very imperfectly known here either to artificers or philosophers. Of the natural productions animate and inanimate we yet have so little intelligence that our books are filled, I fear, with conjectures about things which an Indian Peasant knows by his senses.

Many of those things my first Wish is to see; my second to know by such accounts as a Man like You will be able to give.

As I have not skill to ask proper questions, I have likewise no such access to great men, as can enable me to send[12] you any political information. Of the agitations of an unsettled government, and the struggles of a feeble ministry, care is doubtless taken, to give you more exact accounts than I can obtain.[13] If you are inclined to interest yourself much in publick transactions, it is no misfortune to you, to be so distant from them.

That literature is not totally forsaking us, and that your favourite language is not neglected will appear from the book which I should have pleased myself more with sending if I could have procured it bound—but time was wanting.[14] I beg however, Sir, that you will accept it, from a man very desirous of your regard, and that if you think me able to gratify you by any thing more important, you will employ me.

I am now going to take leave, perhaps a very long leave of my dear Mr. Chambers.[15] That he is going to live where you govern may justly alleviate the regret of parting, and the hope of seeing both Him and You again, which I am not willing to mingle with doubt, must at present content as it can, Sir, Your most humble servant,

SAM. JOHNSON

12. MS: "send" superimposed upon "give" partially erased

13. SJ is mistaken: "In 1774, Lord North had established an unshakeable position both at court and in the house of commons" (J. S. Watson, *The Reign of George III*, 1960, p. 153). North's Ministry lasted until 1782.

14. SJ sent in sheets a copy of William Jones's *Persian Grammar* (1771) (*Life* IV.69 n. 2).

15. *Ante* To Robert Chambers, 30 Sept. 1773, nn. 2, 3.

Robert Chambers

WEDNESDAY 30 MARCH 1774[1]

MS: Johnson House, London.

ADDRESS: To Robert Chambers, Esq.

Dear Sir:

I have waited for You to three this afternoon.[2] I suppose something unexpected has hindred you and am sorry, though I have nothing to say to you which I have not said. I would have been glad to see you once more. I pray God to bless you for Jesus Christs Sake. Farewel.

1. See below, n. 2.

2. "Fortunately, a delay in the departure of the voyage [to India] did permit a final leavetaking on 30 March 1774. Chambers, newly married and harassed by last-minute preparations for the long trip, evidently arrived late for the visit. Johnson, who had not been invited to the private wedding ceremony and whose own indisposition had not permitted him to see Chambers for some time, already suffered from a self-inflicted sense of injury and neglect. He now began to suspect that Chambers had failed him in this final rendezvous and hastily scribbled a bleakly understated note. . . . This note . . . was never mailed to Chambers. Chambers, though late as usual, did keep his appointment" (T. M. Curley, "Johnson, Chambers, and the Law," in *Johnson After Two Hundred Years*, ed. P. J. Korshin, 1986, p. 203). *Ante* To JB, 7 Feb. 1774; 5 Mar. 1774 and n. 2.

George Horne[1]

SATURDAY 30 APRIL 1774

MS: Hyde Collection.

ADDRESS: To the Reverend Dr. Horne of Magdalen College, Oxford.

POSTMARKS: 30 AP, [Undeciphered].

ENDORSEMENT: Dr. Johnson, Apr. 30, 1774.

1. George Horne (1730–92), D.D., President of Magdalen College, Oxford, later Vice-Chancellor of Oxford (1776–80) and Bishop of Norwich (1790–92) (*Alum. Oxon.* II.ii.692). Author of several religious and philosophical works, most important a *Commentary on the Psalms* (1771), Horne had informed SJ in early April that he "purposed to reprint Walton's Lives"; at the same time Horne asked SJ "to contribute to the work" (*Post* To JB, 4 July 1774).

To GEORGE HORNE, 30 *April* 1774

Dear Sir: April 30, 1774

Somebody has observed that there seem to be times when writers of value emerge from oblivion by general consent. Walton's time is at last come. You are reviving him at Oxford, Lord Hail one of[2] the Judges of Scotland appears to have the same design.[3] I once had it too. I had talk with Lord Hail about the manner of doing it with notes; and should wish to know whether he proceeds. Shall I write to him? Or had you rather go on without any communication? Let but the work be done, and do not stay too long for one another.[4]

The Life of Walton has happily fallen into good hands. Sir John Hawkins has prefixed it to the late edition of the Angler, very diligently collected, and very elegantly composed.[5] You will ask his leave to reprint it, and not wish for a better.

I wish that in the leisure of academical retirement more Men would think to review our stores of antiquated literature, and bring back into notice what is undeservedly forgotten. Warton has set a noble example,[6] may he have many to follow him, and none, unless it be you and me, to overtake him. I am, Sir, Your most humble Servant,

SAM. JOHNSON

2. MS: "of" superimposed upon "th"

3. Sir David Dalrymple (1726–92), third Bt., of Hailes, East Lothian, styled "Lord Hailes" as judge of the Court of Session, a position to which he had been appointed in 1766 (*Boswell for the Defence*, ed. W. K. Wimsatt and F. A. Pottle, 1959, p. 354). Hailes, an avid antiquarian, author of *A Catalogue of the Lords of Session* (1767), was at work on a two-volume "Annals of Scotland" (*Life* v.537; *Post* To JB, 4 July 1774 and n. 4). On 17 Aug. 1773 JB had introduced Hailes to SJ, who received the mistaken impression that Hailes intended to publish an edition of Walton's *Lives*. As JB reminded SJ, "While he [Hailes] sat with you in my house, he said, that there should be a new edition of Walton's Lives; and you said, that 'they should be benoted a little.' This was all that passed on that subject" (*Life* II.283; v.48).

4. Neither Hailes nor Horne proceeded with the project (*Post* To JB, 4 July 1774; 1 Oct. 1774).

5. Hawkins's edition of *The Compleat Angler* appeared in 1760. It was accompanied by a lengthy "Life of Walton," compiled in part from notes supplied by William Oldys, SJ's collaborator on the *Catalogus Bibliothecae Harleianae* (B. H. Davis, *A Proof of Eminence: The Life of Sir John Hawkins*, 1973, pp. 79–80).

6. *Ante* To Thomas Warton, 16 July 1754 and n. 1.

James Boswell

TUESDAY 10 MAY 1774

PRINTED SOURCE: JB's *Life*, 1791, I.435.

Dear Sir, May 10, 1774

The lady who delivers this has a law-suit, in which she desires to make use of your skill and eloquence, and she seems to think that she shall have something more of both for a recommendation from me; which, though I know how little you want any external incitement to your duty, I could not refuse her, because I know that at least it will not hurt her, to tell you that I wish her well.[1] I am, Sir, Your most humble servant,

SAM. JOHNSON

1. *Post* To JB, 27 May 1774.

Thomas Cumming[1]

WEDNESDAY 25 MAY 1774

MS: Hyde Collection.

ADDRESS: To Thomas Cumins, Esq., next door to Mrs. Forster's School at Tottenham Green, near Newington, May 25, afternoon.

POSTMARKS: PENNY POST PAYD S WE, 7 O'CLOCK.

Dear Sir: Wednesday, May 25, 1774

I have been talking of your case with my Friend Mr. Levet, who has had great practice, and of whom I have a very high opinion. He thinks you neither have nor ever had a proper

1. Thomas Cumming (d. 1774) of Clerkenwell, prominent Quaker merchant, author of *A Rational Inquiry concerning Prayer* (1742) (*Life* v.497), had been SJ's friend since the early 1740s (Clifford, 1955, p. 232). Known as "the fighting Quaker," Cumming led an expedition to Senegal in 1758; this expedition defeated the French and established England's trading supremacy there (*Life* v.98 n. 1). Cumming died on 29 May at Tottenham (*GM* 1774, p. 287). According to H. L. Piozzi, he "declared on his death-bed to Dr. Johnson, that the pain of an anonymous letter, written in some of the common prints of the day, fastened on his heart, and threw him into the slow fever of which he died" (*Johns. Misc.* I.274).

dropsy. He says that your Lungs are much obstructed and inflamed, but he agrees with me that they are not ulcerated, and that the[2] little flux of blood has nothing in it much to be feared. But as you are brought so low, he thinks your case out of the power of medicine, and to be helped only by proper diet, with occasional helps from slight emetics.

Mrs. Williams, who likewise has good Judgement, desires me to persuade you with all my power to return to Clerkenwel, where you may have her visits and Mr. Levet's, and be more within reach of all that you can want. For this removal You and I know yet a better reason, the necessity of abstracting[3] you from your own thoughts, and of driving by external objects out of your mind, those troublesome and intrusive images which with so little reason, have by taking advantage of a distempered body, harrassed you so long.

I do not say put these painful imaginations out of your head, I know that they have got a dominion which You cannot control; but, I say, get help to dislodge them, come where your friends may amuse and entertain you. Cheerful company and proper diet may yet restore you in less time than You suppose.

You see at least that your present method gives you no help; try another. There[4] is a Man now living whom Mr. Levet restored from ulcerated lungs, after many Physitians had deserted him. I earnestly desire your life, and I have a right to persuade to something. If what we do has no effect You will at least be no loser, for nothing that you now take gives you any relief. Come therefore and try. Do not perish without resistance, but make one effort more; and may that effort be successful. I am, Dear Sir, Your most humble Servant,

SAM. JOHNSON

2. MS: "the the"
3. MS: initial "a" altered from "o"
4. MS: "The"

James Boswell

FRIDAY 27 MAY 1774[1]

MS: Beinecke Library.[2]

⟨ ⟩ This Lady being interested in some suits, desires a letter of introduction to you. That which you have received without understanding it, was written for her, and by mistake given to the post.[3]

She flatters me by telling me,[4] that when You know that I wish her well, you will be more zealous in her causes. I know that you need no incitements to zeal or fidelity, but am willing to do ⟨ ⟩

1. Date supplied by note in unidentified contemporary hand: "Original Letter ⟨in⟩ the Handwriting of Dr. Saml. Johnson, May 27th, 1774."

2. MS: mutilated; half of one page missing

3. *Ante* To JB, 10 May 1774.

4. MS: "m" superimposed upon "y"

John Scott[1]

FRIDAY 27 MAY 1774

MS: Houghton Library.

ADDRESS: To John Scot, Esq. [*added in an unidentified hand*] Broad Street, Ratcliff.

POSTMARKS: PENNY POST PAID, 7 O'CLOCK, [Undeciphered].

Sir: May 27, 1774

I have excited in Mr. Thrale and his Lady the[2] curiosity to see

1. John Scott (1730–83), Quaker poet of Amwell, Hertfordshire, had been introduced to SJ by John Hoole *c.* 1766. During the summer of 1773, SJ spent several days at Scott's estate, accompanied by Hoole and Anna Williams. Despite disagreements on literary and political matters, the two remained on good terms. After Scott's death, SJ agreed to write an account of his life, but died before undertaking the project (L. D. Stewart, *John Scott of Amwell*, 1965, pp. 2, 38, 63–64).

2. MS: "the" superimposed upon "a"

your Garden and Grotto.[3] They purpose to visit your Dryads and Fairies on[4] Tuesday the thirty first of May, if it will not be inconvenient to you, to receive them at that time. It was my purpose to have given you more early notice, but it went out of my thoughts. I am, Sir, your most humble servant,

SAM. JOHNSON

Please to favour me with an answer.

3. Scott's estate at Amwell included a large grotto, which took fifteen years to excavate and embellish. The grotto consisted of seven chambers connected by passages, with pebbles, minerals, and fossils covering the walls (Stewart, *Scott*, pp. 32, 35).

4. MS: "on" altered from "to"

John Scott

THURSDAY 2 JUNE 1774

MS: Hyde Collection.

ADDRESS: To John Scot, Esq., at Amwel near Ware.

POSTMARKS: 2 IV, [Undeciphered].

ENDORSEMENT: Dr. Saml. Johnson.

Dear Sir: Johnson's court, Fleetstreet No. 7, June 2, 1774

On Tuesday the seventh of June, I hope to have the pleasure of introducing some very judicious spectators to your Garden and subterraneous retirements.[1] They will not be prevailed on to do more than dine. If you can be at home be so kind[2] as to let me know, that we may have no uncertainty on either part. I am, Sir, Your most humble Servant,

SAM. JOHNSON

1. *Ante* To John Scott, 27 May 1774 and n. 3.

2. MS: "k" superimposed upon "g"

James Boswell

TUESDAY 21 JUNE 1774

PRINTED SOURCE: JB's *Life*, 1791, I.436.

Dear Sir, Streatham, June 21, 1774

Yesterday I put the first sheets of the "Journey to the Hebrides" to the press.[1] I have endeavoured to do you some justice in the first paragraph.[2] It will be one volume in octavo, not thick.[3]

It will be proper to make some presents in Scotland. You shall tell me to whom I shall give; and I have stipulated twenty five for you to give in your own name.[4] Some will take the present better from me, others better from you. In this, you who are to live in the place ought to direct. Consider it. Whatever you can get for my purpose, send me; and make my compliments to your lady and both the young ones.[5] I am, Sir, your, etc. SAM. JOHNSON

1. SJ had delivered the entire manuscript to the printer, William Strahan—"all except two sheets" (*Post* To JB, 26 Nov. 1774 and n. 1).

2. At the beginning of his *Journey* SJ described JB as "a companion, whose acuteness would help my inquiry, and whose gaiety of conversation and civility of manners are sufficient to counteract the inconveniencies of travel, in countries less hospitable than we have passed" (Fleeman, p. 1).

3. The first edition (octavo) comes to 384 pages of text (*Bibliography*, p. 122).

4. *Post* To JB, 25 Feb. 1775 and n. 1.

5. JB's second daughter, Euphemia (1774–1837), was born 20 May (*Later Years*, p. 95).

Frances Reynolds

TUESDAY 28 JUNE 1774

MS: Hyde Collection.

ENDORSEMENT: addressed to Miss Reynolds.

My dearest Dear: June 28, 1774

I have no suspicion of your being to blame, with respect to me, nor do I want so much apology for what you cannot help. I am afraid that I cannot come on Sunday for I am somehow hurried, but whether I come or not, I shall set the same value upon your invitation and hope we shall never lose any part of the regard that we have for one another. I am, Dear dear Madam, Your most humble Servant, SAM. JOHNSON

James Boswell

MONDAY 4 JULY 1774

PRINTED SOURCE: JB's *Life*, 1791, I.436–37.

Dear Sir, July 4, 1774

I wish you could have looked over my book before the printer, but it could not easily be. I suspect some mistakes; but as I deal, perhaps, more in notions than facts,[1] the matter is not great, and the second edition will be mended, if any such there be.[2] The press will go on slowly for a time, because I am going into Wales to-morrow.[3]

I should be very sorry if I appeared to treat such a character as that of Lord Hailes otherwise than with high respect. I return the sheets, to which I have done what mischief I could; and finding it so little, thought not much of sending them.[4] The narrative is clear, lively, and short.

I have done worse to Lord Hailes than by neglecting his sheets: I have run him in debt. Dr. Horne, the President of Magdalen College in Oxford, wrote to me about three months ago, that he purposed to reprint Walton's Lives, and desired me to contribute to the work: my answer was, that Lord Hailes

1. For the implications of this contrast, see M. M. Lascelles, "Notions and Facts: Johnson and Boswell on their Travels," in *Johnson, Boswell and Their Circle*, 1965, pp. 215–29.

2. The printing of a second edition (with minor revisions) of SJ's *Journey* began in Nov. 1774, thus overlapping with the production of the first edition (W. B. Todd, "The Printing of Johnson's *Journey* [1775]," *Studies in Bibliography* 6, 1954, pp. 250–52).

3. *Post* To Bennet Langton, 5 July 1774 and n. 4.

4. At the author's request, JB had sent part of Lord Hailes's *Annals of Scotland* to SJ for criticism (*Life* II.278). SJ continued to comment on subsequent portions of the work (cf. *Post* To JB, 27 Oct. 1774).

intended the same publication; and Dr. Horne has resigned it to him. His Lordship now must think seriously about it.[5]

Of poor dear Dr. Goldsmith there is little to be told, more than the papers have made publick. He died of a fever, made, I am afraid, more violent by uneasiness of mind.[6] His debts began to be heavy, and all his resources were exhausted. Sir Joshua is of opinion that he owed not less than two thousand pounds. Was ever poet so trusted before?

You may, if you please, put the inscription thus:

Maria Scotorum Regina nata 15—, *a suis in exilium acta* 15—, *ab hospitâ neci data* 15—.[7] You must find the years.

Of your second daughter you certainly gave the account yourself, though you have forgotten it.[8] While Mrs. Boswell is well, never doubt of a boy.[9] Mrs. Thrale brought, I think, five girls running, but while I was with you she had a boy.[10]

I am obliged to you for all your pamphlets, and of the last I hope to make some use.[11] I made some of the former. I am, dear Sir, Your most affectionate servant,

SAM. JOHNSON

My compliments to all the three ladies.

5. *Ante* To George Horne, 30 Apr. 1774 and n. 3.

6. After repeatedly dosing himself with James's Fever Powder, Goldsmith went into convulsions and died on the morning of 4 Apr. (R. M. Wardle, *Oliver Goldsmith*, 1957, pp. 274–76). "When Goldsmith was dying, Dr. Turton said to him, 'Your pulse is in greater disorder than it should be, from the degree of fever which you have: is your mind at ease?' Goldsmith answered it was not" (*Life* III.164).

7. "Mary, Queen of Scots, born in 15—; driven into exile from her own [people] in 15—; handed over to be killed by her host in 15—." On 18 Dec. 1773 JB had written, "You promised me an inscription for a print to be taken from an historical picture of Mary Queen of Scots being forced to resign her crown, which Mr. Hamilton at Rome has painted for me" (*Life* II.270). The inscription included in this letter did not meet with JB's approval (*Life* II.283), and SJ eventually supplied another, along with an English translation (*Life* II.293 n. 2).

8. *Ante* To JB, 21 June 1774, n. 5.

9. JB's first son, Alexander, was born 9 Oct. 1775 (*Boswell: The Ominous Years*, ed. Charles Ryskamp and F. A. Pottle, 1963, p. 163).

10. Ralph Thrale was born 8 Nov. 1773. He was preceded by five girls: Anna Maria, Lucy Elizabeth, Susanna Arabella, Sophia, and Penelope (Hyde, 1977, p. xii).

11. On 24 June JB had complained, "You do not acknowledge the receipt of the

various packets which I have sent to you" (*Life* II.279). It is likely that these "packets" contained the "pamphlets" to which SJ refers, and that JB was doing his best to supply information for use in the *Journey* (Lascelles, "Notions and Facts," p. 219).

Bennet Langton

TUESDAY 5 JULY 1774

MS: Hyde Collection.

ADDRESS: To Bennet Langton, Esqr., at Langton, near Horncastle, Lincoln [*Readdressed in an unidentified hand*] Spilsby.

FRANK: Hfreethrale.

POSTMARKS: 5 IV, FREE, BE.

Dear Sir: July 5, 1774

You have reason to reproach me that I have left your last letter so long unanswered, but I had nothing particular to say. Chambers, you find is gone far,[1] and poor Goldsmith is gone much further.[2] He died of a fever exasperated, as I believe, by the fear of distress. He had raised money and squandred it, by every artifice of acquisition and folly of expence. But let not his frailties be remembred. He was a very great Man.

I have just begun to print my Journey to the Hebrides[3] and am leaving the press to take another journey into Wales, whither Mr. Thrale is going to take possession of at least five hundred a year, fallen to his Lady.[4] All at Streatham that are alive are well.[5]

I have never recovered from the last dreadful Ilness but flat-

1. *Ante* To Robert Chambers, 30 Mar. 1774 and n. 2.

2. *Ante* To JB, 4 July 1774 and n. 6.

3. *Ante* To JB, 21 June 1774 and n. 1.

4. Hester Thrale had inherited the Salusbury family property at Bach-y-Graig, Flintshire (Clifford, 1952, pp. 39, 113). The Thrales and SJ left for Wales on 5 July and returned 30 Sept. (*Life* v.427, 460 n. 2).

5. SJ may have been thinking of the deaths of Hester Salusbury and Lucy Thrale the preceding year.

ter myself that I grow gradually better, much however yet remains to mend. Κύριε ἐλέησον.[6]

If you have the Latin version of *Busy curious thirsty fly,* be so kind as to transcribe and send it,[7] but you need [not] be in haste, for I shall be I know not where, for at least five weeks. I wrote the following tetrastick on poor Goldsmith.

Τὸν τάφον εἰσοράας τὸν 'Ολιβαρίοιο, κονίην
"Αφροσι μὴ σεμνὴν, Ξεῖνε, πόδεσσι πάτει·
Οἶσι μέμηλε φύσις, μέτρων χάρις, ἔργα παλαιῶν,
Κλαίετε ποιήτην, ἱστόρικον, φύσικον.[8]

Please to make my most respectful compliments to all the Ladies, and remember me to young George, and his sister.[9] I reckon George begins to show a pair of heels.

Do not be sullen now, but let me find a letter when I come back. I am, Dear Sir, Your affectionate, humble Servant,

SAM. JOHNSON

6. Κύριε ἐλέησον: "Lord have mercy."

7. SJ had translated "The Fly, An Anacreontick," by William Oldys (*Poems,* pp. 197–98).

8. "Whoe'er thou art, with reverence tread / Where Goldsmith's letter'd dust is laid. / If nature and the historic page, / If the sweet muse thy care engage, / Lament him dead, whose powerful mind / Their various energies combin'd" (Translation by William Seward, in Seward's *Anecdotes,* 1798, II.466). For the correctly accentuated Greek text, see *Poems,* p. 198.

9. SJ refers to George Langton (b. 1772) and his sister Mary (b. 1773) (Fifer, p. lviii n. 29).

Robert Levet

TUESDAY 16 AUGUST 1774

PRINTED SOURCE: JB's *Life,* 1793, II.151.

Dear Sir, Llewenny, in Denbighshire,[1] Aug. 16, 1774

Mr. Thrale's affairs have kept him here a great while, nor do

1. SJ and the Thrales stayed from 28 July to 18 August at Llewenny, the seat of Hester Thrale's cousin, Robert Salusbury Cotton (*Life* V.435 and n. 2, 446). *Post* To Hester Thrale, 7 May 1780 and n. 6.

I know exactly when we shall come hence.[2] I have sent you a bill upon Mr. Strahan.

I have made nothing of the Ipecacuanha, but have taken abundance of pills, and hope that they have done me good.

Wales, so far as I have yet seen of it, is a very beautiful and rich country, all enclosed, and planted. Denbigh is not a mean town.[3] Make my compliments to all my friends, and tell Frank I hope he remembers my advice. When his money is out, let him have more. I am, Sir, Your humble servant,

SAM. JOHNSON

2. *Ante* To Bennet Langton, 5 July 1774 and n. 4.

3. On 1 Aug. SJ and the Thrales "visited Denbigh and the remains of its Castle. The town consists of one main street, and some that cross it. . . . The houses are built some with rough stone, some with brick, and a few are of timber" (*Life* v.437).

James Boswell

SATURDAY 1 OCTOBER 1774

PRINTED SOURCE: JB's *Life*, 1791, I.439.

Dear Sir, London, Octob. 1, 1774

Yesterday I returned from my Welch journey.[1] I was sorry to leave my book suspended so long;[2] but having an opportunity of seeing, with so much convenience, a new part of the island, I could not reject it. I have been in five of the six counties of North Wales; and have seen St. Asaph and Bangor, the two seats of their bishops; have been upon Penmanmaur and Snowden, and passed over into Anglesea. But Wales is so little different from England, that it offers nothing to the speculation of the traveller.[3]

When I came home, I found several of your papers, with

1. *Ante* To Bennet Langton, 5 July 1774 and n. 4.

2. *Ante* To JB, 21 June 1774 and n. 1. "As the author was less accessible to proof, so the press-work was less exigent" (Fleeman, p. xviii).

3. Cf. *Post* To John Taylor, 20 Oct. 1774.

some pages of Lord Hailes's Annals, which I will consider.[4] I am in haste to give you some account of myself, lest you should suspect me of negligence in the pressing business which I find recommended to my care, and which I knew nothing of till now, when all care is vain.[5]

In the distribution of my books I purpose to follow your advice, adding such as shall occur to me. I am not pleased with your notes of remembrance added to your names, for I hope I shall not easily forget them.[6]

I have received four Erse books, without any direction, and suspect that they are intended for the Oxford library.[7] If that is the intention, I think it will be proper to add the metrical psalms,[8] and whatever else is printed in Erse, that the present may be complete. The donor's name should be told.

I wish you could have read the book before it was printed, but our distance does not easily permit it.

I am sorry Lord Hailes does not intend to publish Walton; I am afraid it will not be done so well, if it be done at all.[9]

I purpose now to drive the book forward. Make my compliments to Mrs. Boswell, and let me hear often from you. I am, dear Sir, Your affectionate humble servant,

SAM. JOHNSON

4. *Ante* To JB, 4 July 1774, n. 4.

5. JB had solicited SJ's assistance in securing a pardon for his client John Reid, who had been sentenced to death for sheep-stealing. JB's attempts were unsuccessful, and Reid was executed on 21 Sept. (*Life* II.508; *Later Years*, pp. 101–4).

6. *Ante* To JB, 21 June 1774; *Post* To JB, 25 Feb. 1775 and n. 1.

7. In June JB informed SJ of five books that he had received from the Society for Propagating Christian Knowledge in Scotland: the first Gaelic version of the New Testament (1767), the Gaelic translation of Richard Baxter's *Call to the Unconverted* (1750), *The Confession of Faith . . . Translated into the Irish Language by the Synod of Argyle* (1725), the Gaelic version of John Willison's *The Mother's Catechism for the Young Child* (1752), and Alexander M'Donald's *Galick and English Vocabulary* (1741). As the Society intended, JB forwarded the books to SJ (apparently omitting one). SJ then presented them to the Bodleian Library (*Post* To Philip Fisher, 7 June 1775; L. F. Powell, "Samuel Johnson: An Early 'Friend of the Bodleian,'" *Bodleian Quarterly Record* 5, 1928, pp. 280–81; *Life* II.508).

8. SJ refers to Alexander McFarlane's amended version of the Synod of Argyle's *Caogad* (1753), which comprised the first fifty psalms. According to L. F. Powell, "there is a copy in Bodley, but there is no evidence that it came from Johnson" (*Life* II.508).

9. *Ante* To George Horne, 30 Apr. 1774 and nn. 3, 4.

John Taylor

THURSDAY 20 OCTOBER 1774

MS: Hyde Collection.

Dear Sir: Oct. 20, 1774

Our Journey took up more time than we expected, and we did not come to town till the day after the dissolution of the parliament.[1] We entered North Wales from Chester and went to the extremities of Carnarvonshire, and passed into Anglesea, and came back by Wrexham and Shrewsbury. But Wales has nothing that can much excite or gratify curiosity. The mode of life is entirely English. I am glad that I have seen it, though I have seen nothing, because I now know that there is nothing to be seen.

Mr. Thrale has had a very violent and formidable Opposition which he has very triumphantly overcome.[2] Poor Mrs. Thrale had two day[s] ago a fall from her horse which has cut her face and bruised her body, but she has not miscarried, and will be soon well.[3] Your little Friend Miss is hard at her Italian with Baretti.[4]

I have printed two hundred and forty pages of my Journey to the Hebrides. I hope to have the book out in a Month, and a pretty book, I hope, it will be.[5]

1. Parliament was dissolved 29 Sept.; the Thrales and SJ returned on the 30th (*Ante* To JB, 1 Oct. 1774).

2. Henry Thrale was opposed in his campaign for reelection by supporters of John Wilkes, who incited continuous rioting in Southwark. SJ wrote at least one advertisement on Thrale's behalf, as well as the anti-Wilkes pamphlet, *The Patriot* (J. D. Fleeman, "Dr. Johnson and Henry Thrale, M.P.," in *Johnson, Boswell, and Their Circle*, 1965, pp. 181–82; *Works*, Yale ed. x.387). On 18 Oct. Thrale was officially returned, in second place on the poll (Fleeman, "Dr. Johnson and Henry Thrale," p. 182; Clifford, 1952, pp. 116–17).

3. The accident occurred during a ride from Streatham to Kensington. Hester Thrale was pregnant with her tenth child: Frances Anna, born 4 May 1775 (Hyde, 1977, pp. xii, 108).

4. *Ante* To Hester Thrale, 12 Nov. 1773, n. 5.

5. Signatures B–Q of SJ's *Journey* had been printed. SJ was overly optimistic: printing was not completed until *c.* mid-December, and the book was not distributed for sale until 13 Jan. 1775 (Fleeman, pp. xix, xxii, xxiii).

Your own Advertisements are excellently well done, I know.

To the etc. of the County of Derby.[6]

Having had the honour of being again appointed to represent the County in Parliament, we think it our[7] duty to[8] promise the[9] continuance of that conduct which has recommended us to your choice, and to which we now consider[10] ourselves as still more strictly obliged by our gratitude for that una[ni]mity that by admitting no opposition has spared us the pain of setting worthy men at variance,[11] and of occasioning dissensions among those who have deserved from us that our first care should be their Concord[12] and Happiness. I am, Dear Sir, Your most affectionate etc.

SAM. JOHNSON

6. Apparently Taylor had asked SJ to draft an announcement for two M.P.s who had just been reelected from Derbyshire. They were Lord George Cavendish (?1727–94), one of Taylor's patrons, and Godfrey Bagnall Clarke (*c.* 1742–74) (Namier and Brooke II.201, 216).

7. MS: "not only" del. before "our"

8. MS: "not only" del. before "to"

9. MS: "the" written above "a" del.

10. MS: "and to which we now consider" written above "and having had the uncommon" del.

11. MS: "by our pretensions" del. before comma

12. MS: "happiness and" del. before "Concord"

John Perkins

TUESDAY 25 OCTOBER 1774

MS: Hyde Collection.

ADDRESS: To Mr. Perkins [*added in an unidentified hand*] Three Crown Court, Borough.

ENDORSEMENT: 25 Octr. 1774.

Sir: Oct. 25, 1774

You may do me a very great favour. Mrs. Williams, a Gentlewoman whom You may have seen at Mr. Thrale's, is a petitioner for Mr. Hetherington's Charity; Petitions are this day issued at Christ's Hospital.[1]

1. The Rev. William Hetherington (1698–1778), Rector of Farnham Royal and "probably the richest Clergyman in England" (*Lit. Anec.* IV.294), established his

I am a bad manager of business in a Croud, and if I should send a mean Man, he may be sent away without his errand. I must therefore entreat that you will go, and ask for a Petition for Anna Williams, whose paper of Enquiries was delivered with answers at the counting house of the Hospital on Thursday the 20th. My Servant will attend you thither, and bring the petition to me when you have it.

The Petition, which they are to give us, is a form which they deliver to every petitioner, and which the petitioner is afterwards to fill up, and return to them again. This we must have or we cannot proceed according to their directions. You need, I believe, only ask for a Petition, if they enquire for whom You ask, You can tell them.

I beg pardon for giving you this trouble, but it is a matter of great importance. I am, Sir, Your most humble Servant,

SAM. JOHNSON

---

charity for the blind, administered by governors of Christ's Hospital, in 1774. Anna Williams's application, one of over seven hundred for only fifty vacancies, was unsuccessful (*Life* II.509).

James Boswell

THURSDAY 27 OCTOBER 1774

PRINTED SOURCE: JB's *Life*, 1791, I.440–41.

Dear Sir, London, Octob. 27, 1774

There has appeared lately in the papers an account of a boat overset between Mull and Ulva, in which many passengers were lost, and among them Maclean of Col.[1] We, you know,

1. "*Extract of a Letter from Downe, Oct.* 2. An express arrived here yesterday from the Isle of Mull, with an account of Archibald Murdoch, younger, of Gartincaber, being drowned, crossing one of the ferries in that island. . . . They were within a gun shot of the lands of Ulva and Mull, when the barge was overset by the mismanagement of the Skipper, and nine perished, viz. Mr. Murdoch of Gartincaber, Mr. [Donald] Maclean of Coll, Mr. Fisher from England, and Mr. Mal-

were once drowned;[2] I hope, therefore, that the story is either wantonly or erroneously told. Pray satisfy me by the next post.

I have printed two hundred and forty pages.[3]—I am able to do nothing much worth doing to dear Lord Hailes's book. I will, however, send back the sheets; and hope, by degrees, to answer all your reasonable expectations.[4]

Mr. Thrale has happily surmounted a very violent and acrimonious opposition;[5] but all joys have their abatements: Mrs. Thrale has fallen from her horse, and hurt herself very much.[6] The rest of our friends, I believe, are well. My compliments to Mrs. Boswell. I am, Sir, Your most affectionate servant,

SAM. JOHNSON

---

com McDonald, Drover in Mull, with five attendants" (*London Chronicle*, 8–11 Oct. 1774, p. 346).

2. "In the news-papers" (JB's note). SJ may be referring to the report of their reappearance after having been caught in a "remarkable storm" off of Skye (*Caledonian Mercury*, 30 Oct. 1773, p. 3).

3. *Ante* To John Taylor, 20 Oct. 1774 and n. 5.

4. *Ante* To JB, 4 July 1774, n. 4.

5. *Ante* To John Taylor, 20 Oct. 1774 and n. 2.

6. *Ante* To John Taylor, 20 Oct. 1774 and n. 3.

Thomas Lawrence

SATURDAY 19 NOVEMBER 1774

PRINTED SOURCE: American Art Association, Anderson Galleries, Isham Sale, 4 May 1933, Lot No. 171, p. 32.

Dear Sir: Nov. 19, 1774

I send you the present result of my negotiation.[1] Hardy has no mind to serve us,[2] but I do not intend to give it over. I could

1. The subject of this negotiation has not been determined.

2. Perhaps Sir Charles Hardy (*c.* 1714–80), Kt., M.P. for Rochester (1764–68) and Plymouth (1771–80), a career naval officer who rose through the ranks to become admiral in 1770 (Namier and Brooke II.583).

not get at Lord Sandwich by the way that I intended,[3] I will by some other. I am, Sir, Your most obliged and most humble Servant,

SAM. JOHNSON

3. John Montagu (1718–92), fourth Earl of Sandwich, politician, diplomat, and rake; First Lord of the Admiralty (1771–82).

James Boswell

SATURDAY 26 NOVEMBER 1774

PRINTED SOURCE: JB's *Life*, 1791, I.441.

Dear Sir, Nov. 26, 1774

Last night I corrected the last page of our "Journey to the Hebrides." The printer has detained it all this time, for I had, before I went into Wales, written all except two sheets.[1] "The Patriot" was called for by my political friends on Friday, was written on Saturday, and I have heard little of it.[2] So vague are conjectures at a distance.[3] As soon as I can, I will take care that copies be sent to you, for I would wish that they might be given before they are bought; but I am afraid that Mr. Strahan will send to you and to the booksellers at the same time. Trade is as diligent as courtesy. I have mentioned all that you recom-

1. Cf. *Ante* To JB, 21 June 1774 and n. 1. "The unwritten 'two sheets' is an unclear detail. It seems to mean that the copy occupying sigs. 2A–2B was unwritten, but it is hard to reconcile the text with the signatures at that point in the book. Perhaps SJ meant that he had not written out his copy beyond the point where they left Mull" (Fleeman, p. xviii n. 1).

2. *Ante* To John Taylor, 20 Oct. 1774 and n. 2. *The Patriot* was written on either 1 Oct. or 8 Oct., and published on the 12th. A second edition appeared 5 Nov., and a third the following spring. According to Donald Greene, SJ may mean "that he had not been bothered by ministerial demands for its revision, as with *Thoughts on Falkland's Islands*" (*Works*, Yale ed. x.387).

3. "Alluding to a passage in a letter of mine, where speaking of his 'Journey to the Hebrides,' I say, 'But has not "The Patriot" been an interruption, by the time taken to write it, and the time luxuriously spent in listening to its applauses?'" (JB's note: *Life* II.288 n. 2).

mended. Pray make my compliments to Mrs. Boswell and the younglings. The club has, I think, not yet met.

Tell me, and tell me honestly, what you think and others say of our travels. Shall we touch the continent?[4] I am, dear Sir, Your most humble servant,

SAM. JOHNSON

4. SJ and JB "had projected a voyage together up the Baltick, and talked of visiting some of the more northern regions" (JB's note: *Life* II.288 n. 3). Chapman (I.416 n. 2) contends that, *pace* JB, "travels" must refer to SJ's *Journey*; he also suggests that "touch" may be a mistake for "reach."

William Strahan

WEDNESDAY 30 NOVEMBER 1774

MS: Hyde Collection.

Sir: Nov. 30, 1774

I waited on you this morning having forgotten your new engagement; for this you must not reproach me, for if I had looked upon your present station with malignity, I could not have forgotten it.[1]

I came to consult you upon a little matter that gives me some uneasiness. In one of the pages there is a severe censure of the Clergy of an English Cathedral which I am afraid is just,[2] but I have since recollected that from me it may[3] be thought im-

1. In October Strahan had been elected M.P. for Malmesbury (Namier and Brooke III.489). The new Parliament met for the first time on 29 Nov., and the King's speech took place on the 30th (*Journals of the House of Lords*, 1774–76, XXXIV. 266, 269).

2. SJ refers to the final paragraph of leaf D8: "Let us not however make too much haste to despise our neighbours. There is now, as I have heard, a body of men, not less decent or virtuous than the Scottish council, longing to melt the lead of an English cathedral. What they shall melt, it were just that they should swallow" (1st ed., p. 48; Fleeman, p. lvi). In this passage SJ harshly reproves the Dean and Chapter of Lichfield Cathedral, who had taken preliminary steps toward replacing the leaded roof with slates. Their motive was to raise money for interior renovations (Chapman I.417 n. 2).

3. MS: "may" superimposed upon "is"

proper for the Dean did me a kindness about forty years ago.[4] He is now very old, and I am not young.[5] Reproach can do him no good, and in myself I know not whether it is zeal or wantonness.

Can a leaf be cancelled without too much trouble? Tell me what I should do. I have no settled choice, but I would not refuse to allow the charge.[6] To cancel it seems the surer side. Determine for me. I am, Sir, Your most humble servant,

SAM. JOHNSON

Tell me your mind, if you will cancel it, I will write something to fill up the vacuum.[7] Please to direct to the Borough.

4. In 1735 John Addenbrooke had recommended SJ as tutor to the son of Thomas Whitby (*Johns. Glean.* v.108–10; *Ante* To Richard Congreve, 25 June 1735, n. 16).

5. Cf. *Ante* To Hester Thrale, 5 Aug. 1771.

6. MS: "cost" del. before "charge"

7. The leaf was canceled, and SJ substituted the following passage: "Our own cathedrals are mouldering by unregarded dilapidation. It seems to be part of the despicable philosophy of the time to despise monuments of sacred magnificence, and we are in danger of doing that deliberately, which the Scots did not do but in the unsettled state of an imperfect constitution" (Fleeman, p. 18).

John Hollyer[1]

TUESDAY 6 DECEMBER 1774

MS: Houghton Library.

Sir: Decr. 6, 1774

I take the liberty of writing to You with whom I have no acquaintance and whom I have therefore very little right to trouble, but as it is about a man equally or almost equally related to both of us, I hope You will excuse it.

I have lately received a letter from our Cousin Thomas Johnson complaining of great distress.[2] His distress I suppose

1. I follow A. L. Reade in identifying the recipient of this letter as John Hollyer (*fl.* 1741–84), SJ's cousin, a Coventry wine merchant (*Johns. Glean.* ix.67, 71).

2. *Ante* To Hester Thrale, 14 Aug. 1769, n. 1.

is real, but how can it be prevented. In 1772 about Christmas I sent him thirty pounds, because he thought he could do something in a shop; many have lived who began with less. In the Summer 1773 I sent him ten pounds more, as I had promised him. What was the event? In the spring 1774 He wrote me word that he was in debt for rent, and in want of clothes. That is, he had in about sixteen months consumed forty pounds, and then writes for more without any mention of either misconduct or misfortune. This seems to me very strange, and I shall be obliged to you if you can inform me, or make him inform me how the money was spent, and give me your advice what can be done for him with prudence and efficacy.

He is, I am afraid, not over sensible of the impropriety of his management, for he came to visit me in the summer. I was in the country which perhaps was well for us both; I might have used him harshly, and then have repented.[3]

I have sent a bill for five pounds which you will be so kind to get discounted for him, and see the money properly applyed, and give me your advice what can be done. I am, Sir, Your humble servant,

SAM. JOHNSON

3. Johnson had repeatedly tested SJ's patience by squandering generous gifts of money. SJ's attitude toward his cousin's imprudent behaviour alternated between exasperation and compassion (*Ante* To Lucy Porter, 1 May 1770; *Post* To Thomas Johnson, 16 Dec. 1777).

Thomas Lawrence

TUESDAY 6 DECEMBER 1774

PRINTED SOURCE: Maggs Catalogue No. 343, 1916, Lot No. 291, p. 73.

I begin to have hope that we shall succeed.[1] Be pleased to send me word whether you think anything more necessary.

1. *Ante* To Thomas Lawrence, 19 Nov. 1774.

Hester Thrale

SATURDAY 17 DECEMBER 1774

MS: Hyde Collection.

Madam: Decr. 17, 1774

I have sent you a book, which will, I hope, have the honour of your acceptance. Mr. Strahan does not publish till after the Holidays,[1] and insists that only the King and you shall have it sooner,[2] and that you shall be engaged not to lend it abroad.

There are errata in it[3] which I wish you to mark.[4] I do not forget Carter.[5] I am, Madam, Your most etc.

SAM. JOHNSON

1. *Ante* To John Taylor, 20 Oct. 1774, n. 5.

2. *Post* To William Hunter, 29 Dec. 1774.

3. Hester Thrale's copy lacks the leaf of errata, probably the effect of haste in the bindery (Fleeman, p. xxii).

4. The first edition appeared with a leaf containing twelve lines of errata (*Bibliography Supplement*, p. 151).

5. *Post* To William Strahan, 22 Dec. 1774 and n. 3.

John Hoole

MONDAY 19 DECEMBER 1774

MS: Hyde Collection.

ADDRESS: To Mr. Hool.

ENDORSEMENTS: Dr. Johnson's Letter on the Tragedy of Cleonice, Letter from Dr. Johnson giving his Opinion of the Tragedy of Cleonice, Receiv'd Monday evening, 19th Decem. 1774.

Dear Sir:

I have returned your play which you will find underlined with red where there was a word which I did not like.[1] The red will be washed off with a little water.

1. SJ refers to Hoole's *Cleonice, Princess of Bithynia*, first performed at Covent Garden on 2 Mar. 1775 (*Lond. Stage*, Part IV, iii.1873). As Hoole reported to JB, 17 June 1790: "He [SJ] had a manuscript Tragedy of mine to read, and knew that I was particularly anxious for his opinion, having had great trouble and much

The plot is so well formed, the intricacy[2] so artful, and the disentanglement so easy, the suspense so affecting, and the passionate parts so properly interposed, that I have no doubt of its success.[3] I am, Sir, Your most humble Servant,

SAM. JOHNSON

---

altercation with the Managers and Performers. When he had read part of it, he sent Francis [Barber] to me to let me know that he was then reading the piece, had gone through three acts and was pleased with it. He finished the reading of the whole that evening and immediately wrote me a Note. . . . Surely this was an instance of *attentive, kind* and *gentle* manners" (Waingrow, pp. 326–27).

2. *intricacy*: "state of being entangled; perplexity; involution; complication of facts or notions" (SJ's *Dictionary*). SJ's illustrative quotation from Addison offers an exact parallel to his use of the term in this letter: "The part of Ulysses in Homer's Odyssey is much admired by Aristotle, as perplexing that fable with very agreeable plots and *intricacies*. . . ."

3. *Cleonice* had at best a lukewarm reception: it achieved an acceptable run of nine nights, but "fell a victim to the severity of Criticism, which has capriciously suffered many worse performances to enjoy a better fate" (*Lit. Anec.* II.407; *Lond. Stage*, Part IV, iii.1873–78).

Warren Hastings

TUESDAY 20 DECEMBER 1774

MS: Hyde Collection.

Sir: London, Dec. 20, 1774

Being informed that by the departure of a ship there is now an opportunity of writing to Bengal, I am unwilling to slip out of your memory by my own negligence, and therefore take the liberty of reminding you of my existence, by sending you a book which is not yet made publick.[1]

I have lately visited a region less remote and less illustrious than India, which afforded some occasions for speculation.[2] What occurred to me, I have put into the volume of which I beg your acceptance.

1. *Ante* To John Taylor, 20 Oct. 1774, n. 5; *Ante* To Hester Thrale, 17 Dec. 1774.

2. "I deal, perhaps, more in notions than facts" (*Ante* To JB, 4 July 1774).

Men in your station seldom have presents totally disinterested. My Book is received, let me now make my request.

There is, Sir, somewhere within your Government a young adventurer one Chauncy Laurence, whose father is one of my oldest Friends.[3] Be pleased to show the young man what countenance is fit, whether he wants to be restrained by your authority, or encouraged by your favour. His Father is now president of the College of Physicians, a man venerable for his knowledge, and more venerable for his virtue.

I wish you a prosperous Government, a safe return, and a long enjoyment of plenty and tranquillity. I am, Sir, Your most obedient and most humble Servant,

SAM. JOHNSON

3. Cf. *Ante* To Robert Chambers, 30 Sept. 1773 and n. 4.

William Strahan

THURSDAY 22 DECEMBER 1774

MS: Princeton University Library.

Sir: Dec. 22, 1774

When we meet we talk, and I know not whether I always recollect what I thought I had to say.

You will please to remember that I once asked you to receive an apprentice, who is a scholar, and has always lived in a Clergyman's house, but who is mishapen, though I think not so as to hinder him at the case.[1] It will be expected that I should answer his Friend who has hitherto maintained him, whether I can help him to a place.[2] He can give no money, but will be kept in cloaths.

1. *case*: "the receptacle or frame in which the compositor has his types, divided into compartments for the various letters, figures, and spaces" (*OED*).

2. William Davenport (*c.* 1759–92), the orphan son of a clergyman, lived with the Rev. William Langley in Ashbourne (Llewellynn Jewitt, "Unpublished Episodes in the Life of Dr. Johnson," *GM* 243, 1878, pp. 692, 694). SJ had promised Langley his help in finding Davenport employment with a printer (Langley to

I have another request which it is perhaps not immediately in your power to gratify. I have a presentation to beg for the bluecoat hospital. The boy is a non freeman, and has both his parents living.[3] We have a presentation for a freeman which we can give in exchange.[4] If in your extensive acquaintance you can procure such an exchange, it will be an act of great kindness.[5] Do not let the matter slip out of your mind, for though I try others, I know not any body of so[6] much power to do it. I am, Sir, Your most humble Servant,

SAM. JOHNSON

SJ, 21 Mar. 1774, MS: Bodleian Library). At SJ's urging Strahan hired Davenport (*Post* To John Taylor, 8 Apr. 1775), who continued as one of his compositors until 1783 or 1784 (Jewitt, "Unpublished Episodes," pp. 697, 704).

3. SJ was attempting to assist Charles Carter, Hester Thrale's indigent riding master, by securing his eldest son a place at Christ's Hospital. At this time the governors of the hospital were allowed to make one presentation in three in favor of a child whose father was not a freeman (Hill 1.303 n. 3). Such a presentation was eventually secured, but the boy died before he could enter the school (*Thraliana* 1.117–18; Hyde, 1977, p. 111).

4. Hester Thrale had secured this presentation for Carter's son before it was discovered that he was not a freeman (*Thraliana* 1.117).

5. Cf. *Post* To John Taylor, 22 Dec. 1774.

6. MS: "so" altered from "som"

John Taylor

THURSDAY 22 DECEMBER 1774

PRINTED SOURCE: Hill 1.304–5.

ADDRESS: To the Reverend Dr. Taylor in Ashbourn, Derbyshire.

Dear Sir, London, Dec. 22, 1774

I have upon me in some measure the care of getting a boy into the Bluecoat Hospital,[1] and beg your interest with Mr. Harley or any other man.[2] Our boy is a non-freeman whose parents

1. *Ante* To William Strahan, 22 Dec. 1774 and n. 3.

2. The Hon. Thomas Harley (1730–1804), younger son of the third Earl of Oxford, M.P. for London (1761–74) and former Lord Mayor (1767–68) (Namier

are both living. We have a presentation for a freeman which we can give in exchange.

Charles Congreve is here, in an ill state of health, for advice.[3] How long he has been here I know not. He sent to me one that attends him as an humble friend, and she left me a direction. He told me he knew not how to find me. He is in his own opinion recovering, but has the appearance of a man much broken. He talked to me of theological points, and is going to print a sermon, but I thought he appeared neither very acute nor very knowing.[4] His room was disordered and oppressive, he has the appearance of a man wholly sunk into that sordid self-indulgence which disease, real or imaginary, is apt to dictate. He has lived, as it seems, with no great frequency of recollection. He asked me, and told me he had forgot, whether I was bred at Oxford or at Cambridge. The mind that leaves things so fast behind it, ought to have gone forward at no common rate. I believe he is charitable, yet he seems to have money much in his thoughts; he told me that this ilness would cost him fifty pound, and told it with some appearance of discontent: he seemed glad to see me, and I intend to visit him again. I rather wonder that he sent to me. I mentioned Hector to him whom I saw about ten weeks ago, but he heard the name without emotion or enquiry, nor has ever spoken of any old companions or past occurrences. Is not this an odd frame of understanding? I asked him how long it was since we had seen one another, and he answered me roundly, fifty years. The greatest pleasure that I have had from him is

---

and Brooke II.586–87). Though Harley was not a governor of Christ's Hospital, he was in a position to exert considerable influence (information supplied by S. Freeth, Guildhall Library). Hester Thrale had already written to Harley on behalf of young Carter (*Thraliana* I.117 n. 1).

3. Congreve's ill health, which became increasingly acute, was exacerbated by alcoholism (*Post* To John Taylor, 8 Apr. 1775).

4. In Mar. 1775 SJ informed Thomas Campbell that Congreve's sermon concerned "the nature of moral good & evil." The sermon was "preparing for the press & shd. he [Congreve] die before publication he leaves 50£ for that purpose" (*Dr. Campbell's Diary*, ed. J. L. Clifford, 1947, p. 55). In fact there is no evidence that the sermon ever made its way into print.

to find him pious and orthodox; yet he consorts with John Wesley.

You and I have had ill health, yet in many respects we bear time better than most of our friends. I sincerely wish that you may continue to bear it with as little diminution as is possible either of body or mind, and I think, you return the wish to Dear Sir, Your most humble servant,

SAM. JOHNSON

William Hunter[1]

THURSDAY 29 DECEMBER 1774

MS: Royal College of Surgeons of England (Hunter-Baillie Collection).
NOTE in an unidentified hand: Dr. Hunter.

Sir: Dec. 29, 1774

I am very much obliged by your willingness to present my book to his Majesty.[2] I have not courage to offer it myself, yet I cannot forbear to wish that He may see it, because it endeavours to describe a part of his Subjects, seldom visited, and little known, and his Benevolence will not despise the meanest of his people.[3]

I have sent you a book, to[4] which you are very justly entitled, and beg that it may be admitted to stand in your library however little it may add to its elegance or dignity.[5] I am, Sir, Your most humble Servant,

SAM. JOHNSON

1. William Hunter (1718–83), M.D., F.R.S., F.S.A., anatomist and obstetrician, physician to Queen Charlotte (1764–83).

2. *Ante* To Hester Thrale, 17 Dec. 1774.

3. Cf. *Post* To Hester Thrale, Early Jan. 1775.

4. MS: "to" altered from "of"

5. *Post* To Hester Thrale, Early Jan. 1775.

Henry Thrale

MONDAY 2 JANUARY 1775

MS: Hyde Collection.

Dear Sir: Jan. 2, 1775

I have taken the liberty of enclosing a letter which contains a request of which I cannot know the propriety.[1] Nothing I suppose can be done till the present master of the tap has given notice of his resignation, and whether even then it is fit for you to recommend there may be reason to doubt. I shall tell Heely that I have laid his letter before you, and that he must inform you when he is certain of the intended resignation. You will then act as you judge best. There seems to be nothing unreasonable in Heely's desire. He seems to have a Genius for an alehouse, and if he can get this establishment, may thank his friend that sent him to the Marshalsea.[2]

This, I know, is a happy week; you will revel with your Constituents in plenty and merriment.[3] I must be kept at home by my wicked Mistress, out of the way of so much happiness. You shall however have my good wishes. I hope every man will go from your table more a friend than he came. I am, Sir, Your most humble Servant,

SAM. JOHNSON

1. Humphrey Heeley had asked SJ's help in obtaining the soon-to-be vacant post of "Keeper of the Tap" at Ranelagh House. Heeley acquired the post, which he later resigned (*Life* II.31 n. 1; Hawkins, p. 601).

2. By being imprisoned in the Marshalsea, the debtors prison in Southwark, Heeley had come within Henry Thrale's sphere of influence.

3. Henry Thrale customarily entertained his constituents at the New Year.

Hester Thrale

EARLY JANUARY 1775

MS: Birthplace Museum, Lichfield.

ADDRESS: To Madam Thrale.

Madam:

You must not tell any body but Mr. Thrale that the King fell to reading the book as soon as he got it, when anything struck him, he read aloud to the Queen, and the Queen would not stay to get the King's book, but borrowed Dr. Hunter's.[1] See now. Of the two Queens who has the better tast?[2]

Of all this you must absolutely say nothing to any body.

1. *Ante* To William Hunter, 29 Dec. 1774.

2. Presumably SJ is comparing Queen Charlotte's reaction to Hester Thrale's. The other candidate is the precocious Queeney (Hyde, 1977, p. 75).

James Boswell

SATURDAY 14 JANUARY 1775

PRINTED SOURCE: JB's *Life*, 1791, I.442–43.

Dear Sir, January 14, 1775

You never did ask for a book by the post till now, and I did not think on it. You see now it is done.[1] I sent one to the King, and I hear he likes it.[2]

I shall send a parcel into Scotland for presents, and intend to give to many of my friends. In your catalogue you left out Lord Auchinleck.

Let me know, as fast as you read it, how you like it; and let me know if any mistake is committed, or any thing important left out.[3] I wish you could have seen the sheets. My compli-

1. JB received his copy of SJ's *Journey* ("in thirteen franks") on 18 Jan. It had been mailed in sheets, two sheets to each franked packet. "I have still a kind of childish satisfaction in seeing many packets come to me. . . . I opened the franks with impatience, read a short letter from Mr. Johnson and a part of the book; and, as I had received it the very day on which it was published at London, I was pleased at my being so privileged" (*Boswell: The Ominous Years*, ed. Charles Ryskamp and F. A. Pottle, 1963, pp. 56–57 and n. 7).

2. *Ante* To William Hunter, 29 Dec. 1774; *Ante* To Hester Thrale, Early Jan. 1775.

3. On 19 Jan. JB replied: "I shall only say, that your book has afforded me a high gratification. I shall afterwards give you my thoughts on particular passages.

ments to Mrs. Boswell, and to Veronica, and to all my friends. I am, Sir, Your most humble servant,

SAM. JOHNSON

In the mean time, I hasten to tell you of your having mistaken two names" (*Life* II.291).

William Strahan

SATURDAY 14 JANUARY 1775

MS: Princeton University Library.

Sir: Jan. 14, 1775

Please to send three dozen of the Journey in boards, to Your humble servant,

SAM. JOHNSON

John Taylor

SATURDAY 14 JANUARY 1775

MS: Birthplace Museum, Lichfield.

ADDRESS: To The Rev. Dr. Taylor at Ashbourne, Derbys.

FRANK: Hfreethrale.

POSTMARKS: 14 IY, FREE.

ENDORSEMENTS: 1775, 14 Jany. 75.

Dear Sir: Jan. 14, 1775

I would send you my Journey to the Western Islands, which will be published next Wednesday, but that I do not know into whose care to deliver it for you. It would go commodiously in any parcel which is sent weekly to the tradesmen in your town. Pray send me a direction.

I have been to see Congreve,[1] but he was not at home, and he thinks not, I believe, of coming to me.

1. *Ante* To John Taylor, 22 Dec. 1774.

I hope your health is good. I have hitherto passed the winter with little cold or pain. I am, Sir, your most affectionate,

SAM. JOHNSON

James Macpherson[1]

FRIDAY 20 JANUARY 1775

MS: Hyde Collection.[2]

ADDRESS: To Mr. James Macpherson.

ENDORSEMENT: 20th Janry. 1775, Saml. Johnson.

NOTE in the hand of N. W. Wraxall: Most curious *original Note*. N.W.W.

Jan. 20, 1775

Mr. James Macpherson—I received your foolish and impudent note.[3] Whatever insult is offered me I will do my best to

1. James Macpherson (1736–96), author of *Fragments of Ancient Poetry collected in the Highlands of Scotland* (1760), *Fingal. An Ancient Epic Poem* (1762), and *Temora. An Ancient Epic Poem* (1763). These works purported to be translations of epics by Ossian, a third-century Gaelic bard. From the outset SJ, contrary to widespread opinion, disbelieved their authenticity (*Life* II.513, V.387–89; *Later Years*, p. 71). According to J. D. Fleeman, Macpherson "was not a man likely to appeal to SJ. He was an ambitious Scot who hung about the world of journalism and politics, fastening upon his fellow-countrymen for support. . . . He was evasive and uncandid about 'Ossian' from the first, and this naturally excited SJ's suspicions" (Fleeman, pp. 217–18).

2. Several versions of this letter exist: see Fleeman, p. xxx n. 1 (with the correction that the holograph illustrated in *Life* II.298 is in the Berg Collection, New York Public Library). Given the fame of the controversy and SJ's spirited part in it, the prevalence of copies is not surprising. However, the Hyde MS is indisputably the original: it was addressed, folded, and sealed for delivery by hand; it was endorsed by Macpherson himself; and it was annotated by Nathaniel William Wraxall (1751–1831), who obtained permission from Macpherson's executor to sort through his papers (Fiona Stafford, "Dr. Johnson and the Ruffian: New Evidence in the Dispute between Samuel Johnson and James Macpherson," *Notes and Queries*, Mar. 1989, p. 76 and n. 20).

3. SJ's *Journey* was distributed to the booksellers on 13 Jan. 1775 (Fleeman, p. xxiii). On 15 Jan. Macpherson wrote to William Strahan, taking strong exception to the passage in which SJ implies that the Ossianic poems are fraudulent (*Life* II.511). His demand for a retraction and apology elicited from Strahan the claim that SJ had "meant no *personal affront*" and the promise that "exceptionable Words

repel, and what I cannot do for myself the law will[4] do for me. I will not desist from detecting[5] what I think a cheat, from any fear[6] of the menaces of a Ruffian.

You want me to retract. What shall I retract? I thought your book an imposture from the beginning, I think it upon yet surer reasons an imposture still. For this opinion I give the publick my reasons which I here dare you to refute.

But however I may despise you, I reverence truth and if you can prove the genuineness of the work I will confess it.[7] Your rage[8] I defy, your abilities since your Homer[9] are not so formidable,[10] and what I have heard of your morals disposes me to pay regard not to what you shall say, but to what you can prove.

You may print this if you will.

SAM. JOHNSON

---

shall be left out in all future Editions" (Strahan to Macpherson, 18 Jan. 1775: quoted in Stafford, "Dr. Johnson and the Ruffian," p. 74). A second edition, however, was already in press, and too far advanced to allow for corrections without significant delay and expense. Macpherson then sent SJ a letter by the hand of his friend William Duncan; this letter, which attacked SJ with "the most opprobrious epithets," provoked his defiant response (Sir William Forbes to John Forbes, 15 Feb. 1775, quoted in Fleeman, p. xxx; Stafford, "Dr. Johnson and the Ruffian," p. 75).

4. MS: "will" superimposed upon "sha"

5. MS: "detecting" altered from "detected"

6. MS: "f" superimposed upon "h"

7. Such proof was never forthcoming. "Yet SJ's assertion that there were not 'five hundred lines of which there is any evidence to prove them a hundred years old' . . . is not strictly true, though it is also clear that Macpherson had very little manuscript material upon which to found his compositions. What he produced owed less to MSS than to oral tradition, and his own imagination" (Fleeman, p. 218).

8. MS: "rage" superimposed upon undeciphered erasure

9. In 1773, Macpherson had published an unsuccessful translation of the *Iliad* in Ossianic prose.

10. MS: "since your Homer are not so formidable" superimposed upon undeciphered erasure

James Boswell

SATURDAY 21 JANUARY 1775

PRINTED SOURCE: JB's *Life*, 1791, I.444–45.

Dear Sir, January 21, 1775

I long to hear how you like the book; it is, I think, much liked here. But Macpherson is very furious; can you give me any more intelligence about him, or his Fingal?[1] Do what you can, and do it quickly. Is Lord Hailes on our side?[2]

Pray let me know what I owed you when I left you, that I may send it to you.

I am going to write about the Americans.[3] If you have picked up any hints among your lawyers, who are great masters of the law of nations, or if your own mind suggests any thing, let me know. But mum,—it is a secret.

I will send your parcel of books as soon as I can; but I cannot do as I wish.[4] However, you find every thing mentioned in the book which you recommended.

Langton is here; we are all that ever we were.[5] He is a worthy fellow, without malice, though not without resentment.

Poor Beauclerk is so ill, that his life is thought to be in danger.[6] Lady Di. nurses him with very great assiduity.[7]

1. *Ante* To James Macpherson, 20 Jan. 1775 and n. 1.

2. Hailes told JB that he refused to take sides in the Ossianic controversy (JB to SJ, 2 Feb. 1775, *Life* II.295). Nonetheless, he had gone on record as believing in the authenticity of *Fingal* and *Temora* (*Ancient Scottish Poems*, ed. Hailes, 1770, p. 302).

3. SJ had been requested by Lord North's Ministry to supply an answer to the colonists' "Declaration of Rights," a manifesto issued by the Continental Congress the preceding autumn. By late February he had completed *Taxation No Tyranny*, which was revised by the Government and published 8 Mar. (*Works*, Yale ed. X.401–2, 408; *Post* To William Strahan, 1 Mar. 1775).

4. *Ante* To JB, 14 Jan. 1775; *Post* To JB, 25 Feb. 1775.

5. *Ante* To JB, 5 July 1773 and n. 9.

6. Topham Beauclerk continued very ill (of an undiagnosed "distemper") for several months, but by late March "all the medical people agreed . . . that his life was not in danger" (*Boswell: The Ominous Years*, ed. Charles Ryskamp and F. A. Pottle, 1963, p. 87). Beauclerk lived until 1780 (*Post* To JB, 8 Apr. 1780 and n. 3).

7. In 1767 Beauclerk eloped with Lady Diana Spencer (1734–1808), Viscount-

Reynolds has taken too much to strong liquor, and seems to delight in his new character.

This is all the news that I have; but as you love verses, I will send you a few which I made upon Inchkenneth;[8] but remember the condition, that you shall not show them, except to Lord Hailes, whom I love better than any man whom I know so little. If he asks you to transcribe them for him, you may do it, but I think he must promise not to let them be copied again, nor to show them as mine.

I have at last sent back Lord Hailes's sheets. I never think about returning them, because I alter nothing. You will see that I might as well have kept them. However, I am ashamed of my delay; and if I have the honour of receiving any more, promise punctually to return them by the next post.[9] Make my compliments to dear Mrs. Boswell, and to Miss Veronica. I am, dear Sir, Yours most faithfully,

SAM. JOHNSON

ess Bolingbroke, the elder daughter of the third Duke of Marlborough. They were married in 1768, as soon as Lady Diana could be divorced from Lord Bolingbroke (Fifer, p. xxxviii).

8. *Ante* To Hester Thrale, 23 Oct. 1773, n. 19.

9. *Ante* To JB, 4 July 1774 and n. 4; 1 Oct. 1774; 27 Oct. 1774.

James Boswell

SATURDAY 28 JANUARY 1775

PRINTED SOURCE: JB's *Life*, 1791, I.446.

Dear Sir, January 28, 1775

You sent me a case to consider, in which I have no facts but what are against us, nor any principles on which to reason.[1] It is vain to try to write thus without materials. The fact seems to

1. In his letter of 19 Jan. JB had summarized the case of Dr. Memis and requested SJ's "immediate aid" (*Life* II.291). *Post* To Thomas Lawrence, 7 Feb. 1775 and n. 1; *Post* To JB, 7 Feb. 1775.

be against you, at least I cannot know nor say any thing to the contrary. I am glad that you like the book so well. I hear no more of Macpherson. I shall long to know what Lord Hailes says of it. Lend it him privately. I shall send the parcel as soon as I can. Make my compliments to Mrs. Boswell. I am, Sir, etc.

SAM. JOHNSON

Thomas Lawrence

MONDAY 30 JANUARY 1775

PRINTED SOURCE: Maggs Catalogue No. 291, 1912, Lot No. 2610, p. 40.

I think it will be best for you to write the account of Mr. Laurence's[1] conduct in a few words to me, that I may send it to Mr. Thamier.[2]

1. It is likely that SJ refers to Soulden Lawrence (1751–1814), Dr. Lawrence's eldest son, Fellow of St. John's College, Cambridge (1774–94). Lawrence had already begun the legal career that would lead to a knighthood (1794) and the position of Justice of the Common Pleas (*Alum. Cant.* II.iv.113).

2. Undoubtedly a cataloguer's mistake for "Chamier."

Joseph Palmer[1]

FEBRUARY 1775[2]

MS: Hyde Collection.

Friday Evening

Mr. Johnson sends compliments to Mr. Palmer, and is sorry for the trouble which has been taken by him in making the

1. The Rev. Joseph Palmer (1749–1829), the son of Sir Joshua Reynolds's sister Mary, later (1787–1829) Dean of Cashel (*Alum. Oxon.* II.iii.1061). Palmer had written a tragedy called *Zaphira*, which SJ read and praised. In 1774 it was shown to David Garrick, who declined to produce it (*Letters of Sir Joshua Reynolds*, ed. F. W. Hilles, 1929, pp. 40–42).

2. A copy of this note is included in a letter from Samuel Johnson (son of Elizabeth Reynolds Johnson) to his sister Elizabeth, 9 Mar. 1775 (*Sir Joshua's*

prologue.[3] He needs not proceed, as Mr. Hool thinks himself obliged to use that which he has.

Nephew, ed. S. M. Radcliffe, 1930, pp. 80–83). The premiere of *Cleonice* took place on 2 Mar. (*Ante* To John Hoole, 19 Dec. 1774, n. 1). See below, n. 3.

3. To judge from Samuel Johnson's letter, Joseph Palmer had been asked to contribute a prologue to Hoole's *Cleonice*, which was in rehearsal at Drury Lane. "When He [Palmer] had finish'd it He to His great mortification receiv'd a note from Dr. Johnson. . . . Mr. Hoole has since call'd on him to make an Apology for it, and to desire leave to print it before his play, which he has obtain'd. The Player who was to speak it was so very urgent with Mr. Hoole for the Prologue that He was under the necessity of letting him have one which he had by him" (Radcliffe, *Sir Joshua's Nephew*, pp. 81–82). The printed play has two prologues: the first, "Written by Thomas Vaughan, Esq; Spoken by Mr. Bensley"; the second, "Written by a Friend, to have been spoken in the character of the Tragic Muse."

Hester Thrale

FRIDAY 3 FEBRUARY 1775

MS: Hyde Collection.

Madam: Feb. 3, 1775

So many demands are made upon me, that if you give leave I will stay here till tuesday.[1] My pamphlet has not[2] gone on at all.[3] Please to send by the Bearer the papers on my table, and give my love to my *Brother* and *sisters*.[4] I am, Madam, Your most humble servant,

SAM. JOHNSON

1. MS: "tue" superimposed upon "We"
2. MS: "n" superimposed upon "g"
3. *Ante* To JB, 21 Jan. 1775 and n. 3.
4. "meaning *my Children*" (Piozzi 1.211).

Edmund Hector

SATURDAY 4 FEBRUARY 1775

MS: Hyde Collection.

ADDRESS: To Mr. Hector in Birmingham.

FRANK: Hfreethrale.

POSTMARKS: ⟨4⟩ FE, FREE.

Dear Sir: Febr. 4, 1775

You have such love to be giving, that your Friends ought to learn *how* to refuse. But the china which is ultimately designed for another, I have no right to refuse, and I will not lessen the Lady's pleasure by letting her know any thing of it.[1]

I am glad if my book gave you any pleasure. I hope Mrs. Careless likes it too. The Scotch are angry,[2] and the King says, I must go into that country no more.

Be pleased to direct the Box to me at Henry Thrale's Esq. in Southwarke. I am, Dear Sir, Your most affectionate Servant,

SAM. JOHNSON

1. Hector and his sister, Ann Carless, were planning to make the gift to Hester Thrale (*Post* To Edmund Hector, 23 Mar. 1775).

2. "Opinion did in fact divide along national lines. . . . Complaints ranged over the whole matter of the *Journey* from objections to the comments on treelessness to defences of the authenticity of 'Ossian', and Johnson was attacked for prejudice, discourtesy, and ingratitude" (Fleeman, p. xxxi). For a complete listing of critical responses, see H. L. McGuffie, *Samuel Johnson in the British Press, 1749–1784*, 1976, pp. 136–42.

Hester Thrale

SATURDAY 4 FEBRUARY 1775

MS: Hyde Collection.

ADDRESS: To Mrs. Thrale.

Madam: Febr. 4

Please to send the printed pamphlets that are upon my table.[1]

1. Cf. *Ante* To Hester Thrale, 3 Feb. 1775.

Dr. Worthington[2] is come to town to print a piece about subscription.[3] He is in Cannon Row, Bridge Street. He called on me this morning. He has been come a fortnight.

Mr. Hoole's play is in rehearsal.[4] Pepys[5] and Tigh[6] are reading Jephson to all comers and goers,[7] and it is told how well I liked it; so your spite is spited.[8]

I hope to see you all on Tuesday, but I shall come, I suppose, when you are upon gad, between Breakfast and Dinner.

Eleven of the club dined together and we made many salutary regulations.

Be pleased to frank the letter to

Mr. Hector in Birmingham.

and send it.[9] I am, Madam, Your most humble Servant,

SAM. JOHNSON

2. William Worthington (1703–78), D.D., Prebendary of St. Asaph and York, Vicar of Llanrhaiadr, and author of *The Scripture Theory of the Earth* (1773). SJ and the Thrales had visited Worthington on their Welsh tour in 1774 (*Life* v.453 and n. 2).

3. SJ may be referring to Worthington's *Irenicum, or the Importance of Unity in the Church of Christ Considered* (1775). This identification must remain conjectural at best, for "subscription" could also be "subscriptions": SJ's characteristic terminal hook leaves the reading ambiguous.

4. *Ante* To John Hoole, 19 Dec. 1774 and n. 1.

5. William Weller Pepys (1740–1825), cr. (1801) Bt., Master of Chancery and member of both the Streatham Park and Bluestocking circles (Clifford, 1952, p. 150). According to Hester Thrale, Pepys "is one of my great favourites, and I am very sorry Johnson hates him so. . . . Mr. Pepys however is a Man of Virtue, a Man of Learning, a Man pious, frugal, charitable and kind: has a great many Anecdotes, to enliven his Talk, and dresses gayly to set off his Person" (*Thraliana* I.56).

6. Edward Tighe (*fl.* 1759–97), Irish lawyer and M.P., busily promoted his friend Robert Jephson's forthcoming play, *Braganza* (see below, n. 7). He persuaded Horace Walpole to write an epilogue, and read selections at a Bluestocking party on 29 Jan. (*Walpole's Correspondence*, Yale ed. XXXII.229–30 and nn. 35–38, XL.287 and n. 9).

7. *Braganza*, a tragic drama by the Irish poet and playwright Robert Jephson (1736–1803), was in production at Drury Lane, where it premiered successfully on 17 Feb. "'This Tragedy . . . [was] read by the Author's Friends in most of the great Family's in Town and puff'd up in Such a Manner'" (*Lond. Stage*, Part IV, iii.1869–70).

8. Apparently Hester Thrale had attended one of the public readings of the play and responded critically to SJ.

9. *Ante* To Edmund Hector, 4 Feb. 1775.

Thomas Lawrence

TUESDAY 7 FEBRUARY 1775

MS: Hyde Collection.

ADDRESS: To Dr. Laurence.

Sir: Febr. 7, 1775

One of the Scotch Physicians is now prosecuting a Corporation that in some publick instrument have stiled him *Doctor of Medicine* instead of *Physician.* Boswel desires, being Advocate for the corporation to know whether *Doctor of Medicine* be not a legitimate title, and whether it can be considered as a disadvantageous distinction.[1] I am to write to night,—be pleased to tell me.[2] I am, Sir, your most etc.

SAM. JOHNSON

1. *Ante* To JB, 28 Jan. 1775 and n. 1. Dr. John Memis had sued the managers of the Aberdeen Infirmary for calling him "doctor of medicine" instead of "physician" in a translation of their charter. After gathering information on JB's behalf, SJ dictated to him an opinion in support of the Infirmary's position (*Life* II.372). "Some vanished nuance of medical malice was involved, but Memis's case was found trifling and he had to pay £40 expenses" (*Later Years*, p. 124).

2. *Post* To JB, 7 Feb. 1775.

James Boswell

TUESDAY 7 FEBRUARY 1775

PRINTED SOURCE: JB's *Life*, 1791, I.447–48.

My Dear Boswell, February 7, 1775

I am surprized that, knowing as you do the disposition of your countrymen to tell lies in favour of each other,[1] you can be at all affected by any reports that circulate among them.[2] Mac-

1. Cf. SJ's sentiments in his *Journey*: "A Scotchman must be a very sturdy moralist, who does not love *Scotland* better than the truth: he will always love it better than inquiry; and if falsehood flatters his vanity, will not be very diligent to detect it" (Fleeman, p. 99).

2. On 2 Feb. JB had reported from Edinburgh: "It is confidently told here,

pherson never in his life offered me the sight of any original or of any evidence of any kind, but thought only of intimidating me by noise and threats, till my last answer,—that I would not be deterred from detecting what I thought a cheat, by the menaces of a ruffian,—put an end to our correspondence.[3]

The state of the question is this. He, and Dr. Blair, whom I consider as deceived, say, that he copied the poem from old manuscripts.[4] His copies, if he had them, and I believe him to have none, are nothing. Where are the manuscripts? They can be shown if they exist, but they were never shown. *De non existentibus et non apparentibus*, says our law, *eadem est ratio*.[5] No man has a claim to credit upon his own word, when better evidence, if he had it, may be easily produced. But, so far as we can find, the Erse language was never written till very lately for the purposes of religion. A nation that cannot write, or a language that was never written, has no manuscripts.

But whatever he has, he never offered to show.[6] If old

---

that before your book came out he [Macpherson] sent to you, to let you know that he understood you meant to deny the authenticity of Ossian's poems; that the originals were in his possession; that you might have inspection of them, and might take the evidence of people skilled in the Erse language; and that he hoped, after this fair offer, you would not be so uncandid as to assert that he had refused reasonable proof. That you paid no regard to his message, but published your strong attack upon him; that then he wrote a letter to you, in such terms as he thought suited to one who had not acted as a man of veracity" (*Life* II.295).

3. *Ante* To James Macpherson, 20 Jan. 1775 and n. 3.

4. "The compositions of Ossian are so strongly marked with characters of antiquity, that although there were no external proof to support that antiquity, hardly any reader of judgment and taste, could hesitate in referring them to a very remote aera. . . . the high antiquity of these poems [is] out of question. Especially when we consider, that if there had been any imposture in this case, it must have been contrived and executed in the Highlands of Scotland, two or three centuries ago; as up to this period, both by manuscripts, and by the testimony of a multitude of living witnesses, concerning the uncontrovertible tradition of these poems, they can clearly be traced" (Hugh Blair, *A Critical Dissertation on the Poems of Ossian*, 1763, pp. 16, 19).

5. *De non existentibus et non apparentibus eadem est ratio*: "What cannot be produced must be treated as nonexistent."

6. Macpherson claimed that in 1762 he had left the original manuscripts at the bookshop of his London publisher, Thomas Becket, but that no one had looked at them. In Jan. 1775 Becket published in several London newspapers an adver-

manuscripts should now be mentioned, I should, unless there were more evidence than can be easily had, suppose them another proof of Scotch conspiracy in national falsehood.

Do not censure the expression; you know it to be true.

Dr. Memis's question is so narrow as to allow no speculation; and I have no facts before me but those which his advocate has produced against you.[7]

I consulted this morning the President of the London College of Physicians,[8] who says, that with us, *Doctor of Physick* (we do not say *Doctor of Medicine*) is the highest title that a practicer of physick can have; that *Doctor* implies not only *Physician*, but teacher of physick; that every *Doctor* is legally a *Physician*, but no man, not a *Doctor*, can *practice physick* but by *licence* particularly granted. The Doctorate is a licence of itself. It seems to us a very slender cause of prosecution.

* * * * * *[9]

I am now engaged, but in a little time I hope to do all you would have. My compliments to Madam and Veronica. I am, Sir, Your most humble servant,

SAM. JOHNSON

---

tisement that supported Macpherson's claim (Fleeman, pp. xxxv, 218; *Life* II.294, 510–11).

7. *Ante* to JB, 28 Jan. 1775; *Ante* To Thomas Lawrence, 7 Feb. 1775 and n. 1.

8. *Ante* To Thomas Lawrence, 7 Feb. 1775.

9. In the *Life* JB suppressed a passage that his journal reveals: "He was angry with me for begging to be allowed to read to more people than to Lord Hailes some verses on Inchkenneth which he had sent me. He said, 'Your love of publication is offensive and disgusting, and will end, if it be not reformed, in a general distrust among all your friends'" (*Boswell: The Ominous Years*, ed. Charles Ryskamp and F. A. Pottle, 1963, pp. 63–64).

John Taylor

THURSDAY 9 FEBRUARY 1775

MS: Houghton Library.

ENDORSEMENT: 9 Feby. 1775.

Dear Sir: Febr. 9, 1775

I do not conceive myself able to judge of the question between you and that wild Woman.[1] While I imagined her actuated by zeal for the advancement of her family, and desirous to aggrandise or enrich her brothers,[2] I thought her conduct not unreasonable, but I now consider her as the slave of her own appetites, as a being that acts only but by the grossest motives.

I would have you, if you try the cause, push on the business as fast as you can, that you may rid your mind of anxiety.[3] I am alarmed at what you tell me of your perturbation and uneasiness. When you find any painful idea laying siege to your mind, drive it off immediately, and if you cannot master it, do not trust yourself alone; converse rather with your gardiner or coachman. Those thought[s] with which we know that we have nothing to do, and which haunt us against our will, are always morbid. They are most dangerous in the night, when one can neither rise nor sleep, in that case always have a lamp, and read till you are sleepy. I cannot but think that it would be better for you to change your place.

1. It is likely that SJ refers to the beginning of a protracted legal dispute between Taylor and Mary Rhudde (or "Rudd"), the wife of Anthony Rhudde of Uttoxeter, Staffordshire. Mrs. Rhudde's first husband was Ralph Wood of Market Bosworth, a nephew of Taylor's first wife. Taylor charged the Rhuddes with conspiring to set aside a deed of settlement for certain lands, made by Ralph Wood in Taylor's favor (Thomas Taylor, *Life of John Taylor*, 1910, pp. 64–66; *Life* IV.537). *Post* To John Taylor, 23 Dec. 1775; 7 Mar. 1776; *Post* To Hester Thrale, 14 May 1776.

2. Mary Rhudde's brothers were the antiquarian Thomas Astle and Captain Daniel Astle (*c.* 1743–1826) of the 46th Foot, whom SJ had known since 1765 (*Life* IV.536–37; Waingrow, pp. 180–81).

3. Taylor's dispute with the Rhuddes dragged on into 1780 (Taylor, *Life of John Taylor*, p. 66; *Post* To Hester Thrale, 23 May 1780; 6 June 1780).

I bound young Davenport last tuesday; and hope he will be able to get a living at his trade.[4] I told Miss that I was writing to You, and she sends her compliments.[5]

Take great care of your health both of body and mind and do not let melancholy thoughts lay hold on you. If they once get possession, you may never shake them off. I am, Dear Sir, affectionately yours,

SAM. JOHNSON

4. *Ante* To William Strahan, 22 Dec. 1774 and n. 2; *Post* To John Taylor, 8 Apr. 1775.

5. Cf. *Ante* To John Taylor, 20 Oct. 1774.

James Boswell

SATURDAY 25 FEBRUARY 1775

PRINTED SOURCE: JB's *Life*, 1791, I.456–57.

Dear Sir, Feb. 25, 1775

I am sorry that I could get no books for my friends in Scotland. Mr. Strahan has at last promised to send two dozen to you.[1] If they come, put the names of my friends into them; you may cut them out, and paste them with a little starch in the book.

You then are going wild about Ossian. Why do you think any part can be proved?[2] The dusky manuscript of Egg is probably not fifty years old; if it be an hundred, it proves nothing. The tale of Clanranald has no proof.[3] Has Clanranald

1. Copies of the second edition were presented to Alexander Dick, John Maclaurin, Macleod of Raasay, and Lord Monboddo (Fleeman, p. xxvi).

2. *Ante* To JB, 7 Feb. 1775. On 18 Feb. JB had replied, "After all that has passed, I think the matter is capable of being proved to a certain degree" (*Life* II.309).

3. "I am told that Macpherson got one old Erse MS. from Clanranald, . . . and it is affirmed, that the Gaelick (call it Erse or call it Irish,) has been written in the Highlands and Hebrides for many centuries. . . . There is now come to this

10

You are perhaps imagining that I am withdrawn from the gay and the busy world into regions of peace and pastoral felicity, and am enjoying the reliques of the golden age; that I am surveying Nature's magnificence from a mountain, or remarking her minuter beauties on the flowery bank of a winding rivulet, that I am invigorating myself in the Sunshine, or delighting my imagination with being hidden from the invasion of human evils and human passions, in the darkness of a Thicket, that I am busy in gathering Shells and pebbles on the Shore, or contemplative on a rock, from which I look upon the water and consider how many waves are rolling between me and Streatham. The use of travelling is to regulate imagination by reality, and instead of thinking how things may be, to see them as they are. Here are mountains which I should once have climbed, but to climb steeps is now very laborious, and to descend them dangerous, and I am now content with knowing that by scrambling up a rock, I shall only see other rocks, and a wider circuit of barren desolation. Of Streams we have here a sufficient number, but they murmur not upon pebbles but upon rocks. Of flowers, if Chloris herself were here, I could present her only with the bloom of Heath. Of Lawns and Thickets, he must read, that would know them, for here is little Sun and no Shade. On the Sea I look from my windows, but am not much tempted to the Shore

TO HESTER THRALE, 15–21 SEPTEMBER 1773
(Hyde Collection)

Dear Sir

You have reason to reproach me that I have left your last letter so long unanswered, but I had nothing particular to say. Chambers, you find is gone far, and poor Goldsmith is gone much further. He died of a Fever exasperated, as I believe, by the fear of distress. He had raised money and squandered it, by every artifice of acquisition and folly of expence. But let not his frailties be remembred. He was a very great Man.

I have just begun to print my Journey to the Hebrides and am leaving the press to take another journey into Wales, whither Mr Thrale is going to take possession of at least five hundred a year, fallen

TO BENNET LANGTON, 5 JULY 1774

(Hyde Collection)

Mr James Macpherson — I received your foolish and impudent note. Whatever insult is offered me I will do my best to repel, and what I cannot do for myself the Law shall do for me. I will not desist from detecting what I think a cheat, from any fear of the menaces of a Ruffian.

You want me to retract. What shall I retract? I thought your book an imposture from the beginning, I think it upon yet surer reasons an imposture still. For this opinion I give the publick my reasons which I here dare you to refute.

TO JAMES MACPHERSON, 20 JANUARY 1775

(Hyde Collection)

2d

nity. You have brought into the world a rational Being, ~~and~~ have seen him happy during the little life
that has been granted him, and can have no doubt
but that his happiness is ~~[illegible]~~ now permanent and immutable.

When you have obtained by Prayer such tranquillity
as nature will admit, force your attention, as you
can, upon your accustomed duties, and accustomed entertainments. You can do no more for our dear Boy,
but you must not therefore think less on those whom
your attention may make fitter for the place to
which he is gone. I am

Dearest, dearest Madam

your most affectionate humble Servant,

Lichfield
March 25. 1776

Sam: Johnson

TO HESTER THRALE, 25 MARCH 1776

(Hyde Collection)

told it? Can he prove it? There are, I believe, no Erse manuscripts. None of the old families had a single letter in Erse that we heard of. You say it is likely that they could write. The learned, if any learned there were, could; but knowing by that learning some written language, in that language they wrote, as letters had never been applied to their own. If there are manuscripts, let them be shewn, with some proof that they are not forged for the occasion. You say many can remember parts of Ossian. I believe all those parts are versions of the English, at least there is no proof of their antiquity.

Macpherson is said to have made some translations himself; and having taught a boy to write it, ordered him to say that he had learned it of his grandmother. The boy, when he grew up, told the story. This Mrs. Williams heard at Mr. Strahan's table. Do not be credulous; you know how little a Highlander can be trusted.[4] Macpherson is, so far as I know, very quiet. Is not that proof enough? Every thing is against him. No visible manuscript; no inscription in the language: no correspondence among friends: no transaction of business, of which a single scrap remains in the ancient families. Macpherson's pretence is, that the character was Saxon.[5] If he had not talked unskilfully of *manuscripts*, he might have fought with oral tradition much longer. As to Mr. Grant's information, I suppose he knows much less of the matter than ourselves.[6]

---

city, Ranald Macdonald from the Isle of Egg, who has several MSS. of Erse poetry. . . . This man says, that some of his manuscripts are ancient; . . . one of them which was shewn to me does appear to have the duskyness of antiquity" (JB to SJ, 18 Feb. 1775, *Life* II.309).

4. Cf. *Ante* To JB, 7 Feb. 1775 and n. 1.

5. SJ repeats a point he had made in his *Journey*: "The editor has been heard to say, that part of the poem was received by him, in the Saxon character" (Fleeman, p. 98). According to J. D. Fleeman, "By this SJ must have meant the Old English or 'Anglo-Saxon' letter forms, a style which he rightly regarded as implausible for any Gaelic writing" (Fleeman, p. 219).

6. JB had reported to SJ, "One of the Grants . . . seemed to hope he should be able to convince you of the antiquity of a good proportion of the poems of Ossian" (*Life* II.308–9). JB refers either to Gregory Grant (d. 1803), M.D., a prominent Edinburgh physician, or to Colquhoun Grant (d. 1792), W.S. (*Boswell: The Ominous*

In the mean time, the bookseller says that the sale is sufficiently quick. They printed four thousand.[7] Correct your copy wherever it is wrong,[8] and bring it up. Your friends will all be glad to see you.[9] I think of going myself into the country about May.[10]

I am sorry that I have not managed to send the books sooner. I have left four for you, and do not restrict you absolutely to follow my directions in the distribution. You must use your own discretion.

Make my compliments to Mrs. Boswell; I suppose she is now just beginning to forgive me. I am, dear Sir, Your humble servant,

SAM. JOHNSON

Years, ed. Charles Ryskamp and F. A. Pottle, 1963, p. 67; John Kay, *A Series of Original Portraits*, 1877, II.109–11).

7. "Demand in 1775 was considerable. . . . Not only did the publishers release 4,000 copies on the market, but several other reprints quickly competed for sale" (Fleeman, p. xxvii). However, the fact that copies of the second edition were still available in 1777 suggests that sales may have slackened rather quickly (Fleeman, p. xxv).

8. Cf. *Ante* To Hester Thrale, 17 Dec. 1774 and n. 3.

9. JB arrived in London 21 Mar. and left 22 May (Ryskamp and Pottle, *The Ominous Years*, pp. 86, 158).

10. On 29 May SJ left London for Oxford, Lichfield, and Ashbourne (*Post* To John Taylor, 27 May 1775).

Henry Thrale

c. SUNDAY 26 FEBRUARY 1775[1]

MS: Hyde Collection.

Dear Sir:

I beg that you will be pleased to send me an attestation to Mr.

1. See below, n. 3.

Carter's merit.[2] I am going to morrow,[3] and shall leave the pamflet to shift for itself.[4]

You need only say, that You have sufficient knowledge of Mr. Carter to testify that he is eminently Skilful in the art which he professes, and that he is a man of such decency and regularity of manners, that there will be no danger from his example to the Youth of the Colleges, and that therefore You shall consider it as a favour, if leave may be obtained for him to profess horsemanship in the University. I am, Sir, Your most humble Servant,

SAM. JOHNSON

Please to free[5] this Letter to Mrs. Lucy Porter in Lichfield.

2. In 1751 Henry Hyde (1710–53), Viscount Cornbury, the great-grandson of the first Earl of Clarendon, had bequeathed to Oxford the continuation of Lord Clarendon's *History of the Rebellion* and "the other Remains of his Great Grandfather, in the Hands of Trustees, to be printed at . . . [the University] Press, and directed that the Profits arising from the Sale should be employed towards establishing a Riding School in the University" (*Life* II.527). As part of their campaign to assist Charles Carter and his family (*Ante* To William Strahan, 22 Dec. 1774 and n. 3), the Thrales and SJ were attempting to take advantage of this bequest. They proposed to enable Carter "to profess horsemanship in Oxford, at such prices and under such regulations as shall be fixed by the Magistrates of the University" (SJ's undated draft for Henry Thrale, MS: Harry Ransom Center, University of Texas at Austin). The first step was the "attestation" from Henry Thrale to Nathan Wetherell (*Post* To Hester Thrale, 6 Mar. 1775). "By March 1776 agreement had been reached, but the profits arising from the sale of the *Life of Clarendon* were considered insufficient" and the scheme fell through (*Life* II.527; *Post* To John Douglas, 9 Mar. 1776; *Post* To Hester Thrale, 16 Mar. 1776 and n. 1).

3. SJ left for Oxford *c.* 27 Feb. and returned *c.* 10 Mar. (Hester Thrale to SJ, 1 Mar. 1775, 7 Mar. 1775, MSS: Rylands Library; *Post* To William Strahan, 3 Mar. 1775; *Post* To Hester Thrale, 8 Mar. 1775).

4. *Ante* To JB, 21 Jan. 1775, n. 3.

5. *to free*: "to frank" (*OED*).

Lord North

c. MARCH 1775[1]

1. I follow the dating proposed by Mary Hyde, itself based on information supplied by the late Dr. L. F. Powell and by Dr. J. D. Fleeman ("Not in Chapman," in *Johnson, Boswell and Their Circle*, 1965, p. 308). See below, n. 2.

MS: Hyde Collection.

My Lord:

Having heard that Mr. Onslow intends to vacate the borough of Rye,[2] to which Your Lordship, as I am informed can nominate, I have prevailed on Mr. Crutchley,[3] the Gentleman that waits on You with this, to hear such terms as You shall be pleased to propose for the admission of, My Lord ⟨ ⟩[4]

2. Middleton Onslow (d. 1801), M.P. for Rye (1774–Apr. 1775), was elected "as a stop-gap" until his cousin Thomas (1754–1827), son and heir of the first Earl of Onslow, came of age. Thomas turned twenty-one on 15 Mar. and succeeded Middleton on 20 Apr. (Namier and Brooke III.230).

3. Jeremiah Crutchley (1745–1805), of Sunninghill Park, Berkshire, was the putative illegitimate son of Henry Thrale and an intimate member of the family circle (*Thraliana* I.497 and n. 1). Crutchley subsequently (1784) entered Parliament as M.P. for Horsham (Namier and Brooke II.282). SJ clearly did not know of the "succession" (Onslow to Onslow) that made his appeal to North ineffectual.

4. MS: mutilated; lower portion of sheet torn away

William Strahan

WEDNESDAY 1 MARCH 1775

MS: Hyde Collection.

Sir: [Oxford] March 1, 1775

I am sorry to see that all the alterations proposed are evidence of timidity.[1] You may be sure that I do [not] wish to publish, what those for whom I write do not like to have published.[2]

1. Lord North's government, which had commissioned *Taxation No Tyranny* (*Ante* To JB, 21 Jan. 1775 and n. 3), insisted that several of its most vigorous passages be expurgated. According to Donald Greene, "The revisions were ordered because . . . North's policy at the moment was one of somewhat grudging appeasement" (*Works*, Yale ed. X.402). Five proof pages saved by JB (now in the Hyde Collection) document the extent of these changes. Approximately six pages were deleted, including the original conclusion, with its satirical jibes at "King William" (William Pitt) and "the Whigs of America" (*Works*, Yale ed. X.410, 455).

2. Speaking of the enforced changes, SJ told JB: "It was their [the Ministry's]

But print me half a dozen copies in the original state and lay them up for me.[3] It concludes well enough as it is.

When you print it, if you print it, please to frank one to me here, and frank another to Mrs. Aston at Stow Hill, Lichfield.

The changes are not for the better, except where facts were mistaken. The last paragraph was indeed rather contemptuous, there was once more of it which I put out myself. I am, Sir, your humble Servant,

SAM. JOHNSON

business. If an architect says, I will build five stories, and the man who employs him says, I will have only three, the employer is to decide" (*Life* II.313). Cf. *Post* To William Strahan, 3 Mar. 1775.

3. No copies of the Ur-pamphlet (which Strahan may have declined to print) have been recovered (*Works*, Yale ed. x.402).

William Strahan

FRIDAY 3 MARCH 1775

MS: Hyde Collection.

Sir: University College [Oxford] March 3, 1775

Our post is so unskilfully managed that we can very rarely, if ever, answer a letter from London on the day when we receive it. Your pages were sent back the next post, for there was nothing to do.[1] I had no great difficulty in persuading myself to admit the alterations, for why should I in defense of the ministry provoke those, whom in their own defense they dare not provoke.[2]—But are such men fit to be the governours of kingdoms?

They are here much discouraged by the last motion, and undoubtedly every Man's confidence in Government must be

1. The pages in question were the final proofs of *Taxation No Tyranny* (*Works*, Yale ed. x.410–11). SJ had already corrected an earlier set, partially salvaged by JB (*Ante* To William Strahan, 1 Mar. 1775).

2. *Ante* To William Strahan, 1 Mar. 1775 and n. 1.

diminished,[3] yet if Lives can be saved, some deviation from rigid policy may be excused.[4]

I expect to return some time in the next week, perhaps not till the latter end.[5]

Do not omit to have the presentation pamflets, done and sent to Mrs. Williams, and lay by for me the half dozen which you print without correction,[6] and please to send me one by the post of the corrected books. I am, Sir, Your humble Servant,

SAM. JOHNSON

You will send to Mr. Cooper[7] and such as you think proper either in my name or your own.

3. On 27 Feb. the House of Commons had endorsed Lord North's "Propositions for conciliating the Differences with America." These proposals called for the American colonies to contribute "their proportion to the common defence." In return, Parliament would "forbear . . . to levy any duty, tax, or assessment, or to impose any farther duty, tax, or assessment, except only such duties as it may be expedient to continue to levy or to impose for the regulation of commerce" (*Parliamentary History of England*, 1813, XVIII.319–20, 358). These ineffectual gestures toward appeasement met with widespread disdain. According to Horace Walpole: "The gates of Janus's temple are opened and shut every other day; the porter has a sad time of it, and deserves a reversion for three lives. We are sending the Americans a sprig of olive, lapped up in an Act for a famine next year" (*Walpole's Correspondence*, Yale ed. XXVIII.179).

4. Cf. SJ's sentiments in *Taxation No Tyranny*: "I cannot forbear to wish, that this commotion may end without bloodshed, and that the rebels may be subdued by terrour rather than by violence; and therefore recommend such a force as may take away, not only the power, but the hope of resistance, and by conquering without a battle, save many from the sword" (*Works*, Yale ed. X.451–52).

5. *Ante* To Henry Thrale, *c.* 26 Feb. 1775, n. 3.

6. *Ante* To William Strahan, 1 Mar. 1775 and n. 3.

7. It is likely that SJ refers to Grey Cooper (*c.* 1726–1801), M.P. (1765–90) and Secretary to the Treasury (1765–82), who seems to have acted as liaison between the Ministry and SJ (Namier and Brooke II.250; *Works*, Yale ed. X.401).

Hester Thrale

FRIDAY 3 MARCH 1775

MS: Hyde Collection.

Dear Madam: University College [Oxford] March 3, 1775

I am afraid that something has happened to occupy your mind disagreeably, and hinder you from writing to me, or thinking about me.

The fate of my proposal for our Friend Mr. Carter will be decided on Monday.[1] Those whom I have spoken to are all friends. I have not abated any part of the entrance, or payment, for it has not been thought too much,[2] and I hope he will have scholars.

I am very deaf, and yet cannot well help being much in company, though it is often very uncomfortable. But when I have done this thing, which, I hope, is a good thing, or find that I cannot do it, I wish to live a while under your care and protection.

The imperfection of our post makes it uncertain whether we shall receive letters, sooner than we must send them,[3] this is therefore written while I yet do not know whether you have favoured me or no. I was sufficiently discontented that I heard nothing yesterday. But sure all is well. I am, Dearest Madam, your most obedient and most humble Servant,

SAM. JOHNSON

1. *Ante* To Henry Thrale, *c.* 26 Feb. 1775 and n. 2; *Post* To Hester Thrale, 6 Mar. 1775.

2. Presumably SJ refers to the fees Carter would be authorized to charge his students. Hester Thrale responded, "I am glad there was no need to abate the Price" (7 Mar. 1775, MS: Rylands Library).

3. Cf. *Ante* To William Strahan, 3 Mar. 1775.

William Strahan

MONDAY 6 MARCH 1775

MS: Houghton Library.

Sir: [University College, Oxford] March 6, 1775

I received the pamflet,[1] but not one scrap of a letter. I have

1. *Ante* To William Strahan, 1 Mar. 1775 and n. 1; 3 Mar. 1775.

shown it about the College, and to me at least it is commended. I shall stay here but a little while, and should be glad of about a dozen and half to give to my friends here. Please to send them by the coach on Wednesday, and on thursday I can distribute them, and write me a little piece of a letter. I am, Sir, Your most humble servant,

SAM. JOHNSON

Hester Thrale

MONDAY 6 MARCH 1775

MS: Houghton Library.

Dear Madam: [University College, Oxford] March 6, 1775

Leave was given about two hours ago to Mr. Carter to profess horsemanship in Oxford.[1] It is expected that he wait on the Vicechancellor[2] to receive such directions about hours, and other particulars as may make his exercises consistent with the other parts of education. If he comes before friday I shall attend him.

I have no place for him, but several are mentioned, which he must come and examine. I doubt he must pay rent for that which he has. It is generally believed that he will have a sufficient number of Scholars.

I have wished to hear from you every post, and am uneasy. Sure all is well.

Mr. Thrale's letter to Dr. Wetherel was very efficacious, every body was spoken to, and every [thing] was done by him to promote the design.

You know I owe two guineas to Mr. Carter's expedition, be so kind as to advance them, for I cannot spare them here.

Do write to me. I am, Madam, Your most humble Servant,

SAM. JOHNSON

1. *Ante* To Henry Thrale, *c.* 26 Feb. 1775 and n. 2; *Ante* To Hester Thrale, 3 Mar. 1775.

2. Thomas Fothergill (1716–96), D.D., Provost of Queen's College, Oxford, and Vice-Chancellor (1772–76) (*Alum. Oxon.* II.ii.483; *History of the University of Oxford*, ed. L. S. Sutherland and L. G. Mitchell, 1986, v.889).

Hester Thrale

WEDNESDAY 8 MARCH 1775

MS: Hyde Collection.

ADDRESS: To Henry Thrale, Esq., in Southwark.

POSTMARKS: OXFORD, ⟨9⟩ MR, FREE.

Dear Madam: [University College, Oxford] March 8

Yesterday (March 7) I received from you two letters, of March 1 and March 4. Such is the fidelity of Somebody.[1] I wondered why you forgot me, and did not know but you were angry.

I hope Mr. Carter is coming.[2] Dr. Wetherel is busy thinking on a place for him,[3] and Mr. Scot thinks he can secure him six Scholars to begin with, and says, that rather than the Scheme shall miscarry he will ride himself. I really hope it will do.

If he comes to night, I will take him to the Vice chancellor to morrow,[4] and perhaps to some other of the heads. I shall then have done that for which I came, and hope to get into the tower on friday night.[5]

Poor Boy, what a dreadful death.[6] I hope you will let none of your children go alone into that danger, nor go yourself.

Queeny perhaps is a little lovesick, you will see how she recovers when I come home.[7]

I think Evans to blame in despairing of young Carter, he

1. In at least one instance the post office was the culprit: Hester Thrale's letter of 1 Mar. (MS: Rylands Library) is postmarked "2 MR"; her letter of 4 Mar. has not been recovered.

2. *Ante* To Hester Thrale, 6 Mar. 1775.

3. *Ante* To Hester Thrale, 6 Mar. 1775.

4. *Ante* To Hester Thrale, 6 Mar. 1775, n. 2.

5. At the Thrales' house in Southwark SJ occupied a room above the counting house that was called "the round tower" (Clifford, 1952, p. 68).

6. In her letter of 1 Mar. Hester Thrale had reported, "Harry and his Companions were gone down the Brewhouse Yard ten Minutes before, when a violent Shriek was heard and a Boy said to be scalded—he was got out immediately indeed and carried home, but died the Day after in sad Torment" (MS: Rylands Library).

7. According to her mother, "Hester [Maria] has been very sick indeed and taken up all my Thoughts" (Hester Thrale to SJ, 1 Mar. 1775, MS: Rylands Library).

should persist in his medicines, he can but dye, and young people will recover from great weakness.[8]

Mr. Cadel says that he has yet so many of Mr. Baretti's book unsold,[9] that he is not ready for a new edition, but, will, I suppose, be willing to treat when he has occasion to reprint. I am, Madam, Your most obedient Servant,

SAM. JOHNSON

8. Charles Carter's son was ill with worms. Hester Thrale had informed SJ, "The dying Boy too, though given over by Evans, has still a *voracious Appetite* I hear" (1 Mar. 1775, MS: Rylands Library). SJ and Hester Thrale "applied to the famous man [the apothecary Mr. Evans] at Knightsbridge—but too late, the Creatures had eat into the Intestines and the Boy died" (*Thraliana* 1.117–18). *Ante* To William Strahan, 22 Dec. 1774, n. 3.

9. The book in question may be Giuseppe Baretti's *Introduction to the most useful European Languages*, published by Cadell and Davies in 1772.

Edmund Hector

THURSDAY 23 MARCH 1775

MS: Houghton Library.

ADDRESS: To Mr. Hector at Birmingham.

FRANK: Hfreethrale.

POSTMARKS: 23 MR, FREE, [Undeciphered].

Dear Sir: March 23, 1775

I omitted to return you thanks for your kind present of china, because I knew that Mrs. Thrale would make her own acknowledgments.[1]

I shall think it a favour if you will take opportunity of applying to the Rector of *Kingsnorton* a parish not far from Birmingham,[2] for the dates of the Christenings of the several children of Cornelius Ford, who formerly lived at the *Haunch* in his

1. *Ante* To Edmund Hector, 4 Feb. 1775 and n. 1.

2. The parish of Kings Norton was not a separate living until 1846; from 1771 to 1783 the curate was Thomas Edwards (information supplied by Mrs. H.V.F. Goodger, Parish Archivist, St. Nicolas, Kings Norton).

parish.[3] Of those Children the eldest was Joseph born, I believe, about 1660, and the youngest Nathanael, in all they were eight.[4] My original curiosity is after Sarah, who was my Mother.

I have lately written a pamflet concerning our American disputes, which I will take care to transmit to you.[5]

Be pleased to make my compliments to dear Mrs. Careless.[6] I am, Sir, Your affectionate, humble Servant,

SAM. JOHNSON

3. In 1649 SJ's maternal great-grandmother, Mary Ford, acquired the estate of Haunch Hall, Kings Norton, Worcestershire (now Warwickshire), five miles southwest of the center of Birmingham. "The estate was bought especially" for her son Cornelius Ford (1632–1709) (*Johns. Glean.* III.31; Nikolaus Pevsner and Alexandra Wedgwood, *Warwickshire*, 1966, p. 187). In 1731 the estate was mortgaged by SJ's cousin, the Rev. Cornelius Ford (*Johns. Glean.* III.31).

4. Cornelius Ford (SJ's grandfather) had eight children: Joseph (1662–1720), Benjamin (b. 1663), Phoebe (b. 1665), Mary (b. 1667), Sarah (1669–1759), Samuel (b. 1672), Cornelius (d. 1734), and Nathaniel (1676–1729) (*Reades*, Pedigree XXIX).

5. *Ante* To JB, 21 Jan. 1775, n. 3.

6. *Ante* To Hester Thrale, Early July 1770, n. 11.

John Taylor

THURSDAY 23 MARCH 1775

MS: Hyde Collection.

ADDRESS: To The Rev. Dr. Taylor, Ashbourne, Derbys.

FRANK: Hfreethrale.

POSTMARKS: 23 MR, FREE, [Undeciphered].

ENDORSEMENTS: 1775, 23 March 75.

Dear Sir: March 23, 1775

I am told that your month of residence is April,[1] and that you are making so[me] attempts to defer it, till a further time in Summer. I cannot judge of your convenience, but considering

1. Taylor, as one of twelve prebendaries of Westminster Abbey (*Ante* To John Taylor, 2 Jan. 1743, n. 9), was required to spend one month a year in residence at Westminster (*A House of Kings*, ed. Edward Carpenter, 1966, pp. 214–15).

my own, I wish you to be here in April, because, I think, I can very commodiously accompany you to Derbyshire in May, and the following months will not suit me so well.[2]

I am again gotten into politicks, and have written a pamflet in answer to the American Congress.[3] I shall send it you. I am, Sir, Yours etc.

SAM. JOHNSON

2. Taylor persisted in postponing his "month of residence," and SJ readjusted his travel plans, eventually spending almost a full month at Ashbourne, 29 June–25 July (*Post* To Hester Thrale, 1 July 1775; 26 July 1775; *Post* To John Taylor, 8 Apr. 1775; 13 Apr. 1775; 27 May 1775).

3. *Ante* To JB, 21 Jan. 1775, n. 3.

Benjamin Wheeler[1]

THURSDAY 30 MARCH 1775

MS: Hyde Collection.

Sir: At Mr. Thrale's in Southwark, March 30, 1775

I beg leave to lay before you an inscription which the Editor perceives too late, to have been negligently or unskilfully copied.[2] I have made myself so little acquainted with the lapidary language that I am not willing to venture upon it, nor believe myself able to set it right. If any Gentleman used to read inscriptions will try his Skill upon it, he will do a favour to the authour of the travels, whom I do not know, to the Bookseller who has applied to me,[3] and to, Sir, Your most humble servant,

SAM. JOHNSON

1. Benjamin Wheeler (*c.* 1733–83), D.D., Fellow of Magdalen College, Oxford, Professor of Poetry (1766–76), Sedleian Professor of Natural Philosophy (1767–82), later (1776–83) Regius Professor of Divinity (*Alum. Oxon.* II.iv.1534). SJ refers repeatedly to Wheeler as "my learned friend" (e.g. *Post* To Charles Lawrence, 30 Aug. 1780).

2. *Post* To Benjamin Wheeler, 15 Apr. 1775 and n. 1.

3. The bookseller was Edward Dilly (*Post* To Benjamin Wheeler, 15 Apr. 1775).

Hester Thrale

SATURDAY 1 APRIL 1775

MS: Hyde Collection.

Madam: Apr. 1, 1775

I had mistaken the day on which I was to dine with Mr. Bruce, and hear of Abissinia, and therefore am to dine this day with Mr. Hamilton.[1]

The news from Oxford is that no tenniscourt can be hired at any price, and that the Vicechancellor will not write to the Clarendon Trustees without some previous intimation that his request will not be unacceptable.[2] We must therefore find some way of applying to Lord Mansfield,[3] who with the Archbishop of York,[4] and the Bishop of Chester[5] holds the trust. Thus are we thrown to a vexatious[6] distance. Poor Carter! do not tell him.

The other Oxford news is, that they have sent me a degree of Doctor of Laws, with such praises in the diploma, as,

1. JB recorded in his journal entry for 1 Apr.: "Mr. Johnson had proposed that he and I should dine together this day at the Mitre. But Mr. Thrale sent me a card that the meeting should hold at his house. Mr. Johnson, however, was engaged to dine today with [William] Gerard Hamilton to meet Bruce the traveller, and, I take it, his having this invitation was the reason of Mr. Thrale's card, that Mr. Johnson might get off" (*Boswell: The Ominous Years*, ed. Charles Ryskamp and F. A. Pottle, 1963, pp. 111–12). James Bruce (1730–94), explorer and travel writer, called "Abyssinian Bruce," had traveled for two years in Africa, 1769–71, searching for the source of the Nile. After dining with Bruce, SJ told JB: "Sir, he is not a distinct relater. I should say that he is neither abounding nor deficient in sense. I did not perceive any superior sense" (Ryskamp and Pottle, *The Ominous Years*, p. 114).

2. *Ante* To Henry Thrale, *c.* 26 Feb. 1775 and n. 2; *Ante* To Hester Thrale, 6 Mar. 1775 and n. 2.

3. William Murray (1705–93), first Baron Mansfield (1756), later (1776) first Earl of Mansfield; Lord Chief Justice, Court of King's Bench (1756–88).

4. Robert Hay Drummond (1711–76), D.D. (1745), Archbishop of York (1761–76).

5. William Markham (1719–1807), D.D., Dean of Christ Church, Oxford, Bishop of Chester (1771–77), later (1777–1807) Archbishop of York.

6. MS: "tious" repeated as catchword

perhaps ought to make me ashamed;[7] they are very like your praises. I wonder whether I shall ever show them to you.

Boswel will be with you.[8] Please to ask Murphy[9] the way to Lord Mansfield. Dr. Wetherel who is now here and will be here for some days is very desirous of seeing the Brewhouse. I hope Mr. Thrale will send him an invitation. He does what he can for Carter.[10]

To day I dine with Hamilton, to morrow with Hoole, on[11] Monday with Paradise,[12] on tuesday with Master and Mistress, on Wednesday with Dilly, but come back to the tower.[13] Sic nunquam rediturus labitur annus.[14] I am, Madam, Your most humble servant,

SAM. JOHNSON

Poor Mrs. Williams is very bad, worse than I ever saw her.

7. Writing to the Vice-Chancellor of Oxford on 23 Mar., Lord North had proposed that SJ be awarded an honorary D.C.L. in recognition of his "many learned labours" (*Life* II.331). North may also have wished to reward SJ for the writing of *Taxation No Tyranny* (*Works*, Yale ed. X.408). The degree was conferred on 30 Mar. and SJ received the diploma on the morning of 1 Apr. For the complete text, see *Life* II.332. According to JB, SJ "did not vaunt of his new dignity, but I understood he was highly pleased with it" (Ryskamp and Pottle, *The Ominous Years*, p. 112).

8. See above, n. 1. That evening JB "walked over London bridge to Mr. Thrale's," where he "had a good dinner." The company included Arthur Murphy and Giuseppe Baretti (Ryskamp and Pottle, *The Ominous Years*, p. 113).

9. SJ refers to Arthur Murphy.

10. Cf. *Ante* To Hester Thrale, 6 Mar. 1775.

11. MS: "on" altered from "to"

12. John Paradise (1743–95), F.R.S., later (1776) D.C.L., a scholar and antiquarian especially noted for his linguistic abilities, entertained SJ regularly at his house in Charles Street, Cavendish Square, and joined SJ's Essex Head Club at its foundation in 1783. "Although it is impossible to say when and under what circumstances the acquaintanceship began, it seems likely that it was already well advanced [in 1775]. . . . Of the half a dozen men who might have introduced them the most likely is Bennet Langton" (A. B. Shepperson, *John Paradise and Lucy Ludwell*, 1942, p. 100).

13. *Ante* To Hester Thrale, 8 Mar. 1775 and n. 5.

14. *sic nunquam rediturus labitur annus*: "thus, never returning, the year glides by" (perhaps a reminiscence of Horace, *Odes* II.xiv.1–2, conflated with Tibullus, I.viii.47–48).

Hester Thrale

MONDAY 3 APRIL 1775

PRINTED SOURCE: Chapman II.22.
ADDRESS: To Mrs. Thrale.

Madam: Apr. 3. 1775

I have this morning received an invitation to dine to morrow with Mrs. Montagu, and am to dine on Thursday at Davis's.[1] I wish Mr. Thrale would invite Dr. Wetherel for Friday, but you must have something not flesh.

So I am taken hold of; I would come home at night but you will not let me. I intend not to forget Mr. Carter. You must give Laura a good scolding before her Mistress; if she is turned out of the school, I am afraid she is ruined.[2]

While I sit at this paper I have a summons to dine with the Club on Friday, which I shall be expected to obey.

If Dr. Wetherel were with you to morrow, I could come in the afternoon. He lodges with Perrot and Hodgson over the Crown office Temple.[3] I⟨f⟩ you send me an invitation to bring him some morning it will do. Thursday Morning will fit.

I am, Dearest of all dear Ladies, Your servant and slave, and admirer, and honourer,

SAM. JOHNSON

1. SJ refers to Thomas Davies.

2. In addition to helping Charles Carter and his eldest son, Hester Thrale was doing her best to improve the lot of Laura, Carter's eldest daughter. She herself had taught Laura to read, then "put her to School to learn washing—ironing Lace-mending, clearstarching and such like . . . and then took her into my Nursery" (*Thraliana* I.117). Laura proved too arrogant to be kept as a servant, so she was sent to a boarding school run by Hester Thrale's childhood friend, Elizabeth Thornton Cumyns. There she was "so troublesome and insolent that I know not what we shall do with her" (Hester Thrale to SJ, 1 Apr. 1775, MS: Rylands Library). *Post* To Hester Thrale, 22 May 1775.

3. Crown Office Row, in the Temple precincts on the north side of the Inner Temple Gardens, had been constructed in 1737 (Wheatley and Cunningham I.480).

Thomas Fothergill

FRIDAY 7 APRIL 1775

MS: Beinecke Library. The transcript (in the hand of Thomas Fothergill) used as copy for JB's *Life*.

7 Id. Apr. 1775

Viro reverendo Thomæ Fothergil, S. T. P.
Universitatis Oxoniensis Vicecancellario
S.P.D.
Sam. Johnson.

Multis non est opus, ut Testimonium quo, Te præside, Oxonienses Nomen meum posteris commendârunt, quali animo acceperim compertum faciam.[1] Nemo sibi placens non lætatur; nemo sibi non placet qui vobis, literarum Arbitris, placere potuit. Hoc tamen habet incommodi tantum Beneficium, quod mihi nunquam posthac sine vestræ Famæ detrimento vel labi liceat vel cessare; semperque sit timendum, ne quod mihi tam eximiæ Laudi est, Vobis aliquando fiat Opprobrio. Vale.

1. *Ante* To Hester Thrale, 1 Apr. 1775 and n. 7.

Edward Bentham[1]

SATURDAY 8 APRIL 1775

MS: Hyde Collection.

ENDORSEMENT in an unidentified hand: Dr. S. Johnson, Apr. 8 75, To Dr. Bentham, T.B.

Sir: April 8, 1775

It might perhaps have the appearance of romantick ambition to say, that I regret that want of opposition which made your benevolent eloquence unnecessary, but at least I may [be] al-

1. Edward Bentham (1707–76), D.D., Canon of Christ Church (1754–76), Regius Professor of Divinity (1763–76), and author of *De Studiis Theologicis* (1764). In 1776 SJ and JB visited Bentham at Oxford, and were "much pleased" by his "learned and lively conversation" (*Life* II.445).

lowed to rejoice at the rumour of opposition which has produced from a Mind like yours, such a testimony in my favour.[2] Having so much of your approbation I hope to be admitted to your friendship, and shall applaud myself, if the opinion of my merit which my writings have impressed upon such a judge, is not impaired by more familiar knowledge. I am, Sir, Your most obliged and most humble servant,

SAM. JOHNSON

2. It seems likely that Bentham had anticipated resistance in Convocation to the awarding of SJ's honorary D.C.L. (*Ante* To Hester Thrale, 1 Apr. 1775, n. 7). On 14 Apr. Nathan Wetherell told JB that "he had managed the getting Mr. Johnson's diploma from Oxford, as in so numerous a body some management was required to unite them. I could gather that there were at Oxford some who did not admire and reverence Mr. Johnson as some of us do" (*Boswell: The Ominous Years*, ed. Charles Ryskamp and F. A. Pottle, 1963, p. 144).

John Taylor

SATURDAY 8 APRIL 1775

MS: Berg Collection, New York Public Library.

ADDRESS: To The Revd. Dr. Taylor at Ashborne, Derbys.

FRANK: Hfreethrale.

POSTMARKS: 8 AP, FREE.

ENDORSEMENTS: 1775, 8 April 75.

Dear Sir: April 8, 1775

When shall I come down to you? I believe I can get away pretty early in May, if you have any mind of me; If you have none, I can move in some other direction.[1] So tell me what I shall do.

I have placed young Davenport in the greatest printing house in London, and hear no complaint of him but want of size, which will not hinder him much.[2] He may when he is a journeyman always get a guinea a week.

The patriots pelt me with answers. Four pamflets I think,

1. *Ante* To John Taylor, 23 Mar. 1775, n. 2.

2. *Ante* To William Strahan, 22 Dec. 1774 and n. 2.

already, besides newspapers and reviews, have been discharged against me.[3] I have tried to read two of them, but did not go through them.

Now and then I call on Congreve, though I have little or no reason to think that he wants[4] or wishes to see me. I sometimes dispute with him, but I think he has not studied. He has really ill health, and seems to have given way to that indulgence which sickness is always in too much haste to claim. He confesses a bottle aday.[5] I am, Sir, Your humble Servant,

SAM. JOHNSON

3. "The reception of the work was explosively hostile: within a very few weeks a flood of attacking pamphlets appeared, *An Answer to a Pamphlet Entitled Taxation No Tyranny, Tyranny Unmasked, The Pamphlet Entitled Taxation No Tyranny Candidly Considered,* even one entitled *Taxation Tyranny*" (*Works*, Yale ed. x.408). For a complete listing of pamphlets and newspaper attacks, see *Bibliography*, pp. 125–26; H. L. McGuffie, *Samuel Johnson in the British Press, 1749–1784*, 1976, pp. 150–74.

4. *to want*: "to be without something fit or necessary" (SJ's *Dictionary*).

5. *Ante* To John Taylor, 22 Dec. 1774 and n. 3.

John Taylor

THURSDAY 13 APRIL 1775

MS: Hyde Collection.

ADDRESS: To the Reverend Dr. Taylor in Ashbourne, Derbyshire.

POSTMARK: 13 AP.

ENDORSEMENTS: 1775, 13 April 75.

Dear Sir: Apr. 13, 1775

Your letter did not miscarry. When your enquiry came I consulted Mr. Thrale, who told me, that less than two hundred guineas would not buy a Governours staff.[1] Mrs. Thrale who is more copious, informed me, that you might for a hundred pounds be made a kind of half governour, with so many limitations and restrictions that there would [be] no advantage in

1. Apparently Taylor, always on the lookout for lucrative appointments, was thinking of purchasing himself a directorial position.

it. I then let it out of my head. You may probably do more good with two hundred pounds in other ways.

I hope to pass some time with you in[2] Derbyshire early in the summer.[3] We will concert the visit, if we can, so as to accommodate[4] us both.

How is your health? I have had of late very bad nights, and have taken physick three days together in hope of better.

I hope poor Davenport will do.[5] His temper is well spoken of, and I have recommended him as far as I well can. He is now launched into the world, and is to subsist henceforward by his own powers. The transition from the protection of others to our own conduct is a very awful point of human existence. I am, Sir, Your most humble servant,

SAM. JOHNSON

2. MS: "in" superimposed upon "at"

3. *Ante* To John Taylor, 23 Mar. 1775, n. 2.

4. MS: "acccommodate"

5. *Ante* To William Strahan, 22 Dec. 1774 and n. 2; *Ante* To John Taylor, 8 Apr. 1775.

Benjamin Wheeler

SATURDAY 15 APRIL 1775

MS: Hyde Collection.

ADDRESS: The Revd. Dr. Wheeler, Magdalen College, Oxford.

FRANK: ffree W. Strahan.

POSTMARKS: 15 AP, FREE, [Undeciphered].

Dear Sir: Apr. 15, 1775

The Bookseller has just now brought me the transcript of the Stone at Genoa.[1] I hope that between this paper and Gruter[2]

1. It is almost certain that SJ refers to an inscription (the record of a land dispute in Republican Rome) found outside Genoa in 1506; in the mid-eighteenth century it was kept in the Town Hall (*Corpus Inscriptionum Latinarum*, ed. Theodor Mommsen et al., 1877, v.886–88, No. 7749; information supplied by Professor G. W. Bowersock). There is no record that this inscription (the *Sententia Minuciorum*) was published in England: either the "authour of the travels" (*Ante* To Benjamin Wheeler, 30 Mar. 1775) eliminated the text or his book never appeared.

2. SJ refers to the *Inscriptiones Antiquae Totius Orbis Romani* (1602) by Janus Gruterus (1560–1627).

you will be able to adjust the reading. You will forgive this trouble. I know not where to find Gruter in London, if we knew how to make use of him, and perhaps we could not use him if we had him.

Be pleased to return the papers, when you have finished them, to Mr. Dilly Bookseller in the Poultry.[3] I am, Sir, Your most humble Servant,

SAM. JOHNSON

3. SJ refers to Edward, the elder of the two Dilly brothers.

Bennet Langton[1]

MONDAY 17 APRIL 1775

MS: Hyde Collection.

Dear Sir: Apr. 17, 1775

I have enquired more minutely about the medicine for the rheumatism which I am sorry to hear that you still want. The receipt is this.

Take equal quantities of flour of Sulphur, and *flour* of Mustardseed, make them an electary[2] with honey or treacle; and take a bolus[3] as big as a nutmeg several times a day, as you can bear it, drinking after it a quarter of a pint of the infusion of the root of Lovage.

Lovage in Ray's Nomenclature,[4] is Levisticum, perhaps the Botanists may know the Latin name.

Of this medicine I pretend not to judge. There is all the appearance of its efficacy which a single instance can afford.

1. This letter, which appears in the second edition of the *Life*, is headed "To Bennet Langton, Esq." (1793, II.632).

2. *electuary*: "a form of medicine made of conserves and powders, in the consistence of honey" (SJ's *Dictionary*).

3. *bolus*: "a form of medicine, in which the ingredients are made up into a soft mass, larger than pills, to be swallowed at once" (SJ's *Dictionary*).

4. SJ refers to the *Dictionariolum Trilingue* (1675) by John Ray (1627–1705). In later editions the Dictionary is called *Nomenclator Classicus sive Dictionariolum Trilingue*.

The Patient was very old, the pain very violent, and the relief, I think, speedy and lasting.

My opinion of alterative medicines is not high,[5] but quid tentâsse nocebit?[6] if it does harm, or does no good, it may be omitted, but that it may do good, you have I hope, reason to think is desired, by, Sir, Your most affectionate, humble Servant,

SAM. JOHNSON

5. "Medicines called *alterative*, are such as have no immediate sensible operation, but gradually gain upon the constitution, by changing the humours from a state of distemperature to health. They are opposed to *evacuants*" (explanatory quotation, SJ's *Dictionary*).

6. *sed quid temptare nocebit*: "But what harm will it do to try" (Ovid, *Metamorphoses* I.397, trans. F. J. Miller, Loeb ed.).

Charlotte Lennox

TUESDAY 2 MAY 1775

MS: Houghton Library.

ENDORSEMENT: Doctor Johnson, may be published.

Madam: May 2, 1775

In soliciting subscriptions, as perhaps in many other cases, too much eagerness defeats itself.[1] We must leave our friends to their own motives and their own opportunities. Your subscription can hardly fail of success, but you must wait its progress. By telling your friends how much you expect from them you discourage them, for they finding themselves unequal to your expectation, will rather do nothing and be quiet, than do their utmost, and yet not please. You complain of Miss Reynolds who probably knows not three people whom She can properly solicite. Sir Joshua has made it a rule to act on these occasions only as a Gentleman. When Miss Reynolds used to lay my

1. At the beginning of January SJ had composed *Proposals for Printing by Subscription, Dedicated to the Queen, A New and Elegant Edition, Enlarged and Corrected, of the Original Works of Mrs. Charlotte Lennox*. These *Proposals* appeared in March, but the edition itself was never published (*Works*, Yale ed. I.224; *Life* II.509; M. R. Small, *Charlotte Ramsay Lennox*, 1935, pp. 43, 259).

proposals in the way of the Sitters, he always hid them, and undoubtedly did right.[2]

You tell me of a numerous acquaintance, and of the vain and the gay, who will be proud of standing in the same list with the Queen.[3] Among those whom I know how many are there to whom I should be welcome if I asked them for a Guinea? With the Vain and the Gay I cannot be supposed to have much conversation, nor indeed with any who will enquire the opinion of the court upon the matter.

Do not think that I advise you to desist or to despair. I think you will certainly succeed to a moderate, and probably, to an eminent degree. Your powers are acknowledged, and your character must be respected, if it be not hurt by some ⟨indecencies⟩[4] with respect to religion, of which I have heard complaints.[5]

As to your being a ⟨*four or five words*⟩[6] that concerns only your intimates, and cannot operate upon the subscription. Your manners as far as the publick needs to know, are very elegant and ladylike.

I therefore venture to tell you again, that in my opinion you will have no reason to fear, but you must be a little patient. The work must be done principally by the great Ladies.

I had not written this, but that Mr. Lennox, who if not a good solicitor, is a special teazer, had not told me that he could not go without it. I am, Madam, Your most obedient servant,

SAM. JOHNSON

Once more, I think you will succeed. Send your proposals to every hand without expressing large expectations.

2. It is likely that SJ refers to *Proposals for Printing, by Subscription, the Dramatick Works of William Shakespeare*, dated 1 June 1756 (*Bibliography Supplement*, p. 140).

3. Lennox dedicated the new edition to Queen Charlotte, who had agreed to be a patron (Small, *Charlotte Ramsay Lennox*, p. 44).

4. MS: one word heavily del. and replaced by "peculiarities" in Lennox's hand

5. According to Duncan Isles, "the exact form of religious 'indecency' implied is unknown" ("The Lennox Collection," *Harvard Library Bulletin* 19, 1971, p. 174 n. 147).

6. MS: heavy deletion; "pretty triffler upon occasion" inserted in Lennox's hand

John Macleod of Raasay

SATURDAY 6 MAY 1775

PRINTED SOURCE: JB's *Journal of a Tour to the Hebrides*, 1785, pp. 519–20.

ADDRESS: To the Laird of Raasay.

Dear Sir, London, May 6, 1775

Mr. Boswell has this day shewn me a letter, in which you complain of a passage in "the Journey to the Hebrides." My meaning is mistaken. I did not intend to say that you had personally made any cession of the rights of your house, or any acknowledgement of the superiority of M'Leod of Dunvegan. I only designed to express what I thought generally admitted,—that the house of Rasay allowed the superiority of the house of Dunvegan. Even this I now find to be erroneous, and will therefore omit or retract it in the next edition.[1]

Though what I had said had been true, if it had been disagreeable to you, I should have wished it unsaid; for it is not my business to adjust precedence. As it is mistaken, I find myself disposed to correct it, both by my respect for you, and my reverence for truth.

As I know not when the book will be reprinted, I have desired Mr. Boswell to anticipate the correction in the Edinburgh papers. This is all that can be done.

I hope I may now venture to desire that my compliments may be made, and my gratitude expressed, to Lady Rasay, Mr. Malcolm M'Leod, Mr. Donald M'Queen, and all the gentlemen and all the ladies whom I saw in the island of Rasay; a place which I remember with too much pleasure and too much kindness, not to be sorry that my ignorance, or hasty persuasion, should, for a single moment, have violated its tranquillity.

I beg you all to forgive an undesigned and involuntary injury, and to consider me as, Sir, your most obliged, And most humble servant,

SAM. JOHNSON

1. *Ante* To Hester Thrale, 24 Sept. 1773 and n. 11.

Hester Thrale

TUESDAY 9 MAY 1775

MS: Hyde Collection.

Dearest Lady: May 9, 1775

When I sent last week to enquire after you,[1] Mr. Thrale sent me word that he had a testimonial of your health, *written by Madam's own hand.*[2] I hope You are by this time, strong enough to give me the same pleasure,[3] for next to Mr. Thrale and the young ones, your doing well is of most importance to, Madam, Your most obliged and most humble servant,

SAM. JOHNSON

1. See Appendix II: To Henry Thrale, 6 May 1775.

2. On 4 May Hester Thrale had given birth at Streatham to her tenth child, Frances Anna (Hyde, 1977, p. 117; Clifford, 1952, p. 126).

3. *Post* To Hester Thrale, 12 May 1775.

Hester Thrale

FRIDAY 12 MAY 1775

MS: Clifton College, Bristol.

May 12, 1775

And so, my dearest Mistress, you lie a bed hatching suspicions. I did not mean to reproach you, nor meant any thing but respect, and impatience to know how you did.[1]

I wish I could say or send any thing to divert you, but I have done nothing and seen nothing. I dined one day with Paoli, and yesterday with Mrs. Southwels,[2] and called on Congreve. Mr. Twiss hearing that you talked of despoiling his book of the fine print, has sent you a copy to frame.[3] He is going to

1. *Ante* To Hester Thrale, 9 May 1775. She made a slow recovery from the birth of Frances Anna, remaining "in a highly nervous state throughout May" (Clifford, 1952, p. 126).

2. SJ may be referring to either one of the Southwell sisters. *Ante* To Hester Thrale, 19 Feb. 1773, n. 2.

3. *Travels through Portugal and Spain*, by Richard Twiss (1747–1821), had been

Ireland, and I have given him letters to Dr. Leland, and Mr. Falkner.[4]

Mr. Montague is so ill that the Lady is not visible[5] but yesterday I had I know not how much kiss of Mrs. Abington,[6] and very good looks from Miss Jefferies the Maid of Honour.[7]

Boswel has made me promise not to go to Oxford till he leaves London;[8] I had no great reason for haste, and therefore might as well gratify a Friend. I am always proud and pleased to have my company desired. Boswel would have thought my absence a loss, and I know not who else would have considered my presence as profit. He has entered himself at the Temple, and I joined in his bond.[9] He is to plead before the Lords, and hopes very nearly to gain the cost of his journey.[10] He lives

---

published in April. According to SJ, "they are as good as the first book of travels that you will take up" (*Life* II.345–46). Of the seven copperplates in Twiss's *Travels*, several (including "Prospect of the Alhambra" and "Our Lady of the Fish") are likely candidates for the print to which SJ refers.

4. Twiss's *A Tour of Ireland in 1775* appeared the following year (*Post* To Hester Thrale, 18 May 1776).

5. Elizabeth Montagu's eighty-two-year-old husband Edward had been a complete invalid since the beginning of the year. "His weakness and incapacity had kept his wife in unrelieved attendance"; he died 20 May (*Mrs. Montagu, Queen of the Blues*, ed. Reginald Blunt, 1923, I.297–99).

6. Frances Abington (1737–1815), celebrated comic actress at Drury Lane (1765–82) and Covent Garden (1782–90), created the roles of Lydia Languish in *The Rivals* and Lady Teazle in *The School for Scandal* (*A Biographical Dictionary of Actors, Actresses, Musicians, Dancers, Managers, and Other Stage Personnel in London, 1660–1800*, ed. P. H. Highfill et al., 1973, I.12–17). According to JB, SJ "was, perhaps, a little vain of the solicitations of this elegant and fashionable actress" (*Life* II.321).

7. Elizabeth Jeffries (d. 1802), Maid of Honour from 1770 until her death and a member of Mrs. Abington's social circle (*GM* 1802, p. 94; *Dr. Campbell's Diary*, ed. J. L. Clifford, 1947, p. 76).

8. JB left for Edinburgh 22 May, SJ for Oxford 29 May (*Post* To Hester Thrale, 22 May 1775; *Post* To John Taylor, 27 May 1775).

9. During the first half of May, "as a non-committal step towards coming to the English bar, Boswell began his terms at the Inner Temple, and ate enough meals at commons to fulfil the requirements of one term's residence. . . . As was customary, Boswell had to give a commons bond with two sureties" (*Boswell: The Ominous Years*, ed. Charles Ryskamp and F. A. Pottle, 1963, p. 157 and n. 7).

10. The case of *Alexander et al.* v. *Paterson et al.* had been tried before the Court of Session and appealed to the House of Lords. At JB's request, SJ dictated an

much with his Friend Paoli who says a man must see Wales to enjoy England.

I forgot till now to send Mrs. Gardiner's card. She is got out of her chamber, and has once been in the air. Dr. Laurence says she has been very bad. Mrs. Williams's pimples continue to come out and go in.

The book which is now most read, but which as far as [I] have gone, is but dull, is Grays letters prefixed by Mason to his poems.[11] I have borrowed mine, and therefore cannot lend it, and I can hardly recommend the purchase.

I have offended, and, what is stranger, have justly offended the Nation of Rasay.[12] If they could come hither, they would be as fierce as the Americans. Rasay has written to Boswel an account of the injury done him, by representing his House as subordinate to that of Dunvegan. Boswel has his letter and, I believe, copied my Answer. I have appeased him, if a degraded Chief can possibly be appeased, but it will be thirteen days, days of resentment and discontent, before my recantation can reach him. Many a dirk will imagi[na]tion, during that interval fix in my heart. I really question if at this time my life would not be in danger, if distance did not secure it.

Boswel will find his way to Streatham before he goes, and will detail this great affair.[13] I would have come on Saturday, but that I am engaged to do Dr. Laurence a little service on

---

opinion on the case. Though it was postponed until the autumn, JB earned forty-two guineas in fees (*Life* II.373–74; Ryskamp and Pottle, *The Ominous Years*, p. 370; *Post* To Hester Thrale, 22 May 1775).

11. *The Poems of Mr. Gray. To Which are prefixed Memoirs of his Life and Writings* had appeared in March, edited by Gray's close friend, the Rev. William Mason (1725–97). The *Memoirs* consist chiefly of an ample selection from Gray's letters, much tampered with by Mason (*Correspondence of Thomas Gray*, ed. Paget Toynbee and Leonard Whibley, rev. H. W. Starr, 1971, I.xiv). Initially SJ found these letters "mighty dull" (*Life* III.31), but then revised his opinion: "Gray's letters contain a very pleasing account of many parts of their journey. . . . He that reads his epistolary narration wishes that to travel, and to tell his travels, had been more of his employment" (*Lives of the Poets* III.422, 428).

12. *Ante* To John Macleod, 6 May 1775.

13. On 16 May JB dined at Streatham Park, and left his Hebridean journal for Hester Thrale to read (Hyde, 1972, pp. 29–30).

Sunday. Which day shall I come next week. I hope you will be well enough to see me often. I am, Dearest Madam, Your most humble servant,

SAM. JOHNSON

Hester Thrale

SATURDAY 20 MAY 1775

MS: Hyde Collection.

Dear Madam: May 20, 1775

I will try not to be sullen, and yet when I leave you how shall I help it.[1] ⟨Bos⟩[2] goes away on Monday,[3] I go in a day or two after him,[4] and will try to be well and to be as you would have me. But I hope that when I come back you will teach me the value of liberty.

Nurse tells me that you are all well, and she hopes all growing better. Ralph like other young Gentlemen will travel for improvement.[5]

I have sent you six Guineas and an half, so you may laugh at neglect and parcimony.[6] It is a fine thing to have money. Peyton and Macbean are both starving,[7] and I cannot keep them.[8]

1. "I wish you a safe return, but do not set out sullen when there is nothing to be sullen about" (Hester Thrale to SJ, 20 May 1775, MS: Rylands Library).

2. MS: one word erased; spelling but not identification in doubt

3. MS: "on Monday" written above "to morrow" del.

4. *Ante* To Hester Thrale, 12 May 1775, n. 8.

5. Ralph Thrale, who was "in a miserably declining State," had been sent to Brighton with the hope that sea bathing would improve his health (Hyde, 1977, pp. 115, 118).

6. "A propos please to pay your Debts before we part. . . . There is 27*s* due for Plates" (Hester Thrale to SJ, 20 May 1775, MS: Rylands Library).

7. SJ refers to Alexander Macbean and another former assistant on the *Dictionary,* V. J. Peyton (d. 1776) (Clifford, 1979, pp. 52–54; *Life* 1.187, 536). "Peyton, when reduced to penury, had frequent aid from the bounty of Johnson, who at last was at the expence of burying both him and his wife" (*Life* 1.187). *Post* To Hester Thrale, 1 Apr. 1776.

8. *Post* To Bennet Langton, 21 May 1775.

Must we mourn for the Queen of Denmark?[9] How shall I do for my black cloaths which you have in the chest?[10]

Make my compliments to every body. I am, Madam, Your most humble Servant,

SAM. JOHNSON

9. Caroline Matilda (1751–75), sister of George III and wife (m. 1766) of Christian VII, King of Denmark, died 11 May.

10. *Post* To Hester Thrale, 22 May 1775.

Bennet Langton

SUNDAY 21 MAY 1775

MS: Hyde Collection.

ADDRESS: To Benet Langton, Esq.

Dear Sir: May 21, 1775

I have an old Amanuensis in great distress.[1] I have given what I think I can give, and begged till I cannot tell where to beg again. I put into his hands this morning four guineas. If you could collect three guineas more, it would clear him from his present difficulty. I am, Sir, Your most humble servant,

SAM. JOHNSON

1. *Ante* To Hester Thrale, 20 May 1775 and n. 7. SJ may be referring to either Peyton or Macbean.

Hester Thrale

MONDAY 22 MAY 1775

MS: Hyde Collection.

ADDRESS: To Mrs. Thrale.

Dearest Lady: May 22, 1775

One thing or other still hinders me, besides what is perhaps the great hindrance, that I have no great mind to go.[1] Boswel

1. *Ante* To Hester Thrale, 12 May 1775 and n. 8.

went away at two this morning. Langton, I suppose, goes this week. Boswel got two and forty guineas in fees while he was here.[2] He has, by his Wife's persuasion and mine, taken down a present for his Mother in law.[3]

Pray let me know how the breath does. I hope there is no lasting evil to be feared. Take great care of your self. Why did you take cold? Did you pump into your shoes?[4]

I am not sorry that you read Boswel's Journal.[5] Is it not a merry piece? There is much in it about poor me. Miss, I hear, touches me sometimes in *her* memoirs.

I shall try at Oxford what can be done for Mr. Carter;[6] what can be done for his daughter it is not easy to tell. Does her mother know her own distress, or is she out of her wits with pride, or does Betsy a little exaggerate?[7] It is strange behaviour.

The mourning it seems is general.[8] I must desire that you will let somebody take my best black cloaths out of the chest, and send them. There is nothing in the chest but what may be tumbled. The key is the newest of those two that have the wards channelled. When they are at the borough, my man can fetch them.

But all this while, dear and dear Lady, take great care of yourself.

Do not buy Chandlers travels,[9] they are duller than[10] Twiss's.[11] Wraxal is too fond of words, but you may read

2. *Ante* To Hester Thrale, 12 May 1775 and n. 10.

3. SJ refers to JB's stepmother, Elizabeth Boswell, Lady Auchinleck, with whom his relations were perennially troubled.

4. "because we chid *him* for doing so when he had the Gout on him" (Piozzi I.220).

5. *Ante* To Hester Thrale, 12 May 1775, n. 13. "Almost blinded" by JB's manuscript, Hester Thrale had gone no further than the account of Coll before returning the journal on 18 May (Hyde, 1972, p. 30).

6. *Ante* To Henry Thrale, *c.* 26 Feb. 1775 and n. 2.

7. *Ante* To Hester Thrale, 3 Apr. 1775 and n. 2.

8. *Ante* To Hester Thrale, 20 May 1775 and n. 9.

9. *Travels in Asia Minor* (1775) by Richard Chandler (1738–1810), D.D.

10. MS: "than" altered from "that"

11. *Ante* To Hester Thrale, 12 May 1775 and n. 3.

him.[12] I shall take care that Adair's account of America may be sent you for I shall have it of my own.[13]

Beattie has called once to see me. He lives grand at the Archbishop's.[14]

Dear Lady do not be careless, nor heedless, nor rash, nor giddy. But take care of your health, I am, Dearest Madam, Your most humble servant,

SAM. JOHNSON

Dr. Talbot, which, I think I never told You,[15] has given five hundred pounds to the future infirmary.[16]

12. *A Tour Through Some of the Northern Parts of Europe* (1775), by Nathaniel William Wraxall.

13. James Adair's *History of the American Indians* (1773), published by Edward and Charles Dilly.

14. James Beattie, who had arrived in London on 6 May, was staying with Beilby Porteus (1731–1809), D.D., Rector of Lambeth and Chaplain to the Archbishop of Canterbury. On 13 May Beattie dined with the Archbishop at Lambeth Palace; on 18 May he called on SJ "and sate a while with him" (Beattie's London Diary, MS: Hyde Collection).

15. MS: "Y" superimposed upon "h"

16. Thomas Talbot (d. 1788), D.D., Rector of Ullingswick, Herefordshire, had been campaigning since the early 1760s for the creation of an infirmary in Hereford. In the autumn of 1774 "he subscribed £500 to the cause, and other contributors began to give smaller amounts; a committee was appointed and rules were drawn up; in November, 1775, the Earl of Oxford gave a site on the river; and in March, 1776, the new infirmary was opened to patients" (E. L. McAdam and A. T. Hazen, "Dr. Johnson and the Hereford Infirmary," *Huntington Library Quarterly* 3, 1940, p. 361). McAdam and Hazen argue that SJ contributed substantially to Talbot's *Address to the Nobility, Gentry, and Clergy of the County of Hereford* (Oct. 1774).

Hester Thrale

WEDNESDAY 24 MAY 1775

MS: Hyde Collection.

Dear Madam:

May 24, 1775

I am not gone,[1] nor can well go till I have my black cloaths,

1. To Oxford (*Ante* To Hester Thrale, 12 May 1775 and n. 8).

sending them after me will load me with two suits, and I have no large box.[2] I write this at random, for I hope Frank will find them at the borough.

You were a naughty thing for taking cold but you have suffered for it, and I hope will take warning. How strange it is that I am not gone. Yet one thing or another has hindred me and perhaps, if we knew ourselves, I am not heartily in haste. I had yesterday a kind of fainting fit, but it is gone and over.

For Mr. Carter I will try to do something, but time and opportunity must tell what, for I am sure, I do not know.

Do, send the cloaths if you send them in a wheelbarrow. There are two suits let me have the best. I am, Dearest of all dear Ladies, Your most humble Servant,

SAM. JOHNSON

2. *Ante* To Hester Thrale, 20 May 1775 and n. 9; 22 May 1775.

Hester Thrale

THURSDAY 25 MAY 1775

MS: Current location unknown. Transcribed from a photostat supplied by J. E. Brown.

Dearest Lady: May 25, 1775

The fit was a sudden faintness such as I have had I know not how often; no harm came of it, and all is well.[1] I cannot go till saturday, and then go I will, if I can.[2] My Cloaths Mr. Thrale says must be made like other peoples, and they are gone to the Taylor.[3] If I do not go, you know, how shall I come back again?

I told you, I fancy, yesterday, that I was well, but I thought so little of the disorder, that I know not whether I said any [thing] about it.

1. *Ante* To Hester Thrale, 24 May 1775.
2. *Ante* To Hester Thrale, 12 May 1775, n. 8.
3. *Ante* To Hester Thrale, 24 May 1775.

⟨ ⟩[4] I am, Madam, Your most humble Servant,

SAM. JOHNSON

4. MS: mutilated; approximately one-fifth of the leaf is cut away at the bottom, another one-fifth at the top, such that approximately seven lines of text are missing

Hester Thrale

FRIDAY 26 MAY 1775

MS: Wellcome Historical Medical Library.
ADDRESS: To Mrs. Thrale.

Dearest Lady: May 26, 1775

I have taken the place for Monday.[1] I could not get one for any day sooner. My cloaths came home last night but I could not depend upon them,[2] and therefore could not go to day, and for the two next days the coach is full.

I see no harm in the bark, but as your disorder is now mere weakness, I believe Meat, and Drink, and Air, and Quiet will do all that is wanted. And then, *throw physick to the dogs*.[3]

Will Sir Joseph succeed this time?[4] I am a little afraid, though his Success can have very little effect.[5]

Well then. On Monday I fancy I shall go, and I fancy I shall not wish to stay long away, for I shall always think on Master and Mistress, and all the rest. I am, Madam, your most humble servant,[6]

1. *Ante* To Hester Thrale, 12 May 1775, n. 8; 25 May 1775; *Post* To John Taylor, 27 May 1775.

2. *Ante* To Hester Thrale, 25 May 1775.

3. "Throw physic to the dogs; I'll none of it" (*Macbeth* v.iii.47).

4. Sir Joseph Mawbey (1730–98), Bt., M.P. for Southwark (1761–74), had stood for the county of Surrey in 1774 but was defeated. At the by-election of 14 June 1775, however, he was once again a candidate for the Opposition (Namier and Brooke III.121–22). *Post* To Hester Thrale, 17 June 1775 and n. 8.

5. SJ, a supporter of Lord North's Ministry, did not wish well to one of Sir Joseph's anti-Governmental convictions.

6. MS: mutilated; signature removed

James Boswell

SATURDAY 27 MAY 1775

PRINTED SOURCE: JB's *Life*, 1791, I.495.

Dear Sir: May 27, 1775

I make no doubt but you are now safely lodged in your own habitation, and have told all your adventures to Mrs. Boswell and Miss Veronica.[1] Pray teach Veronica to love me. Bid her not mind mamma.[2]

Mrs. Thrale has taken cold, and been very much disordered, but I hope is grown well. Mr. Langton went yesterday to Lincolnshire, and has invited Nicolaida to follow him.[3] Beauclerk talks of going to Bath. I am to set out on Monday;[4] so there is nothing but dispersion.

I have returned Lord Hailes's entertaining sheets,[5] but must stay till I come back for more, because it will be inconvenient to send them after me in my vagrant state.

I promised Mrs. Macaulay that I would try to serve her son at Oxford.[6] I have not forgotten it, nor am unwilling to perform it. If they desire to give him an English education, it should be considered whether they cannot send him for a year or two to an English school. If he comes immediately from Scotland, he can make no figure in our Universities. The schools in the north, I believe, are cheap; and, when I was a young man, were eminently good.

1. *Ante* To Hester Thrale, 12 May 1775 and n. 8.

2. *Ante* To JB, 27 Nov. 1773 and n. 2.

3. Mr. Nicolaides (*fl.* 1775–82), a friend of John Paradise, was "a learned Greek, nephew of the Patriarch of Constantinople, who fled from some massacre of the Greeks" (John Johnstone, "Memoirs" of Parr, in *The Works of Samuel Parr*, 1828, I.84).

4. *Post* To John Taylor, 27 May 1775.

5. *Ante* To JB, 4 July 1774 and n. 4.

6. On their Hebridean tour SJ and JB had stayed with the Rev. Kenneth Macaulay (1723–79), minister of Cawdor, and his wife Penelope (d. 1799). When they expressed an interest in securing their son Aulay (1762–1842) a place at Oxford, SJ offered to help young Macaulay obtain a servitorship when the time came for him to go to University (*Life* v.122, 505; *Post* To William Adams, 7 Apr. 1778 and n. 3).

There are two little books published by the Foulis,[7] Telemachus[8] and Collins's Poems,[9] each a shilling; I would be glad to have them.

Make my compliments to Mrs. Boswell, though she does not love me. You see what perverse things ladies are, and how little fit to be trusted with feudal estates. When she mends and loves me, there may be more hope of her daughters.

I will not send compliments to my friends by name, because I would be loath to leave any out in the enumeration. Tell them, as you see them, how well I speak of Scotch politeness, and Scotch hospitality, and Scotch beauty, and of every thing Scotch, but Scotch oat-cakes and Scotch prejudices.

Let me know the answer of Rasay,[10] and the decision relating to Sir Allan.[11] I am, my dearest Sir, with great affection, Your most obliged and most humble servant,

SAM. JOHNSON

7. The celebrated Foulis Press of Glasgow was run by the brothers Robert (1707–76) and Andrew (1712–75), whom SJ had met in 1773 (*Life* v.370–71).

8. *Telemachus, a Mask* (1763), by George Graham (1728–67), was published by the Foulis Press in an octavo format in 1767 (Philip Gaskell, *A Bibliography of the Foulis Press,* 2d ed., 1986, pp. 274–75). *Post* To JB, 18 Feb. 1777.

9. *The Poetical Works of Mr. William Collins* (duodecimo, 1771) (Gaskell, *Foulis Press,* p. 303).

10. *Ante* To John Macleod, 6 May 1775; *Ante* To Hester Thrale, 12 May 1775.

11. *Ante* To Hester Thrale, 23 Oct. 1773 and nn. 11, 17.

John Taylor

SATURDAY 27 MAY 1775

MS: Buffalo and Erie County Public Library (J. F. Gluck Collection).

Dear Sir: May 27, 1775

On Monday I purpose to be at Oxford, where I shall perhaps stay a week, from thence I shall come to Birmingham, and so to Lichfield. At Lichfield my purpose is to pass a week or so, but whether I shall stay there in my way to Ashbourne, or in ⟨returning⟩ from it, you may, if you please, determine. When

I come thither I will write to you, or perhaps I may find a letter at Mrs. Porter's. I am, Sir, Your affectionate Servant,

SAM. JOHNSON

Hester Thrale

THURSDAY 1 JUNE 1775

MS: Hyde Collection.

Dear Madam: [University College, Oxford] June 1, 1775

I know well enough what you think, but I am out of your reach. I did not make the epitaph before last night and this morning I have found it too long.[1] I send you it as it is to pacify you, and will make it shorter. It is too long by near half. Tell me what you would be most willing to spare.

Dr. Wetherel went with me to the Vicechancellor,[2] to whom we told the transaction with my Lord of Chester,[3] and the[4] Vicechancellor promised to write to the Archbishop.[5] I told him that he needed have no scruples he was asking nothing for himself, nothing that would make him richer, or them poorer, and that he acted only as a Magistrate and one concerned for the interest of the University. Dr. Wetherel promises to stimulate him.

Don't suppose that I live here, as we live at Streatham. I went this morning to the Chapel at six, and if I was to stay would try to conform to all wholesome rules. Pray let Harry have the peny which I owe him for the last morning.[6]

1. SJ had promised an epitaph for Mrs. Salusbury's memorial tablet, to be placed in St. Leonard's Church, Streatham (Hester Thrale to SJ, 20 May 1775, MS: Rylands Library). The designer of the tablet was Joseph Wilton, who had specified a maximum length of 350 letters or 12 lines; SJ's first version, however, came to 579 letters or 17 lines (*Post* To Hester Thrale, 7 June 1775 [II]). For the (Latin) text as finally engraved, and a translation, see Hyde, 1977, pp. 118–20. *Post* To Hester Thrale, 19 June 1775 and n. 9.

2. SJ refers to Thomas Fothergill.

3. SJ refers to William Markham.

4. MS: "the" superimposed upon "We"

5. SJ refers to Robert Hay Drummond.

6. A penny was due Harry Thrale "for calling Dr. Johnson up" (Piozzi I.224).

Mr. Colson is well,[7] and still willing to keep me, but I shall not delight in being long here. Mr. Smollet of Loch Lomond and his Lady have been here.[8] We were very glad to meet.

Pray let me know how you do, and play no more tricks, if you do, I can yet come back and watch you. I am, Madam, Your most humble servant,

SAM. JOHNSON

7. *Ante* To Hester Thrale, 6 Apr. 1770, n. 2.

8. *Ante* To Hester Thrale, 28 Oct. 1773 and n. 6. Smollet was married to the former Jean Clerk of Pennicuik (*Life* v.564).

Hester Thrale

MONDAY 5 JUNE 1775

MS: Hyde Collection.

Madam: [University College, Oxford] Juin 5, 1775

Trois jours sont passéz sans que [je] reçoive une lettre; point de nouvelles, point d'amitie, point de querelles. Un silence si rare, que veut il? J'ai vous envoyé l'epitaphe, trop longue a la veritè, mais on la raccourcira sans trop de peine.[1] Vous n'en avez dit pas un mot. Peut être que je sois plus heureux ce soir.

J'ai epuisé ce lieu, ou je n'etudie pas, et ou si on ôte l'etude, il n'y a rien, et je ne trouve guere moyen d'echaper. Les voitures qui passent par cy, passent dans la minuit; les chaises de poste me couteront beaucoup.[2] J'envoye querer une passage plus commode.

Je dinerai demain chez le Vicechancelier, j'espere de trouver des choses un peu favorables a nôtre[3] ami infortunè, mais je n'ai null confiance.[4] Je suis, Madame, votre tres obeissant serviteur,

SAM. JOHNSON

1. *Ante* To Hester Thrale, 1 June 1775 and n. 1.

2. *Post* To Hester Thrale, 6 June 1775.

3. MS: "nôtre" repeated as catchword

4. *Ante* To Hester Thrale, 1 Apr. 1775; 1 June 1775.

Hester Thrale

TUESDAY 6 JUNE 1775

MS: Hyde Collection.

ADDRESS: To Henry Thrale, Esq., in Southwark.

POSTMARKS: OXFORD, 7 IV, FREE.

Madam: [University College, Oxford] June 6, 1775

Such is the uncertainty of all human things that Mr. Colson has quarrelled with me.[1] He says, I raise the laugh upon him, and he is an independant man, and all he has is his own, and he is not used to such things.[2] And so I shall have no more good of Colson, of whom I never had any good, but flattery, which my dear Mistress knows I can have at home.

That I had no letters yesterday I do not wonder for yesterday we had no post.[3] I hope something will come to day. Our post is so ill regulated that we cannot receive letters and answer them the same day.

Here I am, and how to get away I do not see for the power of departure otherwise than in a post chaise depends upon accidental vacancies in passing coaches, of which all but one in a week pass through this place at three in the morning.[4] After that one I have sent, but with little hope. Yet I shall be very unwilling to stay here another week.[5]

I supped two nights ago with Mr. Bright, who enquired after Harry and Queeney, to whom I likewise desire to be remembred.

1. *Ante* To Hester Thrale, 1 June 1775.

2. According to Philip Fisher, J. W. Croker's informant, "Coulson was going out on a country living, and talking of it with the same pomp, as to Lord Stowell. . . . Johnson chose to imagine his becoming an archdeacon, and made himself merry . . . at Coulson's expense; at last they got to warm words, and Johnson concluded the debate by exclaiming emphatically—'Sir, having meant you no offence, I will make you no apology'" (JB's *Life*, ed. Croker, 1848, p. 458 n. 1).

3. The post left London every day of the week except Sunday (Howard Robinson, *The British Post Office*, 1948, p. 103).

4. SJ's next stop was Lichfield (*Post* To Hester Thrale, 7 June 1775 [II]; 10 June 1775).

5. Traveling by post chaise, SJ left Oxford for Lichfield (via Birmingham) on 8 June (*Post* To Hester Thrale, 10 June 1775).

Suppose I should grow like my Mistress, and when I am to go forward, think eagerly how and when I shall come back, would that be a strange thing? Love and reverence have always had some tendency to produce conformity.

Where is Mr. Baretti? Are He and Queeney plague and darling as they are used to be?[6] I hope my sweet Queeney will write me a long letter, when I am so settled that she knows how to direct to me, and if I can find any thing for her cabinet I shall be glad to bring it.

What the Vicechancellor says respecting Mr. Carter, if he says any thing, you shall know to morrow, for I shall probably leave him too late for this day's post.[7]

If I have not a little something from you to day, I shall think something very calamitous has befallen us. This is the natural effect of punctuality. Every intermission alarms. Dearest, dear Lady, take care of yourself. You connect us, and rule us, and vex us, and please us; We have all a deep interest in your health, and prosperity. I am, Madam, Your most obliged and most humble Servant,

SAM. JOHNSON

6. Giuseppe Baretti, Queeney's Italian tutor, found his charge "exceedingly bright but hard to control"; Queeney's attitude toward her "Maestro" veered between goodwill and sullenness (Hyde, 1977, p. 79).

7. *Ante* To Hester Thrale, 1 Apr. 1775; 1 June 1775.

Philip Fisher[1]

WEDNESDAY 7 JUNE 1775

MS: Hyde Collection.

ADDRESS: To the Reverend Mr. Fisher.

Sir: [University College, Oxford] June 7, 1775

I beg the favour of you, that you will remember to give the

1. The Rev. Philip Fisher (*c.* 1751–1842), Fellow of University College (1772), later (1803–42) Master of the Charterhouse (*Alum. Oxon.* II.ii.465).

Earse books[2] with the proper message to the librarian,[3] and enable me to return his thanks.

I mentioned them yesterday to the Vicechancellor.[4] I am, Sir, Your most humble servant,

SAM. JOHNSON

2. *Ante* To JB, 1 Oct. 1774 and n. 7.

3. The Rev. John Price (1734–1813), Bodley's Librarian (1768–1813), was "completely attached to the Library, and considered every acquisition to its contents as a personal favour to himself" (*GM* 1813, p. 400).

4. SJ refers to Thomas Fothergill.

Hester Thrale

WEDNESDAY 7 JUNE 1775 (I)

MS: Hyde Collection.

Dearest Madam: [University College, Oxford] July[1] 7, 1775

What can be the reason that I hear nothing from you[2] or from your house? Are you well? Yet while I am asking the question I know not when I shall be able to receive your answer, for I am waiting for the chance of a place in a coach which will probably be come and gone in an hour.[3]

Yesterday the Vicechancellor told me that he has written to the Archbishop of York;[4] His letter, as he represented it to me, was very proper and persuasive. I believe we shall establish Mr. Carter, the riding Master of Oxford.[5]

Still I cannot think why I hear nothing from You.

The Coach is full. I am therefore at full leisure to continue my letter, but I have nothing more to say of business, but that the Vicechancellor is for adding to the ridingschool a house and stable for the master; nor of myself but that I grieve and

1. SJ several times confused June and July (cf. *Post* To Hester Thrale, 8 June 1782; *Post* To William Adams, 11 July 1784).

2. MS: "your"

3. *Ante* To Hester Thrale, 6 June 1775.

4. *Ante* To Hester Thrale, 1 June 1775.

5. *Ante* To Henry Thrale, *c.* 26 Feb. 1775, n. 2.

wonder, and hope and fear about my dear Friends at Streatham. But I may have a letter this afternoon.[6] Sure it will bring me no bad news. You never neglected writing so before. If I have a letter to day I will go away as soon as I can; if I have none, I will stay till this may be answered if I do not come back to town. I am, Madam, Your most obedient servant,

SAM. JOHNSON

6. *Post* To Hester Thrale, 7 June 1775 (II).

Hester Thrale

WEDNESDAY 7 JUNE 1775 (II)

MS: Birthplace Museum, Lichfield.

Dearest Lady: [Oxford] June 7, 1775

Your letter which ought to have come on tuesday came not till wednesday. Well, now I know that there is no harm I will take a chaise and march away towards my own country.

You are but a goose at last. Wilton told you that there is room for 350 letters, which are equivalent to twelve lines.[1] If you reckon by lines the inscription has 17. If by letters 579. So that one way you must expel five lines, the other 229 letters. This will perplex us, there is little that by my own choice I should like to spare, but we must comply with the stone.[2]

Coulson an[d] I are pretty well again.[3] I grudge the cost of going to Lichfield, Frank and I in a postchaise. Yet I think of thundering away to morrow.[4] So you will write your next dear letter to Lichfield.

This letter is written on Wednesday after the receipt of yours, but will not be delivered to the post till to morrow. I

1. *Ante* To Hester Thrale, 1 June 1775 and n. 1.
2. *Post* To Hester Thrale, 19 June 1775 and n. 9.
3. *Ante* To Hester Thrale, 6 June 1775 and n. 2.
4. *Post* To Hester Thrale, 10 June 1775.

wish Ralph better,[5] and my Master and his boys well. I have pretty good nights. I am, Madam, your most humble servant,

SAM. JOHNSON

5. *Ante* To Hester Thrale, 20 May 1775 and n. 5.

Hester Thrale

SATURDAY 10 JUNE 1775

MS: Houghton Library.

Dear Madam: [Lichfield] June 10, 1775

On thursday morning I took a postchaise and intended to have passed a day or two at Birmingham, but Hector had company in his house, and I went on to Lichfield, where I know not yet how long I shall stay, but think of going forward to Ashbourne in a short time.[1]

Neither your letters nor mine seem to have kept due time, if You see the date of the letter in which the epitaph was enclosed, you will find that it has been delayed. I shall adjust the epitaph some way or other.[2] Send me your advice.

Poor Miss Porter has been bad with the gout in her hand. She cannot yet dress herself.

I am glad that Ralph is gone; a new air may do him good.[3] I hope little Miss promises well.[4]

I will write you a longer letter on Monday,[5] being just now called out according to an appointment which I had forgotten. I am, Madam, your most humble servant,

SAM. JOHNSON

1. SJ left for Ashbourne on 29 June (*Post* To Hester Thrale, 1 July 1775).
2. *Ante* To Hester Thrale, 1 June 1775 and n. 1; 7 June 1775 (II).
3. *Ante* To Hester Thrale, 20 May 1775 and n. 5.
4. *Ante* To Hester Thrale, 9 May 1775, n. 2.
5. *Post* To Hester Thrale, 11 June 1775. SJ may have misdated this letter (Chapman II.41 n. 405).

Hester Thrale

SUNDAY 11 JUNE 1775

MS: A. Brooks.

Dearest Lady: [Lichfield] June 11, 1775

I am sorry that my Master has undertaken[1] an impracticable interest, but it will be forgotten before the next election.[2] I suppose he was asked at some time when he could not well refuse.

Lady Smith is settled at last here, and sees company at her new house.[3] I went on saturday. Poor Lucy Porter has her hand in a bag, so disabled by the gout that she cannot dress herself.[4] She does not go out. All your other friends are well.

I go every day to Stowhill; bothe the Sisters are now at home.[5] I sent Mrs. Aston a *taxation*, and sent it nobody else, and Lucy borrowed it. Mrs. Aston since that enquired by a Messenger when I was expected. I can tell nothing of about it, answered Lucy, when he is to be here I suppose she'll know.

Every Body remembers you all; you left a good impression behind you.[6] I hope You will do the same at ⟨Lewes⟩.[7] Do not make them speeches. Unusual compliments to which[8] there is

1. MS: "undertaking"

2. Henry Thrale had offered his support to William Norton (1742–1822), a parliamentary candidate in the Surrey by-election, June 1775. His wife considered this gesture futile as Norton was "vastly unpopular" and unlikely to win the seat (Namier and Brooke I.383–84, III.217; Hester Thrale to SJ, 7 June 1775, MS: Rylands Library).

3. In 1768 Catherine Vyse, eldest daughter of the Rev. William Vyse, married Sir George Smith (1715–69), first Bt., of Stoke, Nottinghamshire. Shortly before SJ's visit Lady Smith had moved into a house in the Close of Lichfield, where she lived until her death (*Johns. Glean.* V.211, XI.436).

4. It was a common practice to cover a gout-stricken hand in a flannel glove (cf. *Walpole's Correspondence*, Yale ed. XXXII.43).

5. SJ refers to Elizabeth Aston and Jane Gastrell.

6. The Thrales had visited Lichfield with SJ in July 1774 (*Life* V.428).

7. MS: one word pasted over; "Lewes" conjecturally restored on the basis of references to a possible trip Hester Thrale was going to make with her cousin, Hester Cotton D'Avenant (*c.* 1748–1822) (Hester Thrale to SJ, 7 June 1775; 16 June 1775, MSS: Rylands Library; *Post* To Hester Thrale, 13 June 1775)

8. MS: "w" superimposed upon "th"

no stated and prescriptive answer embarrass the feeble, who know not what to say, and disgust the wise, who knowing them to be false, suspect them to be hypocritical. Did I think when I sat down to this paper that I should write a lesson to my Mistress, of whom I think with so much admiration?

As to Mr. Carter I am inclined to think that our project will succeed. The Vice-chancellor is really in earnest. He remarked to me how necessary it must be to provide in places of education a sufficient variety of innocent amusements, to keep the young Men from pernicious pleasures.

When I did not hear from you, I thought whether it would not be proper to come back, and look for you. I know not what might have happened.

Consider the epitaph, which, you know, must be shortened and tell what part you can best spare.[9] Part of it which tells the birth and marriage is formulary, and can be expressed only one way; the character we can make longer or shorter, and since it is too long, may choose what we shall take away. You must get the dates for which you see spaces left.

You never told me,[10] and I omitted to enquire how you were entertained by ⟨Boswel's Journal⟩.[11] One would think the Man had been hired to be a spy upon me. He was very diligent and caught opportunities of writing from time to time. You may now conceive yourself tolerably well acquainted with the expedition. Folks want me to go to Italy, but I say you are not for it.[12] However write often to, Madam, Your most obliged and most humble Servant,

SAM. JOHNSON

9. *Ante* To Hester Thrale, 1 June 1775 and n. 1.

10. Cf. *Ante* To Hester Thrale, 22 May 1775 and n. 5.

11. MS: "Boswel's Journal" in H. L. Piozzi's hand on a slip of paper pasted over approximately two words of text (a reading supported by discernible traces of SJ's original)

12. In the spring of 1774 the Thrales and SJ had planned a trip to Italy, with Giuseppe Baretti as the courier, but "the project was abandoned in the end because of Mrs. Thrale's worries about her Welsh property" (Hyde, 1977, p. 88). It was revived again in 1776 (*Post* To JB, 5 Mar. 1776 and n. 2).

Hester Thrale

TUESDAY 13 JUNE 1775

MS: Hyde Collection.

Dearest Lady: Lichfield, June 13, 1775

I now write at Mrs. Cobb's where I have dined and had custard. She and Miss Adey send their compliments. Nothing considerable has happened since I wrote, only I am sorry to see Miss Porter so bad;[1] and I am not well pleased to find that after a very comfortable intermission, the old flatulence distressed me again last night. The world is full of ups and downs, as I think I once told you before.

Lichfield is full of Box clubs.[2] The Ladies have one for their own sex. They have incorporated themselves under the appellation of the amicable Society, and pay each twopence a week to the box. Any woman who can produce the weekly twopence is admitted to the Society, and when any of the poor subscribers is in want, she has six shillings a week, and I think when she dies five pounds are given to her children. Lucy is not one, nor Mrs. Cobb. The subscribers are always quarrelling, and every now and then a Lady in a fume withdraws her name. But they are an hundred pounds beforehand.

Mr. Green has got a cast of Shakespeare,[3] which he holds to be a very exact resemb[l]ance.

There is great lamentation here for the death of Coll.[4] Lucy is of opinion that he was wonderfully handsome.

Boswel is a favourite, but he has lost ground, since I told them that he is married, and all hope is over.

Be so kind as to let me know when you go to Lewes[5] and

1. *Ante* To Hester Thrale, 11 June 1775.

2. *box club*: "a primitive form of provident society, the members of which were assisted from funds raised by sending round the collecting-box among the members" (*English Dialect Dictionary*, ed. Joseph Wright, 1981, I.367).

3. *Ante* To Lucy Porter, 12 July 1768, n. 2.

4. *Ante* To JB, 27 Oct. 1774 and n. 1.

5. *Ante* To Hester Thrale, 11 June 1775 and n. 7. On 16 June Hester Thrale replied, "Mrs. D'Avenant is not yet stout enough to travel so far" (MS: Rylands Library).

when you come back that I may not fret for want of a letter, as I fretted at Oxford.[6] Pay my respects to my dear Master. I am, Madam, Your most humble servant,

SAM. JOHNSON

6. *Ante* To Hester Thrale, 7 June 1775 (I).

Edmund Allen

SATURDAY 17 JUNE 1775

MS: Hyde Collection.

ADDRESS: To Mr. Allen, Printer, in Boltcourt, Fleetstreet, London.

POSTMARKS: LITCHFIELD, 19 IV.

Dear Sir: Lichfield, June 17, 1775

I wrote to you and to Sir Joshua yesterday, but wrote by the bypost,[1] and lest it should have miscarried have written again, and inclosed a [letter] which You may take to Sir Joshua.[2] You will see by it that your success is earnestly desired, by, Sir, Your most humble Servant,

SAM. JOHNSON

1. "The word 'bypost' appears at first to refer to any service of less importance than that of the main roads, and a by-letter would be one carried on a subsidiary route" (Howard Robinson, *The British Post Office*, 1948, p. 65).

2. SJ supported Allen's candidacy for the post of Printer to the Royal Academy. However, his letters came too late to be of use: at the Council's meeting on 16 June Thomas Davies received the appointment (F. W. Hilles, "Johnson and Boswell Notes," *JNL* 17, Mar. 1957, p. 3). *Post* To Edmund Allen, 19 June 1775.

Hester Thrale

SATURDAY 17 JUNE 1775

MS: Hyde Collection.

Dear Madam: Lichfield, June 17, 1775

Write to me something every post, for on the stated day my

head runs upon a letter.[1] I will answer Queeney. Bad nights came again, but I took Mercury, and hope to find good effects. I am distresfully and frightfully deaf. Querelis jam satis datum.[2]

So we shall have a fine house in the winter,[3] as we already have in the summer.[4] I am not sorry for the appearance of a little superfluous expence. I have not yet been at Ashbourne, and yet I would fain flatter myself that you begin to wish me home, but do not tell me so, if it be not true, for I am very well at Stowhill.

Mrs. Porter will be glad of a memorial from you, and will keep the workbag carefully, but has no great use for it, her present qualifications for the niceties of[5] needlework, being dim eyes and lame fingers.

Of the harvest about us, it is said, that the much is expected from the wheat, more indeed than can be easily remembred. The Barley is promising enough but not uncommonly exuberant. But this is of itself a very good account, for no grain is ever dear, when wheat is cheap. I hope therefore that my Master may without fear or danger build this year, and dig the next. I do not find that in this part of the country rain has been much wanted.

If you go with Mrs. D'Avenant,[6] do not forget me amidst the luxuries of absolute dominion, but let me have kind letters full of yourself, of your own hopes and your own fears, and your own thoughts, and then go where you will. You will find your journey however but a barren business; it is dull to live neither scolding nor scolded, neither governing nor governed.[7] Now try.

1. The post left London for Lichfield on Tuesday, Thursday, and Saturday evenings; a letter regularly took two days to arrive.

2. *Querelis iam satis datum*: "there have now been enough complaints."

3. Henry Thrale was enlarging the house at Southwark.

4. Henry Thrale was continuing his "long succession of improvements" at Streatham Park—improvements that included not only the library wing but a parlor and a summerhouse (Clifford, 1952, p. 49 and n. 1; *Ante* To Hester Thrale, 23 Mar. 1773, n. 2).

5. MS: "of" repeated as catchword

6. *Ante* To Hester Thrale, 11 June 1775, n. 7; 13 June 1775 and n. 5.

7. The two women planned to "*leave our Husbands* at home," thereby allowing

I expected that when the interest of the county had been divided, Mawbey would have had very [little] difficulty and am glad to find that Norton opposes him with so much efficacy, pray send me the result.[8] I am, Madam, Your most obedient Servant,

SAM. JOHNSON

themselves the "luxuries of absolute dominion" (Hester Thrale to SJ, 7 June 1775, MS: Rylands Library).

8. At the by-election on 14 June, Sir Joseph Mawbey was returned top of the poll, defeating William Norton and the son of the previous M.P., Sir Francis Vincent (*Ante* To Hester Thrale, 26 May 1775, n. 4; 11 June 1775, n. 2).

Edmund Allen

MONDAY 19 JUNE 1775

MS: Hyde Collection.

ADDRESS: To Mr. Allen, Printer, in Boltcourt, Fleetstreet, London.

POSTMARKS: LICHFIELD, 21 IV.

Dear Sir: Litchfield, June 19, 1775

I have recommended you, as you desire, both to Sir Joshua, and to Mr. Davies, and hope that you will find the effect of my good will.[1] I had it not in my thoughts that Mr. Davies could ask for the place being no printer. They will both have their letters by the post that brings this.

Please to make my compliments to Mrs. Allen. Whenever you think I can do you any good, make no difficulty to call upon, Sir, Your most humble Servant,

SAM. JOHNSON

1. *Ante* To Edmund Allen, 17 June 1775 and n. 2.

Hester Thrale

MONDAY 19 JUNE 1775

MS: Birthplace Museum, Lichfield.

Dear Madam: Lichfield, June 19, 1775

I hope it is very true that Ralph mends, and wish you were gone to see that you might come back again.[1]

Queeney revenges her long tasks upon Mr. Baretti's hen, who must sit on Duck eggs a week longer than on her own. I hope she takes great care of my Hen, and the Guinea hen and her pretty little brood.[2]

I was afraid Mawbey would succeed, and have little hope from the scrutiny.[3] Did you ever[4] know a scrutiny change the account?

Miss Adey does not run after me, but I do not want her, here are other Ladies.

Invenies alium, si te hic fastidit Alexis.[5]

Miss Turton grows old; and Miss Vyse has been ill, but I believe, she came to me as soon as she got out. And I can always go to Stow hill. So never grieve about me. Only flatulencies are come again.

Do you read Boswel's Journals?[6] He moralised, and found my faults, and laid them up to reproach me. Boswel's narrative is very natural, and therefore very entertaining, he never made any scruple of showing it to me. He is a very fine fellow. He has established Rasa's Chieftainship in the Edinburgh pa-

1. On 16 June Hester Thrale had written, "They say Ralph mends. I long to go see" (MS: Rylands Library). *Ante* To Hester Thrale, 20 May 1775 and n. 5.

2. "Queeney says I must tell you how a Guinea hen that was missing and we thought her lost, is come home with twelve young ones" (Hester Thrale to SJ, 16 June 1775, MS: Rylands Library).

3. In her letter of 16 June, Hester Thrale had reported Sir Joseph Mawbey's victory (*Ante* To Hester Thrale, 17 June 1775, n. 8); she also told SJ, "There is however to be a Scrutiny" (MS: Rylands Library). In his *Dictionary* SJ defines *scrutiny* as "enquiry; search; examination with nicety."

4. MS: "ever" altered from "even"

5. *Invenies alium si te hic fastidit, Alexim*: "You will find another Alexis, if this one scorns you" (Virgil, *Eclogues* II.73, trans. H. R. Fairclough, Loeb ed.).

6. Cf. *Ante* To Hester Thrale, 22 May 1775; 11 June 1775.

pers, and quieted all commotion in the Hebridean world.[7] These little things are great to little Man.[8]

Small letters will undoubtedly gain room for more words, but words are useless if they cannot be read.[9] The lines need not all be kept distinct, and some words I shall wish to leave out, though very few.[10] It must be revised before it is engraved. I always told you that Mr. Thrale was a man take him for all in all, you ne'er will look upon his like.[11] But you never mind him nor me, till time forces conviction into your steely bosom.[12] You will perhaps find all right about the house and the windows.[13]

Pray always suppose that I send my respects to Master, and Mr. Baretti, and Queeney, and Harry, and Susey, and Sophy.

Poor Lucy mends very slowly,[14] but she is very good humoured, while I do just as she would have me.

Lady Smith has got a new postchaise, which is not nothing to talk on at Lichfield. Little things here serve for conversation. Mrs. Aston's Parrot pecked my leg, and I heard of it some time after at Mrs. Cobb's.

—We deal in nicer things
Than routing armies, and dethroning Kings.

7. *Ante* To Hester Thrale, 24 Sept. 1773 and n. 11; *Ante* To John Macleod, 6 May 1775.

8. "These little things are great to little man" (Goldsmith, *The Traveller*, l. 42).

9. "Mr. Thrale . . . has found out that the Letter of the Epitaph [for Mrs. Salusbury] may be made less, and then the Stone will hold more; he will not have your Writing or my Mother's Praises curtailed he says" (Hester Thrale to SJ, 16 June 1775, MS: Rylands Library).

10. A draft of the epitaph in SJ's hand shows both deletions and additions (MS: Rylands Library). See J. D. Wright, "Some Unpublished Letters to and from Dr. Johnson," *Bulletin of the John Rylands Library* 16, 1932, pp. 60–61. The inscription as finally engraved contains 547 letters, as compared with 579 letters in the original version (Hyde, 1977, p. 119; *Ante* To Hester Thrale, 7 June 1775 [II]).

11. "A was a man, take him for all in all: / I shall not look upon his like again" (*Hamlet* I.ii.187–88).

12. Hester Thrale confessed to SJ that her attitude toward the candidates in the Surrey by-election had been mistaken: "My Master is apt to be right and I apt to be perverse and self opinionated" (16 June 1775, MS: Rylands Library).

13. *Ante* To Hester Thrale, 17 June 1775, n. 3.

14. *Ante* To Hester Thrale, 10 June 1775.

A week ago Mrs. Cobb gave me sweetmeats to breakfast, and I heard of it last night at Stowhill.

If you are for small talk.

—Come on, and do the best you can
I fear not you, nor yet a better man.

I could tell[15] you about Lucy's two cats, and Brill her brothers old dog, who is gone deaf, but the day would fail me. Suadentq cadentia sidera somnum.[16] So said Aeneas but I have not yet had my diner. I have begun early for what would become of the nation if a Letter of this importance should miss the post? Pray write to, Dear Madam, your most obedient and most humble servant,

SAM. JOHNSON

15. MS: "t" superimposed upon "c"

16. *suadentque cadentia sidera somnos*: "the setting stars invite to sleep" (*Aeneid* II.9, trans. H. R. Fairclough, Loeb ed.).

Hester Thrale

WEDNESDAY 21 JUNE 1775

MS: Hyde Collection.

Dear Madam: Lichfield, June 21, 1775

Now I hope you are thinking. Shall I have a letter today from Lichfield? Something of a letter You will have how else can I expect that you should write? and the morning on which I should miss a letter, would be a morning of uneasiness, notwithstanding all that would be said or done by the Sisters of Stowhill, who do and say whatever good they can. They give me good words, and cherries, and strawberries. Lady Smith, and her Mother[1] and Sister[2] were visiting there yesterday, and Lady Smith took her tea before her Mother.

1. Catherine Vyse (d. 1792), widow of William Vyse and daughter of Richard Smalbroke (1672–1749), Bishop of Lichfield (*Johns. Glean.* V.210).

2. *Ante* To Lucy Porter, 18 June 1768, n. 5.

Mrs. Cobb is to come to Miss Porters this afternoon. Miss Adey comes little near me. Mr. Langley of Ashbourne was here to day in his way to Birmingham, and every body talks of you.

The Ladies of the amicable society are to walk in a few days from the townhall to the Cathedral in procession to hear a sermon.[3] They walk in Linen gowns, and each has a stick with an acorn, but for the acorn they could give no reason, till I told them of the civick crown.[4]

I have just had your sweet letter, and am glad that you are to be at the regatta.[5] You know how little I love to have you left out of any shining part of life. You have every right to distinction and should therefore be distinguished. You will see a show with philosophick superiority, and therefore may see it safely. It is easy to talk of sitting at home contented when others are seeing or making shows. But not to have been where it is supposed, and seldom supposed falsely, that all would go if they could; To be able [to] say nothing when every one is talking; to have no opinion when every one is judging; to hear exclamations of rapture without power to depress; to listen to falsehoods without right to contradict, is, after all, a state of temporary inferiority, in [which] the mind is rather hardened by stubornness, than supported by fortitude. If the

3. *Ante* To Hester Thrale, 13 June 1775. "On Thursday last, being St. Peter's Day, was celebrated the Annual Festival of the Original Female Society established at Lichfield. At Half-past Ten o'clock, about One Hundred young Women, neatly dressed, walked in Procession, from the Guildhall to the Cathedral, where a most excellent Sermon, suitable to the Occasion, was preached. . . . After the Sermon, the Society returned to the Hall to Dinner, and the Evening concluded with a Ball" (*Aris's Birmingham Gazette*, 3 July 1775: quoted in William Bennett, *Doctor Samuel Johnson and the Ladies of the Lichfield Amicable Society, 1775*, 1934, pp. 5–6).

4. The "civic wreath" or "civic crown," a garland of oak leaves with acorns, "is supposed to represent the Roman crown conferred upon public benefactors, especially upon those who had saved the life of a citizen" (Henry Gough and James Parker, *A Glossary of the Terms Used in Heraldry*, 1894, pp. 100–101).

5. This "novel entertainment," the first regatta ever held in England, took place 23 June (*GM* 1775, p. 302). "It was beautiful to see the Thames covered with boats, barges and streamers, and every window and housetop loaded with spectators. I suppose so many will not meet again till the day of judgment" (*Walpole's Correspondence*, Yale ed. XXXII.237). *Post* To Hester Thrale, 23 June 1775; 26 June 1775 and n. 1.

world be worth winning let us enjoy it,[6] if it is to be despised let us despise it by conviction. But the world is not to be despised but as it is compared with something better. Company is in itself better than solitude and pleasure better than indolence. Ex nihilo nihil fit,[7] says the moral as well as natural philosopher. By doing nothing and by knowing nothing no power of doing good can be obtained. He must mingle with the world that desires to be useful. Every new scene impresses new ideas, enriches the imagination, and enlarges the powers of reason, by new topicks of comparison. You that have seen the regatta will have images which we who miss it must want, and no intellectual images are without uses. But when you are in this scene of splendour and gayety, do not let one of your fits of negligence steal upon you. Hoc age,[8] is the great rule whether you are serious or merry, whether you are stating the expences of your family, l[e]arning science or duty from a folio, or floating on the Thames in a fancied dress. Of the whole entertainment let me not hear so copious nor so true an account from any body as from you. I am, Dearest Madam, Your most obedient and most humble Servant,

SAM. JOHNSON

6. "If the World be worth thy Winning, / Think, O think, it worth Enjoying" (Dryden, *Alexander's Feast*, ll.102–3).

7. *ex nihilo nihil fit*: "nothing comes of nothing" (proverbial).

8. *hoc age*: "come, get on with it!" (*Oxford Latin Dictionary*).

Hester Thrale

FRIDAY 23 JUNE 1775

MS: Houghton Library.

Dear Madam: June 23, 1775

So now you have been at the regatta, for I hope you got tickets somewhere, else you wanted me, and I shall not be sorry, because you fancy You can do so well without me, but however I hope you got tickets, and were dressed fine and fanciful, and made a fine part of the fine show, and heard musick, and said good things, and staid on the water four hours after midnight, and came well home, and slept, and dreamed of the regatta, and waked, and found yourself in bed, and thought now it is all over, only I must write about it to Lichfield.[1]

We make a hard shift here to live on without a regatta. The cherries are ripe at Stowhil, and the currants are ripening, and the Ladies are very kind to me. I wish however you would go to Surry[2] and come back, though I think it wiser to stay till the improvement in Ralph may become perceptible,[3] else you will be apt to judge by your wishes and your imagination. Let us in the mean time hope the best. Let me but know when you go, and when you come back again.[4]

If you or Mr. Thrale would write to Dr. Wetherel about Mr. Carter, it will please Wetherel, and keep the business in motion. They know not otherwise how to communicate news if they have it.

As to my hopes and my wishes I can keep them to myself. They will perhaps grow less, if they are laughed at. I needed not tell them, but that I have little else to write, and I needed not write but that I do not like to be without hearing from you, because I love the Thrales and the Thralites. I am, Madam, your most humble servant,

SAM. JOHNSON

1. *Ante* To Hester Thrale, 21 June 1775 and n. 5; *Post* To Hester Thrale, 26 June 1775 and n. 1.

2. SJ's "Surry" is a mistake for "Sussex" (*Ante* To Hester Thrale, 11 June 1775 and n. 7).

3. *Ante* To Hester Thrale, 20 May 1775 and n. 5.

4. *Post* To Hester Thrale, 1 July 1775, n. 4.

Hester Thrale

MONDAY 26 JUNE 1775

MS: Hyde Collection.

Dear Madam: [Lichfield] June 26, 1775

That the regatta disappointed you is neither wonderful nor new, all pleasure preconceived and preconcerted ends in disappointment;[1] but disappointment when it involves neither shame nor loss is as good as success, for it supplies as many images to the mind, and as many topicks to the tongue. I am glad it failed for another reason which looks more sage, than my reasons commonly try to look. This, I think, is Queeney's first excursion into the regions of pleasure, and I should not wish to have her too much pleased. It is as well for her to find that pleasures have their pains, and that bigger Misses who are at Ranelaugh when she is in bed, are not so much to be envied as they would wish to be, or as they may be represented.

So you left out the Rices[2] and I suppose they did not go. It will be a common place for you and Queeney fourscore years hence; and my Master and you may have recourse to it sometimes. But I can only listen. I am glad that you were among the finest.

Nothing was the matter between me and Miss Seward. We are well enough now. Miss Porter went yesterday to Church from which she has been kept a long time. I fancy, that I shall go on thursday to Ashbourne,[3] but do not think that I shall stay very long.[4] I wish you were gone to Surry[5] and come well

1. "Now for the regatta, of which, Baretti says, the first notion was taken from Venice, where the gondoliers practice rowing against each other perpetually, and I dare say 'tis good diversion where the weather invites, and the water seduces to such entertainments;—here, however, it was not likely to answer; and I think nobody was pleased" (Piozzi, *Letters* 1.247). The water was rough, it rained, and the refreshments were inadequate (Piozzi, *Letters* 1.248–52; *GM* 1775, p. 315).

2. *Ante* To Hester Thrale, 17 May 1773, n. 3.

3. *Post* To Hester Thrale, 1 July 1775.

4. *Post* To Hester Thrale, 26 July 1775.

5. *Ante* To Hester Thrale, 23 June 1775, n. 2.

back again, and yet I would not have you go too soon. Perhaps I do not very [well] know what I would have, it is a case not extremely rare. But I know I would hear from you by every post, and therefore I take care that you should every post day hear from me. I am, Madam, Your most humble Servant,

SAM. JOHNSON

Hester Thrale

SATURDAY 1 JULY 1775

MS: Hyde Collection.

Dear Madam: Ashbourne, July 1, 1775

On thursday I came to Dr. Taylor's, where I live as I am used to do, and as You know.[1] He has gotten nothing new, but a very fine looking glass, and a Bull bitch. The less Bull is now grown the bigger. But I forgot; he has bought old Shakespeare the Racehorse for a Stalion. He has likewise some fine iron gates which he will set up somewhere.[2] I have not yet seen the old Horse.

You are very much enquired after, as well here as at Lichfield.

This I suppose will go after You to Sussex, where I hope you will find every thing either well, or mending.[3] You never told me whether you took Queeney with You;[4] nor ever so much as told me the name of the little one.[5] Maybe, you think, I don't care about you.

I behaved myself so well at Lichfield, that Lucy says I am grown better, and the Ladies at Stow hill, expect I should come

1. On their trip to Wales in 1774, SJ and the Thrales stayed in Ashbourne, 15–20 July (*Life* v.430–32).

2. *Post* To Hester Maria Thrale, 4 Sept. 1777.

3. *Ante* To Hester Thrale, 20 May 1775 and n. 5; 23 June 1775 and n. 2.

4. "I receive your Letter tonight, I go to Sussex tomorrow Morning: I so little think of leaving Queeney behind that I forgot to say She went with me" (Hester Thrale to SJ, 3 July 1775, MS: Rylands Library).

5. *Ante* To Hester Thrale, 9 May 1775, n. 2.

back thither before I go to London, and offer to entertain me if Lucy refuses.[6]

I have this morning received a letter from Mrs. Chambers of Calcutta. The Judge has a sore eye and could not write. She represents all as going on very well, only Chambers does not now flatter himself that he shall do much good. I am, Madam, Your most humble Servant,

SAM. JOHNSON

6. *Post* To Hester Thrale, 26 July 1775.

Hester Thrale

EARLY JULY 1775[1]

MS: Birthplace Museum, Lichfield.[2]

⟨ ⟩ Your dissertation upon Queeney is very deep.[3] I know not what to say to the chief question. Nature probably has some part in human characters, and accident has some part, which has most we will try to settle when we meet.

⟨ ⟩ as to hold a horse, and that is in the possession of ⟨old⟩ Shakespeare. However, I am sure Mr. Langton will g⟨*one or two words*⟩ and he is but a little further off. When Liz. is tr⟨avelling⟩ one hundred and thirty miles, he may as well tra-⟨vel twen⟩ty more to find a welcome.[4] If every thing fails ⟨*five to seven words*⟩ or Christmas ⟨ ⟩

1. Dated on the basis of references to "Liz." and "Shakespeare": see below, n. 4.

2. In order to conceal the comments on JB and his Hebridean journal in SJ's letter of 19 June, H. L. Piozzi cut out a section from another letter (possibly the original of No. 120, *Letters* I.258–61) and pasted it over the offending paragraph; the result was the suppression of one passage and the interpolation of another. The surviving text of the mutilated letter consists of one complete paragraph from the recto and fragmentary sentences from the verso.

3. As R. W. Chapman suggests (II.48), this "dissertation" may have been related to incidents at the Regatta (*Ante* To Hester Thrale, 21 June 1775; 23 June 1775; 26 June 1775).

4. In her letter of 29 June, Hester Thrale informed SJ that Charles Carter was being forced by a creditor to sell two of his horses, Prince and Lizard. In order to prevent the loss of Lizard, who would be particularly valuable to the projected

riding school at Oxford, Mrs. Thrale thought of buying him herself, if she could find someone to stable him. "This is what I have half a hope of from Dr. Taylor . . . and Lizard would recompense his Charity by leaving him a beautiful Colt or Filley for a Favourite" (MS: Rylands Library). SJ replies that the only possible stable at Taylor's is already occupied by the racehorse Shakespeare (*Ante* To Hester Thrale, 1 July 1775), and suggests instead that Lizard might be stabled at Bennet Langton's estate in Lincolnshire. *Post* To Hester Thrale, 13 July 1775.

Hester Thrale

c. MONDAY 3 JULY 1775

PRINTED SOURCE: Piozzi, *Letters* i.258–61.[1]

Now, thinks my dearest Mistress to herself, sure I am at last gone too far to be pestered every post with a letter: he knows that people go into the country to be at quiet; he knows too that when I have once told the story of Ralph,[2] the place where I am affords me nothing that I shall delight to tell, or he will wish to be told; he knows how troublesome it is to write letters about nothing; and he knows that he does not love trouble himself, and therefore ought not to force it upon others.

But, dearest Lady, you may see once more how little knowledge influences practice, notwithstanding all this knowledge, you see, here is a letter.

Every body says the prospect of harvest is uncommonly delightful; but this has been so long the Summer talk, and has been so often contradicted by Autumn, that I do not suffer it to lay much hold on my mind. Our gay prospects have now for many years together ended in melancholy retrospects. Yet I am of opinion that there is much corn upon the ground.

1. H. L. Piozzi has placed this (undated) letter between those of 1 July and 6 July 1775; internal references, as well as Hester Thrale's side of the correspondence, fully support her implied dating. It is possible that the letter originally contained the sentences referring to Queeney and Lizard (*Ante* To Hester Thrale, Early July 1775).

2. *Ante* To Hester Thrale, 20 May 1775 and n. 5; *Post* To Hester Thrale, 6 July 1775, n. 5.

Every dear year encourages the farmer to sow more and more, and favourable seasons will be sent at last. Let us hope that they will be sent now.

The Doctor and Frank are gone to see the hay. It was cut on Saturday, and yesterday was well wetted; but to day has its fill of sunshine. I hope the hay at Streatham was plentiful, and had good weather.

Our lawn is as you left it, only the pool is so full of mud that the water-fowl have left it. Here are many calves, who, I suppose, all expect to be great bulls and cows.

Yesterday I saw Mrs. Diot at church,[3] and shall drink tea with her some afternoon.

I cannot get free from this vexatious flatulence, and therefore have troublesome nights, but otherwise I am not very ill. Now and then a fit; and not violent. I am not afraid of the waterfall. I now and then take physick; and suspect that you were not quite right in omitting to let blood before I came away. But I do not intend to do it here.

You will now find the advantage of having made one at the regatta.[4] You will carry with you the importance of a publick personage, and enjoy a superiority which, having been only local and accidental, will not be regarded with malignity. You have a subject by which you can gratify general curiosity, and amuse your company without bewildering them. You can keep the vocal machine in motion, without those seeming paradoxes that are sure to disgust; without that temerity of censure which is sure to provoke enemies; and that exuberance of flattery which experience has found to make no friends. It is the good of publick life that it supplies agreeable topicks and general conversation. Therefore wherever you are, and whatever you see, talk not of the Punick war;[5] nor of the depravity of

3. During their stay in Ashbourne, in July 1774, SJ and the Thrales had exchanged visits with Catherine Herrick Dyott (1724–1810) and her husband Richard (1723–87), a well-to-do Staffordshire landowner (*Life* v.430–31, 581).

4. *Ante* To Hester Thrale, 21 June 1775 and n. 5; 23 June 1775; 26 June 1775.

5. In her *Anecdotes* H. L. Piozzi recorded: "As ethics or figures, or metaphysical reasoning, was the sort of talk he most delighted in, so no kind of conversation pleased him less I think, than when the subject was historical fact or general polity.

human nature; nor of the slender motives of human actions; nor of the difficulty of finding employment or pleasure; but talk, and talk, and talk of the regatta, and keep the rest for, dearest Madam, Your, etc.

'What shall we learn from *that* stuff (said he)? . . .' He never (as he expressed it) desired to hear of the *Punic war* while he lived: such conversation was lost time (he said), and carried one away from common life" (*Johns. Misc.* 1.201–2).

Hester Thrale

THURSDAY 6 JULY 1775

MS: Hyde Collection.

Dear Madam: Ashbourne, July 6, 1775

Dr. Taylor says he shall be very glad to see you all here again,[1] if you have a mind of retirement. But I told him that he must not expect you this summer, and [he] wants to know—why?

I am glad you have read Boswel's journal because it is something for us to talk about,[2] and that you have seen the Hornecks, because that is a publick theme.[3] I would have you see and read and hear, and talk it all, as occasion offers.

Pray thank Queeney for her letter. I still hope good of poor Ralph, but sure never poor rogue was so troubled with his teeth.[4] I hope occasional bathing, and keeping him about two minutes with his body immersed, may promote the discharge from his head, and set his little brain at liberty.[5] Pray give my

1. *Ante* To Hester Thrale, 1 July 1775, n. 1.

2. *Ante* To Hester Thrale, 22 May 1775 and n. 5.

3. "It is the good of publick life that it supplies agreeable topicks and general conversation" (*Ante* To Hester Thrale, *c.* 3 July 1775).

4. On 3 July Hester Thrale reported: "This Post has brought me disagreeable Accounts of poor Ralph; he has had another Struggle with his Teeth it seems, a Fever and Diarrhea but is mending again" (MS: Rylands Library).

5. Ralph suffered from a congenital disorder of the brain, either hydrocephalus (increased fluid in the ventricles of the brain) or hydranencephaly (distorted development of the brain and skull due to a bag of clear fluid which forms

service to my dear friend Harry, and tell him that Mr. Murphy does not love him better than I do.

I am inclined to be of Mr. Thrale's mind about the changes in the State.[6] A dissolution of the pa[r]liament would in my opinion, be little less than a dissolution of the government, by the encouragement which it would [give to] every future faction to disturb the publick tranquillity.[7] Who would ever want places and power if perseverence in falsehood, and violence of outrage were found to be certain and infallible means of procuring them? Yet I have so little confidence in our present statesmen, that I know not whether any thing is less likely, for being either absurd or dangerous.

About your estate I have little to say. Why it should not be settled upon your children I do not see, and I do not see on the other side, why you should diminish your own power over it. I think there is hardly sufficient reason for you, as distinct from Mr. Thrale, either to promote or oppose the[8] settlement. To oppose it, if he desires it, there can be surely no reason. I love you all too well, not to wish that whatever is[9] done, may be best. It will be prudent to hear Mr. Scrase's opinion.[10] In matters of business the most experienced man must have great authority. I am, dearest Lady, Your most humble Servant,

SAM. JOHNSON

---

between the brain and the skull). On 13 July he died at Brighton (Hyde, 1977, pp. 115–16, 122–25).

6. It is uncertain what "changes" SJ and Henry Thrale had in mind. Lord North's Ministry was firmly in power, despite the troubles in America (the news of Lexington and Concord had reached England at the end of May). By the end of the summer "there was indeed a massive strengthening of Lord North's political position" (J. S. Watson, *The Reign of George III*, 1960, p. 203).

7. Parliament was not dissolved until 1780.

8. MS: "the" superimposed upon "it"

9. MS: "is" superimposed upon "be"

10. "With quixotic impetuosity Mrs. Thrale wished to settle her Welsh property permanently on her eldest son, with 'remainder' to the sons of her daughters, or other heirs of her husband. When Scrase mildly suggested that should Thrale and her children die she might presumably have children by a second husband, she was shocked at the idea. . . . Scrase urged that no absolute entail be set up" (Clifford, 1952, pp. 128–29).

Hester Thrale

SUNDAY 9 JULY 1775[1]

PRINTED SOURCE: Chapman II.59–60.

Dear Madam: Ashbourne, July 1775

I am sorry that my poor little friend Ralph goes on no better. We must see what time will do for him.[2]

I hope Harry is well. I had a very pretty letter from Queeney, and hope she will be kind to my Hen and her ten chickens, and mind her Book.[3]

I forget whether I tell some things, and may perhaps tell them twice, but the matter is not great, only, as you observe, the more we write, the less we shall have to say, when we meet.

Are we to go all to Brighthelmston in the Autumn, or have you satiated yourself with this visit?[4] I have only one reason for wishing you to go, and that reason is far enough from amounting to necessity.[5]

That Dr. Delap's simplicity should be forgiven for his benevolence is very just, and I will not ⟨now⟩ say anything in opposition to your kind resolution.[6] It is pity that any good man should ever from violence be ridiculous.[7]

This letter will be short, for I am so much disordered by

1. I follow Chapman (II.59) in viewing this partially dated letter as that to which SJ refers in his letter of 11 July ("I have written twice to You, on the 6th and the 9th").

2. *Ante* To Hester Thrale, 6 July 1775, nn. 4, 5.

3. *Ante* To Hester Thrale, 19 June 1775 and n. 2.

4. For several days the previous week, Hester Thrale had been tending Ralph in Brighton (Hester Thrale to SJ, MSS: Rylands Library 539.45, 539.46). The Thrales and SJ did not visit Brighton that fall, traveling instead to France (Clifford, 1952, p. 130; *Post* To Robert Levet, 18 Sept. 1775).

5. Cf. *Post* To Hester Thrale, 24 July 1775. It is possible that SJ wished to consult with Charles Scrase (who lived in Brighton) on the settlement of Hester Thrale's Welsh property (*Ante* To Hester Thrale, 6 July 1775 and n. 10).

6. The Rev. John Delap (1725–1812), D.D., Rector of Iford and Kingston, Sussex (1765–1812), was a poet, playwright, and friend of the Thrales, who had introduced him to SJ. During SJ's breakdown in 1766 the Thrales "waited on him one morning, and heard him, in the most pathetic terms, beg the prayers of Dr. Delap, who had left him as we came in" (*Johns. Misc.* I.234).

7. It is not clear to what incident SJ refers.

indigestion of which I can give no account, that it is difficult to write more than that I am, Dearest Lady, Your most humble Servant,

SAM. JOHNSON

Hester Thrale

TUESDAY 11 JULY 1775[1]

MS: Hyde Collection.

Dear Madam: Ashbourne

I am sure I write and write, and every letter that comes from you charges me with not writing. Since I wrote to Queeney I have written twice to You, on the 6th and the 9th, be pleased to let me know whether You have them or have them not.[2] That of the 6th you should regularly have had on the 8th, yet your letter of the 9th seems not to mention it, all this puzzles me.

Poor dear ⟨*one word*⟩.[3] He only grows dull because he is sickly; age has not yet begun to impair him, nor is he such a chameleon as to take immediately the colour of his company. When You see him again, you will find him reanimated. Most men have their bright and their cloudy days, at least they have days when they put their powers into act, and days when they suffer them to repose.

Fourteen thousand pounds make a sum sufficient for the establishment of a family, and which in whatever flow of riches, or confidence of prosperity deserves to be very seriously considered.[4] I hope a great part of [it] has paid debts, and no

1. See below, final paragraph.

2. *Ante* To Hester Thrale, 6 July 1775; 9 July 1775.

3. MS: one word erased; the traces do not support any of the conjectural identifications: "Delap" (Piozzi 1.271); "Berenger" (Piozzi, *Letters*, annotated copy at Trinity College, Cambridge); "Seward" (Hill 1.346 n. 1.)

4. Hester Thrale replied, "I will keep the Story of the 14000£ till we meet, so I will all Family Concerns" (MS: Rylands Library 538.13). The source of the money has not been determined. It is unlikely to have represented profits from

small part bought Land. As for gravelling and walling and digging, though I am not much delighted with them, yet something indeed much must be allowed to every man's taste. He that is growing rich has a right to enjoy part of the growth his own way. I hope to range in the[5] walk, and row upon the water, and devour fruit from the wall.

Dr. Taylor wants to be gardening. He means to buy a piece of ground in the neighborhood, and surround it with a Wall, and build a Gardeners house upon it, and have fruit, and be happy. Much happiness it will not bring him, but what can he do better? If I had money enough what would I do. Perhaps, if You and Master did not hold me I might go to Cairo, and down the Red Sea to Bengal, and take a ramble in India. Would this be better than building and planting. It would surely give more variety to the eye, and more amplitude to the mind. Half fourteen thousand would send me out to see other forms of existence and bring me back to describe them.

I answer this the day on which[6] I had yours of the 9th that is on the 11th. Let me know when it comes. I am, Madam, Your most humble Servant,

SAM. JOHNSON

---

the brewery, which did not reach £14,000 until the following year, when the price of malt had fallen (Peter Mathias, *The Brewing Industry in England, 1700–1830,* 1959, p. 268).

5. MS: "the" superimposed upon "his"

6. MS: "w" superimposed upon "th"

Hester Thrale

WEDNESDAY 12 JULY 1775

MS: Hyde Collection.

Dear Madam: Ashbourn, Wednesday, July 12, 1775

On Monday I was not well, but I grew better at night, and before morning was, as the Doctors say, out of danger.

We have no news here, except that on saturday Lord

Scarsdale dined with the Doctor.[1] He is a very gentlemanlike man. On Sunday Mr. Green paid a visit from Lichfield, and having nothing to say, said nothing and went away.

Our great Cattle, I believe, go on well,[2] but our deer have died, all but five does and the poor Buck.[3] We think the ground too wet for them.

I have enclosed a letter from Mrs. Chambers partly, perhaps wholly, for Mr. Baretti's amusement and gratification, though he has probably a much longer letter of his own, which he takes no care to send me.[4]

Mr. Langley and the Doctor still continue at variance, and the Doctor is afraid, and Mr. Langley not desirous of a reconciliation. I therefore step over at bytimes; and of bytimes I have enough.[5]

Mrs. Dale has been ill, and at fourscore has recovered.[6] She is much extenuated, but having the Summer to favour her, will, I think, renew her hold on life.

To the Diots I yet owe a visit. Mr. Gell is now rejoicing at fifty seven for the birth of an heir male.[7]—I hope here is news. Mr. Okeover[8] and the Doctor seem to be making preparations for war.

1. Nathaniel Curzon (1726–1804), fifth Bt., of Kedleston, Derbyshire, M.P. for Clitheroe (1748–54) and Derbyshire (1754–61), cr. (1761) first Baron Scarsdale (Namier and Brooke II.287). *Post* To Hester Thrale, 20 Sept. 1777 and n. 4.

2. *Ante* To Hester Thrale, 1 July 1775; *c.* 3 July 1775.

3. *Ante* To Hester Thrale, 15 July 1771.

4. Before her marriage Frances Wilton Chambers had studied Spanish with Giuseppe Baretti (Baretti, *Lettere Sparse*, ed. Franco Fido, 1976, p. 108).

5. *by-time*: "time not occupied by one's main work or pursuits; spare time, odd hours" (*OED*).

6. During their visit to Ashbourne in 1774, SJ and the Thrales had visited "old Mrs. Dale" (*c.* 1694–1783), the mother (or possibly grandmother, d. 1777) of Robert Dale (1749–1835), son-in-law of Richard and Catherine Dyott (*Life* v.431, 581).

7. Philip Gell (*c.* 1723–95), of Hopton Hall, Derbyshire, had married Dorothy Milnes (1758–1808) in May 1774 (*Life* v.431 n. 4, 581). Their son and heir, Philip, (1775–1842), was born 9 July (*The Reliquary* 11, 1870–71, plate xxxi).

8. In July 1774 SJ and the Thrales had dined with Edward Walhouse Okeover (*c.* 1752–93), of Okeover Hall, Staffordshire, near Ashbourne (*Life* v.430, 580; A. M. Broadley, *Doctor Johnson and Mrs. Thrale*, 1910, pp. 167 n. 1, 168).

Now I flatter myself that you want to know something about me. My spirits are now and then in an uneasy flutter, but upon the whole, not very bad.

We have here a great deal of rain, but this is a very rainy region. I hear nothing but good of the harvest; but the expectation is[9] higher of the wheat than of the barley, but I hope there will be barley enough for us and Mr. Scrase, and Lady Lade, and something still to spare.[10] I am, Dearest, Sweetest Lady, Your most obedient Servant,

SAM. JOHNSON

Be pleased to send[11] Mrs. Chambers's Letter to Mrs. Williams.

9. MS: "of"

10. In 1772 Charles Scrase and Ann Lade had lent thousands of pounds apiece when the brewery almost failed. These debts had yet to be paid off (Peter Mathias, *The Brewing Industry in England, 1700–1830*, 1959, p. 267; *Ante* To Hester Thrale, 15 Oct. 1772, n. 3).

11. MS: "sent"

Hester Thrale

THURSDAY 13 JULY 1775

MS: Rosenbach Museum and Library.

Dearest Madam: [Ashbourne] July 13, 1775

In return for your three letters I do not find myself able to send you more than two;[1] but if I had the prolixity of an emperour, it should be all at your service.

Poor Ralph. I think what they purpose to do for his relief is right, but that it will be efficacious I cannot promise.[2]

Your anxiety about your other Babies is, I hope, superfluous.[3] Miss and Harry are as safe as ourselves, they have outlived the age of weakness; their fibres are now elastick, and

1. It is likely that SJ refers to this letter and its immediate predecessor, sent in the same cover.

2. *Ante* To Hester Thrale, 6 July 1775 and n. 5.

3. "It is the horrible Apprehension of losing the others by the same cruel Disease that haunts my affrighted Imagination and makes me look upon them with an Anxiety scarce to be endured" (Hester Thrale to SJ, 9 July 1775, MS: Rylands Library).

their headachs when they have them are from accidental causes, heat, or indigestion.

If Susy had been at all disposed to this horrid malady, it would have laid hold on her, in her[4] early state of laxity and feebleness. That native vigour which has carried her happily through so many obstructions to life and growth, will, I think, certainly preserve her from a disease, most likely to fall only on the weak.

Of the two small ladies it can only be said, that there is no present appearance of danger, and of fearing evils merely possible there is no end.[5] We are told by the Lord of Nature that "for the day its own evil is sufficient."[6]

Now to lighter things, and those of weight enough to another. I am still of opinion, that we shall bring the Oxford riding School to bear.[7] The Vicechancellor is indeed un Esprit foible,[8] and perhaps too easily repressed, but Dr. Wetherel is in earnest. I would come back through Oxford, but that at this time there is nobody there. But I will not desist. I think to visit them next term.

Do not let poor Lizard be degraded for five pounds.[9] I sent you word that I would spend something upon him, and indeed for the money which it would cost to take him to Taylor or Langton and fetch him back, he may be kept while he stands idle, a long time in the Stable.

Mrs. Williams has been very ill, and it would do her good, if you would send a message of enquiry, and a few strawberries or currants.

Mr. Flints little girl is alive and well, and pretty, as, I hope, yours, my dear Lady, will long continue.[10]

4. MS: "her" repeated as catchword

5. SJ refers to Sophia (b. 1771) and Frances Anna (b. 1775).

6. "Sufficient unto the day is the evil thereof" (Matthew 6:34).

7. *Ante* To Henry Thrale, *c.* 26 Feb. 1775, n. 2.

8. SJ refers to Thomas Fothergill.

9. *Ante* To Hester Thrale, Early July 1775, n. 4. On 9 July Hester Thrale had informed SJ that "nobody would bid above five pounds for him" (MS: Rylands Library).

10. In her letter of 9 July Hester Thrale had inquired: "Pray tell me if your

The hay harvest is here very much incommoded by daily showers, which, however, seem not violent enough to beat down the corn.

I cannot yet fix the time of coming home.[11] Dr. Taylor and I spend little time together, yet he will not yet be persuaded to hear of parting. I am, Dearest Lady, Your most obliged and obedient,

SAM. JOHNSON

Relation Mr. [Thomas] Flint has all his Children alive? there was a sweet little Girl among them very like my poor Lucy" (MS: Rylands Library). This comment echoes her diary entry for 15 July 1774: "In the afternoon Mr. Johnson took me to drink tea with a relation of his, a Mrs. Flint who lives in this town [Ashbourne] and has a daughter so like my poor Lucy that it brought tears to my eyes" (A. M. Broadley, *Dr. Johnson and Mrs. Thrale*, 1910, p. 169). The daughter in question was Martha Flint (b. 1767) (*Johns. Glean.* IX.29).

11. SJ left Ashbourne for Lichfield on 25 July and returned to London sometime in mid-to-late August (*Post* To Hester Thrale, 26 July 1775; *Post* To JB, 27 Aug. 1775).

Hester Thrale

SATURDAY 15 JULY 1775

PRINTED SOURCE: Chapman II.67–68.

Dear Madam: Ashbourne, July 15, 1775

You are so kind, every post, that I now regularly expect your favours. You have indeed more materials for writing than I; here are only I and the Doctor, and of him I see not much. You have Master, and young Master, and Misses ⟨about 3 words erased⟩ besides Geese, and Turkies, and Ducks, and Hens.

The Doctor says, that if Mr. Thrale comes so near as Derby, without seeing us, it will be a sorry trick.[1] I wish, for my part, that he may return soon, and rescue the fair captives from the

1. Henry Thrale had business to transact in Derby (Hester Thrale to SJ, 9 July 1775, MS: Rylands Library).

tyranny of B⟨arett⟩i. Poor B⟨arett⟩i![2] do not quarrel with him, to neglect him a little will be sufficient.[3] He means only to be frank, and manly, and independent, and perhaps, as you say, a little wise. To be frank he thinks is to be cynical, and to be independent, is to be rude. Forgive him, dearest Lady, the rather, because of his misbehaviour, I am afraid, he learned part of me. I hope to set him hereafter a better example.

Your concern for poor Ralph, and your resolution to visit him again, is too parental to be blamed.[4] You may perhaps do good, you do at least your duty, and with that we must be contented, with that indeed, if we attained it, we ought to be happy; but who ever attained it?

You have perceived by my letters, that without knowing more than that the Estate was unsettled, I was inclined to a settlement. I am likewise for an entail. But we will consult men of experience, for that which is to hinder my dear Harry from mischief when he comes of age, may be done with mature deliberation.[5]

You have not all the misery in the world to yourself, I was last night almost convulsed with flatulence, after having gone to Bed I thought so well—but it does not much trouble me when I am out of bed. To your anxiety about your children I wrote lately what I had to say.[6] I blame it so little, that I think you should add a small particle of anxiety about me, for I am, Dearest Madam, Your most obedient servant,

SAM. JOHNSON

2. H. L. Piozzi makes this identification in both annotated sets of her *Letters* (Lichfield and Trinity College, Cambridge).

3. From the beginning of Giuseppe Baretti's tenure at Streatham Park, he and Hester Thrale had been at odds. "Not a Servant, not a Child did he leave me any Authority over; if I would attempt to correct or dismiss them, there was instant Appeals to Mr. Baretti, who was sure always to be against me in every Dispute" (*Thraliana* 1.43).

4. *Ante* To Hester Thrale, 6 July 1775, n. 5. On 13 July Hester Thrale returned to Brighton, only to find Ralph dead (Clifford, 1952, p. 127).

5. *Ante* To Hester Thrale, 6 July 1775 and n. 10.

6. *Ante* To Hester Thrale, 13 July 1775.

Hester Thrale

MONDAY 17 JULY 1775

MS: Hyde Collection.

Dear Madam: [Ashbourne] July 17, 1775

The post is come without a letter; now could I be so sullen—but *He must be humble who would please.*[1] Perhaps you are gone to Brighthelmston, and so could not write.[2] However it be, this I feel, that I have no letter but then I have sometimes had two, and if I have as many letters as there come posts, nobody will pity me if I were to complain.

How was your hay made? The Doctor has had one part well housed; another wetted and dried till it is hardly worth the carriage; and now many acres newly mown, that have hitherto had good weather. This may be considered as a foreign article; the domestick news is that our Bulbitch has puppies, and that our six calves are no longer to be fed by hand, but to live on grass.

Mr. Langley has[3] made some improvements in his garden.[4] A rich man might do more; but what he has done is well.

You have never in all your letters touched but once upon my Master's summer projects. Is he towering into the air, and tending to the center? Is he excavating the earth, or covering its surface with edifices? Something he certainly is doing, and something he is spending. A Genius never can be quite Still. I do not murmur at his expences, a good Harvest will supply them.[5]

We talk here of Polish oats,[6] and Siberian barley,[7] of which

1. "She shou'd be humble, who wou'd please: / And She must suffer, who can love" (Matthew Prior, "Chloe Jealous," ll. 19–20).

2. *Ante* To Hester Thrale, 15 July 1775, n. 4.

3. MS: "has" altered from "had"

4. MS: "gar" repeated as catchword

5. Cf. *Ante* To Hester Thrale, 11 July 1775.

6. *Poland oat*: "known by its thick white husk, awnless chaff, solitary grains, short white kernel, and short stiff straw. It requires a dry warm soil, but is very prolific" (J. C. Loudon, *Encyclopaedia of Agriculture*, 3d ed., 1835, II.826). *Post* To Hester Thrale, 20 July 1775.

7. *Siberian barley* (*Hordeum coeleste*): "a variety of early barley with broader leaves

both are said to be more productive, and to ripen in less time, and to afford better grain than the English. I intend to procure specimens of both, which we will try in some spots of our own ground.

The Doctor has no great mind to let me go. Shall I teaze him and plague him till he is weary of me? I am, I hope, pretty well, and fit to come home. I shall[8] be expected by all my Ladies to return through Lichfield,[9] and to stay there a while, but if I thought you wanted me, I hope, you know what would be[10] done, by, Dearest, dearest Madam, Your most humble Servant,

SAM. JOHNSON

---

and reckoned more productive than the other [*Hordeum vulgare*]. It is much grown in the north of Europe, and was introduced to this country [Great Britain] in 1768, but is believed to be now [1835] lost or merged in the parent species" (Loudon, *Encyclopaedia*, II.823).

8. MS: "s" superimposed upon "m"

9. *Post* To Hester Thrale, 24 July 1775.

10. MS: "be" altered from "by"

William Strahan

THURSDAY 20 JULY 1775

MS: Hyde Collection.

ADDRESS: To William Strahan, Esq., M.P., in London.

POSTMARKS: ASHBOURNE, 22 IY, FREE.

Sir: Ashbourn, July 20, 1775

As I know your curiosity to be active, and your intelligence exact,[1] I should think it a favour if you would communicate to me your opinion of the stability of our Ministry at home, and the likelihood of our success in America.[2] I suppose nothing told in the papers is true, and therefore do not suffer them to disturb me; yet I should be glad of some information on which I could rest my mind.

1. As a member of Parliament, Strahan presumably would have access to information more reliable than that provided in the newspapers.

2. *Ante* To Hester Thrale, 6 July 1775, n. 6.

If you can find time to write on saturday, as I wish, be pleased to direct hither, if you delay a post, direct to Lichfield.[3] Make my compliments to dear Mrs. Strahan. I am, Sir, Your most humble servant,

SAM. JOHNSON

3. *Post* To Hester Thrale, 24 July 1775; 26 July 1775.

Hester Thrale

THURSDAY 20 JULY 1775

MS: Hyde Collection.

Dear Madam: Ashbourn, July 20, 1775

Poor Ralph! he is gone, and nothing remains but that you comfort yourself with having done your best.[1] The first wish was that he might live long to be happy and useful; the next, that he might not suffer either long pain or ⟨long discomfort⟩.[2] The second wish has been granted. Think now only on those which are left you. I am glad that you went to Brighthelmston, for your journey is a standing proof to you of your affection and diligence.[3] We can hardly be confident of the state of our own minds, but as it stands attested by some external action; we are seldom sure that we sincerely meant what we omitted to do.

Dr. Taylor says that Mr. Thrale has not used us well, in coming so near without coming nearer.[4] I know not what he can say for himself, but I know that he can take shelter in sullen silence.

There is, I think, still the same prospect of a plentiful harvest. We have in this part of the kingdom had rain to swell the grain, and sunshine to ripen it. I was yesterday to see the Dr.'s

1. *Ante* To Hester Thrale, 6 July 1775, n. 5.
2. MS: two words heavily del.
3. *Ante* To Hester Thrale, 15 July 1775, n. 4.
4. *Ante* To Hester Thrale, 15 July 1775 and n. 1.

Poland Oats.[5] They grow, for a great part, four feet high, with a stalk equal in bulk and strength to Wheaten Straw. We were of opinion that they must be reaped, as the lower joints would be too hard for fodder. We will try them.

Susy was always my little girl; see what she is come to, you must keep her in mind of me, who was always on her side. Of Mrs. Fanny I have no knowledge.[6]

You have two or three of my Letters to answer, and I hope you will be very copious and distinct, and tell me a great deal of your mind; a dear little mind it is, and I hope always to love it better, as I know it more. I am, Madam, Your most humble servant,

SAM. JOHNSON

5. *Ante* To Hester Thrale, 17 July 1775 and n. 6.

6. It is likely that SJ refers to the newborn Frances Anna. Cf. *Ante* To Hester Thrale, 1 July 1775.

Hester Thrale

FRIDAY 21 JULY 1775

MS: Hyde Collection.

Dear Lady: Ashbourn, July 21, 1775

When you write next, direct to Lichfield, for I think to move that way on tuesday,[1] and in no long time to turn homewards, when we will have a serious consultation, and try to do every thing for the best.

I shall be glad of a letter from dear Queeney, and am not sorry that she wishes for me. When I come we will enter into an alliance defensive at least.

Mr. Baretti very elegantly sent his pupil's letter to Mrs. Williams without a cover, in such a manner that she knew not whence it was transmitted.[2]

1. *Post* To Hester Thrale, 26 July 1775.

2. *Ante* To Hester Thrale, 12 July 1775 and n. 4.

I do not mean to bleed but with your concurrence,[3] though I am troubled with eruptions, which I cannot suppress by frequent physick.

As my Master staid only one day, we must forgive him, yet he knows he staid only one day because he thought it not worth his while to stay two.[4]

You and Baretti are friends again.[5] My dear Mistress has the quality of being easily reconciled, and not easily offended. Kindness is a good thing in itself; and there are few things that are worthy of anger, and still fewer that can justify malignity.

Nothing remains for the present but that you sit down placid and content, disposed to enjoy the present and planning the proper use of the future liberalities of Providence. You have really much to enjoy, and without any wild indulgence of imagination much to expect. In the mean time, however, life is gliding away, and another state is hastening forwards. You were but five and twenty when I knew you first,[6] and you are now—What I shall be next September I confess I have lacheté enough to turn aside from thinking.

I am glad that you read Boswel's journal,[7] you are now sufficiently informed of the whole transaction, and need not regret that you did not make the tour of the Hebrides.

You have done me honour in naming me your Trustee, and have very judiciously chosen Cator.[8] I believe our fidelity will

3. Cf. *Ante* To Hester Thrale, *c.* 3 July 1775.

4. *Ante* To Hester Thrale, 15 July 1775 and n. 1; 20 July 1775. Hester Thrale had written to SJ that her husband "staid but one Day" in Derby (20 July 1775, MS: Rylands Library).

5. *Ante* To Hester Thrale, 15 July 1775 and n. 3. On 18 July Hester Thrale reported to SJ, "Baretti has been very good, and taken Care of my little ones like a Nurse while I was away, and has not failed writing me etc. and I am sorry I was so peevish with him" (MS: Rylands Library).

6. When SJ and the Thrales first met, 9 Jan. 1765, Hester was twenty-three (Hyde, 1977, pp. 2, 19).

7. *Ante* To Hester Thrale, 22 May 1775 and n. 5.

8. *Ante* To Hester Thrale, 6 July 1775, n. 10. In her letter of 18 July, Hester Thrale informed SJ that she had appointed him a trustee of the estate, along with John Cator (1728–1806), of Beckenham, Kent, timber merchant and M.P. for

not be exposed to any strong temptations. I am, Madam, your most humble Servant,

SAM. JOHNSON

Wallingford (1772–80) (Namier and Brooke II.198–99). Although she found Cator loud and vulgar, Hester Thrale valued his loyalty and business acumen (Hyde, 1977, p. 129).

Hester Thrale

MONDAY 24 JULY 1775

MS: Hyde Collection.

Dear Madam: [Ashbourne] July 24, 1775

Be pleased to return my thanks to Queeney for her pretty little letter. I hope the Peacock will recover. It is pity we cannot catch the fellow, we would make him drink at the pump. The victory over the poor wild cat delights me but little. I had rather he had taken a chicken than lost his life.

To morrow I go to Lichfield. My company would not any longer make the Doctor happy. He wants to be rambling with his Ashbourn Friends. And it is perhaps time for me to think of coming home. Which way I shall take, I do not know.

Miss says that you have recovered your spirits, and that you all are well. Pray do not grudge the trouble of[1] telling me so your own self, for I do not find my attention to you and your sensations, at all lessened, by this time of absence which always appears to my imagination much longer than when I count it.

Now to morrow I expect to see Lucy Porter, and Mrs. Adey, and to hear how they have gone on at Lichfield. And then for a little I shall wander about, as the birds of passage circle and flutter, before they set out on the main flight.

I have been generally without any violent disorder of either mind or body, but every now and then ailing, but so that I could keep it to myself.

1. MS: "of" repeated as catchword

Are we to go to Brighthelmston this autumn?[2] I do not enquire with any great solicitude. You know one reason, and it will not be easy to find another, except that which brings all thither that go, unwillingness to stay at home, and want of power to supply with either business or amusement, the cravings of the day. From this distress all that know either You or me, will suppose that we might rescue ourselves, if we would, without the help of a bath in the morning and an assemb[l]y at night. I am, Madam, Your most humble servant,

SAM. JOHNSON

2. *Ante* To Hester Thrale, 9 July 1775 and n. 5.

Hester Thrale

WEDNESDAY 26 JULY 1775

MS: Hyde Collection.

Dear Madam: Lichfield, July 26, 1775

Yesterday I came hither; after dinner I went to Stow hill; there I was pampered, and had an uneasy night; Physick to day put me out of order; and for some time I forgot that this is post night.

Nothing very extraordinary has happened at Lichfield since I went away. Lucy Porter is better, and has got her lame hand out of the bag.[1] The rest of your friends I have not seen.

Having staid long enough at Ashbourn I was not sorry to leave it. I hindred some of Taylors diversions and he supplied me with very little. Having seen the neighbouring places I had no curiosity to gratify, and having few new things, we had little new talk.

When I came I found Lucy at her book. She had Hammond's commentary on the Psalms before her.[2] He is very

1. *Ante* To Hester Thrale, 11 June 1775 and n. 4.

2. SJ refers to *Paraphrase and Annotations upon . . . the Psalms* (1659) by Henry Hammond (1605–60), D.D., Chaplain to Charles I. SJ was "extremely fond of Dr.

learned, she says, but there is enough that any body may understand.

Now I am here I think myself a great deal nearer London than before, for though the distance is not very different, I am here in the way of Carriages, and can easily get to Birmingham, and so to Oxford, but I know not which way I shall take, but some way or other I hope to find that may bring me back again to Streatham; and then I shall see what have been my Master's goings on; and will try whether I shall know the old places.

As I lift up my head from the paper I can look into Lucy's Garden. Her walls have all failed.[3] I believe she has had hardly any fruit but Gooseberries, but so[4] much verdure looks pretty in a town.

When you read my letters I suppose you are very proud to think how much you excel in the correspondence: but you must remember that your materials are better. You have a family, and friends, and hopes, and fears, and wishes, and aversions, and all the ingredients that are necessary to the composition of a Letter. Here sit poor I, with nothing but my own solitary individuality; doing little, and suffering no more than I have often suffered; hearing nothing that I can repeat; seeing nothing that I can relate; talking, when I do talk, to those whom you can not regard, and at this moment hearing the curfew which you cannot hear.[5] I am, Dearest, dearest Lady, Your most humble servant,

SAM. JOHNSON

Hammond's Works, and sometimes gave them as a present to young men going into orders: he also bought them for the library at Streatham" (*Johns. Misc.* II.19).

3. Presumably SJ means that the espaliered trees had not been fruitful (Cf. *Ante* To Hester Thrale, 11 July 1775).

4. MS: "so" repeated as catchword

5. The church bells of St. Mary's, Lichfield's civic church, rang at eight o'clock every evening to signal the curfew (information supplied by Dr. G. W. Nicholls).

Hester Thrale

SATURDAY 29 JULY 1775

MS: Hyde Collection.

Madam: [Lichfield] July 29, 1775

The rain caught me at Stowhill, and kept me till it is very late. I must however write for I am enjoined to tell you how much Mrs. Lucy was pleased with your present, and to entreat you to excuse her from writing because her hand is not yet recovered.[1] She is very glad of your notice, and very thankful.

Lucy may thank you if she will, but you shall have no thanks from me, for Wisdom—and critical eruptions—and advanced life— Such Stuf.[2] I remember to have read in a book called the *Catholicon*,[3] that all evil begins *ab undecimo*.[4] What then must be the evil of *three times eleven* or thirty three.[5] However I have burnt the letter.

What you tell me of your *Reste*[6] and ten-thousand pounds, has more sense in it. Will it not be now in our power to pay Mr. Scrase?[7]

I am very desirous that Mr. Lester should be sent for a few weeks to Brighthelmston.[8] Air, and Vacancy, and novelty, and the consciousness of his own value, and the pride of such distinction, and delight in Mr. Thrale's kindness would as Cheney

1. *Ante* To Hester Thrale, 10 June 1775; 17 June 1775.

2. The context makes it almost certain that this "Stuf" appeared in a letter (unrecovered) from Hester Thrale. Her reflections on "advanced life" may well have been sparked by SJ's comments in his letter of 21 July.

3. It is likely that SJ refers to the *Catholicon* of Giovanni Balbi, "the most important of the Latin dictionaries of the Middle Ages. . . . Its text includes a Latin grammar, but the greatest part of it consists of a huge etymological dictionary which in fact amounts to an encyclopedia" (R. N. Schwab, "Some Signs of Stereotyping of the Yale Vellum Copy of the Mainz *Catholicon*," *Yale University Library Gazette* 63, 1988, p. 8). Balbi's *Catholicon*, compiled in the thirteenth century, was first printed in 1460; SJ may well have consulted the copy in the Bodleian Library.

4. *ab undecimo*: "from the eleventh (year)"

5. In Jan. 1775 Hester Thrale had turned thirty-four.

6. *Ante* To Hester Thrale, 24 May 1773, n. 11. Cf. *Post* To Hester Thrale, 22 May 1776.

7. *Ante* To Hester Thrale, 12 July 1775 and n. 10.

8. "Mr. Lester" was "one of the chief Clerks" at the Brewery (Piozzi 1.291).

phrases it, afford all the relief that human art can give, or human nature receive.[9] Do not read this slightly, you may prolong a very useful life.

Whether the pineapples be ripe or rotten, whether the Duke's Venison be baked or roasted, I begin to think it time I were at home. I have staid till perhaps nobody wishes me to stay longer except the Ladies on the hill, who offer me a lodging, and though not ill, am unsettled enough to wish for change of place, even though that change were not to bring me to Streatham. But thither I hope I shall quickly come, and find you all well, and gay, and happy, and catch a little gayety and health, and happiness among you. I am, Dearest of all dear Ladies, Your most humble servant,

SAM. JOHNSON

9. "To these I *seriously* affirm, that this *Method*, strictly and for Time sufficient pursued, will afford all the *Ease* which human *Art* can give, or human *Nature* receive" (George Cheyne, *The Natural Method of Curing the Diseases of the Body, and the Disorders of the Mind Depending on the Body*, 1742, [A4v]).

Hester Thrale

TUESDAY 1 AUGUST 1775

MS: Hyde Collection.

Dear Madam: [Lichfield] August 1, 1775

I wonder how it could happen. I forgot that the post went out yester night, and so omitted to write.[1] I therefore send this by the bypost,[2] and hope it will come that I may not lose my regular letter.

This was to have been my last letter from this place but Lucy says I must not go this week. Fits of tenderness with Mrs. Lucy are not common, but she seems now to have a little paroxysm, and I was not willing to counteract it. When I am to go I shall take care to inform you. The Lady at Stowhill says,[3] how comes

1. Mail left Lichfield for London on Monday, Wednesday, and Saturday evenings.

2. *Ante* To Edmund Allen, 17 June 1775, n. 1.

3. SJ refers to Elizabeth Aston.

Lucy to be such a sovereign; all the tow[n] besides could not have kept you.

America now fills every mouth, and some heads; and a little of it shall come into my letter. I do not much like the news. Our troops have indeed the Superiority, five and twenty hundred have driven five thousand from their intrenchment but the Americans fought skilfully; had coolness enough in the battle to carry off their men; and seem[4] to have retreated orderly for they were not persued.[5] They want nothing but confidence in their leaders and famili[ari]ty with danger. Our business is to persue their main army, and disperse it by a decisive battle and then waste the country till they sue for peace. If we make war by parties and detachments, dislodge them from one place, and exclude them from another, we shall by a local, gradual, and ineffectual war, teach them our own knowledge, harden their obstinacy, and strengthen their confidence, and at last come to fight on equal terms of skill and bravery, without equal numbers.

Mrs. Williams wrote me word, that you had honoured her with a visit, and *behaved lovely.*

Mr. Thrale left off digging his pool, I suppose for want of water.[6] The first thing to be done is by digging in three or four places to try how near the springs will rise to the surface; for though we cannot hope to be always full, we must be sure never to be dry.

Poor Sir Linch! I am sorry for him. It is sad to give a family of children no pleasure but by dying.[7] It was said of Otho.[8]

4. MS: "seems"

5. News of the battle of Bunker Hill (17 June) reached London on 25 July (*Walpole's Correspondence,* Yale ed. XXIV.119 n. 1). Over 1,000 British troops were killed or wounded, almost half the army of 2,300 men. By contrast, the American forces (estimated at 3,500) suffered casualties of between 400 and 600 men (R. M. Ketchum, *The Battle for Bunker Hill,* 1962, pp. 144, 147; J. R. Elting, *The Battle of Bunker's Hill,* 1975, p. 38).

6. *Ante* To Hester Thrale, 11 July 1775.

7. Sir Lynch Salusbury Cotton (1705–75), fourth Bt., of Llewenny, Denbighshire, and Combermere, Cheshire, M.P. for Denbighshire (1749–74), Hester Thrale's miserly uncle, had treated his children with a signal lack of "Tenderness and Attention" (*Thraliana* I.46, 103; Namier and Brooke II.260).

8. Otho (A.D. 32–69), Roman governor of Lusitania, became emperor in Jan.

Hoc tantum fecit nobile quod perijt.[9] It may be changed to Sir Linch, hoc tantum fecit utile.

If I could do Mr. Carter any good at Oxford, I could easily stop there, for through it, if I go by Birmingham I am likely to pass; but the place is now a sullen solitude. Whatever can be done, I am ready to do; but our operations must for the present be at London. I am, Madam, Your most humble servant,

SAM. JOHNSON

69, having arranged the assassination of his predecessor, Galba. However, Otho's rule was immediately challenged by Vitellius, whose troops were victorious in Apr. 69. Otho then committed suicide.

9. *fine tamen laudandus erit, qui morte decora / hoc solum fecit nobile, quo perrit*: "Yet for his end shall he be deserving praise, who by an honourable death did this one noble deed—he died" (Ausonius, *De XII Caesaribus*, ll. 35–36, trans. H.G.E. White, Loeb ed.). SJ substitutes *utile* ("useful") for *nobile*.

Hester Thrale

WEDNESDAY 2 AUGUST 1775

MS: Birthplace Museum, Lichfield.

Madam: Lichfield, August 2, 17⟨75⟩

I dined to day at Stowhill, and am come away to write my letter. Never surely was I such a writer before. Do you keep my letters? I am not of your opinion that I shall not like to read them hereafter, for though there is in them not much history of mind or any thing else, they will, I hope, always be in some degree the records of a pure and blameless friendship, and in some hours of languour and sadness may revive the memory of more cheerful times.

Why you should suppose yourself not desirous hereafter to read the history of your own mind I do not see.[1] Twelve years

1. In 1773 SJ told JB "that he had twelve or fourteen times attempted to keep a journal of his life, but never could persevere. . . . 'The great thing to be recorded, (said he), is the state of your own mind'" (*Life* II.217). SJ later repeated this idea in conversation with Hester Thrale: "A man loves to review his own mind. That is the use of a diary, or journal" (*Life* III.228).

on which you now look, as on a vast expanse of life will probably be passed over uniformly and smoothly, with very little perception of your progress, and with very few remarks upon the way. That accumulation of knowledge which you promise to yourself, by which the future is to look back upon the present, with the superiority of manhood to infancy, will perhaps never be attempted, or never will be made, and you will find as millions have found before you, that forty five has made little sensible addition to thirty three.[2]

As the body after a certain time gains[3] no encrease of height, and little of strength, there is likewise a period though more variable by external causes, when the mind commonly attains its stationary point, and very little advances its powers of reflection, judgement, and ratiocination. The body may acquire new modes of motion, or new dexterities of mechanick operation, but its original strength receives not improvement; the mind may be stored with new languages, or new sciences, but its power of thinking remains nearly the same, and unless it attains new subjects of meditation, it commonly produces thoughts of the same force and the same extent,[4] at very distant intervals of life, as the tree unless a foreign fruit be ingrafted gives year after year productions of the same form and the same flavour.

By intellectual force or strength of thought is meant the degree of power which the mind possesses of surveying the[5] subject of meditation with its circuit of concomitants, and its train of dependence.

Of[6] this power which all observe to be very different in dif-

2. Forty-five was commonly assumed to be the age beyond which "a man did not improve" (*Life* IV.431). However, in conversation with Thomas Barnard SJ disagreed with this notion (and implicitly contradicted his remarks to Hester Thrale). Barnard responded with a set of witty verses, whose first stanza reformulates the opinion that touched off their "altercation": "I lately thought no man alive, / Could e'er improve past forty-five, / And ventured to assert it; / The observation was not new, / But seem'd to me so just and true, / That none could controvert it" (*Life* IV.115 n. 4, 432).

3. MS: "g" altered from "s"

4. MS: "extent" altered from "extend"

5. MS: undeciphered del. before "the"

6. MS: "Of" altered from "If"

ferent minds, part seems the gift of nature, and part the acquisition of experience. When the powers of nature have attained their intended energy, they can be no more advanced. The shrub can never become a tree. And it is not unreasonable to suppose that [they] are before the middle of life in their full vigour.

Nothing then remains but practice and experience; and perhaps why they do so little may be worth enquiry.

But I have just looked and find it so late, that I will enquire against the next postnight.[7] I am, Madam, your most humble servant,

SAM. JOHNSON

7. *Ante* To Hester Thrale, 1 Aug. 1775, n. 1.

Elizabeth Desmoulins

SATURDAY 5 AUGUST 1775

MS: Hyde Collection.

ADDRESS: To Mrs. Desmoulins in Chelsea.

POSTMARK: PENY POST PAYD T MO, 7 O'CLOCK, COLES.

ENDORSEMENT: Dr. Johnson about Dr. Hawkesworth.

Madam: Lichfield, August 5, 1775

Mr. Garrick has done as he is used to do. You may tell him that Dr. Hawkesworth and I never exchanged any letters worth publication; our notes were commonly to tell when we should be at home, and I believe were seldom kept on either side. If I have any thing that will do any honour to his memory, I shall gladly supply it, but I remember nothing.[1] I am, Madam, Your humble Servant,

SAM. JOHNSON

1. It is possible that Garrick may have been involved in plans for a posthumous edition of Hawkesworth's works, though there is no mention of such a project in his letters. *Post* To John Ryland, 21 Sept. 1776; 14 Nov. 1776; 12 Apr. 1777.

Hester Thrale

SATURDAY 5 AUGUST 1775

MS: Pierpont Morgan Library.

Dear Madam: Lichfield, Aug. 5, 1775

Instead of forty reasons for my return one is sufficient; That you wish for my company. I purpose to write no more till you see me. The Ladies at Stowhill, and Greenhill[1] are unanimously of opinion, that it will be best to take a postchaise, and not be troubled with the vexations of a common carriage. I will venture to suppose the Ladies at Streatham to be of the same mind.

You will now expect to be told why you will not be so much wiser as you expect when you have lived twelve years longer.[2]

It is said and said truly, that Experience is the best teacher, and it is supposed that as life is lengthened, experience is encreased. But a closer inspection of human life will discover that time often passes without any incidents which can much enlarge knowledge or rectify judgement. When we are young, we learn much, because we are universally ignorant, we observe every thing because every [thing] is new. But after some years the occurrences of daily life are exhausted; one day passes like another, in the same scene of appearances, in the same course of transactions; we have to do what we have often done, and what we do not try because we do not wish to do much better, we are told what we already know, and therefore what repetition cannot make us know with greater certainty.

He that has early learned much, perhaps[3] seldom makes with regard to life and manners much addition to his knowledge, Not only because as more is known there is less to learn, but because a mind stored with images and principles, turns inwards for its own entertainment, and is employed in sorting

1. Mary Cobb lived with her niece, Mary Adey, at The Friary, Green Hill, Lichfield—"a sweet old sequestered place close by the town" (*Boswell: The Ominous Years*, ed. Charles Ryskamp and F. A. Pottle, 1963, p. 293; *Reades*, p. 229 and n. 3).

2. *Ante* To Hester Thrale, 2 Aug. 1775.

3. MS: "berhaps"

those ideas which run into confusion, and in recollecting those which are stealing away, practices by which wisdom may be kept but not gained. The merchant who was at first busy in acquiring[4] money, ceases to grow richer, from the time when he make it his business only to count it.

Those who have families or employments are engaged in business of little difficulty but of great importance, requiring rather assiduity of practice than subtilty of speculation, occupying the attention with images too bulky for refinement, and too obvious for research. The right is already known, what remains is only to follow it. Daily business adds no more to wisdom, than daily lesson to the learning of the teacher. But of how few lives does not stated duty claim the greater part.

Far the greater part of human minds never endeavour their own improvement. Opinions once received from instruction or settled by whatever accident, are seldom recalled to examination; having been once supposed to be right, they are never discovered to be erroneous, for no application is[5] made of any thing that time may present, either to shake or to confirm them. From this acquiescence in preconceptions none are wholly free, between fear of uncertainty, and dislike of labour every one rests while he might yet go forward, and they that were wise at thirty three, are very little wiser at forty five.

Of this Speculation you are perhaps tired, and would rather hear of Sophy. I hope before this comes, that her head will be easier, and your head less filled with fears and troubles, which you know are to be indulged only to prevent evil, not to encrease it.[6]

Your uneasiness about Sophy is probably unnecessary, and at worst your other children are healthful, and your affairs

4. MS: "gain-" del. before "acquiring"

5. MS: "is" superimposed upon "of"

6. On 2 Aug. Hester Thrale recorded in her "Family Book": "Sophie has terrified me into Agonies; She came down this Morning drooping and dismal and complaining of her Head—I concluded Sentence was already past, and that She was about to follow her Brother and Sisters, so I fairly sate me down to cry—but it ended in nothing, She eat a good Dinner, and when the Dancing Master came was as alert as usual" (Hyde, 1977, pp. 127–28).

prosperous. Unmingled good cannot be expected, but as we may lawfully gather all the good within our reach we may be allowed to lament after that which we lose. I hope your losses are at an end, and that as far as the condition of our present existence permits, your remaining life will be happy. I am, Madam, Your most obliged and most humble Servant,

SAM. JOHNSON

James Boswell

SUNDAY 27 AUGUST 1775

PRINTED SOURCE: JB's *Life*, 1791, I.496–97.

Dear Sir, London, August, 27, 1775

I am now returned from the annual ramble into the middle counties. Having seen nothing that I had not seen before, I have nothing to relate. Time has left that part of the island few antiquities; and commerce has left the people no singularities. I was glad to go abroad, and, perhaps, glad to come home; which is, in other words, I was, I am afraid, weary of being at home, and weary of being abroad. Is not this the state of life? But, if we confess this weariness, let us not lament it; for all the wise and all the good say, that we may cure it.

For the black fumes which rise in your mind,[1] I can prescribe nothing but that you disperse them by honest business or innocent pleasure, and by reading sometimes easy and sometimes serious. Change of place is useful; and I hope that your residence at Auchinleck will have many good effects. * * * * * *.[2]

That I should have given pain to Rasay, I am sincerely sorry; and am therefore very much pleased that he is no longer un-

1. JB had informed SJ: "My mind has been somewhat dark this summer. I have need of your warming and vivifying rays; and I hope I shall have them frequently. I am going to pass some time with my father at Auchinleck" (*Life* II.381).

2. JB's directions to the printer of the *Life* indicate that a passage beginning "You never" has been deleted (MS: Beinecke Library).

easy.[3] He still thinks that I have represented him as personally giving up the Chieftainship. I meant only that it was no longer contested between the two houses, and supposed it settled, perhaps, by the cession of some remote generation, in the house of Dunvegan. I am sorry the advertisement was not continued for three or four times in the papers.

That Lord Monboddo and Mr. Macqueen should controvert a position contrary to the imaginary interest of literary or national prejudice, might be easily imagined;[4] but of a standing fact there ought to be no controversy: If there are men with tails, catch an *homo caudatus*;[5] if there was writing of old in the Highlands or Hebrides, in the Erse language, produce the manuscripts. Where men write, they will write to one another, and some of their letters, in families studious of their ancestry, will be kept. In Wales there are many manuscripts.

I have now three parcels of Lord Hailes's history, which I purpose to return all the next week:[6] that his respect for my little observations should keep his work in suspense, makes one of the evils of my journey. It is in our language, I think, a new mode of history, which tells all that is wanted, and, I suppose, all that is known, without laboured splendour of language, or affected subtilty of conjecture. The exactness of his dates raises my wonder. He seems to have the closeness of Henault without his constraint.[7]

Mrs. Thrale was so entertained with your "Journal," that she almost read herself blind.[8] She has a great regard for you.

Of Mrs. Boswell, though she knows in her heart that she does not love me, I am always glad to hear any good, and hope

3. *Ante* To John Macleod, 6 May 1775; *Ante* To Hester Thrale, 12 May 1775.

4. JB had reported: "Mr. Donald Macqueen and Lord Monboddo supped with me one evening. They joined in controverting your proposition, that the Gaelick of the Highlands and Isles of Scotland was not written till of late" (*Life* II.380–81).

5. *Ante* To Hester Thrale, 25 Aug. 1773 and n. 14.

6. *Ante* To JB, 4 July 1774, n. 4.

7. Charles Jean François Hénault (1685–1770), historian and playwright, President of the Première Chambre des Enquêtes and author of the immensely successful *Nouvel Abrégé chronologique de l'histoire de France* (1744). *Post* To JB, 10 Jan. 1776.

8. *Ante* To Hester Thrale, 22 May 1775, n. 5.

that she and the little dear ladies will have neither sickness nor any other affliction. But she knows that she does not care what becomes of me, and for that she may be sure that I think her very much to blame.

Never, my dear Sir, do you take it into your head to think that I do not love you; you may settle yourself in full confidence both of my love and my esteem; I love you as a kind man, I value you as a worthy man, and hope in time to reverence you as a man of exemplary piety. I hold you as Hamlet has it, "in my heart of heart,"[9] and, therefore, it is little to say, that I am, Sir, Your affectionate humble servant,

SAM. JOHNSON

9. "Give me that man / That is not passion's slave, and I will wear him / In my heart's core, ay, in my heart of heart / As I do thee" (*Hamlet* III.ii.71–74).

John Hoole

MONDAY 28 AUGUST 1775

MS: Hyde Collection.

ADDRESS: To Mr. Hoole.

ENDORSEMENT: On my third accident of breaking my kneepan.

Dear Sir: August 28, 1775

You are very unfortunate, or very careless. But take great care not to lay any stress upon your knee till it is quite strong. To recover from such hurts so often I take to be uncommon, to recover again can hardly be expected, if you should again do yourself the same mischief.

I am very much obliged by your kind invitation, and return my sincere thanks to you and Mrs. Hoole, but it so happens, that I am engaged to go to Brighthelmston, I think, on Monday.[1] If that design be laid aside, you may expect, Sir, Your most etc.

SAM. JOHNSON

1. *Ante* To Hester Thrale, 9 July 1775, n. 4. The Thrales and SJ intended to go to Brighton; plans changed, however, and on 15 Sept. they left for France (*Post* To Lucy Porter, 9 Sept. 1775; *Post* To JB, 14 Sept. 1775).

Hester Thrale

TUESDAY 29 AUGUST 1775

MS: Houghton Library.

Madam: Aug. 29, 1775

Here is a rout and bustle; and a bustle, and a rout; as if nobody had ever before forgotten where a thing was laid. At l[e]ast there is no great harm done both Colson and Scot have copies; and real haste there is none.[1] You will find it some day this week and any day will serve, or perhaps we can recollect it between us.

About your memory we will, if you please, have some serious talk. I fret at your forgetfulness, as I do at my own. We will try to mend both; yours at least is, I should hope, remediable. But, however it happens, we are of late never together.

Am I to come to morrow to the Borough, or will any call on me? This sorry foot! and this sorry Doctor Laurence who says it is the Gout! But then he thinks every thing the gout, and so I will try not to believe him. Into the sea, I suppose, you will send it, and into the sea I design it shall go.[2]—Can you remember, dear Madam, that I have a lame foot? I am sure I cannot forget it, if you had one so painful you would *so* remember it. Pain is good for the memory. I am, Dear Madam, Your most humble servant,

SAM. JOHNSON

1. SJ's references to John Coulson and William Scott suggest that the missing papers related to the scheme for an Oxford riding school under Charles Carter's direction (Cf. *Ante* To Hester Thrale, 8 Mar. 1775).

2. *Ante* To John Hoole, 28 Aug. 1775 and n. 1.

James Boswell

WEDNESDAY 30 AUGUST 1775

PRINTED SOURCE: JB's *Life*, 1791, I.498.

Sir, August 30, 1775

If in these papers, there is little alteration attempted, do not suppose me negligent. I have read them perhaps more closely than the rest; but I find nothing worthy of an objection.[1]

Write to me soon, and write often, and tell me all your honest heart. I am, Sir, Your's affectionately,

SAM. JOHNSON

1. SJ refers to the "three parcels of Lord Hailes's history" (*Ante* To JB, 27 Aug. 1775).

Lucy Porter

SATURDAY 9 SEPTEMBER 1775

MS: Pembroke College, Oxford. A copy in the hand of Thomas Harwood.

Dear Madam, London, Sept. 9, 1775

I have sent your Books by the Carrier, and in Sandys's Travels you will find your glasses.[1]

I have written this post to the ladies at Stow-hill, and you may, the day after you have this, or at any other time, send Mrs. Gastrel's Books.

Be pleased to make my Compliments to all my good friends.

I hope the poor dear hand is recovered, and you are now able to write, which, however, you need not do, for I am going to Brighthelmston,[2] and when I come back, will take care to tell you. In the mean time take great care of your health, and

1. SJ had sent Lucy Porter two books: *A Relation of a Journey begun in 1610* (1615) by George Sandys (1578–1644) and *Paraphrase and Annotations on the New Testament* (1653) by Henry Hammond (1605–60). *Post* To Lucy Porter, *c.* 23 Dec. 1775.

2. *Ante* To John Hoole, 28 Aug. 1775 and n. 1.

drink as much as you can. I am, Dearest Love, Your most humble servant,

SAM. JOHNSON

James Boswell

THURSDAY 14 SEPTEMBER 1775

MS: Beinecke Library. The transcript (in the hand of Veronica Boswell, with corrections by JB) used as copy for JB's *Life*.

My Dear Sir: Septr. 14th 1775

I now write to you, lest in some of your freaks and humours you should fancy yourself neglected. Such fancies I must entreat you never to admit, at least never to indulge, for my regard for you is so radicated[1] and fixed that it is become part of my mind, and cannot be effaced but by some cause uncommonly violent. Therefore, whether I write, or not, set your thoughts at rest—I now write to tell you that I shall not very soon write again, for I am to set out to morrow on another journey.[2]

* * * *

Your friends are all well at Streatham and in Leicester fields.[3] Make my compliments to Mrs. Boswell if she is in good humour with me. I am, Sir, etc.

SAM. JOHNSON

1. *radicate*: "to root, to plant deeply and firmly" (SJ's *Dictionary*).

2. *Ante* To John Hoole, 28 Aug. 1775 and n. 1; *Post* To Robert Levet, 18 Sept. 1775 and n. 1.

3. SJ refers to Sir Joshua Reynolds and his nieces (*Post* To Frances Reynolds, 15 Feb. 1779, n. 2).

Robert Levet

MONDAY 18 SEPTEMBER 1775

PRINTED SOURCE: JB's *Life*, 1793, II.257.

Dear Sir, Sept. 18, 1775, Calais

We are here in France, after a very pleasing passage of no more than six hours.[1] I know not when I shall write again,[2] and therefore I write now, though you cannot suppose that I have much to say. You have seen France yourself.[3] From this place we are going to Rouen, and from Rouen to Paris, where Mr. Thrale designs to stay about five or six weeks.[4] We have a regular recommendation to the English resident,[5] so we shall not be taken for vagabonds.[6] We think to go one way and return another,[7] and see[8] as much as we can, I will try to speak a little French; I tried hitherto but little, but I spoke sometimes.[9] If I heard better, I suppose I should learn faster. I am, Sir, Your humble servant,

SAM. JOHNSON

1. The travelers (Henry and Hester Thrale, SJ, Queeney, and Giuseppe Baretti) sailed from Dover the morning of the 17th. Hester Thrale recorded in her journal, "The Weather was lovely—the Ship all our own, the Sea smooth" (*The French Journals of Mrs. Thrale and Doctor Johnson*, ed. Moses Tyson and Henry Guppy, 1932, p. 70). They arrived in time for dinner and a tour of the Capuchin monastery (Tyson and Guppy, *French Journals*, p. 71).

2. *Post* To Robert Levet, 22 Oct. 1775.

3. "Mr. Levett, though an Englishman by birth, became early in life a waiter at a coffee-house in Paris" (*GM* 1785, p. 101).

4. Later on the 18th they left Calais and traveled to Paris via St. Omer, Arras, Amiens, and Rouen, arriving on the 28th. They left Paris on 1 Nov. (Tyson and Guppy, *French Journals*, pp. 72–89, 149).

5. *resident*: "an agent, minister, or officer residing in any distant place with the dignity of an ambassador" (SJ's *Dictionary*).

6. In Paris the Thrales "applied . . . to the English Ambassador" for "his Protection" (Tyson and Guppy, *French Journals*, p. 128). From 1772 to 1778 the Ambassador was David Murray (1727–96), seventh Viscount Stormont, later (1793) second Earl of Mansfield.

7. The party traveled back from Paris to Calais via Chantilly, Noyon, Cambrai, Douai, Lisle, and Dunkirk (Tyson and Guppy, *French Journals*, pp. 149–61).

8. I follow Hill (*Life* II.385) and Chapman (II.86) in emending "for" (JB's *Life*, 1793, II.257) to "see."

9. "When Johnson was in France, he was generally very resolute in speaking Latin. It was a maxim with him that a man should not let himself down, by speaking a language which he speaks imperfectly" (*Life* II.404).

Robert Levet

SUNDAY 22 OCTOBER 1775

PRINTED SOURCE: JB's *Life*, 1793, II.257–58.

Dear Sir, Paris, Oct. 22, 1775

We are still here, commonly very busy in looking about us. We have been to day at Versailles. You have seen it, and I shall not describe it.[1] We came yesterday from Fontainbleau, where the Court is now. We went to see the King and Queen at dinner, and the Queen was so impressed by Miss, that she sent one of the gentlemen to enquire who she was.[2] I find all true that you have ever told me of Paris. Mr. Thrale is very liberal, and keeps us two coaches, and a very fine table; but I think our cookery very bad.[3] Mrs. Thrale got into a convent of English nuns, and I talked with her through the grate,[4] and I am very kindly used by the English Benedictine friars.[5] But upon the

1. To judge from SJ's journal entry, he was more impressed with the menagerie at Versailles than with the palace itself (*Works*, Yale ed. I.241–43).

2. On 19 Oct. Hester Thrale recorded in her journal: "Monsieur & Madame [the future Louis XVIII and his wife, Marie Joséphine of Savoy] dine together in another Room. . . . They likewise sat like two people stuffed with straw; and only spoke to enquire after our Niggey [Queeney], about whom the Queen had likewise before been very inquisitive" (*The French Journals of Mrs. Thrale and Doctor Johnson*, ed. Moses Tyson and Henry Guppy, 1932, p. 125).

3. In his journal SJ described French cuisine as "gross," a verdict confirmed by Hester Thrale: "No Meat here has the Taste of Meat in England; Onions & Cheese prevail in all the Dishes, & overpower the natural Taste of the Animal excepting only when it stinks indeed, which is not infrequently the Case" (Tyson and Guppy, *French Journals*, p. 130).

4. Hester Thrale spent most of 16 Oct. with the Austin nuns of Notre Dame de Sion, Rue des Fossés St. Victor. The Abbess was the niece of Arabella Fermor, "Belinda" of Pope's *Rape of the Lock* (Tyson and Guppy, *French Journals*, pp. 120–22).

5. On 3 Oct. Cecilia Strickland, an old friend of Hester Thrale, took the travelers to visit "a Convent of English Benedictine Monks"—the monastery of St. Edmund the King in Paris (Tyson and Guppy, *French Journals*, pp. 59–60, 97). SJ and Hester Thrale struck up a friendship with the Prior, Father William Cowley, who arranged a cell at the monastery for SJ's use (*French Journals*, pp. 99, 110; *Works*, Yale ed. I.231, 247, 250; *Life* II.402; Waingrow, p. 82 n. 3). SJ spent his last day in Paris at the monastery and "parted very tenderly from the Prior and Frier

whole I cannot make much acquaintance here, and though the churches, palaces, and some private houses are very magnificent, there is no very great pleasure after having seen many, in seeing more; at least the pleasure, whatever it be, must some time have an end, and we are beginning to think when we shall come home. Mr. Thrale calculates that as we left Streatham on the fifteenth of September, we shall see it again about the fifteenth of November.[6]

I think I had not been on this side of the sea five days before I found a sensible improvement in my health. I ran a race in the rain this day, and beat Baretti. Baretti is a fine fellow, and speaks French, I think, quite as well as English.

Make my compliments to Mrs. Williams; and give my love to Francis, and tell my friends that I am not lost. I am, dear Sir, Your affectionate humble, etc.

SAM. JOHNSON

[Joseph] Wilkes" (*Works,* Yale ed. 1.253; J. M. Osborn, "Dr. Johnson and the Contrary Converts," privately printed for The Johnsonians, 1954, pp. 6–7 and n.*).

6. The travelers landed at Dover on 11 Nov. and returned to Streatham on the 13th (Hyde, 1977, p. 143).

James Boswell

THURSDAY 16 NOVEMBER 1775

PRINTED SOURCE: JB's *Life,* 1791, 1.499–500.

Dear Sir, November 16, 1775

I am glad that the young Laird is born,[1] and an end, as I hope, put to the only difference that you can ever have with Mrs. Boswell.[2] I know that she does not love me, but I intend to persist in wishing her well till I get the better of her.

1. On 24 Oct. JB had written to inform SJ of the birth of his son and heir Alexander on 9 Oct. (*Life* II.386).

2. Margaret Boswell objected strongly to JB's insistence on exclusively male succession to the Auchinleck estates, fearing that he would disinherit his daughters (*Boswell: The Ominous Years,* ed. Charles Ryskamp and F. A. Pottle, 1963, pp. 184–86). *Post* To JB, 15 Jan. 1776; 3 Feb. 1776; 9 Feb. 1776.

Paris is, indeed, a place very different from the Hebrides, but it is to a hasty traveller not so fertile of novelty, nor affords so many opportunities of remark. I cannot pretend to tell the publick any thing of a place better known to many of my readers than to myself.[3] We can talk of it when we meet.

I shall go next week to Streatham, from whence I purpose to send a parcel of the "History" every post.[4] Concerning the character of Bruce, I can only say, that I do not see any great reason for writing it, but I shall not easily deny what Lord Hailes and you concur in desiring.[5]

I have been remarkably healthy all the journey, and hope you and your family have known only that trouble and danger which has so happily terminated. Among all the congratulations that you may receive, I hope you believe none more warm or sincere, than those of, dear Sir, Your most affectionate,

SAM. JOHNSON

3. In his letter of 24 Oct. JB had inquired, "Shall we have '*A Journey to Paris*' from you in the winter?" (*Life* II.386).

4. *Ante* To JB, 4 July 1774, n. 4; 27 Aug. 1775.

5. Hailes had requested JB's assistance in persuading SJ to compose a "character" of Robert the Bruce for inclusion in the *Annals* (*Life* II.386).

Edmund Hector

THURSDAY 16 NOVEMBER 1775

MS: Hyde Collection.

ADDRESS: To Mr. Hector in Birmingham.

POSTMARK: 16 NO.

Dear Sir: Fleetstreet, Nov. 16, 1775

On tuesday I returned from a ramble about France, and about a month's stay at Paris.[1] I have seen nothing that much delighted or surprised me. Their palaces are splendid, and their Churches magnificent in their structure, and gorgeous in their

1. *Ante* To Robert Levet, 18 Sept. 1775 and n. 4; 22 Oct. 1775 and n. 6.

ornaments, but the city in general makes a very mean appearance.

When I opened my letters, I found that you had very kindly complied with all my requests. The Bar may be sent in a box directed to me at Henry Thrale Esq. in Southwark. The whole company that you saw went to France together,[2] and the Queen was so pleased with our little girl, that she sent to enquire who she was.[3]

We are all well, but I find, my dear Sir, that you are ill. I hope it dos not continue true that you are almost a cripple. Would not a warm bath have helped you? Take care of yourself for my sake as well as that of your other Friends. I have the best claim to your attention, if priority be allowed any advantages. Dear Mrs. Careless, I know, will be careful of you. I can only wish you well, and of my good wishes you may be always certain, for I am, Dear Sir, Your most affectionate,

SAM. JOHNSON

2. On their return from Wales in 1774, SJ and the three Thrales (Henry, Hester, and Queeney) had breakfasted in Birmingham with Hector (*Life* v.458).

3. *Ante* To Robert Levet, 22 Oct. 1775 and n. 2.

Lucy Porter

THURSDAY 16 NOVEMBER 1775

MS: Hyde Collection.

Dear Madam: Nov. 16, 1775

This week I came home from Paris.[1] I have brought you a little box which I thought pretty, but I know not whether it is properly a snuffbox, or a box for some other use.[2] I will send it when I can find an opportunity. I have been through the whole Journey remarkably well. My fellow travellers were the

1. *Ante* To Robert Levet, 22 Oct. 1775 and n. 6.

2. At the "palais marchand" on 17 Oct. SJ had purchased "a snufbox" for twenty-four livres (*Works*, Yale ed. 1.237).

same whom you saw at Lichfield, only we took Baretti with us.[3] Paris is not so fine a place as you would expect. The palaces and Churches however are very splendid and magnificent, and what would please you, there are many very fine pictures, but I do not think their way of life commodious or pleasant.

Let me know how your health has been all this while. I hope the fine summer has given you strength sufficient to encounter the Winter.

Make my compliments to all my friends, and if your fingers will let you, write to me, or let your maid write, if it be troublesome to you.[4] I am, Dear Madam, your most affectionate, humble servant,

SAM. JOHNSON

3. On the way to Wales in July 1774, SJ had introduced Henry, Hester, and Queeney Thrale to Lucy Porter (*Life* v.428).

4. Lucy Porter had been suffering from gout in her hand (*Ante* To Hester Thrale, 10 June 1775).

John Taylor

THURSDAY 16 NOVEMBER 1775

MS: Berg Collection, New York Public Library.

ENDORSEMENTS: 1775, 16 Novr. 1775, abt. the French.

Dear Sir: London, Nov. 16, 1775

I came back last tuesday from France.[1] Is not mine a kind of life turned upside down. Fixed to a spot when I was young, and roving the world when others are contriving to sit still, I am wholly unsettled. I am a kind of ship with a wide sail, and without an anchor.

Now I am come home, let me know how it is with you. I hope you are well, and intend to keep your residence this year.[2] Let

1. *Ante* To Robert Levet, 22 Oct. 1775 and n. 6.

2. *Ante* To John Taylor, 23 Mar. 1775 and nn. 1, 2.

me know the month, and I will contrive to be about you. Our Friendship has now lasted so long, that it is valuable for its antiquity. Perhaps neither has any other companion to whom he can talk of his early years. Let me particularly know the state of your health. I think mine is the better for the journey. The French have a clear air and a fruitful soil, but their mode of common life is gross, and incommodious, and disgusting. I am come home convinced that no improvement of general use is to be gained among them. I am, Dear Sir, Your affectionate servant,

SAM. JOHNSON

Jane Burke

MID-TO-LATE NOVEMBER 1775

MS: Sheffield City Libraries (Fitzwilliam MSS).

ENDORSEMENT in the hand of Edmund Burke: Mrs. Burke on her Fathers death, From Dr. Johnson.

Madam:

Among those who really share your pleasures and your troubles, give me leave to condole with you upon the death of a Friend whom I loved much, and whom you undoubtedly loved much more.[1] His death has taken from us the benefit of his counsel, and the delight of his conversation, but it cannot without our own fault, deprive us of the influence of his virtues, or efface the pleasing remembrance of his Worth, his Integrity, and his Piety. I am, Madam, your most humble Servant,

SAM. JOHNSON

1. Jane Burke's father, Dr. Christopher Nugent, died 12 Nov. 1775 (*Burke's Correspondence* III.236). SJ presumably received the news of Nugent's death soon after his return to London on the 14th.

Elizabeth Montagu

FRIDAY 15 DECEMBER 1775

PRINTED SOURCE: JB's *Life*, ed. Croker, 1831, III.295.

Madam, 15th Dec. 1775

Having, after my return from a little ramble to France, passed some time in the country,[1] I did not hear, till I was told by Miss Reynolds, that you were in town; and when I did hear it, I heard likewise that you were ill. To have you detained among us by sickness is to enjoy your presence at too dear a rate. I suffer myself to be flattered with hope that only half the intelligence is now true, and that you are now so well as to be able to leave us, and so kind as not to be willing. I am, madam, your most humble servant,

SAM. JOHNSON

1. SJ had been staying at Streatham Park for approximately three weeks (*Ante* To JB, 16 Nov. 1775).

Elizabeth Montagu

SUNDAY 17 DECEMBER 1775

MS: Hyde Collection.

Madam: Decr. 17, 1775

All that the esteem and reverence of mankind can give you, has been long in your possession, and the little that I can add to the voice of Nations, will not much exalt you; of that little however you are, I hope, very certain.

I wonder, Madam, if you remember Coll in the Hebrides?[1] The Brother and Heir of poor Coll has just been to visit me,[2]

1. Presumably Elizabeth Montagu had not met "Young Coll" in person (*Ante* To Hester Thrale, 30 Sept. 1773, n. 37; *Ante* To JB, 27 Oct. 1774 and n. 1), but had read SJ's account of him in the *Journey.*

2. Alexander Maclean (1753–1835), who had studied with his brother Donald

and I have engaged to dine with him on Thursday.[3] I do not know his lodging, and cannot send him a message, and must therefore suspend the honour which You are pleased to offer, to, Madam, Your most humble Servant,

SAM. JOHNSON

at King's College, Aberdeen, became fourteenth Laird of Coll on the death of his father in 1786 (Fleeman, pp. 196, 268).

3. *Post* To JB, 23 Dec. 1775.

Elizabeth Montagu

THURSDAY 21 DECEMBER 1775

MS: Princeton University Library.

Madam, Thursday, Dec. 21, 1775

I know not when any letter has given me so much pleasure or vexation, as that which I had yesterday the honour of receiving. That You, Madam, should wish for my company, is surely a sufficient reason for being pleased; that I should delay twice,[1] what I had so little right to expect even once, has so bad an appearance, that I can only hope to have it thought, that I am ashamed.

You have kindly allowed me to name aday. Will You be pleased, Madam to accept of me any day after Tuesday? Till I am favoured with your answer, or despair of so much condescention, I shall suffer no engagement[2] to fasten itself upon me. I am, Madam, your most obliged and most humble Servant,

SAM. JOHNSON

1. *Ante* To Elizabeth Montagu, 17 Dec. 1775.
2. MS: "gagement" repeated as catchword

James Boswell

SATURDAY 23 DECEMBER 1775

PRINTED SOURCE: JB's *Life*, 1791, I.515–16.

Dear Sir, December 23, 1775

Never dream of any offence, how should you offend me?[1] I consider your friendship as a possession, which I intend to hold till you take it from me, and to lament if ever by my fault I should lose it. However, when such suspicions find their way into your mind, always give them vent, I shall make haste to disperse them, but hinder their first ingress if you can. Consider such thoughts as morbid.

Such illness as may excuse my omission to Lord Hailes I cannot honestly plead. I have been hindered I know not how, by a succession of petty obstructions. I hope to mend immediately, and to send next post to his Lordship. Mr. Thrale would have written to you if I had omitted; he sends his compliments, and wishes to see you.

You and your lady will now have no more wrangling about feudal inheritance.[2] How does the young Laird of Auchinleck?[3] I suppose Miss Veronica is grown a reader and discourser.

I have just now got a cough, but it has never yet hindered me from sleeping: I have had quieter nights than are common with me.

I cannot but rejoice that Joseph has had the wit to find the way back.[4] He is a fine fellow, and one of the best travellers in the world.

1. In his journal for 18 Dec. JB recorded: "I was uneasy that I had not heard from Dr. Johnson for a long time. I feared that he was ill or had perhaps heard of my defending the Americans and was angry with me. I wrote to him this evening and to Mr. Thrale in case of his being ill" (*Boswell: The Ominous Years*, ed. Charles Ryskamp and F. A. Pottle, 1963, pp. 201–2).

2. *Ante* To JB, 16 Nov. 1775 and n. 2.

3. *Ante* To JB, 16 Nov. 1775 and n. 1.

4. JB's Bohemian servant, Joseph Ritter, had attended the travelers on their Hebridean tour. JB described Ritter as "a fine stately fellow above six feet high, who had been over a great part of Europe, and spoke many languages. He was the

Young Col brought me your letter.[5] He is a very pleasing youth. I took him two days ago to the Mitre, and we dined together. I was as civil as I had the means of being.[6]

I have had a letter from Rasay, acknowledging, with great appearance of satisfaction, the insertion in the Edinburgh paper.[7] I am very glad that it was done.

My compliments to Mrs. Boswell, who does not love me; and of all the rest, I need only send them to those that do; and I am afraid it will give you very little trouble to distribute them. I am, my dear, dear Sir, Your affectionate humble servant,

SAM. JOHNSON

---

best servant I ever saw" (*Hebrides*, p. 33). "After having left me for some time, he [Ritter] had now returned to me" (JB's note, *Life* II.411 n. 2).

5. *Ante* To Elizabeth Montagu, 17 Dec. 1775 and n. 2. JB had supplied Maclean with a letter of introduction dated 5 Dec. (*Life* II.406).

6. "Mr. Maclean returned with the most agreeable accounts of the polite attention with which he was received by Dr. Johnson" (*Life* II.406).

7. *Ante* To Hester Thrale, 24 Sept. 1773 and n. 11; *Ante* To John Macleod, 6 May 1775.

Lucy Porter

c. SATURDAY 23 DECEMBER 1775

MS: Hyde Collection.

ADDRESS: To Mrs. Lucy Porter in Lichfield.

FRANK: Hfreethrale.

POSTMARKS: 2⟨3⟩ DE, FREE, [Undeciphered].

Dear Madam: Dec. 1775

Some weeks ago I wrote to You to tell you that I was just come home from a ramble,[1] and hoped that I should have heard from you; I am afraid Winter has laid hold on your fingers and hinders you from writing. However let somebody write, if you cannot, and tell me how you do, and a little of what has

1. *Ante* To Lucy Porter, 16 Nov. 1775.

happened at Lichfield among our Friends. I hope you are all well. When I was in France, I thought myself growing young,[2] but am afraid that cold weather will take part of my new vigour from me. Let us however take care of ourselves and lose no part of our health by negligence.

I never knew whether you received the Commentary on the New Testament, and the Travels, and the glasses.[3]

Do, my dear Love, write to me, and do not let us forget each other. This is the season of good wishes, and I wish you all good. I have not lately seen Mr. Porter, nor heard of him.[4] Is he with you?

Be pleased to make my compliments to Mrs. Adey, and Mrs. Cobb, and all my friends, and when I can do you any good let me know. I am, Dear Madam, Yours most affectionately,

SAM. JOHNSON

2. Cf. *Ante* To Robert Levet, 22 Oct. 1775; *Ante* To JB, 16 Nov. 1775.

3. *Ante* To Lucy Porter, 9 Sept. 1775 and n. 1.

4. SJ refers to Joseph Porter.

John Taylor

SATURDAY 23 DECEMBER 1775

MS: Free Library of Philadelphia.

ADDRESS: To The Revd. Dr. Taylor at Ashborne, Derbys.

FRANK: Hfreethrale.

POSTMARKS: 23 DE, FREE.

ENDORSEMENTS: 1775, 23 Decr. 75.

Dear Sir: Dec. 23, 1775

Of your affair with Mrs. Wood I can form no judgement.[1] I suppose you have the opinions of the Counsellors. I do not see how a man can settle the succession to his estate beyond his

1. *Ante* To John Taylor, 9 Feb. 1775 and n. 1.

own power of revocation, except by something equivalent to a sale of the reversion, and the mode I think must be that of putting the Buyer in actual possession, and taking from him a lease for life. But of this I know very little. Other modes may be equally binding. I do not know how Mrs. Wood is provided for in your contract with Mr. Wood, on that, I think, something may depend. She has no right, that is, no natural or customary right beyond her life. By getting the estate forever she defeats the claims of consanguinity.

If the Lawyers judge your claim untenable, or even disreputable, I would not have you bring it into the courts. You do not want it, and need not to care much about it. I am, Sir, Your most etc.

SAM. JOHNSON

James Boswell

WEDNESDAY 10 JANUARY 1776

PRINTED SOURCE: JB's *Life*, 1791, II.1–2.

Dear Sir, Jan. 10, 1776

I have at last sent you all Lord Hailes's papers.[1] While I was in France, I looked very often into Henault; but Lord Hailes, in my opinion, leaves him far, and far, behind.[2] Why I did not dispatch so short a perusal sooner, when I look back, I am utterly unable to discover: but human moments are stolen away by a thousand petty impediments which leave no trace behind them. I have been afflicted, through the whole Christmas, with the general disorder, of which the worst effect was a cough, which is now much mitigated, though the country, on which I look from a window at Streatham, is now covered with a deep snow. Mrs. Williams is very ill: every body else is as usual.

Among the papers, I found a letter to you, which I think

1. *Ante* To JB, 4 July 1774, n. 4.

2. *Ante* To JB, 27 Aug. 1775 and n. 7.

you had not opened; and a paper for "The Chronicle," which I suppose it not necessary now to insert.[3] I return them both.

I have, within these few days, had the honour of receiving Lord Hailes's first volume, for which I return my most respectful thanks.[4]

I wish you, my dearest friend, and your haughty lady, (for I know she does not love me,) and the young ladies, and the young Laird, all happiness. Teach the young gentleman, in spite of his mamma, to think and speak well of, Sir, Your affectionate humble servant,

SAM. JOHNSON

3. For twenty-five years (1766–90) JB habitually "inserted" a wide variety of articles, letters, poems, and notices in the *London Chronicle*. These contributions were usually anonymous or pseudonymous (*Lit. Car.*, pp. 236–50).

4. *Annals of Scotland*, Volume I, was officially published by John Murray on 15 Jan. (*Walpole's Correspondence*, Yale ed. xv.140 and nn. 1, 2).

James Boswell

MONDAY 15 JANUARY 1776

PRINTED SOURCE: JB's *Life*, 1791, II.4.

Dear Sir, London, Jan. 15, 1776

I was much impressed by your letter,[1] and, if I can form upon your case any resolution satisfactory to myself, will very gladly impart it: but whether I am quite equal to it, I do not know. It is a case compounded of law and justice, and requires a mind versed in juridical disquisitions. Could you not tell your whole

1. JB and his father were disputing the terms of an entail both wished to create for the family estates. Lord Auchinleck "had declared a predilection for heirs general, that is, males and females indiscriminately," while JB "had a zealous partiality for heirs male, however remote" (*Life* II.414; cf. *Ante* To JB, 16 Nov. 1775 and n. 2). Angered by JB's recalcitrance, Lord Auchinleck had threatened to disinherit him and withhold a legacy to Margaret Boswell and the children. On 2 Jan. JB wrote "a long, serious, and earnest letter to Dr. Johnson upon the subject of the settlement of our estate . . . and entreated a full opinion from him. He had formerly confirmed me in my resolution to be steadfast to heirs male for ever" (*Boswell: The Ominous Years*, ed. Charles Ryskamp and F. A. Pottle, 1963, p. 211).

mind to Lord Hailes?[2] He is, you know, both a Christian and a Lawyer. I suppose he is above partiality, and above loquacity; and, I believe, he will not think the time lost in which he may quiet a disturbed, or settle a wavering mind. Write to me, as any thing occurs to you; and if I find myself stopped by want of facts necessary to be known, I will make enquiries of you as my doubts arise.

If your former resolutions should be found only fanciful, you decide rightly in judging that your father's fancies may claim the preference; but whether they are fanciful or rational, is the question. I really think Lord Hailes could help us.

Make my compliments to dear Mrs. Boswell; and tell her, that I hope to be wanting in nothing that I can contribute, to bring you all out of your troubles. I am, dear Sir, most affectionately, Your humble servant,

SAM. JOHNSON

2. When consulted, Hailes replied that JB need not fight to uphold the principle of "strict male succession" in defiance of his father's wishes (*Later Years*, p. 120). *Post* To JB, 3 Feb. 1776; 9 Feb. 1776.

John Taylor

MONDAY 15 JANUARY 1776

MS: Hyde Collection.

ADDRESS: To The Revd. Dr. Taylor at Ashborne, Derbys.

FRANK: Hfreethrale.

POSTMARKS: 16 IA, FREE.

ENDORSEMENTS: 1776, 15 Jany. 76.

Dear Sir: London, Jan. 15, 1776

You gave me but an uncomfortable account of your health, and as I have not heard from you since, I am afraid you are worse, let me know whether you are well, and when we shall see You.

You will not wonder, that I am curious about your cause.[1]

1. *Ante* To John Taylor, 9 Feb. 1775 and n. 1; 23 Dec. 1775.

My advice still is, if you are likely to lose it, that you should not try it; but as I know not the nature of the settlement, I cannot tell whether you are likely to lose it. It is easy to conceive that such a woman would have power enough over such a man, to dictate his will. Have You had the opinions of Dunning,[2] and the rest of your council? If you have you will begin to judge what you may expect. Do not let an event to disturb you, about which you have so little need to care. I am, Sir, Your most humble servant,

SAM. JOHNSON

2. John Dunning (1731–83), of Ashburton, Devon, M.P. for Calne (1768–82), later (1777) a member of The Club. "The foremost advocate of his day," Dunning remained in Opposition until entering Lord Rockingham's Administration in 1782, when he was raised to the peerage as Baron Ashburton. In 1780 he was instrumental in launching the movement to diminish "the influence of the Crown" (Namier and Brooke II.367–68).

James Boswell

SATURDAY 3 FEBRUARY 1776

PRINTED SOURCE: JB's *Life*, 1791, II.4–7.

Dear Sir, Feb. 3, 1773[1]

I am going to write upon a question which requires more knowledge of local law, and more acquaintance with the general rules of inheritance, than I can claim; but I write, because you request it.[2]

Land is, like any other possession, by natural right wholly in the power of its present owner; and may be sold, given, or bequeathed, absolutely or conditionally, as judgement shall direct, or passion incite.

But natural right would avail little without the protection of law; and the primary notion of law is restraint in the exercise

1. JB placed this letter immediately after that of 15 Jan. 1776. The misprint was corrected in the seventh edition of the *Life*.

2. *Ante* To JB, 15 Jan. 1776 and n. 1.

of natural right. A man is therefore, in society, not fully master of what he calls his own, but he still retains all the power which law does not take from him.

In the exercise of the right which law either leaves or gives, regard is to be paid to moral obligations.

Of the estate which we are now considering, your father still retains such possession, with such power over it, that he can sell it, and do with the money what he will, without any legal impediment. But when he extends his power beyond his own life, by settling the order of succession, the law makes your consent necessary.

Let us suppose that he sells the land to risk the money in some specious adventure, and in that adventure loses the whole: his posterity would be disappointed; but they could not think themselves injured or robbed. If he spent it upon vice or pleasure, his successors could only call him vicious and voluptuous; they could not say that he was injurious or unjust.

He that may do more, may do less. He that, by selling or squandering, may disinherit a whole family, may certainly disinherit part, by a partial settlement.

Laws are formed by the manners and exigencies of particular times, and it is but accidental that they last longer than their causes: the limitation of feudal succession to the male arose from the obligation of the tenant to attend his chief in war.

As times and opinions are always changing, I know not whether it be not usurpation to prescribe rules to posterity, by presuming to judge of what we cannot know; and I know not whether I fully approve either your design or your father's, to limit that succession which descended to you unlimited. If we are to leave *sartum tectum*[3] to posterity, what we have without any merit of our own received from our ancestors, should not choice and free-will be kept unviolated? Is land to be treated with more reverence than liberty?—If this consideration should

3. *sartum tectum*: literally, "mended roof"; used as a legal term to signify "wind-tight and water-tight, in a state of good repair" (*Oxford Latin Dictionary*).

restrain your father from disinheriting some of the males, does it leave you the power of disinheriting all the females?

Can the possessor of a feudal estate make any will? Can he appoint, out of the inheritance, any portions to his daughters? There seems to be a very shadowy difference between the power of leaving land, and of leaving money to be raised from land; between leaving an estate to females, and leaving the male heir, in effect, only their steward.

Suppose at one time a law that allowed only males to inherit, and during the continuance of this law many estates to have descended, passing by the females, to remoter heirs. Suppose afterwards the law repealed in correspondence with a change of manners, and women made capable of inheritance; would not then the tenure of estates be changed? Could the women have no benefit from a law made in their favour? Must they be passed by upon moral principles for ever, because they were once excluded by a legal prohibition? Or may that which passed only to males by one law, pass likewise to females by another?

Your mention your resolution to maintain the right of your brothers.[4] I do not see how any of their rights are invaded.

As your whole difficulty arises from the act of your ancestor, who diverted the succession from the females, you enquire, very properly, what were his motives, and what was his intention; for you certainly are not bound by his act more than he intended to bind you, nor hold your land on harder or stricter terms than those on which it was granted.

Intentions must be gathered from acts. When he left the estate to his nephew, by excluding his daughters, was it, or was it not, in his power to have perpetuated the succession to the males? If he could have done it, he seems to have shewn, by omitting it, that he did not desire it to be done; and, upon your own principles, you will not easily prove your right to destroy that capacity of succession which your ancestors have left.

4. "Which term I applied to all the heirs male" (JB's note).

If your ancestor had not the power of making a perpetual settlement; and if, therefore, we cannot judge distinctly of his intentions, yet his act can only be considered as an example; it makes not an obligation. And, as you observe, he set no example of rigorous adherence to the line of succession. He that overlooked a brother, would not wonder that little regard is shewn to remote relations.

As the rules of succession are, in a great part, purely legal, no man can be supposed to bequeath any thing, but upon legal terms; he can grant no power which the law denies; and if he makes no special and definite limitation, he confers all the powers which the law allows.

Your ancestor, for some reason, disinherited his daughters; but it no more follows that he intended his act as a rule for posterity, than the disinheriting of his brother.

If therefore, you ask by what right your father admits daughters to inheritance, ask yourself, first, by what right you require them to be excluded?

It appears, upon reflection, that your father excludes nobody; he only admits nearer females to inherit before males more remote; and the exclusion is purely consequential.

These, dear Sir, are my thoughts, immethodical and deliberative; but, perhaps, you may find in them some glimmering of evidence.[5]

I cannot, however, but again recommend to you a conference with Lord Hailes, whom you know to be both a Lawyer and a Christian.[6]

Make my compliments to Mrs. Boswell, though she does not love me. I am, Sir, Your affectionate servant,

SAM. JOHNSON

5. *evidence*: "the state of being evident; clearness" (SJ's *Dictionary*).
6. *Ante* To JB, 15 Jan. 1776 and n. 2.

John Wesley

TUESDAY 6 FEBRUARY 1776

MS: Pembroke College, Oxford. A copy in the hand of Thomas Harwood.
HEADING: Dr. Johnson to the Rev. John Wesley.

Sir: Feb. 6, 1776

When I received your Commentary on the Bible,[1] I durst not at first flatter myself that I was to keep it, having so little claim to so valuable a present; and when Mrs. Hall informed me of your kindness, was hindered from time to time from returning you those thanks, which I now intreat you to accept.

I have thanks likewise to return for the addition of your important suffrage to my argument on the American question.[2] To have gained such a mind as yours, may justly confirm me in my own opinion. What effect my paper has had upon the publick, I know not; but I have no reason to be discouraged. The Lecturer was surely in the right, who, though he saw his audience slinking away, refused to quit the Chair, while Plato staid.[3] I am, Reverend Sir, Your most humble Servant,

SAM. JOHNSON

1. It is likely that Wesley had given SJ his *Explanatory Notes upon the Old Testament* (1765) and the fourth edition of his *Explanatory Notes upon the New Testament* (1768); these had been printed as a four-volume set by William Pine of Bristol (Frank Baker, "John Wesley, Biblical Commentator," *Bulletin of the John Rylands University Library* 71, 1989, pp. 118–19).

2. In his *Calm Address to our American Colonies*, published the previous autumn, Wesley had "extracted the chief arguments" from SJ's *Taxation No Tyranny* (*Life* v.466).

3. As the poet Antimachus read his epic poem, all of the audience except Plato departed. Antimachus continued, saying, "Plato alone is as good as a hundred thousand" (Cicero, *Brutus* 191, trans. G. L. Hendrickson, Loeb ed.). Cf. *Post* To Hester Thrale, 18 Mar. 1779.

James Boswell

FRIDAY 9 FEBRUARY 1776

PRINTED SOURCE: JB's *Life*, 1791, II.7–9.

Dear Sir, February 9, 1776

Having not any acquaintance with the laws or customs of Scotland, I endeavoured to consider your question upon general principles,[1] and found nothing of much validity that I could oppose to this position. "He who inherits a fief unlimited by his ancestor, inherits the power of limiting it according to his own judgement or opinion." If this be true you may join with your father.

Further consideration produced another conclusion, "He who receives a fief unlimited by his ancestors, gives his heirs some reason to complain if he does not transmit it unlimited to posterity." For why should he make the state of others worse than his own, without a reason? If this be true, though neither you nor your father are about to do what is quite right, but as your father violates (I think) the legal succession least, he seems to be nearer the right than yourself.

It cannot but occur that "Women have natural and equitable claims as well as men, and these claims are not to be capriciously or lightly superseded or infringed." When fiefs implied military service, it is easily discerned why females could not inherit them; but that reason is now at an end. As manners make laws, manners likewise repeal them.

These are the general conclusions which I have attained. None of them are very favourable to your scheme of entail, nor perhaps to any scheme. My observation, that only he who acquires an estate may bequeath it capriciously, if it contains any conviction includes this position likewise, that only he who acquires an estate may entail it capriciously. But I think it may

1. *Ante* To JB, 15 Jan. 1776 and n. 1; 3 Feb. 1776. On 30 Jan. JB had written to SJ, enclosing Lord Hailes's opinion of the entail and "begging to hear from him again, upon this interesting question" (*Life* II.419; *Boswell: The Ominous Years*, ed. Charles Ryskamp and F. A. Pottle, 1963, p. 226).

be safely presumed, that "he who inherits an estate inherits all the power legally concomitant." And that "He who gives or leaves unlimited an estate legally limitable, must be presumed to give that power of limitation which he omitted to take away, and to commit future contingencies to future prudence." In these two positions I believe Lord Hailes will advise you to rest;[2] every other notion of possession seems to me full of difficulties, and embarrassed with scruples.[3]

If these axioms be allowed, you have arrived now at full liberty without the help of particular circumstances, which, however, have in your case great weight. You very rightly observe, that he who passing by his brother gave the inheritance to his nephew, could limit no more than he gave, and by Lord Hailes's estimate of fourteen years purchase, what he gave was no more than you may easily entail according to your own opinion, if that opinion should finally prevail.

Lord Hailes's suspicion that entails are encroachments on the dominion of Providence, may be extended to all hereditary privileges and all permanent institutions; I do not see why it may not be extended to any provision but for the present hour, since all care about futurity proceeds upon a supposition, that we know at least in some degree what will be future. Of the future we certainly know nothing; but we may form conjectures from the past; and the power of forming conjectures, includes, in my opinion, the duty of acting in conformity to that probability which we discover. Providence gives the power of which reason teaches the use. I am, dear Sir, Your most faithful servant,

SAM. JOHNSON

I hope I shall get some ground now with Mrs. Boswell; make my compliments to her, and to the little people.

Don't burn papers; they may be safe enough in your own box,—you will wish to see them hereafter.

2. *Ante* To JB, 15 Jan. 1776 and n. 2.

3. "Scruples," according to SJ, "made many men miserable, but few men good" (*Johns. Misc.* II.152–53). Cf. *Post* To JB, 15 Feb. 1776; 5 Mar. 1776.

Hester Thrale

SUNDAY 11 FEBRUARY 1776

MS: Hyde Collection.

Dear Madam: Febr. 11, 1776

All goes well on both sides of our project.[1] Mr. Carter will show you my letters. I will go down to Oxford with him when he goes again; for the Vicechancellor thinks it will serve him.[2]

Mrs. Montague laments that she did not let you in.

I desire that you will put my watch into dear Misses custody, I left it in my chamber.

I will come on Tuesday before dinner. Your most humble,

SAM. JOHNSON

1. *Ante* To Henry Thrale, *c.* 26 Feb. 1775, n. 2.

2. SJ refers to Thomas Fothergill.

Archibald Hamilton

TUESDAY 13 FEBRUARY 1776

MS: Hyde Collection.

ADDRESS: To Mr. Hamilton.

Dear Sir: Febr. 13, 1776

I am afraid that by altering the first article of the Dictionary at your desire, I have given occasion to an unhappy difference between you and Dr. Calder, who has been with me, and seems to think himself in danger of losing the revision of the work.[1]

1. *Ante* To John Hawkesworth, 20 Jan. 1773 and nn. 2, 3. On 10 Feb. Calder had reported to SJ that, having reviewed SJ's criticisms and those of other referees, the proprietors of Chambers's *Cyclopaedia* (who included Hamilton and William Strahan) had decided "not to print the Work under my direction, and to apply to the Chancellor to set aside our agreement." Calder requested SJ's help in reversing this judgment (John Nichols, *Illustrations of the Literary History of the Eighteenth Century*, 1822, IV.809–10). Although he tried to make peace, SJ was unable to prevent the firing of Calder. *Post* To John Calder, 19 Feb. 1776.

For this consequence I ⟨should⟩ be very deeply sorry. I considered the redundance which I lopped away not as the consequence of negligence or inability, but as the [result] of superfluous diligence naturally exerted on the first article. He that does too much, soon learns to do less.

By his own account, however, it appears that [he] has shown what I think an improper degree of turbulence and impatience. I have advised him, and he has promised, to be hereafter less tenacious of his own determination, and more pliable to the direction of the proprietors, and the opinion of those whom they may consult. I entreat therefore that all the past may be forgotten, that he may stand where he stood before, and be permitted to proceed with the work in which he is engaged.

Do not refuse this request to, Sir, your most humble Servant,

SAM. JOHNSON

James Boswell

THURSDAY 15 FEBRUARY 1776

PRINTED SOURCE: JB's *Life*, 1791, II.9–10.

Dear Sir, Feb. 15, 1775[1]

To the letters which I have written about your great question I have nothing to add.[2] If your conscience is satisfied, you have now only your prudence to consult. I long for a letter, that I may know how this troublesome and vexatious question is at last decided.[3] I hope that it will at last end well. Lord Hailes's letter was very friendly, and very seasonable,[4] but I think his

1. JB placed this letter immediately after that of 9 Feb. 1776. The misprint was corrected in the fourth edition of the *Life*.

2. *Ante* To JB, 15 Jan. 1776; 3 Feb. 1776; 9 Feb. 1776.

3. The Auchinleck entail was finally made out with the estate settled on heirs male of JB's great-grandfather, followed by all heirs whatsoever (*Later Years*, pp. 135–36).

4. *Ante* To JB, 9 Feb. 1776, n. 1.

aversion from entails has something in it like superstition. Providence is not counteracted by any means which Providence puts into our power. The continuance and propagation of families makes a great part of the Jewish law, and is by no means prohibited in the Christian institution, though the necessity of it continues no longer. Hereditary tenures are established in all civilised countries, and are accompanied in most with hereditary authority. Sir William Temple considers our constitution as defective, that there is not an unalienable estate in land connected with a peerage:[5] and Lord Bacon mentions as a proof that the Turks are Barbarians, their want of *Stirpes*, as he calls them, or hereditary rank.[6] Do not let your mind, when it is freed from the supposed necessity of a rigorous entail, be entangled with contrary objections, and think all entails unlawful, till you have cogent arguments, which I believe you will never find; I am afraid of scruples.[7]

I have now sent all Lord Hailes's papers,[8] part I found hidden in a drawer in which I had laid them for security, and had forgotten them. Part of these are written twice, I have returned both the copies. Part I had read before.

Be so kind as to return Lord Hailes my most respectful thanks for his first volume; his accuracy strikes me with wonder; his narrative is far superiour to that of Henault, as I have formerly mentioned.[9]

I am afraid that the trouble, which my irregularity and delay has cost him, is greater, far greater, than any good that I can do him will ever recompense, but if I have any more copy, I will try to do better.

5. SJ refers to the essay *Of Popular Discontents*, in which Temple proposes a way of diminishing corruption in the House of Lords. Temple suggests that the Crown create no more peers unless each new peer agrees to entail an estate sufficient to support the honor (*The Works of Sir William Temple, Bt.*, 1814, III.62).

6. In his *Advertisement touching an Holy War* (1629) Bacon calls the Turkish Empire a "cruel tyranny, bathed in the blood of their emperors upon every succession; . . . no nobles, no gentlemen, no freemen, no inheritance of land, no stirp of ancient families" (*Works of Francis Bacon*, ed. James Spedding, R. L. Ellis, and D. D. Heath, 1870, VII.22).

7. *Ante* To JB, 9 Feb. 1776 and n. 3.

8. *Ante* To JB, 4 July 1774, n. 4.

9. *Ante* To JB, 27 Aug. 1775 and n. 7; 10 Jan. 1776 and n. 4.

Pray let me know if Mrs. Boswell is friends with me, and pay my respects to Veronica, and Euphemia, and Alexander. I am, Sir, Your most humble servant,

SAM. JOHNSON

John Taylor

SATURDAY 17 FEBRUARY 1776

MS: Berg Collection, New York Public Library.

ADDRESS: Revd. Dr. Taylor, Ashbourn, Derbyshire.

FRANK: ffree W. Strahan.

POSTMARKS: 17 FE, FREE, R·I.

ENDORSEMENTS: 1776, 17 Feby. 76, very good.

Dear Sir, Febr. 17, 1776

The Case which You sent me contains such vicissitudes of settlement and rescission[1] that I will not pretend yet to give any opinion about it.[2] My advice is, that it be laid before some of the best Lawyers, and branched out into queries, that the answer may be more deliberate, and the necessity of considering made greater.

Get it off your hands and out of your head as fast as you can.[3] You have no evidence to wait for; all that can be done may be done soon.

Your health is of more consequence. Keep yourself cheerful. Lye in Bed with a lamp, and when you cannot sleep, and are beginning to think, light your candle and read. At least light your candle, a man is perhaps never so much harrassed by his own mind in the light as in the dark.[4]

Poor Caleb Harding is dead.[5] Do's not every death of a Man

1. *rescission*: "the act of cutting off; abrogation" (SJ's *Dictionary*).

2. *Ante* To John Taylor, 9 Feb. 1775 and n. 1; 23 Dec. 1775; 15 Jan. 1776.

3. Cf. *Ante* To John Taylor, 9 Feb. 1775.

4. Cf. *Ante* To John Taylor, 9 Feb. 1775.

5. Caleb Hardinge (d. 1776), M.D., F.R.S., Physician Extraordinary to George II. "He was a man of singular habits and whims, but of infinite humour and wit. . . . His conversation was coveted by the most accomplished wits and scholars of his

long known begin to strike deep? How few dos the Man who has lived sixty years now know of the friends of his youth? At Lichfield there are none but Harry Jackson and Sedgwick,[6] and Sedgwick when I left him, had a dropsy.

I am, I think, better than usual, and hope you will grow better too. I am, Sir, Your most affectionate,

SAM. JOHNSON

age" (John Nichols, *Illustrations of the Literary History of the Eighteenth Century*, 1818, III.4). Hardinge had been a schoolmate of SJ and Taylor at the Lichfield Grammar School (*Johns. Glean.* III.130–32).

6. SJ may be referring to Henry Sedgwick, who was baptized at St. Mary's, Lichfield, about four months before him (*Johns. Glean.* III.130).

John Calder

MONDAY 19 FEBRUARY 1776

MS: Rare Book and Manuscript Library, Columbia University.

ADDRESS: To Dr. Calder.

Sir: Febr. 19, 1776

I saw Mr. Strahan on Saturday, and find that Mr. Hamilton had shown him my letter.[1] Mr. Strahan is, as I feared, so angry, and so resolute, that I could not impress him in your favour, nor have any hope from him. If any thing is done, it must be with the other proprietors.[2] I am sorry for it. I am, Sir, Your very humble servant,

SAM. JOHNSON

1. *Ante* To Archibald Hamilton, 13 Feb. 1776.

2. *Ante* To Archibald Hamilton, 13 Feb. 1776 and n. 1.

James Boswell

SATURDAY 24 FEBRUARY 1776

MS: Beinecke Library. The transcript (in JB's hand) used as copy for JB's *Life*.

Dear Sir, Feb. 24, 1776

I am glad that what I could think or say has at all contributed to quiet your thoughts.[1] Your resolution not to act, till your opinion is confirmed by more deliberation, is very just. If you have been scrupulous, do not now be rash. I hope that as you think more, and take opportunities of talking with men intelligent in questions of property, you will be able to free yourself from every difficulty.

When I wrote last, I sent, I think, ten packets.[2] Did you receive them all?

You must tell Mrs. Boswell that I suspected her to have written without your knowledge, and therefore did not return any answer, lest a clandestine correspondence should have been perniciously discovered. I will write to her soon.[3] * * * * * *. I am, dear Sir, Most affectionately yours,

SAM. JOHNSON

1. "I wrote to Dr. Johnson on the 20th of February, complaining of melancholy, and expressing a strong desire to be with him; informing him that the ten packets [of Hailes's *Annals*] came all safe; that Lord Hailes was much obliged to him, and said he had almost wholly removed his scruples against entails" (*Life* II.423).

2. *Ante* To JB, 15 Feb. 1776; Cf. *Ante* To JB, 14 Jan. 1775, n. 1.

3. "My wife wrote also [4 Jan.] to Dr. Johnson a very sensible, clear letter on the subject of my male succession, entreating his interest with me, that I might agree to my father's settlement; and she did not try to have heirs whatsoever brought in directly. I was much pleased with her letter" (*Boswell: The Ominous Years*, ed. Charles Ryskamp and F. A. Pottle, 1963, p. 214). *Post* To Margaret Boswell, 16 May 1776.

James Boswell

TUESDAY 5 MARCH 1776

PRINTED SOURCE: JB's *Life*, 1791, II.11.

Dear Sir, March 5, 1776

I have not had your letter half an hour; as you lay so much weight upon my notions, I should think it not just to delay my answer.[1]

1. On 29 Feb. JB, who had been suffering from "low spirits," recorded in his

I am very sorry that your melancholy should return, and should be sorry likewise if it could have no relief but from my company. My counsel you may have when you are pleased to require it; but of my company you cannot in the next month have much, for Mr. Thrale will take me to Italy, he says, on the first of April.[2]

Let me warn you very earnestly against scruples. I am glad that you are reconciled to your settlement, and think it a great honour to have shaken Lord Hailes's opinion of entails.[3] Do not, however, hope wholly to reason away your troubles; do not feed them with attention, and they will die imperceptibly away. Fix your thoughts upon your business, fill your intervals with company, and sunshine will again break in upon your mind. If you will come to me, you must come very quickly, and even then I know not but we may scour the country together, for I have a mind to see Oxford and Lichfield before I set out on this long journey.[4] To this I can only add, that I am, dear Sir, Your most affectionate humble servant,

SAM. JOHNSON

---

journal: "I . . . wrote an earnest letter to Dr. Johnson; but was sensible that I might appear weak and troublesome to him. I trusted to his kindness for me, and his knowledge from experience of dejection of mind" (*Boswell: The Ominous Years*, ed. Charles Ryskamp and F. A. Pottle, 1963, p. 241).

2. Encouraged by the success of their expedition to France, the Thrales were planning an extended trip through Italy, with Giuseppe Baretti as principal *cicerone*. According to Baretti, the trip was due to begin on 8 Apr. However, the death of Harry on 23 Mar. caused the Thrales to cancel (Clifford, 1952, pp. 134–38). *Post* To Hester Thrale, 9 Apr. 1776.

3. *Ante* To JB, 9 Feb. 1776 and n. 3; 15 Feb. 1776.

4. JB arrived in London 15 Mar. On 19 Mar. he and SJ set out for Oxford; on 21 Mar. they left for Lichfield, traveling via Birmingham, and arrived on the 22nd (Ryskamp and Pottle, *The Ominous Years*, pp. 253, 275, 282–83; *Post* To Hester Thrale, 23 Mar. 1776).

John Douglas[1]

WEDNESDAY 6 MARCH 1776

MS: British Library.

ADDRESS: To the Reverend Dr. Douglas.

ENDORSEMENT: Sam. Johnson, March 6th 1776.

Sir: March 6th 1776

This Gentleman has been approved by the Vicechancellor and Proctors of Oxford, as a Man properly qualified to profess Horsemanship in that place.[2] The Trustees of the Clarendon legacy have consented to issue Money for the erection of a Riding house, and the Bishop of Chester[3] delays the payment till he knows the state of the account between the Trustees and the University, for he says very reasonably, that he knows not to give, till he knows how much they have.

Upon application to the Dean of Hereford,[4] I was told that you, dear Sir, have in your hand the accounts between them. If You would be pleased to examine them, and appoint this Gentleman a time when he may wait on you for the result to carry to the Bishop you will put an end to a business, in which I have interested myself very much, as it will restore prosperity to a family that has suffered great difficulties a long time. I am, Dear Sir, Your most humble Servant,

SAM. JOHNSON

1. John Douglas (1721–1807), D.D., F.R.S., Canon of Windsor, later Bishop of Carlisle (1787–91) and Salisbury (1791–1807). Douglas had edited the *Diary and Letters of Henry, Second Earl of Clarendon* (1763); L. F. Powell surmises that he was also the editor of the *Life of Lord Clarendon* (1759), profits from the sale of which were supposed to fund the riding school. According to Powell, Douglas's "editorship would explain why it was that he had in his hands the accounts between the Trustees and the University relating to this book" (*Life* II.528). *Post* To John Douglas, 9 Mar. 1776; *Post* To Nathan Wetherell, 12 Mar. 1776.

2. *Ante* To Henry Thrale, *c.* 26 Feb. 1775 and n. 2; *Ante* To Hester Thrale, 6 Mar. 1775.

3. SJ refers to William Markham.

4. SJ refers to Nathan Wetherell.

Edmund Hector

THURSDAY 7 MARCH 1776

MS: Hyde Collection.

Dear Sir: March 7, 1776

Some time ago You told me that you had unhappily hurt yourself; and were confined, and You have never since let me hear of your recovery. I hope however that you are grown, at least are growing well. We must be content now to mend very gradually, and cannot make such quick transitions from sickness to health, as we did forty years ago. Let me know how you do, and do not imagine that I forget you.

I forget whether I told you that at the latter end of the summer I rambled over part of France. I saw something of the vintage, which is all I think that they have to boast above our country, at least, it is their great natural advantage. Their air I think is good, and my health mended in it very perceptibly.[1]

Our Schoolfellow Charles Congreve is still in town, but very dull, very valetudinary, and very recluse, willing, I am afraid, to forget the world, and content to be forgotten by it, to repose in that sullen sensuality, into which men naturally sink, who think disease a justification of indulgence, and converse only with those who hope to prosper by indulging them.[2] This is a species of Beings with which your profession must have made you much acquainted, and to which I hope acquaintance has made you no friend. Infirmity will come but let us not invite it; Indulgence will allure us, but let us turn resolutely away. Time cannot be always defeated, but let us not yield till we are conquered.

I had the other day a letter from Harry Jackson who says nothing, and yet seems to have something which he wishes to say. He is very poor.[3] I wish something could be done for him.

I hope dear Mrs. Careless is well, and now and then does

1. *Ante* To Robert Levet, 22 Oct. 1775; *Ante* To John Taylor, 16 Nov. 1775.

2. *Ante* To John Taylor, 22 Dec. 1774, n. 3; 8 Apr. 1775.

3. *Ante* To John Taylor, 17 Feb. 1776.

not disdain to mention my name. It is happy when a Brother and Sister live to pass their time at our age together. I have nobody to whom I can talk of my first years. When I go to Lichfield I see the old places, but find nobody that enjoyed them with me. May She and You live long together. I am, Dear Sir, Your affectionate, humble servant,

SAM. JOHNSON

John Taylor

THURSDAY 7 MARCH 1776

MS: Pierpont Morgan Library.
ENDORSEMENT: 9 March 1776.

Dear Sir: March 7, 1776

You will not write to me, nor come to see me, and You will not have me within reach long for We are going to Italy in the Spring.[1]

I called the other day upon poor Charles Congreve, whom I had not seen for many Months.[2] He took no notice of my absence, nor appeared either glad or sorry to see me, but answered every thing with monosyllables, and seemed heavy and drowsy, like a man muddled with a full meal; at last I enquired the hour, which gave him hopes of being delivered from me, and enabled him to bounce up with great alacrity and inspect his watch. He sits in a room about ten feet square, and though he takes the air every day in his chaise, fancies that he should take cold in any other house, and therefore never pays a visit.

Do you go on with your suit?[3] If you do, you had surely better come to town and talk with Council.[4] Unless skilful men

1. *Ante* To JB, 5 Mar. 1776 and n. 2.
2. Cf. *Ante* To Edmund Hector, 7 Mar. 1776.
3. *Ante* To John Taylor, 17 Feb. 1776.
4. *Ante* To John Taylor, 15 Jan. 1776; 17 Feb. 1776; *Post* To Hester Thrale, 14 May 1776.

give you hopes of success, it will be better not to try it, for ma[n]y will triumph in your ill success. But supposing that by the former compact between you and Wood, she had it for her life, She had as much as she ought to have. I never well understood the settlement which he and you concerted between you. Do you know what is become of her, and how she and the ⟨Buyer⟩[5] live together? What a wretch it is!

I would be glad to take my usual round and see my friends before I set out, but am afraid it will hardly be convenient,[6] therefore write to me. I am, Dear Sir, Your most humble servant,

SAM. JOHNSON

5. MS: one word heavily del.

6. *Ante* To JB, 5 Mar. 1776 and n. 4; *Post* To JB, 12 Mar. 1776.

John Douglas

SATURDAY 9 MARCH 1776

MS: Berg Collection, New York Public Library.

ADDRESS: To The Revd. Dr. Douglas at Windsor.

FRANK: Hfreethrale.

POSTMARKS: 9 MR, FREE.

ENDORSEMENT: Dr. Johnson, 1776; Sam. Johnson March 9, 1776.

Dear Sir: March 9, 1776

The Vicechancellor and Proctors of Oxford have approved, a Master of Horsemanship recommended by me, as a proper man to put in practice the design for which Lord Clarendon[1] left a provision. The Trustees have been consulted and have agreed to issue Money for the erection of a Ridinghouse, and the business is at a stand only till the Bishop of Chester can be informed how [much] money the Book has produced. For this information I have [been] directed by the Dean of Hereford,

1. "Clarendon" should be "Cornbury" (*Ante* To Henry Thrale, *c.* 26 Feb. 1775, n. 2; *Post* To Nathan Wetherell, 12 Mar. 1776).

the late Vicechancellor to apply to You;[2] and I make it my earnest request that you will be pleased to lay out your first hours of leisure upon the settlement of the account,[3] and transmit the result either to the Bishop, or to, Sir, Your most humble servant,

SAM. JOHNSON

2. *Ante* To John Douglas, 6 Mar. 1776 and n. 1.

3. *Post* To Nathan Wetherell, 12 Mar. 1776 and n. 3.

James Boswell

TUESDAY 12 MARCH 1776

PRINTED SOURCE: JB's *Life*, 1791, II.12.

Dear Sir, March 12, 1776

Very early in April we leave England,[1] and in the beginning of the next week I shall leave London for a short time;[2] of this I think it necessary to inform you, that you may not be disappointed in any of your enterprises. I had not fully resolved to go into the country before this day.

Please to make my compliments to Lord Hailes; and mention very particularly to Mrs. Boswell my hope that she is reconciled to, Sir, Your faithful servant,

SAM. JOHNSON

1. *Ante* To JB, 5 Mar. 1776 and n. 2.

2. *Ante* To JB, 5 Mar. 1776, n. 4.

Nathan Wetherell

TUESDAY 12 MARCH 1776

MS: Beinecke Library. The transcript (in JB's hand) used as copy for JB's *Life*.[1]

HEADING: Dr. Johnson To Mr. Wetherell about establishing Mr. Carter a riding master at Oxford.

1. On 21 Mar. 1776 JB, while in Oxford with SJ, recorded in his journal: "Dr.

March 12, 1776

Few things are more unpleasant than the transaction of business with men who are above knowing or caring what they have to do, such as the Trustees for Lord Cornbury's institution will perhaps appear when you have read Dr. Douglas's letter.[2]

The last part of the Doctor's letter is of great importance.[3] The complaint which he makes I have heard long ago, and did not know but it was redressed.[4] It is unhappy that a practice so erroneous has not yet been altered; for altered it must be or our press will be useless with all it's privileges. The Booksellers who like all other men have strong prejudices in their own favour are enough inclined to think the practice of printing and selling books by any but themselves an encroachment on the rights of their fraternity and have need of stronger inducements to circulate academical publications than those of one another; for of that mutual cooperation by which the general trade is carried on, the University can bear no part. Of those whom he neither loves nor fears and from whom he expects no reciprocation of good offices, why should any man

---

Wetherell had read in my presence part of a letter from Dr. Johnson, giving advice as to the sale of University books and explaining with his pointed perspicuity the trade of bookselling. I wished to have a copy of it, and Dr. Wetherell agreed to let me have it if Dr. Johnson consented. I obtained his consent last night, and this morning got the letter and copied it" (*Boswell: The Ominous Years*, ed. Charles Ryskamp and F. A. Pottle, 1963, p. 283).

2. *Ante* To Henry Thrale, *c.* 26 Feb. 1775, n. 2; *Ante* To John Douglas, 6 Mar. 1776; 9 Mar. 1776.

3. In this letter, which "related to the management of the Clarendon Press" (JB's MS note), John Douglas presumably replied to SJ's letters of 6 and 9 Mar.

4. "I suppose the complaint was, that the trustees of the Oxford press did not allow the London booksellers a sufficient profit upon vending their publications" (JB's note, *Life* II.425). In more precise terms, Oxford University Press was guilty of providing less than generous discounts to the London booksellers who distributed its publications; the result was that sales were crippled. To illustrate his argument that more substantial discounts are in order, SJ proceeds to trace "the progress of a book of which the retail price is assumed to be twenty shillings" (R. W. Chapman, "Authors and Booksellers," in *Johnson's England*, ed. A. S. Turberville, 1933, 1952, II.314).

promote the interest but for profit. I suppose with all our scholastick ignorance of mankind we are still too knowing to expect that the Booksellers will erect themselves into Patrons and buy and sell under the influence of a disinterested zeal for the promotion of Learning.[5]

To the Booksellers if we look for either honour or profit from our press, not only their common profit but something more must be allowed, and if Books printed at Oxford are expected to be rated at a high price, that price must be levied on the publick, and paid by the ultimate purchaser not by the intermediate Agents. What price shall be set upon the Book is to the Booksellers wholly indifferent provided that they gain a proportionate profit by negotiating the Sale.

Why Books printed at Oxford should be particularly dear I am however unable to find. We pay no rent; we inherit many of our instruments and materials; lodging and victuals are cheaper than at London and therefore workmanship ought at least not to be dearer. Our expences are naturally less than those of Booksellers, and in most cases communities are content with less profit than individuals.

It is perhaps not considered through how many hands a Book often passes, before it comes into those of the reader, or what part of the profit each hand must retain as a motive for transmitting it to the next.

We will call our primary Agent in London Mr. Cadel who receives our books from us, gives them room in his warehouse and issues them on demand. By him they are sold to Mr. Dilly a wholesale Bookseller who sends them into the Country, and the last seller is the Country Bookseller.[6] Here are three prof-

5. SJ's opinion of the booksellers tended to vary. To JB he praised them "as generous liberal-minded men" and "considered them as the patrons of literature" (*Life* 1.304–5).

6. According to John Feather, whose commentary places SJ's account of trade practices in the context of the contemporary distribution system: "Johnson assumes that the Press will deliver its books to one bookseller, Cadel, who will warehouse them for the wholesaler, Dilly; Dilly will then sell them to the country bookseller" (*The Provincial Book Trade in Eighteenth-Century England*, 1985, p. 56). But as R. W. Chapman observes: "Johnson's account is . . . simplified to his pur-

its to be paid between the Printer and the Reader, or in the stile of commerce between the Manufacturer and the Consumer; and if any of these profits is too penuriously distributed the process of commerce is intercepted.

We are now come to the practical question, What is to be done? You will tell me with reason that I have said nothing till I declare how much according to my opinion of the ultimate price ought to be distributed through the whole Succession of Sale.

The deduction I am afraid will appear very great. But let it be considered before it is refused. We must allow for profit between thirty and thirty five per cent, between six and seven shillings in the pound, that is for every book which costs the last buyer twenty shillings we must charge Mr. Cadel with something less than fourteen. We must set the copies at fourteen shillings each and superadd what is called the quarterly book or for every hundred books so charged we must deliver an hundred and four.[7]

The profit will then stand thus.

Mr. Cadel who runs no hazard and gives no credit will be paid for warehouse room and attendance by a shilling profit on each Book, and his chance of the quarterly Book.

Mr. Dilly who buys the Book for fifteen shillings and who will expect the quarterly book if he takes five and twenty will sell it to his country customer at sixteen and sixpence by which

---

pose. The real Cadell had a shop in the Strand, and sold his books over the counter. The real Dilly we know to have been a publisher, for he was Boswell's. The various functions doubtless over-lapped. . . . The ordinary course of trade is what Johnson had in mind" (Chapman, "Authors and Booksellers," p. 315).

7. "The country bookseller was given a discount of about 17½% on the retail price, from which, of course, he had to cover his costs as well as make a profit. Allowing for the quarterly copies, Cadel has 1s.0d. in the pound, and Dilly 10%, each to cover both costs and profit. Johnson was accurately reflecting the practices of the trade" (Feather, *Provincial Book Trade*, p. 57). SJ assumes, moreover, that "the publisher will charge 70% of the retail price to his immediate customer, whether wholesaler or retailer. If a wholesaler was used, his profit came out of the bookseller's discount; generally, however, the country bookseller could expect between 17½% and 30%" (Feather, *Provincial Book Trade*, p. 57).

at the hazard of loss and the certainty of long credit, he gains the regular profit of ten per cent which is expected in the wholesale trade.

The Country Bookseller buying at Sixteen and Sixpence and commonly trusting a considerable time gains but three and sixpence, and if he trusts a year, not much more than two and sixpence, otherwise than as he may perhaps take as long credit as he gives.

With less profit than this, and more you see he cannot have, the Country Bookseller cannot live; for his receipts are small, and his debts sometimes bad.

Thus Dear Sir I have been incited by Dr. Douglas's letter to give you a detail of the circulation of Books which perhaps every man has not had opportunity of knowing and which those who know it, do not perhaps always distinctly consider. I am, etc.

SAM. JOHNSON

Hester Thrale

SATURDAY 16 MARCH 1776

MS: Hyde Collection.

Dearest Madam: March 16, 1776

When You have read the two letters which I have enclosed you will, I am afraid, be of opinion that the last spark of hope is now extinguished.[1] If the 150£ could be had, which is doubtful, the condition upon which it will be offered, of employing it in some purchase permanently useful, we cannot perform, and on any other terms they cannot honestly grant it.

You will be pleased to return this letter that I may show it to Dr. Wetherel, at Oxford. I shall not go till tuesday, for Gwin

1. The intricate and sustained attempt to assist Charles Carter had finally been defeated (*Ante* To Henry Thrale, *c.* 26 Feb. 1775, n. 2). One of the two letters enclosed by SJ was presumably John Douglas's reply (*Ante* To John Douglas, 6 Mar. 1776; 9 Mar. 1776; *Ante* To Nathan Wetherell, 12 Mar. 1776 and n. 3).

neglected to get places in the coach.[2] Boswel will either accompany or[3] follow me.[4]

In the Closet there is an Italian Palmerin of England,[5] and the key of the Closet is in the tabledrawer at the window. Please to send it me.

Poor Carter's case is truly worthy of commiseration. Peyton was not worse this morning.[6] Heely has yet got no employment.[7]

Sunt lacrymae rerum, et mentem mortalia tangunt,[8] I am, Madam, Your most obliged and most humble Servant,

SAM. JOHNSON

2. *Post* To Hester Thrale, 4 Aug. 1777, n. 2.

3. MS: "or" repeated as catchword

4. JB accompanied SJ to Oxford, and thence to Lichfield and Ashbourne (*Boswell: The Ominous Years*, ed. Charles Ryskamp and F. A. Pottle, 1963, pp. 275–301).

5. *Il Palmerino d'Inghilterra* (1553–54), an Italian translation from the Spanish version (1547–48) of a Portuguese original (*c.* 1544), has been attributed to Francisco de Moraes (*c.* 1500–1572) (*Life* III.468). On 27 Mar. JB recorded in his journal: "He had with him upon this jaunt a volume of *Il Palmerino d'Inghilterra*, a romance praised by Cervantes. But Dr. Johnson did not like it much. He read it for the language, by way of preparation for Italy" (Ryskamp and Pottle, *The Ominous Years*, p. 301).

6. *Ante* To Hester Thrale, 20 May 1775, n. 7.

7. *Ante* To Henry Thrale, 2 Jan. 1775 and n. 1.

8. *sunt lacrimae rerum et mentem mortalia tangunt*: "Here, too, there are tears for misfortune and mortal sorrows touch the heart" (Virgil, *Aeneid* I.462, trans. H. R. Fairclough, Loeb ed.).

John Taylor

SATURDAY 23 MARCH 1776

MS: Hyde Collection.

ENDORSEMENT: 23 March, 1776.

Dear Sir: Lichfield, Saturday, March 23, 1776

I came hither last night, and found your Letter. You will have a note from me on Monday, yet I thought it better to send a Messenger to day. Mr. Boswel is with me, but I will take care that he shall hinder no business, nor shall he know more than you would have him.[1] Send when you please, we shall be ready.[2] I am, Sir, Your humble servant,

SAM. JOHNSON

If you care not to send, let me know, we will take a chaise.

1. On 26 Mar., while SJ and JB were staying at Ashbourne, Taylor informed JB that he and SJ "were to talk together of some difficulties as to the title-deeds of an estate which he had bought" (*Boswell: The Ominous Years*, ed. Charles Ryskamp and F. A. Pottle, 1963, p. 300). *Ante* To John Taylor, 7 Mar. 1776. Presumably the two men discussed the suit the following morning, while JB was being shown round Ashbourne by Taylor's clerk (Ryskamp and Pottle, *The Ominous Years*, p. 300).

2. On 26 Mar. SJ and JB were conveyed from Lichfield to Ashbourne "in Dr. Taylor's large post-chaise drawn by four stout plump horses, and driven by two jolly postilions" (Ryskamp and Pottle, *The Ominous Years*, p. 299).

Hester Thrale

SATURDAY 23 MARCH 1776

MS: Hyde Collection.

Dear Madam: Lichfield, March 23, 1776

On Thursday we set out so late that we got only to Henley,[1] early in the morning on Friday we reached Birmingham. I dined with some Quaker Friends,[2] and sent Mr. Boswel with Hector to Bolton's,[3] while I sat with Mrs. Careless. When it

1. On 21 Mar. SJ and JB left Oxford for Birmingham and Lichfield. Traveling through Blenheim Park and Stratford-upon-Avon, they spent the night at Henley, a Warwickshire village about thirteen miles from Birmingham (*Boswell: The Ominous Years*, ed. Charles Ryskamp and F. A. Pottle, 1963, pp. 283–86).

2. SJ and JB dined with Sampson Lloyd (1728–1807), founder of Lloyd's Bank, and his wife Rachel (1745–1814) (*Life* II.456, 535). JB reported, "These Quakers were opulent people and kept a good table" (Ryskamp and Pottle, *The Ominous Years*, p. 288).

3. Matthew Boulton (1728–1809), manufacturer and engineer, collaborated with James Watt in the development of the steam engine. Returning from his trip to Wales in 1774, SJ had visited Boulton's factory, called "Soho," on the outskirts of Birmingham (*Life* II.536–57). To JB "Boulton seemed to be a clever, fine fellow.

was dark we went to Lichfield. To day Mr. Boswel went to Mr. Garrick,[4] who showed him the City, while I waited on Mrs. Aston. I have taken him to Mr. Green's, and to morrow he sees the Cathedral. We shall struggle hard to be with you in the next week. I am, Madam, Your most humble servant,

SAM. JOHNSON

. . . 'I sell, Sir, . . . what all the world desires to have—power'" (Ryskamp and Pottle, *The Ominous Years*, p. 289).

4. Peter Garrick (1710–95), elder brother of the actor and a Lichfield wine merchant, pleased JB "with his resemblance to his brother David, and at the same time by a calmness and tranquillity. He was David with a sourdine [mute]: the same instrument, but not so loud or sharp" (Ryskamp and Pottle, *The Ominous Years*, p. 291).

Hester Thrale

MONDAY 25 MARCH 1776

MS: Hyde Collection.

Dear Madam: Lichfield, March 25, 1776

This letter will not, I hope, reach you many days before me, in a distress which can be so little relieved, nothing remains for a friend but to come and partake it.[1]

Poor dear sweet little Boy. When I read the letter this day to Mrs. Aston, she said "Such a death is the next to Translation." Yet, however I may convince myself of this, the tears are in my eyes, and yet I could not love him as You loved him, nor reckon upon him for a future comfort, as You and his Father reckoned upon him.

He is gone, and we are going. We could not have enjoyed him long, and shall not long be separated from him. He has probably escaped many such pangs as You are now feeling.

1. The news of Harry Thrale's death (*Ante* To JB, 5 Mar. 1776, n. 2) reached SJ at breakfast 25 Mar. in a letter written by John Perkins; the letter concluded, "I need not say how much they wish to see you in London" (*Life* II.468–69). After stopping at Ashbourne, SJ returned 29 Mar. (*Life* II.473, III.5).

Nothing remains but that with humble confidence We resign ourselves to almighty Goodness, and fall down without irreverent murmurs before the Sovereign Distributer of good and evil, with hope that though sorrow endureth for a night, yet joy may come in the Morning.[2]

I have known you, Madam, too long to think that you want any arguments for submission to the supreme will, nor can my consolations have any effect but that of showing that I wish to comfort you. What can be done You must do for yourself. Remember first that your Child is happy, and then, that he is safe not only from the ills of this world, but from those more formidable dangers which extend their mischief to eternity. You have brought into the world a rational Being, have[3] seen him happy during the little life that has been granted him, and can have no doubt but that his Happiness is now[4] permanent and immutable.

When You have obtained by Prayer such tranquillity as nature will admit, force your attention, as you can, upon your accustomed duties, and accustomed entertainments. You can do no more for our dear Boy, but you must not therefore think less on those whom your attention may make fitter for the place to which he is gone. I am, Dearest, dearest Madam, your most affectionate, humble Servant,

SAM. JOHNSON

2. "Heaviness may endure for a night, but joy cometh in the morning" (Psalm 30:5, Book of Common Prayer). In substituting "sorrow" for "heaviness" SJ may have had in mind the gloss on this verse in the Douay Version: "The state of a just man's life is often changed from sorow to comforte, and from comforte to sorow."

3. MS: "and" del. before "have"

4. MS: "now" written above "own" del.

Hester Thrale

SATURDAY 30 MARCH 1776

MS: Hyde Collection.

ADDRESS: To Mrs. Thrale.

Dear Madam: March 30, 1776

Since, as Mr. Baretti informs us our dear Queeney is grown better, I hope you will by degrees recover your tranquillity.[1] Only by degrees and those perhaps sufficiently slow, can the pain of an affliction like yours be abated. But though effects are not wholly in our power, yet Providence always gives us something to do; many of the operations of nature may by human diligence be accelerated or retarded. Do not indulge your sorrow, try to drive it away by either pleasure or pain; for opposed to what you are feeling many[2] pains will become pleasures. Remember the great precept. *Be not solitary, be not idle.*[3]

But above all resign yourself and your children to the Universal Father, the Authour of Existence, and Governour of the Universe, who only knows what is best for all, and without whose regard not a Sparrow falls to the Ground.[4]

That I feel what friendship can feel I hope I need not tell you. I loved him as I never expect to love any other little boy, but I could not love him as a parent. I know that such a loss is a laceration of the mind. I know that a whole system of hopes, and designs, and expectations is swept away at once, and nothing left but bottomless vacuity.[5] What you feel, I have felt, and hope that your disquiet will be shorter than mine.

Mr. Thrale sent me a letter from Mr. Boswel, I suppose, to be inclosed.[6] I was this day with Mrs. Montague, who with

1. When SJ, immediately upon returning from Ashbourne, arrived at the Thrales' Southwark house, he found Hester Thrale, Giuseppe Baretti, and Queeney, who was ill, on the verge of departure for Bath (Hyde, 1972, pp. 36–37). They had returned to London by 7 Apr. (Clifford, 1952, p. 138).

2. MS: "many" altered from "may"

3. *Ante* To Hester Thrale, 12 Nov. 1773, n. 3.

4. "Are not two sparrows sold for a farthing? And one of them shall not fall on the ground without your Father" (Matthew 10:29).

5. Cf. SJ's letter of consolation to Thomas Lawrence, 20 Jan. 1780.

6. Not knowing of Hester Thrale's imminent departure, JB had sent his letter of condolence (addressed "To Mrs. Thrale" and dated "Friday, 29 March 1776") via the penny post to Southwark (MS: Hyde Collection). By the time it arrived, the party of three had left for Bath (see above, n. 1). Presumably SJ mailed JB's letter together with his in a separate cover franked by Henry Thrale. Writing to

every body else laments your misfortune. I am, Dearest Madam, Your most dutiful servant,

SAM. JOHNSON

SJ from Bath on 1 Apr., Hester Thrale acknowledged receipt of JB's letter (MS: Rylands Library).

Hester Thrale

MONDAY 1 APRIL 1776

MS: Hyde Collection.

ADDRESS: To Mrs. Thrale.

Dearest Madam: Apr. 1, 1776

When You were gone Mr. Thrale soon sent me away.[1] I came next day, and was made to understand that when I was wanted I should be sent for; and therefore I have not gone yesterday or to day, but I will soon go again whether invited or not.

You begin now I hope to be able to consider that what has happened might have had great aggravations. Had you been followed in your intended travels by an account of this afflictive deprivation,[2] where could have [been] the end of doubt, and surmise, and suspicion, and self condemnation, you could not easily have been reconciled to those whom you left behind, or those who had persuaded you to go. You would [have] believed that he died by neglect, and that your presence would have saved him. I was glad of your letter from Marlborough,[3] and hope You will try to force yourself to write. If grief either caused or aggravated poor Queeney's ilness, you have taken

1. SJ and JB arrived in London during the late morning of 29 Mar. They parted company, SJ hastening off to Southwark and the Thrales. By teatime, however, he was back in his house: Hester Thrale, Queeney, and Giuseppe Baretti had left for Bath, and Henry Thrale apparently did not wish his company (*Boswell: The Ominous Years*, ed. Charles Ryskamp and F. A. Pottle, 1963, p. 305).

2. *Ante* To JB, 5 Mar. 1776 and n. 2.

3. Presumably the travelers had stopped at Marlborough, Wiltshire, on their way to Bath. The letter to which SJ refers has not been recovered.

the proper method for relieving it. Young minds easily receive new impressions.

Poor Peyton expired this morning.[4] He probably during many years for which he sat starving by the bed of a Wife not only useless, but almost motionless, condemned by[5] poverty to personal attendance, and by the necessity of such attendance chained down to poverty, he probably thought often how lightly he should tread the path of life without his burthen. Of this thought the admission was unavoidable, and the indulgence might be forgiven to frailty and distress. His Wife died at last, and before she was buried he was seized by a fever, and is now going to the grave.

Such miscarriages when they happen to those on whom many eyes are fixed, fill histories and tragedies and tears have been shed for the sufferings, and wonder excited by the fortitude of those who neither did nor suffered mor[e] than Peyton.

I was on Saturday at Mrs. Montague's who expressed great sensibility of your loss, and have this day received an invitation to a supper and a ball, but I returned my acknowledgement to the Ladies, and let them know, that I thought, I should like the ball better another week.[6] I am, Dear Madam, Your most obedient servant,

SAM. JOHNSON

4. *Ante* To Hester Thrale, 20 May 1775, n. 7; 16 Mar. 1776.

5. MS: "by" superimposed upon "to"

6. In 1776 Easter fell on 7 Apr. Cf. *Ante* To John Taylor, 17 Apr. 1772.

James Boswell

WEDNESDAY 3 APRIL 1776

PRINTED SOURCE: JB's *Life*, 1791, I.454.

Mr. Johnson does not see why Mr. Boswell should suppose a Scotchman less acceptable than any other man. He will be at the Mitre.[1]

1. On 3 Apr. 1776 JB sent SJ a note, "asking if he would meet me at dinner at

the Mitre, though a friend of mine, a Scotchman, was to be there" (*Life* II.307). The dinner at the tavern duly took place; the "Scotchman" in question was Alexander Murray (1736–95), Solicitor-General of Scotland (1775–83), later (1783) raised to the Bench as Lord Henderland (*Life* III.8; Namier and Brooke III.183).

John Taylor

THURSDAY 4 APRIL 1776

MS: Hyde Collection.

ADDRESS: To the Reverend Dr. Taylor in Ashbourn, Derbyshire.

POSTMARK: 4 AP.

ENDORSEMENTS: 1776, 4 Apr. 76.

No. 8 Bolt court, Fleetstreet (not Johnson's Court),[1]

Dear Sir: Apr. 4, 1776

I was sorry, and so was Mr. Boswel, that we were summoned away so soon.[2] Our effort of travelling in the Evening was useless, We did not get home till friday morning.[3] Mrs. Thrale and her girl are gone to Bath.[4] The blow was very heavy upon them.

The Expedition however still proceeds, so that I shall be but a short time here.[5] If Mr. Longdon will be so kind as to send the barley next week,[6] I can deliver to Boswel, I wish he would

1. SJ had just moved from No. 7 Johnson's Court to No. 8 Bolt Court, where he lived until his death. On 16 Mar. JB, who was taken aback by the change of dwelling, reported: "When I found his new house a much better one, I was cheered. He had good rooms and a pretty little spot of background" (*Boswell: The Ominous Years*, ed. Charles Ryskamp and F. A. Pottle, 1963, p. 255).

2. SJ and JB had cut short their stay at Ashbourne in order that SJ might return to London and console the Thrales. They arrived at Ashbourne on 26 Mar. and left the following afternoon (Ryskamp and Pottle, *The Ominous Years*, pp. 299–301).

3. On their hurried return trip to London, SJ and JB spent two nights on the road, the first at Loughborough and the second at St. Albans (*Life* III.2, 4–5).

4. *Ante* To Hester Thrale, 30 Mar. 1776, n. 1.

5. *Ante* To JB, 5 Mar. 1776, n. 2.

6. Robert Longden (*c.* 1731–1802), "a civil and rather spruce Squire" of Ashbourne, who supplemented his landed income by dealing in cheese (*Life* III.504–5). The barley in question is in all likelihood that discussed in To Hester

[put] a peck more in a separate bag, for I would not break the main bulk, and yet I cannot well help it, unless I have a little more.

Mr. Boswel is in the room, and sends his respects. Let me know whether you design to come hither before I am to go, and if you come we will contrive to pass a few hours together.[7] I am, Sir, Your most humble servant,

SAM. JOHNSON

Thrale, 17 July 1775; it was intended for experimental planting at Streatham Park.

7. Although the Italian trip was canceled, SJ did accompany the Thrales to Bath on 15 Apr. On 3 May, however, he returned to London in order to meet with Taylor (Clifford, 1952, pp. 139–40; *Post* To John Taylor, 13 Apr. 1776; 29 Apr. 1776; *Post* To Hester Thrale, 6 May 1776).

Hester Thrale

THURSDAY 4 APRIL 1776

MS: Hyde Collection.

Dearest Madam: April 4, 1776

I am glad to hear of pretty Queeney's recovery, and your returning tranquillity.[1] What we have suffered ought to make us remember what we have escaped. You might at as short a warning have been taken from your children, or Mr. Thrale might have been taken from us all.

Mr. Thrale, when he dismissed me, promised to call on me;[2] he has never called, and I have never seen him.[3] He said that he would go to the house,[4] and I hope he has[5] found something that laid hold on his attention.

1. Writing from Bath, Hester Thrale had reported on her restorative activities and Queeney's improved health (1 Apr. 1776, MS: Rylands Library).

2. *Ante* To Hester Thrale, 1 Apr. 1776.

3. On 5 Apr., Good Friday, Henry Thrale called on SJ, stayed several hours, and then attended church with him (*Works*, Yale ed. 1.258).

4. Presumably SJ refers to the House of Commons, then in session.

5. MS: "has" altered from "was"

I do not wish you to return, while the novelty of the place does any good either to You or Queeney, and longer I know you will not stay, there is therefore no need of soliciting your return.[6] What gratification can be extracted from so sad an event, I derive from observing that Mr. Thrale's behaviour has united you to him by additional endearments. Every evil will be more easily born while you fondly love one another, and every good will be enjoyed with encrease of delight *past compute* to use the phrase of Cumberland.[7] May your love of each other always encrease. I am, Dearest Madam, Your most obedient servant,

SAM. JOHNSON

6. *Ante* To Hester Thrale, 30 Mar. 1776, n. 1.

7. Richard Cumberland (1732–1811), playwright, poet, and novelist, "the Terence of England" (Goldsmith, "Retaliation," l. 62). In SJ's somewhat ambiguous judgment, "Mr. Cumberland is a Million" (*Post* To Hester Thrale, 21 Oct. 1779). In his *Memoirs* Cumberland claims, "I . . . knew him [SJ] well, respected him highly, loved him sincerely"; according to other contemporary testimony, however, Cumberland never became an intimate member of the Johnsonian circle (*Johns. Misc.* II.72–78). Hester Thrale praised his "genteel" appearance and his "elegant" manner, but concluded that "he is a Man one cannot love" (*Thraliana* I.135).

Hester Thrale

TUESDAY 9 APRIL 1776

MS: Hyde Collection.

Dear Madam: Apr. 9, 1776

Mr. Thrale's alteration of purpose is not weakness of resolution; it is a wise man's compliance with the change of things, and with the new duties which the change produces.[1] Whoever expects me to be angry will be disappointed. I do not even grieve at the effect, I grieve only at the cause.[2]

1. On 5 Apr. plans for the Italian expedition were still in force, though Henry Thrale appeared to JB "to have some difficulty about going" (*Boswell: The Ominous Years*, ed. Charles Ryskamp and F. A. Pottle, 1963, p. 317). Sometime during the next three days, however, he decided against the trip.

2. "I wondered to see him bear, with a philosophical calmness, what would

Your business for the present is to seek for ease, and to go where you think it most likely to be found. There cannot yet be any place in your minds for mere curiosity. Whenever I can contribute to your tranquillity, I shall readily attend, and hope never to add to the evils that[3] may oppress You. I will go with You to Bath, or stay with you at home.[4]

I am very little disappointed. I was glad to go, to places of so much celebrity, but had promised to myself no raptures, no[r] much improvement. Nor is there any thing to be expected worth such a sacrifice as You might make.

Keep yourself busy, and you will in time grow cheerful; new prospects may open, and new enjoyments may come within your reach. I surely cannot but wish all evil removed from a house, which has afforded my miseries all the succour which attention and benevolence could give. I am sorry not to owe so much, but to repay so little. What I can do, you may with great reason expect from, Dearest Madam, Your most obliged and most humble servant,

SAM. JOHNSON

---

have made most people peevish and fretful. I perceived, however, that he had so warmly cherished the hope of enjoying classical scenes, that he could not easily part with the scheme" (*Life* III.28).

3. MS: "that" superimposed upon "of"

4. *Ante* To John Taylor, 4 Apr. 1776, n. 7.

Lord Hertford[1]

THURSDAY 11 APRIL 1776

MS: Hyde Collection. A copy in the hand of Sir George Rose.

ENDORSEMENT: Mr. Saml. Johnson to the Earl of Hertford requesting apartments at Hampton Court,[2] 11th May 1776.

1. Francis Seymour Conway (1718–94), second Baron Conway, cr. (1750) first Earl of Hertford, later (1793) Marquis of Hertford. Hertford served as Lord Chamberlain from 1766 to 1782 and again briefly in 1783.

2. In 1760 George III instituted "grace-and-favour" apartments, which provided free accommodations at Hampton Court Palace to those people who had

My Lord, Bolt Court, Fleet Street, Ap. 11, 1776

Being wholly unknown to your Lordship, I have only this apology to make for presuming to trouble you with a request, that a stranger's petition, if it cannot be easily granted, can be easily refused.

Some of the apartments are now vacant, in which I am encouraged to hope, that by application to your Lordship, I may obtain a residence. Such a grant would be considered by me as a great favour, and I hope that to a man who has had the honour of vindicating his Majesty's Government,[3] a retreat in one of his houses, may be not improperly or unworthily allowed.[4]

I therefore request, that your Lordship will be pleased to grant such rooms in Hampton Court as shall seem proper, to, my Lord, Your Lordship's most obedient and most humble servant,

SAM. JOHNSON

---

given notable service to the Crown in one form or another. To occupy any apartment, one required written authority from the Lord Chamberlain—hence SJ's letter to Lord Hertford (R. J. Minney, *Hampton Court*, 1972, p. 217; Roy Nash, *Hampton Court*, 1983, p. 175).

3. Presumably SJ refers to his political tracts, and in particular to *Taxation No Tyranny* (*Ante* To JB, 21 Jan. 1775, n. 3; *Post* To Hester Thrale, 6 May 1776 and n. 2).

4. Hertford turned down SJ's request: "Lord C. [Chamberlain] presents his compliments to Mr. Johnson, and is sorry he cannot obey his commands, having already on his hands many engagements unsatisfied" (MS copy, Hyde Collection).

Frances Reynolds

THURSDAY 11 APRIL 1776

MS: Hyde Collection.

ENDORSEMENT: Dr. Johnson, April 11, 76.

Dearest Madam: Apr. 11, 1776

To have acted with regard to you in a manner either unfriendly or disrespectful would give me great pain, and I hope will be always very contrary to my intention. That I staid away was merely accidental. I have seldom dined from home; and I did not think my opinion necessary to your information in any proprieties of behaviour.

The poor Parents of the child are much grieved, and much dejected. The Journey to Italy is put off,[1] but they go to[2] Bath on Monday. A visit from you will be well taken, and I think your intimacy is such, that You may very properly pay it in a morning.[3] I am sure it will be thought seasonable and kind, and wish you not to omit it. I am, Dear Madam, Your most humble Servant,

SAM. JOHNSON

1. *Ante* To JB, 5 Mar. 1776, n. 2; *Ante* To Hester Thrale, 9 Apr. 1776, n. 1.

2. MS: "to" altered from "the"

3. *Post* To Frances Reynolds, 15 Apr. 1776.

John Taylor

SATURDAY 13 APRIL 1776

MS: University of Rochester Library.

ADDRESS: To the Reverend Dr. Taylor in Ashbourn, Derbyshire.

POSTMARK: 13 AP.

ENDORSEMENTS: 1776, 13 Apr. 76.

Bolt court (not Johnson's court) Fleetstreet,

Dear Sir: Apr. 13, 1776[1]

I have not yet carried the cases.[2] I would have the value of the Estate truly told. This trial takes up the Attorney general for the present,[3] and there is little hope of his attention to any

1. *Ante* To John Taylor, 4 Apr. 1776, n. 1.

2. *Post* To JB, *c.* 22 Apr. 1776. In accordance with SJ's advice, Taylor was soliciting legal opinions of his case (*Ante* To John Taylor, 15 Jan. 1776; 17 Feb. 1776; *Post* To Hester Thrale, 14 May 1776).

3. Edward Thurlow (1731–1806), first Baron Thurlow (1778), Attorney-General (1771–78), later (1778–92) Lord Chancellor. Thurlow was involved in trying Elizabeth Chudleigh (*c.* 1720–88), Dowager Duchess of Kingston, for bigamy (on

thing else. And upon the whole, I do not see that there is any haste. The opinion is as good and as useful a month hence, unless you found Mr. Rudd alienating the land.[4] I am going with Mr. Thrale to Bath on Monday. Our Italian Journey is deferred to another year, perhaps totally put off on their part. They are both extremely dejected. I think, his grief is deepest. If you put off your coming to town, I will give You notice when we return, but if your coming is necessary, I will come from Bath to meet you.[5] I am, Sir, Your most humble Servant,

SAM. JOHNSON

---

the grounds that she was the legal wife of the Earl of Bristol when she married the Duke). The trial before the House of Lords began 15 Apr., and the Duchess was declared guilty on 23 Apr. However, as Horace Walpole reported, "After a paltry defence and an oration of fifty pages, which she herself had written and pronounced well, the sages in spite of the Attorney-General, who brandished a hot iron, dismissed her with the simple injunction of paying her fees" (*Walpole's Correspondence*, Yale ed. XXVIII.266).

4. *Ante* To John Taylor, 7 Mar. 1776.

5. *Ante* To John Taylor, 4 Apr. 1776, n. 7.

Frances Reynolds

MONDAY 15 APRIL 1776

MS: Hyde Collection.

ADDRESS: To Miss Reynolds.

ENDORSEMENT: Dr. Johnson, April 15, 76.

Dearest Madam: Apr. 15, 1776

When You called on Mrs. Thrale, I find by enquiry that she was really abroad;[1] the same thing happenned to Mrs. Montague, of which I beg you to inform her, for she went likewise by my opinion. The Denial, if it had been feigned would not have pleased me. Your visits however are kindly paid, and very kindly taken.

Pray tell Sir Joshua, that I have examined Mr. Thrales Man,

1. *Ante* To Frances Reynolds, 11 Apr. 1776.

and find no foundation for the Story of the Alehouse and mulled Beer. He was at the play two nights before, with one of the chief men in the Brewhouse, and came home at the regular time. This, I believe is true, for Mrs. Thrale told me that she had sent him to his friend Murphy's play,[2] and if more had been to be told, I should then have heard it.

We are going to Bath this morning, but I would not part without telling you the real state of your visit. I am, dearest Madam, Your most humble Servant,

SAM. JOHNSON

2. Apparently rumors had been circulating that Harry Thrale's health was undermined by a post-theatre visit to a tavern. The true story is that Harry had been permitted to attend (in the company of one of the brewery clerks) a performance of Arthur Murphy's *The Way to Keep Him* at Drury Lane. According to Hester Thrale's account, her son "came home . . . half mad with delight, and in such Spirits Health and Happiness that nothing ever exceeded" (Hyde, 1977, p. 149). The following day, 22 Mar., Harry was in perfect health; on the 23rd he died (Hyde, 1977, p. 151).

James Boswell

c. MONDAY 22 APRIL 1776[1]

MS: Beinecke Library. The transcript (in the hand of Veronica Boswell) used as copy for JB's *Life*.

Dear Sir: [Bath]

Why do you talk of neglect? When did I neglect you?If you will come to Bath we shall all be glad to see you; come therfore as soon as you can.[2]

But I have a little business for you at London. Bid Francis look in the paper drawer of the Chest of Drawers in my Bed-

1. According to JB's Register, this letter was received 23 Apr. 1776 (MS: Beinecke Library).

2. "I had never seen that beautiful city [Bath], and wished to take the opportunity of visiting it, while Johnson was there. Having written to him, I received the following answer" (*Life* III.44). JB joined SJ and the Thrales on 26 Apr. He had returned to London by 1 May (*Life* III.45 and n. 1).

chamber, for two cases,[3] one for the Attorney General,[4] and one for the Soliciter General.[5] They lye, I think at the top of my papers, otherwise they are some where else, and will give me more trouble.

Please to write me immediately if they can be found. Make my compliments to all our Friends round the world and to Mrs. Williams at home. I am, Sir, your etc.

SAM. JOHNSON

Search for the papers as soon as you can that if it is necessary, I may write to you again before you come down.

3. *Ante* To John Taylor, 13 Apr. 1776 and n. 2.

4. SJ refers to Edward Thurlow.

5. SJ refers to Alexander Wedderburn.

John Taylor

MONDAY 29 APRIL 1776

MS: Hyde Collection.

ADDRESS: To the Reverend Dr. Taylor.

ENDORSEMENTS: 1776, 29 April 76.

Dear Sir: Bath, Apr. 29, 1776

I am glad that you are come up, for it is very difficult to do business at a distance.[1] My purpose is to hasten to you. I suppose I shall be in London on friday or on saturday, and we will then drive the matter forwards. I am, Dear Sir, Your most humble Servant,

SAM. JOHNSON

1. *Ante* To John Taylor, 4 Apr. 1776, n. 7; 13 Apr. 1776.

Hester Thrale

MONDAY 6 MAY 1776

MS: Houghton Library.

Dearest Madam: May 6, 1776

On friday night, as you know, I left you about eleven o'clock. The Moon shone but I did not see much of the way, for I think, I slept better than I commonly do in bed. My Companions were civil men, and we despatched our journey very peaceably. I came home at about seven on Saturday very little fatigued.

To day I have been at home. To morrow I am to dine, as I did yesterday with Dr. Taylor, on Wednesday I am to dine with Oglethorpe, and[1] Thursday with Paoli. He that sees before him to his third dinner, has a long prospect.

My political tracts are printed, and I bring Mr. Thrale a copy when I come. They make but a little book.[2]

Count Manucci is in such haste to come that I believe he will [not] stay for me; if he would I should like to hear his remarks on the road.[3]

Mr. Baretti has a cold and hoarseness, and Mrs. Williams says that I have caught a cold this afternoon. I am, Madam, your most humble servant,

SAM. JOHNSON

1. MS: "and and"

2. The octavo edition of *Political Tracts* (1776) collected SJ's four pamphlets of the 1770s: *The False Alarm*, *Thoughts on the Late Transactions Respecting Falkland's Islands*, *The Patriot*, and *Taxation No Tyranny* (*Bibliography*, p. 127).

3. Giovanni Tommaso (1750–1814), Conte Manucci, a Florentine nobleman whom the Thrales and SJ had met in Paris the previous year. Manucci, who arrived in England on 14 Feb., was a guest at Streatham Park, where he witnessed the sudden death of Harry Thrale. He was then invited to join the family in Bath (*The Piozzi Letters*, ed. E. A. Bloom and L. D. Bloom, 1989, 1.154 n. 10; *The French Journals of Mrs. Thrale and Doctor Johnson*, ed. Moses Tyson and Henry Guppy, 1932, pp. 64–66; Hyde, 1977, pp. 147, 152). Manucci planned to accompany SJ back to Bath, but SJ, delayed by Taylor's legal business, finally counseled him to go by himself (*Post* To Hester Thrale, 14 May 1776; 16 May 1776).

Hester Thrale

SATURDAY 11 MAY 1776

MS: Hyde Collection.

Dear Madam: May 11, 1776

That you may have no superfluous uneasiness I went this afternoon to visit the two Babies at Kensington, and found them indeed a little spotted with their disorder, but as brisk and gay as health and youth can make them.[1] I took a paper of Sweetmeats, and spread them on the table. They took great delight[2] to show their governess the various animals that were made of sugar, and when they had eaten as much as was fit, the rest were laid up for tomorrow.

Susy sends her duty and love with great propriety. Sophy sends her duty to You, and her love to Queeney and Papa. Mr. Evans came in after me.[3] You may set your heart quite at rest, no babies can be better than they appear to be. Dr. Taylor went with me, and we staid a good while. He likes them very much. Susy said her Creed in French.

Dr. Taylor says I must not come back till his business is adjusted, and indeed it would not be wise to come away without doing what I came hither only to do. However I expect to be dismissed in a few days, and shall bring Manucci with me.[4]

I dined yesterday with ⟨Langton and Lady R.⟩ ⟨*two words*⟩ just going to bed. His three children are very lovely.[5] ⟨Boswel⟩ longs to teach him a little economy. I know not how his money goes, for I do not think that Mrs. Williams and I had our due share of the nine guineas.[6]

1. When the rest of the family left for Bath, Susanna and Sophia were put under the care of Elizabeth Cumyns in Kensington. In her letter to SJ of 8 May, Hester Thrale reported that the two children had contracted chicken pox (MS: Rylands Library; Hyde, 1977, p. 158).

2. MS: "delight" altered from "desire"

3. SJ refers to James Evans.

4. *Ante* To Hester Thrale, 6 May 1776 and n. 3.

5. The three children of Bennet Langton and Lady Rothes were George (b. 1772), Mary (b. 1773), and Diana (b. 1774) (Fifer, p. lviii n. 29).

6. Presumably SJ means that Langton, who had been given a present of nine

He begins to reproach himself with neglect of George's education,[7] and censures that idleness or that deviation by the indulgence of which he has left uncultivated such a fertile mind. I advised him to let the child alone, and told him that the matter was not great, whether he could read at the end of four years or of five, and that I thought it not proper to harrass a tender mind with the violence of painful attention.[8] I may perhaps procure both father and son a year of quiet, and surely I may rate myself among their benefactors. I am, Madam, Your most humble Servant,

SAM. JOHNSON

---

guineas, had not spent an appropriate amount of that sum on the dinner served to his guests.

7. Langton's eldest child, born 8 Mar. 1772 (Fifer, p. lviii n. 29).

8. According to SJ: "Endeavouring to make children prematurely wise is useless labour. Suppose they have more knowledge at five or six years old than other children, what use can be made of it? . . . Too much is expected from precocity, and too little performed" (*Life* II.407–8).

Hester Thrale

TUESDAY 14 MAY 1776

MS: Hyde Collection.

Dear Lady: May 14, 1776

Since my visit to the Younglings[1] nothing has happenned but[2] a little disappointment in Dr. Taylor's affairs which, he says, must keep me here a while longer. Mr. Wedderburn has given his opinion to day directly against us.[3] He thinks of the claim much as I think. We sent this afternoon for a solicitor, another Scrase,[4] who gave the same sentence with Wedderburn, and

1. *Ante* To Hester Thrale, 11 May 1776.

2. MS: "but" altered from "by"

3. *Ante* To JB, *c.* 22 Apr. 1776 and n. 5.

4. SJ appears to mean that he and Taylor consulted a solicitor (name unspecified) who is comparable to the wise and trustworthy Charles Scrase.

with less delicacy. The Dr. tried to talk him into better notions, but to little purpose, for a man is not much believed in his own cause. At last finding the Dr. somewhat moody I bid him not be disturbed, for he could not be injured till the death of Mrs. Rudd, and her life was better than his. So I *comforted and advised him.*[5]

I know not how You intend to serve me, but I expect a letter to morrow, and I do not see why Queeney should forget me.

Manucci must, I believe, come down without me.[6] I am ashamed of having delayed him so long, without being able to fix a day; but you know, and must make him know that the fault is not mine.

Boswel goes away on thursday, very well satisfied with his journey. Some great men have promised to obtain him a place, and then a fig for my father, and his new wife.[7]

I have not yet been at Borough, nor know when I shall go unless you send me. There is in the exhibition of Exeter exchange, a picture of the house at Streatham, by one Laurence, I think, of the Borough.[8] This is something, or something like.

Mr. Welch sets out for France to morrow, with his younger

5. "And thus we comforted him, and advised him" (Mr. Mowbray to John Belford, 7 Sept., Samuel Richardson, *Clarissa*, 1748, VII.215). This quotation was part of Hester Thrale's standard epistolary repertoire (Hester Thrale to SJ, 10 Apr. 1773, MS: Rylands Library; Hester Thrale to Frances Burney, 1779, *Diary and Letters of Madame D'Arblay*, ed. Austin Dobson, 1904, I.158).

6. *Ante* To Hester Thrale, 6 May 1776 and n. 3.

7. In 1776 JB "had real hopes of obtaining something through Mountstuart's 'noble Tory interest.' . . . It was essential for Boswell to get an independency, a post paying a few hundred a year, while Lord Auchinleck was still alive, not merely because he wanted to get free from his father but because once he inherited Auchinleck he could not claim a pressing need for money. And Maecenas [Mountstuart] did make gestures, talked to the Duke of Queensberry, who was to talk to the Prime Minister, Lord North" (*Later Years*, pp. 127–28). Despite all these efforts, however, JB did not secure the much desired "place."

8. Thomas Lawrence, a landscape painter specializing in views of London, was an honorary exhibitioner at the Society of Artists, 1770–76 (Ellis Waterhouse, *The Dictionary of British 18th Century Painters*, 1981, p. 219). In 1772 his address was given as "179, High Street, Borough." In 1776 Lawrence exhibited "A View of the House of H. Thrale, Esq., Streatham, Surry" (Algernon Graves, *The Society of Artists of Great Britain, 1760–1791*, 1907, p. 144).

daughter. He has leave of absence for a year, and seems very much delighted with the thought of travelling, and the hope of health.[9] I am, Madam, Your most humble servant,

SAM. JOHNSON

9. Saunders Welch (1710–84), who had served as J.P. for Westminster since 1755, was an old and close friend of SJ, who told JB that he had "attended Mr. Welch in his office for a whole winter, to hear the examinations of the culprits" (*Life* III.216). SJ also contributed an introduction to Welch's *Proposal . . . to Remove the Nuisance of Common Prostitutes* (1758). "Mr. Welch's health being impaired, he was advised to try the effect of a warm climate; and Johnson, by his interest with Mr. Chamier, procured him leave of absence to go to Italy, and a promise that the pension or salary of two hundred pounds a year, . . . should not be discontinued. Mr. Welch accordingly went abroad, accompanied by his daughter Anne" (*Life* III.216–17). *Post* To Saunders Welch, 3 Feb. 1778.

Margaret Boswell

THURSDAY 16 MAY 1776

PRINTED SOURCE: JB's *Life*, 1791, II.93–94.

Madam, May 16, 1776

You must not think me uncivil in omitting to answer the letter with which you favoured me some time ago.[1] I imagined it to have been written without Mr. Boswell's knowledge, and therefore supposed the answer to require, what I could not find, a private conveyance.

The difference with Lord Auchinleck is now over; and since young Alexander has appeared, I hope no more difficulties will arise among you;[2] for I sincerely wish you all happy. Do not teach the young ones to dislike me, as you dislike me yourself; but let me at least have Veronica's kindness, because she is my acquaintance.

You will now have Mr. Boswell home;[3] it is well that you

1. *Ante* To JB, 24 Feb. 1776 and n. 3.

2. *Ante* To JB, 15 Jan. 1776, n. 1; 15 Feb. 1776, n. 3.

3. JB left London for Edinburgh early on the morning of 17 May (*Boswell: The Ominous Years*, ed. Charles Ryskamp and F. A. Pottle, 1963, p. 352).

have him, he has led a wild life.[4] I have taken him to Lichfield, and he has followed Mr. Thrale to Bath.[5] Pray take care of him, and tame him. The only thing in which I have the honour to agree with you is, in loving him; and while we are so much of a mind in a matter of so much importance, our other quarrels will, I hope, produce no great bitterness. I am, Madam, Your most humble servant,

SAM. JOHNSON

4. The tone of this remark is similar to that of SJ's observation during the course of the Dilly-Wilkes dinner: "I turned him [JB] loose at Lichfield, my native city, that he might see for once real civility: for you know he lives among savages in Scotland, and among rakes in London" (*Life* III.77). *Post* To Hester Thrale, 16 May 1776 and n. 3.

5. *Ante* To John Taylor, 23 Mar. 1776; *Ante* To JB, *c.* 22 Apr. 1776, n. 2.

Joshua Reynolds

THURSDAY 16 MAY 1776

MS: Hyde Collection.

ADDRESS: To Sir Joshua Reynolds.

ENDORSEMENT: Dr. Johnson.

Dear Sir: May 16, 1776

I have been kept away from You, I know not well how, and of these vexatious hindrances I know not when there will be an end. I therefore send you the poor dear Doctor's epitaph.[1] Read it first yourself, and if You then think it right, show it to the Club.[2] I am, you know, willing enough to be corrected.[3] If

1. SJ had written a Latin epitaph for Oliver Goldsmith's monument in Westminster Abbey.

2. A number of members of The Club, Reynolds included, requested certain "additions and alterations," and asked that the epitaph be written in English and not in Latin. They drafted their comments in the form of a "round robin," which JB reproduces in his biography (*Life* III., facing page 83).

3. "Sir Joshua agreed to carry it [the round robin and an accompanying address] to Dr. Johnson, who received it with much good humour, and desired Sir Joshua to tell the gentlemen, that he would alter the Epitaph in any manner they

you think any thing much amiss, keep it to yourself, till we come together. I have sent two copies, but prefer the card.[4] The dates must be settled by Dr. Percy.[5] I am, Sir, Your most humble Servant,

SAM. JOHNSON

pleased, as to the sense of it; but *he would never consent to disgrace the walls of Westminster Abbey with an English inscription*" (*Life* III.84–85).

4. By "copies" SJ means "versions," one of which (the epitaph he himself prefers) was written on a card. For the difference between the two texts, *Post* To Joshua Reynolds, 22 June 1776 and n. 2.

5. There was some confusion over Goldsmith's birthday. The inscription gives it as 1731, but modern scholarship has established the correct date as 1730 (*Life* III.83 and n. 1).

Hester Thrale

THURSDAY 16 MAY 1776

MS: Hyde Collection.

Dear Madam: May 16, 1776

This is [my] third letter.[1] Well—sure I shall have something to morrow. Our business stands still. The Doctor says I must not go; and yet my stay does him no good. His Solicitor says he is sick, but I suspect he is sullen.[2] The Doctor in the mean time has his head as full as yours at an Election. Livings and preferments, as if he were in want with twenty children, run in his head. But a man must have his head on something small or great.

For my part, I begin to settle and keep company with grave aldermen. I dined yesterday in the poultry with Mr. Alderman Wilkes, and Mr. Alderman Lee, and Counsellor Lee, his Brother.[3] There sat you the while, so sober, with your Wood-

1. *Ante* To Hester Thrale, 11 May 1776; 14 May 1776. Hester Thrale had last written on 8 May (MS: Rylands Library).

2. *Ante* To Hester Thrale, 14 May 1776.

3. JB had engineered a meeting between SJ and John Wilkes at a dinner party given by the Dilly brothers the previous evening; for JB's classic narrative set piece,

wards[4] and your Harringtons[5] and my Aunt[6] and her turnspit. And when they are[7] gone, you think by chance on Johnson what is he doing? What should he be doing? he is breaking jokes with Jack Wilkes upon the Scots. Such Madam, are the vicissitudes of things. And there was Mrs. Knowles the Quaker that works the sutile pictures, who is a great admirer of your conversation.[8] She saw you at Mr. Shaw's, at the election time. She is a staffordshire Woman, and I am to go and see her. Staffordshire is the nursery of arts, where the[y] grow up till they are transplanted to London.

Yet it is strange that I hear nothing from you. I hope you are not angry, or sick. Perhaps you are gone without me for spite to see places. That is natural enough, for evil is very natural, but I shall vex, unless it does you good.

Steevens seems to be connected with Tyrwhit in publishing Chatterton's poems; he came very anxiously to know the result of our enquiries, and though he says, he always thought them forged, is not quite pleased to find us so fully convinced.[9]

---

see *Life* III.64–79. The Dillys' "patriotick" guests included William Lee (1739–95), merchant and diplomat, the only American ever elected an alderman of London; Lee was accompanied by his brother Arthur (1740–92), M.D., who served as a confidential agent for the Continental Congress.

4. Francis Woodward (d. 1785), M.D., a prominent Bath physician.

5. Henry Harington (Harrington) (1727–1816), M.D., not only practiced medicine but also served as alderman and magistrate of Bath and founded the Bath Harmonic Society.

6. It is probable that SJ refers to Sidney Arabella Cotton. *Post* To Hester Thrale, 22 Sept. 1777, n. 9.

7. MS: "a" superimposed upon "w"

8. Mary Morris Knowles (1733–1807), "the amiable accomplished Quaker," wife of the Rev. Thomas Knowles (1723–1802), D.D., Rector of Ickworth, Suffolk, was a highly accomplished needlewoman—so accomplished that Queen Charlotte had commissioned from her tapestry portraits of the King and the young princes (*Boswell: The Ominous Years*, ed. Charles Ryskamp and F. A. Pottle, 1963, p. 350). In *Idler* No. 13, SJ had referred to "a kind of 'sutile pictures' which imitate tapestry" (*Works*, Yale ed. II.44).

9. George Steevens was assisting Thomas Tyrwhitt (1730–86), F.R.S., Fellow of Merton College and a pioneering Chaucer scholar, in editing the poems attributed by Thomas Chatterton (1752–70) to one Thomas Rowley, a fifteenth-century priest. Chatterton claimed to have discovered the "Rowley" manuscripts in the archives of St. Mary Redcliffe, Bristol. On 29 Apr. SJ and JB had traveled from

I have written to Manucci to find his own way,[10] for the *Law's delay*[11] makes it difficult for me to guess when I shall be, able to [be] otherwise than by my inclination, Madam, Your most humble servant,

SAM. JOHNSON

Bath to Bristol in order to "enquire upon the spot, into the authenticity of '*Rowley's* Poetry'" (*Life* III.50). After examining the putative originals, SJ pronounced them forgeries. "Steevens was . . . closely identified with the publication, and, whatever his real views were on the authenticity of the poems, he was naturally not a little annoyed to find that the Literary Dictator, whose denunciation of Macpherson's fabrications was fresh in men's minds, had, after 'ocular demonstration,' pronounced against Rowley" (L. F. Powell, "Thomas Tyrwhitt and the Rowley Poems," *RES* 7, 1931, p. 318). In Aug. 1776 Steevens and Tyrwhitt visited Bristol together, examined the manuscripts, and decided to proceed with the project (Powell, "Thomas Tyrwhitt," p. 321). Tyrwhitt's *Poems Supposed to Have Been Written at Bristol, by Thomas Rowley* duly appeared in 1777 and went rapidly into a second edition. To the third edition (1778) Tyrwhitt added an appendix that exposed the poems as an imposture.

10. *Ante* To Hester Thrale, 6 May 1776 and n. 3.

11. "The pangs of dispriz'd love, the law's delay" (*Hamlet* III.i.72).

Hester Thrale

SATURDAY 18 MAY 1776

MS: Hyde Collection.

Dear Madam: May 18, 1776

Then You are neither sick nor angry.[1] Don't let me be defrauded of Queeney's Letter.[2] Yesterday Seward was with me, and told me what he knew of you. All good. To day I went to look into my places at the borough. I called on Mr. Perkins in the counting house. He crows, and triumphs; as We go on, we shall double our business. The best brown malt he can have

1. *Ante* To Hester Thrale, 16 May 1776. In *Letters* (1788), H. L. Piozzi includes a letter to SJ, written from Bath and dated 16 May; the holograph has not been recovered. The published version begins, "I had no notion of your staying away from us so long, or you should not surely have wanted a letter" (I.327).

2. "Farewel, dear Sir, and expect a long letter from Queeney" (Piozzi, *Letters* I.332).

laid in at thirty and sixpence, and great stores he purposes to buy. Dr. Taylor's business stagnates but he resolves not to wait on it much longer. Surely I shall get down to you next week.[3]

Boswel went away on thursday night,[4] with no great inclination to travel northward, but who can contend with destiny? He says, he had had a very pleasant journey;[5] he paid another visit, I think, to Mrs. Rudd,[6] before he went home to his own deary. He carries with him two or three good resolutions, I hope they will not mould upon the road. Who can be this new friend of mine?[7] The letter you sent me was from Mr. Twisse, and the book, if any came, is Twisse's travels to Ireland,[8] which you will, I hope, unty and read.

I enclose some of the powders lest you should lose your patient by delay. I am, Madam, Your most humble servant,

SAM. JOHNSON

3. The Thrales had returned from Bath before SJ was able to disengage himself (*Post* To Henry Thrale, 3 June 1776).

4. *Ante* To Margaret Boswell, 16 May 1776, n. 3.

5. *Ante* To Margaret Boswell, 16 May 1776.

6. Margaret Caroline Rudd (*c.* 1745–97), courtesan and adventuress, achieved a career comparable to that of Defoe's Roxana. After acquiring (and subsequently blackmailing) a series of wealthy protectors, with whom she lived under various pseudonyms, Rudd became the mistress of Daniel Perreau, "a man of expensive tastes but no certain occupation"; together with Perreau and his brother Robert, she "soon became involved in criminal transactions on a large scale" (*Boswell: The Ominous Years*, ed. Charles Ryskamp and F. A. Pottle, 1963, pp. 353–54). The Perreaus and Rudd forged bonds and promissory notes, and when they were apprehended, Rudd became a witness for the Crown against the brothers. The Perreaus were found guilty and executed at Tyburn, 17 Jan. 1776; Rudd was tried separately on 8 Dec. 1775 and acquitted. JB, who "could not resist coming to grips with a woman of such extraordinary address and insinuation," visited Rudd on 22 Apr. and again on 14 May (*Later Years*, pp. 134–35; Ryskamp and Pottle, *The Ominous Years*, p. 344).

7. "We have a flashy friend here already, who is much your adorer; I wonder how you will like *him*? An Irishman he is; very handsome, very hot-headed" (Piozzi, *Letters* 1.329). At Bath the Thrales had met Richard Musgrave (1746–1818), later (1782) first Bt., of Tourin, Co. Waterford.

8. *Ante* To Hester Thrale, 12 May 1775, n. 4.

Hester Thrale

WEDNESDAY 22 MAY 1776

MS: Hyde Collection.

Dear Madam: May 22, 1776

On friday and saturday I dined with Dr. Taylor who is in discontent, but resolved not to stay much longer to hear the opinions of Lawyers who are all against him.[1] Who can blame him for being weary of them?

On Sunday I dined at Sir Joshua's house on the hill,[2] with the Bishop of St. Asaph.[3] The Dinner was good, and the Bishop is knowing and conversible. Yesterday at the Doctor's again—very little better—in the evening came in Dr. Crane,[4] who enquired after you.

All this while the Doctor is hurt only in his vanity. He thought he had supplanted Mrs. Wood,[5] and Mrs. Wood has found the means of defeating him. He really wanted nothing more than to have the power of bequeathing a reversion to Mr. Green's Son, who is very nearly related to Wood.[6] This purity of intention however he cannot prove, and the transaction in itself seems pactum iniquum.[7] I do not think that he can, or indeed that he ought to prevail.

1. *Ante* To Hester Thrale, 14 May 1776.

2. Reynolds divided his time between the house and studio on Leicester Square and Wick House, Richmond Hill, completed in 1772 (Derek Hudson, *Sir Joshua Reynolds*, 1958, pp. 110–11).

3. Jonathan Shipley (1714–88), D.D., Bishop of St. Asaph (1769–88), whom SJ and the Thrales had visited on their Welsh trip of 1774 (*Life* v.437). Shipley was an eloquent advocate of independence for the American colonies and toleration of Protestant dissenters. In 1776 Reynolds painted Shipley's portrait; in 1780 Shipley was elected to The Club (Fifer, p. xx).

4. Edward Crane (1696–1777), LL.D., Prebendary of Westminster (1748–77), had been a close friend of Hester Thrale's father, John Salusbury (*Thraliana* I.284–85).

5. *Ante* To John Taylor, 9 Feb. 1775, n. 1.

6. SJ refers to Thomas Webb Greene (1763–1842), the son of Richard Greene (*Johns. Glean.* VIII.135). It is not clear how Greene was related to Taylor's nephew Ralph Wood, Mrs. Wood's first husband.

7. *pactum iniquum*: "an inequitable agreement" (perhaps a distant reminiscence of Cicero's *Verrine Orations* II.iii.38).

Woodward,[8] I hear, is gone to Bristol, in deep dudgeon at Barret's declaration against Chatterton's productions.[9] You have now only Harington,[10] whom you can only make a silent admirer. I hope my friend buzzes a little about you to keep me in your head,[11] though I think, I do my part pretty well myself. There are very few writers of more punctuality.

I wish Queeney joy of her new watch, and next time I write intend myself the honour of directing my letter to her. Her hand is now very exact, and when use has made it free, may be very beautiful.

I am glad of Mr. Thrale's resolution to take up his restes[12] in person. He is wise in keeping the trade in his own hands, and appearing on proper occasions as the principal agent. Every man has those about him who wish to sooth him into inactivity and delitescence,[13] nor is there[14] any sem[b]lance of kindness more vigorously to be repelled, than that which voluntarily offers a vicarious performance of the tasks of life, and conspires with the natural love of ease against diligence and perseverance.

While I was holding my pen over the last period I was called down to Father Wilks the Benedictine,[15] and Father Brewer, a Doctor of the Sorbon, who are come to England, and are now wandering over London. I have invited them to dine with me to morrow.[16] Father Cowley is well, and Mrs. Strickland is at

8. SJ refers to Francis Woodward.

9. William Barrett (1733–89), surgeon and antiquarian of Bristol, owned several of the manuscript poems attributed by Chatterton to Thomas Rowley (*Ante* To Hester Thrale, 16 May 1776 and n. 9). According to L. F. Powell, SJ's reference to Barrett's "declaration" cannot be explained, particularly given the fact that Barrett based part of his *History and Antiquities of the City of Bristol* (1789) upon the "Rowley" manuscripts. SJ may have in mind Barrett's doubts concerning one of Chatterton's fabrications, the biography of William Canynge (Powell, "Thomas Tyrwhitt and the Rowley Poems," *RES* 7, 1931, pp. 319–20).

10. SJ refers to Henry Harington.

11. *Ante* To Hester Thrale, 18 May 1776 and n. 7.

12. *Ante* To Hester Thrale, 24 May 1773, n. 11.

13. *delitescence*: "the condition of lying hid; latent state, concealment, seclusion" (*OED*).

14. MS: "there" altered from "therefore"

15. *Ante* To Robert Levet, 22 Oct. 1775, n. 5.

16. *Post* To Hester Thrale, 23 May 1776.

Paris.[17] More news than this I have not yet learned. They stay, I think, here but a little time.

I have sent your last parcel of powders, and hope soon to come myself. I am, Madam, Your most humble Servant,

SAM. JOHNSON

17. Cecilia Towneley Strickland (1741–1814), widow of Charles Strickland (1734–70) of Sizergh Castle, Westmoreland, was a childhood friend of Hester Thrale (*The Piozzi Letters*, ed. E. A. Bloom and L. D. Bloom, 1989, i.81 n. 1). Cecilia Strickland, who spent several weeks with the Thrales and SJ during their trip to France, had introduced them to the English Benedictines in Paris (*The French Journals of Mrs. Thrale and Doctor Johnson*, ed. Moses Tyson and Henry Guppy, 1932, pp. 59–60).

Hester Thrale

THURSDAY 23 MAY 1776

MS: Lawrence G. Blackmon.

Dear Madam: May 23, 1776

The Doctor's affairs have driven us so close that I have left it to hazard whether I can get a place or not.[1] If I cannot, I will send the key of my drawers by one of the Coachmen, and promise him that you will pay him two Shillings if he delivers it properly. You will then be pleased to look yourself into the drawers, and the closet by the beds head, and in the table drawer. The books to be returned are *Pastor fido*,[2] and *Vita Tychonis*.[3] The rest are mine own, and to come home.

I hope to be with you, if not, I shall long to see you return.[4]

Yesterday Father Wilkes the Benedictine, and another of the same Monastry dined with me.[5] Mr. Barretti luckily came in. I am, Madam, Your most humble servant,

SAM. JOHNSON

1. SJ speaks of reserving a place on the coach to Bath.

2. *Il pastor fido* (1589) by Giovanni Battista Guarini (1538–1612).

3. SJ may be referring to *Tychonis Brahei . . . vita* (1654), an account by Pierre Gassendi of the Danish astronomer Tycho Brahe.

4. *Ante* To Hester Thrale, 18 May 1776, n. 3.

5. *Ante* To Hester Thrale, 22 May 1776.

William Adams

WEDNESDAY 29 MAY 1776

MS: Hyde Collection.

Sir: May 29, 1776

The Gentleman who brings this is a learned Benedictine,[1] in whose monastery I was treated at Paris with all the civilities, which the Society had means or opportunity of Showing. I dined in their refectory, and studied in their library, and had the favour of their company to other places, as curiosity led me. I therefore take the liberty of recommending him to You, Sir, and to Pembroke college, to be shown that a lettered Stranger is not treated with less regard at Oxford than in France, and hope that You and my fellow collegians will not be unwilling to acknowledge some obligation for benefits conferred on one who has had the honour of Studying amongst you. I am, Sir, Your most humble Servant,

SAM. JOHNSON

1. SJ refers to Father Joseph Wilkes (*Ante* To Hester Thrale, 22 May 1776).

Henry Thrale

MONDAY 3 JUNE 1776

MS: Hyde Collection.

Dear Sir: June 3, 1776

You are all, I suppose, now either at one home or the other, and all, I hope, well. My Mistress writes as if she was afraid I should make too much haste to see her.[1] Pray tell her, that

1. "Upon leaving home in April, the Thrales had dismissed most of their servants, and they were now faced with the prospect of securing a new staff" (Clifford, 1952, p. 141). On 30 May Hester Thrale had written from Southampton,

there is no danger. The Lameness of which I made mention in one of my notes, has improved to a very serious and troublesome fit of the gout. I creep about and hang by both[2] hands. Johnny Wilcocks might be my running Footman.[3] I enjoy all the dignity of lameness. I receive Ladies and dismiss them sitting. *Painful Preeminence*.[4]

Baretti is at last mentioned in one of the reviews, but in a manner that will not give him much delight. They are neither angry nor civil.[5]

Catcot has been convinced by Barret, and has written his recantation to Tyrrwhit, who still persists in his edition of the poems,[6] and perhaps is not much pleased to find himself mistaken.

You are now, I suppose, busy about your *restes*,[7] I heartily wish you, dear Sir, a happy perambulation, and a good ac-

---

where they had stopped on their way back from Bath, "If you have any pity for me do not come home [to Streatham] till I have got my house a little to rights, and if you can hear of a *Butler* or a *Footman* or a *Maid*, or almost anything do send them to me" (MS: Rylands Library).

2. MS: "both" altered from "bothe"

3. SJ may be referring to the actor, "Mr. Wilcocks" or "Willcox," who specialized in comic parts at Lincoln's Inn Fields and various London fairs (Sybil Rosenfield, *The Theatre of the London Fairs in the 18th Century*, 1960, pp. 32, 85, 89). Wilcocks's roles included that of Boniface, the Lichfield innkeeper in Farquhar's *The Beaux Stratagem*, who boasts of having "a good running trade" (I.i).

4. "Am I distinguished from you but by toils, / Superior toils, and heavier weight of cares? / Painful pre-eminence!" (Addison, *Cato* III.v.21–23).

5. Giuseppe Baretti's *Easy Phraseology for the Use of Young Ladies* had been noticed in the *Monthly Review* for May 1776: "In other respects this book, barring the Author's vanity, which breaks out continually, is not the most contemptible of the kind" (54, 1776, p. 423).

6. Thomas Chatterton had consigned the "originals" of the "Rowley" manuscripts to George Symes Catcott (1729–*c.* 1802), a Bristol pewterer. When SJ and JB visited Bristol to examine the manuscripts, Catcott, "who was as zealous for Rowley, as Dr. Hugh Blair was for Ossian . . . with a triumphant air of lively simplicity called out, 'I'll make Dr. Johnson a convert'" (*Life* III.50). Just as with Barrett's "declaration" (*Ante* To Hester Thrale, 22 May 1776 and n. 9), this reference to a "recantation" cannot be satisfactorily accounted for (L. F. Powell, "Thomas Tyrwhitt and the Rowley Poems," *RES* 7, 1931, p. 320). See also *Ante* To Hester Thrale, 16 May 1776 and n. 9.

7. *Ante* To Hester Thrale, 24 May 1773, n. 11; 22 May 1776.

count of the trade, and hope that You and My Mistress as you come by, will call upon, Sir, Your most humble servant,

SAM. JOHNSON

Dr. Taylor went away last Monday.[8]

8. *Ante* To Hester Thrale, 22 May 1776.

Hester Thrale

TUESDAY 4 JUNE 1776[1]

PRINTED SOURCE: Piozzi, *Letters* 1.338–39.

Dear Madam, June 4, at night

The world is indeed full of troubles, and we must not chuse for ourselves. But I am not sincerely sorry that in your present state of mind you are going to be immediately a mother.[2] Compose your thoughts, diversify your attention, and attend your health.

If I can be of any use, send for me; I think I can creep to the end of the court, and climb into a coach, though perhaps not very easily;[3] but if you call me, very willingly. If you do not send for me, let me, pray let me know as oft as you can how you do.

I am glad that my master is at his *restes*,[4] they will help to fill up his mind.

Pray let me know often how you do. I am, dearest Lady, Your, etc.

1. H. L. Piozzi's placement of this letter between those of 3 June 1776 and 5 June 1776 is confirmed by the references to SJ's gout, Henry Thrale's *restes*, and Hester Thrale's pregnancy; her dating is supported as well by the opening sentence of To Hester Thrale, 5 June 1776.

2. Hester Thrale was pregnant with her eleventh child, Cecilia, born 8 Feb. 1777 (Hyde, 1977, p. xii).

3. SJ's "fit of the gout" continued (*Ante* To Henry Thrale, 3 June 1776).

4. *Ante* To Hester Thrale, 24 May 1773, n. 11; 22 May 1776.

Hester Thrale

WEDNESDAY 5 JUNE 1776

MS: Hyde Collection.

Dearest Lady: June 5, 1776

You will have a note which I wrote last night.[1] I was thinking as I lay awake that you might be worse, but I hope you will be every moment better and better.[2] I have never had any overpowering pain, nor been kept more awake than is usual to me; but I am a very poor creeper upon the earth, catching at any thing with my hands to spare my feet.[3] In a day or two I hope to be as fit for Streatham as for any other place. Mr. Thrale it seems called last night when I was in bed, and yet I was not in bed till near twelve, for I sit up lest I should not sleep. He must keep well, for he is the pillar of the House,[4] and you must get well or the house will hardly be worth propping. I am, Dearest Madam, Your most humble servant,

SAM. JOHNSON

1. *Ante* To Hester Thrale, 4 June 1776.

2. As well as being pregnant, Hester Thrale was ill with cholera morbus, the name given to an acute and severe form of gastroenteritis with a high mortality rate (Hyde, 1977, p. 160 and n. 39).

3. *Ante* To Henry Thrale, 3 June 1776.

4. *Post* To Hester Thrale, 4 Nov. 1779 and n. 4.

Hester Thrale

THURSDAY 6 JUNE 1776[1]

MS: Hyde Collection.

My dear Lady: June 6

How could you so mistake me?[2] I am very desirous that the

1. Dated with reference to SJ's letters of 3 and 5 June 1776.

2. At this point the sequence of correspondence between SJ and Hester Thrale is in some doubt: the printed text of To Hester Thrale, 4 June 1776, appears to

whole business should be as You would have it,[3] only cheerfulness at that time is reckoned a good thing.

My feet grow better,[4] and I hope, if you send a carriage, to mount it on Monday. This gout has a little depressed me, not that I have suffered any great pain; I have been teized rather than tortured; but the tediousness and the imbecillity have been unpleasant. However I now recover strength and do not yet despair of kicking the Moon.

Could not you send me something out of your garden? Things have been growing, and You have not been consuming them. I wish I had a great bunch of asparagus for Sunday.

Take great care of our Queeney, and of yourself,[5] and encourage yourself in bustle and variety, and cheerfulness. I will be ready to come as soon as I can, but the pain is now twinging me. Let me know, my sweetest Lady, very often how you do. I thought it late before I heard to day. I am, Dear Madam, your most humble servant,

SAM. JOHNSON

---

be incomplete, and in her datelines Hester Thrale was neglecting to specify either month or year. This letter seems to respond to one dated "Thursday Morning," which appears in turn to respond to SJ's of 4 June. If this conjecture is correct, then SJ's "How could you so mistake me?" relates to a question from Hester Thrale: "How can you say what you do about the *great Affair*, and yet be so sincerely kind to me as you are?" (MS: Rylands Library 539.59). However, the nature of the "*great Affair*" cannot be conclusively established; it may have been Hester Thrale's pregnancy and her ardent wish for a son and heir.

3. "We were wishing for a Son" (Piozzi 1.340).

4. *Ante* To Henry Thrale, 3 June 1776.

5. *Ante* To Hester Thrale, 5 June 1776 and n. 2.

Hester Thrale

SATURDAY 8 JUNE 1776[1]

MS: Hyde Collection.

1. Dated with reference to SJ's letters of 3 and 5 June, and to the reconstructed sequence of correspondence from 3 through 9 June.

Dear Madam: June 8

My feet disappointed me last night; I thought they would have given me no disturbance, but going up stairs, I fancy, fretted them, and they would not let me be easy. On Monday I am afraid I shall be a poor walker, but well enough to talk, and to hear you talk.[2] And then, you know, what care We?

Mr. Hector called on me yesterday, he is at Sayer's printshop in Fleet-street,[3] and would take an invitation to diner very kindly.[4]

Poor Mr. Levet has fallen down and hurt himself dangerously.

Of the Monks I can give no account. I had them to dinner,[5] and gave each of them the *Political tracts*[6] and furnished Wilkes with [a] letter, which will, I believe, procure him a proper reception at Oxford.[7] I am, Dearest Lady, Your most—and most etc.

SAM. JOHNSON

2. *Ante* To Hester Thrale, 6 June 1776.

3. Robert Sayer (*c.* 1725–94), print, map, and chart seller at 53 Golden Buck, Fleet Street, 1745–94 (Ian Maxted, *The London Book Trades, 1775–1800*, 1977, p. 199).

4. In a letter begun on Saturday, 8 June, and completed on Sunday the ninth, Hester Thrale replied, "Mr. Hector has a Card sent him, less from Compliment than true kindness" (MS: Rylands Library 540.60).

5. *Ante* To Hester Thrale, 22 May 1776; 23 May 1776.

6. *Ante* To Hester Thrale, 6 May 1776 and n. 2.

7. *Ante* To William Adams, 29 May 1776.

Frances Reynolds

SATURDAY 15 JUNE 1776

MS: Hyde Collection.

ADDRESS: To Miss Reynolds.

ENDORSEMENT: Dr. Johnson, June 15, 76.

My dearest Dear: June 15, 1776

When I am grown better,[1] which is, I hope, at no great dis-

1. *Ante* To Henry Thrale, 3 June 1776.

tance, for I mend gradually, We will take a little time to ourselves, and look over your dear little production,[2] and try to make it such as we may both like. I will not forget it, nor neglect it, for I love your tenderness. I am, Dear Madam, your most humble Servant,

SAM. JOHNSON

2. Apparently SJ refers to one of Frances Reynolds's literary projects. Cf. *Post* To Frances Reynolds, 16 June 1780; 21 July 1781; 8 Apr. 1782.

Frances Reynolds

FRIDAY 21 JUNE 1776

MS: British Library.

ADDRESS: To Miss Reynolds.

ENDORSEMENT: Dr. Johnson, June 21, 76.

Dear Madam: June 21, 1776

You are as naughty as You can be.[1] I am willing enough to write to you when I have any thing to say. As for my disorder, as Sir Joshua saw me, I fancied he would tell you, and that I needed not tell you myself.

Of Dr. Goldsmith's Epitaph, I sent Sir Joshua two copies,[2] and had none myself. If he has lost it, he has not done well.[3] But I suppose I can recollect it, and will send it to you.[4] I am, Madam, your most humble servant,

SAM. JOHNSON

1. Frances Reynolds had complained: "You saw by my last letter that I knew nothing of your illness, and it was unkind of you not to tell me what had been the matter with you; and you should have let me know how Mrs. Thrale and all the family were; but that would have been a sad transgression of the rule you have certainly prescribed to yourself of writing to some sort of people just such a number of lines" (Frances Reynolds to SJ, 21 June 1776, JB's *Life*, ed. J. W. Croker, 1831, III.446).

2. *Ante* To Joshua Reynolds, 16 May 1776 and nn. 1, 4.

3. Frances Reynolds had requested a copy to send to Dr. Beattie, for "my brother says he has lost Dr. Goldsmith's epitaph" (Croker, *Life*, 1831, III.446).

4. *Post* To Joshua Reynolds, 22 June 1776.

All the Thrales are well, and Mrs. Thrale has a great regard for Miss Reynolds.

Bennet Langton

SATURDAY 22 JUNE 1776

MS: Hyde Collection.

ADDRESS: To Benet Langton, Esq.

Dear Sir: June 22, 1776

I am better, but gain ground slowly.[1] However, at this rate of amendment, I can probably wait on You at the latter end of next week.

I hope that Lady Rothes and all the pretty little people are well.[2] When you would see me favour me with a not[e] at Mr. Thrale's. I am, Sir, Your most humble Servant,

SAM. JOHNSON

1. *Ante* To Henry Thrale, 3 June 1776.

2. *Ante* To Hester Thrale, 11 May 1776 and n. 5. On 26 June Lady Rothes gave birth to a fourth child, Jane (Fifer, p. lviii n. 29).

Joshua Reynolds

SATURDAY 22 JUNE 1776

MS: Hyde Collection.

ADDRESS: To Sir Joshua Reynolds.

ENDORSEMENT in the hand of Frances Reynolds: Dr. Johnson, June 22, 76, To Sir Joshua.

Sir: June 22, 1776

Miss Reynolds has a mind to send the Epitaph to Dr. Beattie, I am very willing, but having no copy, cannot immediately recollect it. She tells me you have lost it.[1] Try to recollect and put

1. *Ante* To Joshua Reynolds, 16 May 1776 and n. 1; *Ante* To Frances Reynolds, 21 June 1776 and n. 3.

down as much as you retain; you perhaps may have kept what I have dropped. The lines for which I am at a loss, are something of *Rerum civilium sivè naturalium.*[2] It was a sorry trick to lose it, help me if you can. I am, Sir, Your most humble Servant,

SAM. JOHNSON

The Gout grows better, but slowly.

2. SJ is trying to reconstruct the version that was not chosen for the Abbey epitaph. It praises Goldsmith as *Rerum, sive naturalium, sive civilium, / elegans, at gravis scriptor*: "a writer elegant yet weighty on subjects either natural or civil" (MS: Earl of Crawford and Balcarres; on deposit at National Library of Scotland, printed collections).

John Taylor

TUESDAY 25 JUNE 1776[1]

MS: Berg Collection, New York Public Library.

ADDRESS: To the reverend Dr. Taylor in Ashbourne, Derbyshire.

POSTMARK: 25 IV.

ENDORSEMENTS: 1776, 23 June 76.

Dear Sir: June 23, 1776

The Gout is now grown tolerable; I can go up stairs pretty well, but am yet aukward in coming down.

Some time ago I had a letter from the solicitor,[2] in which he mentioned our cause with respect enough, but persists in his opinion, as I suppose, your Attorney has told you.[3] He is however convinced that nothing fraudulent was intended:[4] I would be glad to hear what the Attorney says.[5]

1. (Re)dated with reference to the polling for the Chamberlainship (see below, n. 8) and the postmark.

2. SJ refers to Solicitor-General Alexander Wedderburn. *Ante* To Hester Thrale, 14 May 1776.

3. *Ante* To Hester Thrale, 14 May 1776 and n. 4.

4. Cf. *Ante* To Hester Thrale, 22 May 1776.

5. SJ may be referring to Taylor's attorney or to the Attorney-General, Edward Thurlow (*Ante* To John Taylor, 13 Apr. 1776 and n. 3).

Mr. Thrale would glad[l]y have seen you at his house. They are all well.

Whether I shall wander this summer, I hardly know, If I do, tell me when it will be the best time to come to you.[6]

I hope you persevere in drinking, my opinion is that I have drank too little, and therefore have the gout, for it is of my own acquisition, as[7] neither my father had it nor my mother.

Wilkes and Hopkins have now polled two days,[8] and I hear that Wilkes is two hundred behind.[9]

Of this Sudden Revolution in the Prince's household, the original cause is not certainly known. The quarrel began between Lord Holderness, and Jackson, the part of Jackson was taken by the Bishop, and all ended in a total change.[10] I am, Sir, Your affectionate etc.

SAM. JOHNSON

6. SJ's travels during the remainder of 1776 were limited to a fall trip to Brighton (*Post* To Robert Levet, 23 Sept. 1776; 21 Oct. 1776).

7. MS: "a" superimposed upon "f"

8. On 24 June "the Sheriffs . . . informed the Livery [of the City of London] that there were two candidates for the Chamberlainship, Mr. Hopkins, the present Chamberlain, and Mr. Wilkes. The two candidates were then separately put up for the choice of the Livery, when the shew of hands was so apparently equal, that the Sheriffs were unable to determine who had the majority; they therefore put them up a second time, when they declared the majority was in favour of Mr. Wilkes; but a poll was immediately demanded by the friends of Mr. Hopkins" (*GM* 1776, p. 285). John Wilkes's opponent was Benjamin Hopkins (*c.* 1734–79), M.P. (1771–74), underwriter, and a director of the Bank of England (Namier and Brooke II.639–40).

9. When the poll closed on 28 June, Hopkins had defeated Wilkes by 2,610 to 1,513 votes (*GM* 1776, p. 285).

10. At the end of May there had been, in Edmund Burke's phrase, a "Nursery revolution": the Prince of Wales's governor—Robert Darcy (1718–78), fourth Earl of Holdernesse—resigned, and the King then dismissed both the Prince's preceptor, William Markham, Bishop of Chester, and his sub-preceptor, Cyril Jackson (1746–1819) (*Burke's Correspondence* III.269; Stanley Ayling, *George the Third*, 1972, p. 220). According to Horace Walpole: "No reason whatever was assigned for so total a change, which did not allay the astonishment. It is now known that on Lord Holderness's return from the south of France he found a great alienation from him in the minds of his royal pupils, which he attributed to Jackson. This grew so bad, that after vainly complaining of Jackson, and as vainly having obtained reproof, the Bishop, who seemed to be the instigator of the manoeuvre and subsequent *disobedience*, was turned out with his instrument, and the Earl saw it hopeless to try to recover his authority" (*Walpole's Correspondence*, Yale ed. XXIV.217–18).

James Boswell

TUESDAY 2 JULY 1776

PRINTED SOURCE: JB's *Life*, 1791, II.94–95.

Dear Sir, July 2, 1776

These black fits, of which you complain, perhaps hurt your memory as well as your imagination. When did I complain that your letters were too long?[1] Your last letter, after a very long delay, brought very bad news. [Here a series of reflections upon melancholy, and—what I could not help thinking strangely unreasonable in him who had suffered so much from it himself—a good deal of severity and reproof, as if it were owing to my own fault, or that I was, perhaps, affecting it from a desire of distinction].

Read Cheyne's "English Malady;"[2] but do not let him teach you a foolish notion that melancholy is a proof of acuteness. * * * * *.

To hear that you have not opened your boxes of books is very offensive.[3] The examination and arrangement of so many volumes might have afforded you an amusement very seasonable at present, and useful for the whole of life. I am, I confess, very angry that you manage yourself so ill. * * * * *.

I do not now say any more, than that I am, with great kindness and sincerity, dear Sir, Your humble servant,

SAM. JOHNSON

1. "You have formerly complained that my letters were too long" (JB to SJ, 25 June 1776, *Life* III.86). In a footnote to the *Life* JB added, "Baretti told me that Johnson complained of my writing very long letters to him when I was upon the continent; which was most certainly true; but it seems my friend did not remember it" (III.86 n. 4).

2. *The English Malady, or a Treatise of Nervous Diseases of All Kinds* (1733), a popular treatise on hypochondria by George Cheyne (1671–1743), M.D. SJ, who owned a copy of Cheyne's book, had already recommended it in conversation with JB on 7 Apr. 1776 (*Life* III.26–27; Greene, 1975, p. 48).

3. The balance due JB for expenses incurred during the Hebridean tour was paid by SJ in the form of various books (*Life* III.86 n. 2; *Post* To JB, 6 July 1776). In his letter of 25 June, JB had reported, "The boxes of books which you sent to me are arrived; but I have not yet examined the contents" (*Life* III.86).

It was last year determined by Lord Mansfield, in the Court of King's Bench, that a negro cannot be taken out of the kingdom without his own consent.[4]

4. SJ refers to the controversial case involving an escaped slave, James Somerset, whose master had recaptured him in England and attempted to take him to Jamaica. In 1772 Lord Mansfield's ruling in favor of Somerset established the doctrine that "slaves enjoyed the benefits of freedom while they stood on English soil" (J. S. Watson, *The Reign of George III, 1760–1815*, 1960, p. 57). JB was active in a similar case pending before the Court of Session in Scotland (*Life* III.86, 200, 202–3, 212; *Post* To JB, 22 July 1777 and nn. 17, 18).

James Boswell

SATURDAY 6 JULY 1776

PRINTED SOURCE: JB's *Life*, 1791, II.95–96.

Dear Sir, July 6, 1776

I make haste to write again, lest my last letter should give you too much pain.[1] If you are really oppressed with overpowering and involuntary melancholy, you are to be pitied rather than reproached. * * * * *.

Now, my dear Bozzy, let us have done with quarrels and with censure. Let me know whether I have not sent you a pretty library.[2] There are, perhaps, many books among them which you need never read through; but there are none which it is not proper for you to know, and sometimes to consult. Of these books, of which the use is only occasional, it is often sufficient to know the contents, that, when any question arises, you may know where to look for information.

Since I wrote, I have looked over Mr. Maclaurin's plea, and think it excellent.[3] How is the suit carried on? If by subscrip-

1. *Ante* To JB, 2 July 1776.

2. *Ante* To JB, 2 July 1776 and n. 3.

3. John Maclaurin (1734–96), Scots advocate, was involved with JB in the cause that paralleled the Somerset case (*Ante* To JB, 2 July 1776 and n. 4; *Post* To JB, 22 July 1777 and n. 17; *Boswell in Extremes*, ed. C. M. Weis and F. A. Pottle, 1970, p. 183 n. 7). JB had sent SJ "Mr. Maclaurin's paper for the negro, who claims his freedom in the Court of Session" (*Life* III.86).

tion, I commission you to contribute, in my name, what is proper. Let nothing be wanting in such a case. Dr. Drummond,[4] I see, is superseded. His father would have grieved;[5] but he lived to obtain the pleasure of his son's election, and died before that pleasure was abated.[6]

Langton's lady has brought him a girl,[7] and both are well; I dined with him the other day. * * * * *.

It vexes me to tell you, that on the evening of the 29th of May I was seized by the gout, and am not quite well. The pain has not been violent, but the weakness, and tenderness were very troublesome, and what is said to be very uncommon, it has not alleviated my other disorders. Make use of youth and health while you have them; make my compliments to Mrs. Boswell. I am, my dear Sir, Your most affectionate

SAM. JOHNSON

4. SJ refers to Alexander Monro Drummond.

5. SJ refers to William Drummond.

6. According to JB, Alexander Drummond "was a young man of such distinguished merit, that he was nominated to one of the medical professorships in the College of Edinburgh, without solicitation, while he was at Naples. Having other views, he did not accept of the honour" (*Life* III.88 n. 1).

7. *Ante* To Bennet Langton, 22 June 1776, n. 2. When Jane Langton was christened in August, SJ stood godfather (Fifer, pp. 71–72).

Francis Fowke[1]

THURSDAY 11 JULY 1776

MS: British Library (India Office).

ENDORSEMENT in the hand of Joseph Fowke: 11 July 1776, Dr. Saml. Johnson to my Brother.

HEADING in an unidentified hand: To Francis Fowke.

1. Francis Fowke, one of the two surviving brothers of Joseph Fowke (see below, n. 2). Francis Fowke appears to have been an attorney in Malmesbury (A. B. Sharma, "The Fowkes and the Lawrences," *Indian Journal for 18th Century Studies* 1, 1986, p. 31). He has previously been confused with Joseph's son and colleague, who was also named Francis.

London, Bolt court, Fleetstreet,

Sir: July 11, 1776

I received some weeks ago a collection of papers concerning the trial of my dear Friend Joseph Fowke,[2] of whom I cannot easily be induced to think otherwise than well, and who seems to have been much injured by the prosecution and the Sentence. His first desire is that I would prepare his narratives for the press; his second, that if I cannot gratify him by publication, I[3] would transmit them to you.

To a compliance with his first request, I have this objection, that I live in a[4] reciprocation of civility with Mr. Hastings, and therefore cannot properly diffuse a narrative intended[5] to bring upon him the censure of the publick. Of two adversaries it would be rash to condemn either upon the evidence of the other; and a common friend must keep himself suspended at least till he has heard both.

I am therefore ready to transmit you the papers, which have been seen only by myself, and beg to be informed how they may be conveyed to you. I see no legal objection to the publication, and of prudential reasons Mr. Fowke and you will be allowed to be fitter judges.

If you would have me send them, let me have proper directions, if a Messenger is to call for them give me notice by the post that they may be ready for delivery.

2. Joseph Fowke (1716–1806), merchant and administrator, entered the service of the East India Company in 1736; in 1751 he was appointed a member of the Council at Madras. In 1752 Fowke resigned and went to live "very prettily in London, till his wife died. After her death, he took to dissipation and gaming, and lost all he had" (*Life* III.20). SJ, who had become well acquainted with Fowke in London, thought of accompanying him when Fowke returned to India, where he intended to recoup his fortunes. In 1771 Fowke settled in Calcutta, where he joined the faction that was attempting to undermine the governorship of Warren Hastings. Hastings, in retaliation, had Fowke tried for conspiracy. In 1775 Fowke was found innocent of working against Hastings, but was then convicted of conspiracy against one of the Governor-General's supporters, Richard Barwell. The consequent disgrace, as well as Hastings's personal hostility, ruined Fowke's prospects in India (Sharma, "The Fowkes and the Lawrences," pp. 29–31; information supplied by Professor Thomas Curley).

3. MS: "that" del. before "I"

4. MS: "a" superimposed upon "r"

5. MS: "indended"

To do my dear Mr. Fowke any good would give me great pleasure, I hope for some opportunity of performing the duties of Friendship to him, without violating them with regard to another. I am, Sir, your most humble Servant,

SAM. JOHNSON

Frances Reynolds

SATURDAY 3 AUGUST 1776[1]

MS: Hyde Collection.

ADDRESS: To Mrs. Reynolds.

ENDORSEMENT: Dr. Johnson.[2]

Dearest Madam: Aug. 3

To do what you desire with your restrictions is impossible. I shall not see Mrs. Thrale till tuesday in the afternoon. If I write, I must give a stronger reason than you care to allow. The company is already very numerous, but yet there might I suppose be found room for a girl, if the proposal could be made. Even writing if you allow it, will hardly do, the penny post does not go on Sunday, and Mr. Thrale does not always come to town on Monday. However let me know what you would have done. I am, Madam, Your most humble servant,

SAM. JOHNSON

1. I follow Hill (I.411) and Chapman (II.149) in assigning this letter to 1776 on calendrical grounds: it was probably written on a Saturday, possibly on a Sunday, and this fact, combined with the record of SJ's residence in London, makes that year the only persuasive candidate. Furthermore, as both Hill and Chapman point out, the letter may well have accompanied To Joshua Reynolds, 3 Aug. 1776.

2. MS: mutilated; rest of endorsement torn away

Joshua Reynolds

SATURDAY 3 AUGUST 1776

MS: Hyde Collection.

ADDRESS: To Sir Joshua Reynolds.

ENDORSEMENT: Dr. Johnson.

Sir: Aug. 3, 1776

A young Man whose name is Paterson offers himself this evening to the Academy.[1] He is the Son of a Man for whom I have long had a kindness, and who is now abroad in distress. I shall be glad that you will be pleased to show him any little countenance, or pay him any small distinction.[2] How much it is in your power to favour or to forward a young man I do not know, nor do I know how much this candidate deserves favour by his personal merit, or what hopes his proficiency may now give of future eminence. I recommend him as the Son of my Friend. Your character and station enable you to give a young man great encouragement by very easy means. You have heard of a Man who asked no other favour of Sir Robert Walpole, than that he would bow to him at his levee.[3] I am, Sir, Your most humble Servant,

SAM. JOHNSON

1. Charles Paterson (b. 1760), the son of Samuel Paterson and SJ's godchild (S. C. Hutchison, "The Royal Academy Schools, 1768–1830," *The Walpole Society* 38, 1962, p. 142; *Ante* To Samuel Paterson, 6 Apr. 1772, n. 1).

2. On 4 Oct. 1776 Charles Paterson was admitted as a student of painting to the Royal Academy Schools. Details of his subsequent career have not been uncovered (information supplied by Mr. Nicholas Savage, Royal Academy of Arts). SJ continued to exert himself on Paterson's behalf. *Post* To Joshua Reynolds, 2 June 1783; *Post* To Ozias Humphry, 5 Apr. 1784.

3. Sir Robert Walpole (1676–1745), Earl of Orford (1742), First Lord of the Treasury (1715–17, 1721–42) and first Prime Minister of Great Britain. The anecdote in question has not been traced.

Unidentified Correspondent[1]

SATURDAY 31 AUGUST 1776

MS: Johnson House, London.

Sir: Aug. 31, 1776

Mr. Stockdale desires me to mention to You a small literary project, of which, I hope, You will have no ill opinion.

He proposes to write, in three octavo volumes, a short history of Spain.[2] We have none in our language but translations. It is a very interesting story, and contains many important revolutions and events. I have given Mr. Stockdale such hints as occurred to me. Of his abilities for the performance You must judge by his works. I am, Sir, Your most humble Servant,

SAM. JOHNSON

1. The likeliest candidates are William Strahan and Thomas Cadell.
2. No record of such a publication has been uncovered.

John Taylor

TUESDAY 3 SEPTEMBER 1776

MS: Hyde Collection.

ADDRESS: To the reverend Dr. Taylor in Ashbourne, Derbyshire.

POSTMARK: 3 SE.

ENDORSEMENTS: 1776, 3 Septr. 76, good.

Dear Sir: Sept. 3, 1776

I received on saturday the three opinions.[1] That of the Attorney[2] is violent and peremptory, and perhaps not very well considered. The Solicitor's[3] is upon the review still against us. Mr. Maddox[4] seems to have studied the question more diligently.

1. *Ante* To John Taylor, 13 Apr. 1776, n. 2.
2. SJ refers to Edward Thurlow.
3. SJ refers to Alexander Wedderburn.
4. Perhaps the solicitor described by SJ as "another Scrase" (*Ante* To Hester Thrale, 14 May 1776 and n. 4).

There are some legal niceties in his opinion which I do not understand; but he rests his hopes of our finding, what we cannot find, some proof that the recovery was suffered, and the will made under undue influence. The persuasion of a Wife can never be judged either coercive or fraudulent. She obtained by the common means of blandishment and importunity, a preference which the Event shows her not to have deserved. Her marriage has produced a complete justification of your conduct, by showing that she is not to be trusted with an inheritance.

With the consciousness of having endeavoured well, and the certainty that those endeavours must now be generally approved, I think we are now to be contented. There seems to be no encouragement given us to try the question. You have lost nothing, for You were to have gotten nothing for yourself. The Greens will be disappointed.[5]

What can the Attorney mean by such an emphatical mention of the heir at law? If Wood had power to make a will, that will bars the heir, if he had not the power, how does it bar You? I think his opinion hasty if not negligent.

One reason for doing no more is that the Proprietor appearing to be so weak a man, every attempt to direct his conduct, may be in very strong colours represented as fraudulent; and you can hardly lose the cause without loss of character. You must judge for yourself. I think we should be quiet. I am, Dear Sir, Your most etc.

SAM. JOHNSON

5. *Ante* To Hester Thrale, 22 May 1776 and n. 6.

John Ryland

SATURDAY 21 SEPTEMBER 1776

MS: Hyde Collection.

ADDRESS: To Mr. Ryland.

Sir: Sept. 21, 1776

I have procured this play to be read by Mrs. Thrale, who declares that no play was ever more nicely secured from the objection of indelicacy.[1]

If it can be got upon the stage, it will I think, succeed, and may get more money, than will be raised by the impression of the other works.

In selling the copy[2] to the printer, the liberty of inserting it in the volumes may be retained. I am, Sir, Your most humble servant,

SAM. JOHNSON

1. SJ, together with John Ryland (John Hawkesworth's brother-in-law) and Mary Hawkesworth (his widow), had undertaken an edition of Hawkesworth's collected works. According to Mrs. Hawkesworth, SJ had her husband's "papers in hand before June 14, 1776 . . . and she cites Johnson's procrastination as the barrier to publication. . . . Mary Hawkesworth apparently received papers from Johnson by August 27, 1777, but for unexplained reasons no collected edition of Hawkesworth's works appeared" (J. L. Abbott, *John Hawkesworth*, 1982, pp. 192–93). *Post* To John Ryland, 14 Nov. 1776; 12 Apr. 1777. The play in question appears to have been unpublished and unperformed; it therefore cannot be Hawkesworth's original comedy, *Edgar and Emmeline* (produced at Drury Lane in Jan. 1761), or his two adaptations (of Dryden's *Amphitryon*, 1756, and Thomas Southerne's *Oroonoko*, 1759) (Abbott, *Hawkesworth*, pp. 73, 78–80, 82–84).

2. *copy*: "property in 'copy,' copyright" (*OED*).

Robert Levet

MONDAY 23 SEPTEMBER 1776

MS: Hyde Collection.

ADDRESS: To Mr. Levett.

Dear Sir: Sept. 23, 1776

Mr. Thrale to enquire after You,[1] and this is the answer. You must contrive to be more particular when we return. We are going to Brighthelmston, but shall hardly stay long so late in

1. *Ante* To Hester Thrale, 8 June 1776.

the year.[2] Francis and his Wife[3] have both given great satisfaction by their behaviour. I am, Sir, Your humble Servant,

SAM. JOHNSON

2. SJ returned to London 30 Oct. (*Post* To John Hoole, 30 Oct. 1776).

3. On 28 Jan. 1773 Francis Barber had married Elizabeth Ball (*c.* 1755–1816) (John Ingledew, "Some New Light on Francis Barber, Samuel Johnson's Servant," *Notes and Queries* 31, 1984, p. 8).

William Strahan

MONDAY 14 OCTOBER 1776

MS: Hyde Collection.

Sir: Oct. 14, 1776

I wrote to You about ten days ago, and sent you some copy.[1] You have not written again. That is a sorry trick.

I am told that you are printing a Book for Mr. Professor Watson of Saint Andrews,[2] if upon any occasion, I can give any help, or be of any use, as formerly in Dr. Robertsons publication,[3] I hope you will make no scruple to call upon me, for I shall be glad of an opportunity to show that my reception at Saint Andrews has not been forgotten.[4] I am, Sir, Your humble servant,

SAM. JOHNSON

1. *Post* To JB, 11 Mar. 1777 and n. 3.

2. Robert Watson's *History of the Reign of Philip the Second, King of Spain* appeared in 1777, "printed for W. Strahan; and T. Cadell."

3. Apparently SJ had assisted Strahan in correcting William Robertson's *History of Charles V*, printed and published by Strahan in 1769. Strahan also corrected works by two of his other Scots authors, Adam Smith and David Hume (J. A. Cochrane, *Dr. Johnson's Printer*, 1964, pp. 51, 54, 129, 162–63). Arthur Sherbo draws attention to the fact that SJ had three copies of Robertson's *History of America* (published by Strahan in 1777) in his library (*JN* 20, Sept. 1960, p. 11).

4. *Ante* To Hester Thrale, 25 Aug. 1773; *Post* To Hester Thrale, 20 May 1779 and n. 3.

Robert Levet

MONDAY 21 OCTOBER 1776

PRINTED SOURCE: JB's *Life*, 1793, II.461–62.

Dear Sir: Brighthelmstone, Oct. 21, 1776

Having spent about six weeks at this place, we have at length resolved upon returning. I expect to see you all in Fleet-street on the 30th of this month.[1]

I did not go into the sea till last Friday, but think to go most of this week, though I know not that it does me any good. My nights are very restless and tiresome, but I am otherwise well.

I have written word of my coming to Mrs. Williams. Remember me kindly to Francis and Betsy.[2] I am, Sir, Your humble servant,

SAM. JOHNSON

1. *Post* To John Hoole, 30 Oct. 1776.

2. *Ante* To Robert Levet, 23 Sept. 1776 and n. 3.

John Hoole

WEDNESDAY 30 OCTOBER 1776

MS: Hyde Collection.

Dear Sir: Oct. 30, 1776

I am just come from Brighthelmston, and have heard of dear Mrs. Hoole's dreadful ilness. I am just told that she is thought better, and sincerely wish her a complete recovery.[1] Take care of your own hea[l]th in the mean time. Mrs. Williams sends her compliments. I am, Sir, Your most humble servant,

SAM. JOHNSON

1. *Post* To John Hoole, 9 Nov. 1776.

John Hoole

SATURDAY 9 NOVEMBER 1776

MS: Hyde Collection.

ENDORSEMENT: Dr. Johnson to J. Hoole.

Dear Sir: Novemb. 9, 1776

I hope You believe us to partake very sincerely of the happiness which you enjoy in dear Mrs. Hooles recovery.[1] Let us know from time to time how she advances.

Mrs. Williams enjoyned me to caution her against taking cold, and I hope, without a prompter, that every thing hurtful will be avoided, and every thing useful practiced by both of you. I hope soon to see you both well and merry. I am, Dear sir, Your humble servant,

SAM. JOHNSON

1. *Ante* To John Hoole, 30 Oct. 1776.

John Ryland

THURSDAY 14 NOVEMBER 1776

MS: Hyde Collection.

ADDRESS: To Mr. Ryland.

Dear Sir: Nov. 14, 1776

The selection made in this parcel is indicated partly in a catalogue by the words *print* or *omit*, and partly by[1] the same words written in red ink at the top of those pieces which are not in the catalogue.[2] I purpose to send the rest very soon, and I believe You and I must then have two or three interviews to adjust the order in which they shall stand. I am, Sir, Your most humble servant,

SAM. JOHNSON

1. MS: "be"
2. *Ante* To John Ryland, 21 Sept. 1776 and n. 1.

James Boswell

SATURDAY 16 NOVEMBER 1776

PRINTED SOURCE: JB's *Life*, 1791, II.98–99.

Dear Sir, Bolt-court, Nov. 16, 1776

I had great pleasure in hearing that you are at last on good terms with your father.[1] Cultivate his kindness by all honest and manly means. Life is but short; no time can be afforded but for the indulgence of real sorrow, or contests upon questions seriously momentous. Let us not throw any of our days away upon useless resentment, or contend who shall hold out longest in stubborn malignity. It is best not to be angry, and best, in the next place, to be quickly reconciled. May you and your father pass the remainder of your time in reciprocal benevolence!

* * * * * *

Do you ever hear from Mr. Langton? I visit him sometimes, but he does not talk. I do not like his scheme of life;[2] but, as I am not permitted to understand it, I cannot set any thing right that is wrong. His children are sweet babies.[3]

I hope my irreconcileable enemy, Mrs. Boswell, is well. Desire her not to transmit her malevolence to the young people. Let me have Alexander, and Veronica, and Euphemia, for my friends.

Mrs. Williams, whom you may reckon as one of your well-wishers, is in a feeble and languishing state, with little hope of growing better. She went for some part of the autumn into the country, but is little benefited; and Dr. Lawrence confesses that his art is at an end. Death is, however, at a distance; and what more than that can we say of ourselves? I am sorry for

1. "I again wrote to Dr. Johnson on the 21st of October, informing him, that my father had, in the most liberal manner, paid a large debt [£1,000] for me, and that I had now the happiness of being upon very good terms with him" (*Life* III.92–93 and n. 1).

2. Cf. *Ante* To Hester Thrale, 11 May 1776; *Post* To JB, 3 July 1778.

3. *Ante* To Bennet Langton, 22 June 1776, n. 2; *Ante* To Hester Thrale, 11 May 1776, n. 5.

her pain, and more sorry for her decay. Mr. Levett is sound, wind and limb.

I was some weeks this autumn at Brighthelmston.[4] The place was very dull, and I was not well: the expedition to the Hebrides was the most pleasant journey that I ever made. Such an effort annually would give the world a little diversification.

Every year, however, we cannot wander, and must therefore endeavour to spend our time at home as well as we can. I believe it is best to throw life into a method, that every hour may bring its employment, and every employment have its hour. Xenophon observes, in his "Treatise of Oeconomy," that if every thing be kept in a certain place, when any thing is worn out or consumed, the vacuity which it leaves will shew what is wanting;[5] so if every part of time has its duty, the hour will call into remembrance its proper engagement.

I have not practised all this prudence myself, but I have suffered much for want of it;[6] and I would have you, by timely recollection and steady resolution, escape from those evils which have lain heavy upon me. I am, my dearest Boswell, Your most humble servant,

SAM. JOHNSON

4. *Ante* To Robert Levet, 21 Oct. 1776.

5. "And so, my dear, if you do not want this confusion, and wish to know exactly how to manage our goods, and to find with ease whatever is wanted . . . let us choose the place that each portion should occupy. . . . Thus we shall know what is safe and sound and what is not; for the place itself will miss whatever is not in it, and a glance will reveal anything that wants attention, and the knowledge where each thing is will quickly bring it to hand" (Xenophon, *Oeconomicus* VIII.10, trans. E. C. Marchant, Loeb ed.).

6. "Yet the chief cause of my deficiency has been a life immethodical and unsettled, which breaks all purposes, confounds and suppresses memory, and perhaps leaves too much leisure to imagination" (*Works*, Yale ed. I.162).

Thomas Percy

SUNDAY 1 DECEMBER 1776

MS: Victoria and Albert Museum (Dyce-Forster Collection).
ADDRESS: To the Reverend Dr. Percy.

Dear Sir: Dec. 1, 1776

Mr. Langton and I shall wait on You at St. James's on Tuesday.[1]

I must entreat your attention to a business of more importance. The Duke[2] is President of the Middlesex hospital;[3] Could You obtain from him the admission of a Patient, the Son of Mr. Thomas Coxeter, a Gentleman and a Man of Letters?[4] The unhappy Man inherits some claim from his father to particular notice; and has all the claims common to others, of disease and want.

I shall apply no where else till I hear from you;[5] Be pleased to answer this request as soon as You can. I am, Sir, Your most humble Servant,

SAM. JOHNSON

1. During his month of waiting as Chaplain to the King, Percy was entitled to invite his friends to dine at the Chaplain's table at St. James's (A.C.C. Gaussen, *Percy: Prelate and Poet*, 1908, p. 173).

2. SJ refers to Percy's patron, the first Duke of Northumberland.

3. Middlesex Hospital, Mortimer Street, London, was begun in 1755 but not completed until 1775. Originally it contained only eighteen beds (Wheatley and Cunningham II.537).

4. Presumably SJ refers to Thomas Coxeter the younger (*Ante* To Henry Thrale, Mar. 1771; *Post* To Thomas Percy, 2 Dec. 1776).

5. MS: "you" repeated as catchword

Thomas Percy

MONDAY 2 DECEMBER 1776

PRINTED SOURCE: Hill I.414–15.
ADDRESS: To the Reverend Dr. Percy.

Dec. 2, [1776]

Thomas Coxeter[1] of little Carter lane, in Doctors Commons.

His disease I could not gather from his sister's accounts so as to name it.[2] He has had a scorbutick[3] humour which I believe has fallen back upon his vitals.

I have got a cold which, I hope, will not hinder me from dining at your table,[4] and returning you thanks for this favour.

1. *Ante* To Thomas Percy, 1 Dec. 1776 and n. 4.
2. *Ante* To Henry Thrale, Mar. 1771, n. 3.
3. *scorbutick*: "diseased with the scurvy" (SJ's *Dictionary*).
4. *Ante* To Thomas Percy, 1 Dec. 1776 and n. 1.

Thomas Percy

MONDAY 16 DECEMBER 1776

MS: Historical Society of Pennsylvania.

Reverend Sir, Dec. 16, 1776

At this time when donatives are distributed at Northumberland House, with such unexampled liberality, I beg leave to recommend Mrs. Elizabeth Coxeter,[1] a Gentlewoman, and very poor, as not unfit to partake of the Duke's beneficence.[2] I am, Sir, Your most humble servant,

SAM. JOHNSON

I am just come home, and am going to Dr. Laurence.

1. *Ante* To Henry Thrale, Mar. 1771, n. 3; *Ante* To Thomas Percy, 2 Dec. 1776.
2. MS: "beneficence" superimposed upon "liberality" partially erased

James Boswell

SATURDAY 21 DECEMBER 1776

PRINTED SOURCE: JB's *Life*, 1791, II.99–100.

Dear Sir, Dec. 21, 1776

I have been for some time ill of a cold,[1] which, perhaps, I made an excuse to myself for not writing, when in reality I knew not what to say.

The books you must at last distribute as you think best,[2] in my name, or your own, as you are inclined, or as you judge most proper.[3] Every body cannot be obliged, but I wish that nobody may be offended. Do the best you can.

I congratulate you on the increase of your family, and hope that little David is by this time well,[4] and his mamma perfectly recovered. I am much pleased to hear of the re-establishment of kindness between you and your father.[5] Cultivate his paternal tenderness as much as you can. To live at variance at all is uncomfortable; and variance with a father is still more uncomfortable. Besides that, in the whole dispute you have the wrong side; at least you gave the first provocations, and some of them very offensive. Let it now be all over. As you have no reason to think that your new mother has shown you any foul play, treat her with respect, and with some degree of confidence;[6] this

1. *Ante* To Thomas Percy, 2 Dec. 1776.

2. On 16 Nov. JB informed SJ that William Strahan had finally sent him twelve presentation copies of SJ's *Journey*—considerably fewer than the twenty-five originally promised (*Life* III.94; *Ante* To JB, 21 June 1774). These copies were intended, *inter alios*, for Sir Alexander Dick, Lord Hailes, and Lord Monboddo (Fleeman, p. xxv n. 7; *Life* III.102).

3. JB's inscription in Dick's copy reads: "This Book was sent to me by the Authour Dr. Samuel Johnson to be presented to Sir Alexander Dick of Prestonfield Baronet, at whose seat he was agreeably entertained. James Boswell" (Fleeman, p. xxv n. 7).

4. David Boswell, JB's fourth child and second son, was born 15 Nov. in frail condition (*Boswell in Extremes*, ed. C. M. Weis and F. A. Pottle, 1970, p. 55).

5. *Ante* To JB, 16 Nov. 1776 and n. 1.

6. On 14 Feb. 1777 JB replied: "I do not suspect my Stepmother of foul play in money matters. But I beleive she estranges my Father from me and mine, with an assiduity that is too successful" (MS: Beinecke Library).

will secure your father. When once a discordant family has felt the pleasure of peace, they will not willingly lose it. If Mrs. Boswell would but be friends with me, we might now shut the temple of Janus.[7]

What came of Dr. Memis's cause?[8] Is the question about the negro determined?[9] Has Sir Allan any reasonable hopes?[10] What is become of poor Macquarry?[11] Let me know the event of all these litigations. I wish particularly well to the negro and Sir Allan.

Mrs. Williams has been much out of order; and though she is something better, is likely, in her physician's opinion, to endure her malady for life, though she may, perhaps, die of some other.[12] Mrs. Thrale is big, and fancies that she carries a boy;[13] if it were very reasonable to wish much about it, I should wish her not to be disappointed. The desire of male heirs is not appendant only to feudal tenures.[14] A son is almost necessary to the continuance of Thrale's fortune; for what can misses do with a brewhouse? Lands are fitter for daughters than trades.

Baretti went away from Thrale's in some whimsical fit of disgust, or ill-nature, without taking any leave.[15] It is well if he finds in any other place as good an habitation, and as many

7. SJ alludes to the Roman custom of keeping the doors to the Temple of Janus open during times of war.

8. *Ante* To Thomas Lawrence, 7 Feb. 1775 and n. 1; *Ante* To JB, 7 Feb. 1775.

9. *Ante* To JB, 2 July 1776, n. 4; *Post* To JB, 22 July 1777, nn. 17, 18.

10. *Ante* To Hester Thrale, 23 Oct. 1773 and nn. 11, 17.

11. *Ante* To Hester Thrale, 23 Oct. 1773 and n. 7.

12. Cf. *Ante* To JB, 16 Nov. 1776.

13. *Ante* To Hester Thrale, 4 June 1776, n. 2.

14. SJ alludes to JB's preference for strict male succession (*Ante* To JB, 16 Nov. 1775, n. 2).

15. The relationship between Hester Thrale and Giuseppe Baretti had never been an easy one (*Ante* To Hester Thrale, 15 July 1775, n. 3). In the aftermath of Harry Thrale's death, a violent quarrel erupted, which was imperfectly patched over (Hyde, 1977, p. 163). "The final break came the first week in July 1776. Thrown into a frenzy by various arguments over servants and guests, the Italian quietly packed his effects to be sent after him to London, and on the morning of July 6 stalked off to the city" (Clifford, 1952, p. 144).

conveniences.[16] He has got five-and-twenty guineas by translating Sir Joshua's Discourses into Italian,[17] and Mr. Thrale gave him an hundred in the spring;[18] so that he is yet in no difficulties.

Colman has bought Foote's patent, and is to allow Foote for life sixteen hundred pounds a year, as Reynolds told me, and to allow him to play so often on such terms that he may gain four hundred pounds more.[19] What Colman can get by this bargain, but trouble and hazard, I do not see. I am, dear Sir, Your humble servant,

SAM. JOHNSON

16. Until his reconciliation with the Thrales in Sept. 1780, Baretti lived a hand-to-mouth existence, subsisting on the proceeds from various literary projects and on the patronage of John Cator (Lacy Collison-Morley, *Giuseppe Baretti*, 1909, pp. 307–14; *Thraliana* I.456–58).

17. Baretti's *Delle arti del disegno*, a translation of the first seven of Reynolds's *Discourses on Painting*, was published in 1778.

18. In compensation for time and money expended on preparations for the Italian tour, Henry Thrale had presented Baretti with a hundred guineas (Clifford, 1952, p. 139).

19. Samuel Foote (1721–77), comic actor, manager, and playwright, was thrown (in Feb. 1766) from a horse owned by the Duke of York. This accident necessitated the amputation of Foote's leg. In recompense, York used his influence to obtain a royal patent authorizing Foote to operate the Haymarket Theatre during the summer season. In Oct. 1776 Foote leased this patent to George Colman for £1,600 a year, in addition to £500 for any of Foote's unpublished plays that should be produced. Foote also agreed to act only at the Haymarket (*A Biographical Dictionary of Actors, Actresses, Musicians, Dancers, Managers, and Other Stage Personnel in London, 1660–1800*, ed. P. H. Highfill et al., 1978, V.324, 342–43, 352).

Joseph Nollekens[1]

TUESDAY 24 DECEMBER 1776

MS: Hyde Collection.

1. Joseph Nollekens (1737–1823), R.A., prominent sculptor, was most in demand for his busts and monuments, although he himself preferred to produce allegorical figures (Margaret Whinney, *English Sculpture, 1720–1830*, 1971, p. 113). It is likely that Nollekens entered the Johnsonian circle through his marriage to the daughter of Saunders Welch (see below, n. 3).

Sir: Dec. 24, 1776

I have sent the inscription. Where there are dots : : : there must be a space left for the dates which we have [not] yet got at.[2] My compliments and good wishes come with this both to You and Mrs. Nollikens,[3] from, Sir, Your most humble servant,

SAM. JOHNSON

2. SJ refers to Goldsmith's epitaph (*Ante* To Joshua Reynolds, 16 May 1776 and nn. 1, 5). Nollekens sculpted the monument in Westminster Abbey (Margaret Whinney, *Sculpture in Britain, 1530–1830*, 1964, p. 160).

3. Mary Welch (*c.* 1743–1817), second daughter of Saunders Welch, married Nollekens in 1772 (H. W. Liebert, "Johnson's Head," privately printed for The Johnsonians, 1960; *GM* 1817, p. 190).

William Strahan

TUESDAY 24 DECEMBER 1776

MS: Hyde Collection.

ADDRESS: To William Strahan, Esq.

Sir: Dec. 24, 1776

I have read over Dr. Blair's first sermon, with more than approbation.[1] To say it is good is to say too little.

Be so kind as to frank this Letter to Mrs. Lucy Porter in Lichfield.

I intended to have come to you to day but something has hindred me. I will come on Saturday or Monday, or both. I am, Sir, Your most humble servant,

SAM. JOHNSON

1. When Hugh Blair first proposed to Strahan that he publish an edition of Blair's sermons, Strahan's response was negative. However, Strahan had given SJ a sample sermon to read; upon receiving the strong recommendation contained in this letter, he changed his mind and purchased the collection for one hundred pounds. The sermons proved to be a great success, and two further volumes appeared. Ultimately Strahan paid Blair a total of £1,100 (*Life* III.97–98; *Boswell in Extremes*, ed. C. M. Weis and F. A. Pottle, 1970, p. 165).

INDEX

This is an index of proper names alone; the comprehensive index to the entire edition appears in Volume v. The following abbreviations are used: Bt. (Baronet), Kt. (Knight), ment. (mentioned). Peers are listed under their titles, with cross references from the family name.

Entries for each of SJ's correspondents begin with a comprehensive listing of all letters to the individual in question. Page numbers for footnotes refer to pages on which the footnotes begin, although the item which is indexed may be on a following page.

The index was compiled mainly by Phyllis L. Marchand with the assistance of Marcia Wagner Levinson and Judith A. Hancock.

B

D

E

F

G

H

M

N

O

P

Q

R

S

T

V

W

Y